Language Socialization
in Bilingual and Multilingual Societies

Bilingual Education and Bilingualism

Series Editors: Professor Nancy H. Hornberger, *University of Pennsylvania, Philadelphia, USA* and Professor Colin Baker, *University of Wales, Bangor, Wales, Great Britain*

Other Books in the Series
At War With Diversity: US Language Policy in an Age of Anxiety
   James Crawford
Child-Rearing in Ethnic Minorities
   J.S. Dosanjh and Paul A.S. Ghuman
Cross-linguistic Influence in Third Language Acquisition
   J. Cenoz, B. Hufeisen and U. Jessner (eds)
English in Europe: The Acquisition of a Third Language
   Jasone Cenoz and Ulrike Jessner (eds)
Identity and the English Language Learner
   Elaine Mellen Day
An Introductory Reader to the Writings of Jim Cummins
   Colin Baker and Nancy Hornberger (eds)
Japanese Children Abroad: Cultural, Educational and Language Issues
   Asako Yamada-Yamamoto and Brian Richards (eds)
Language and Literacy Teaching for Indigenous Education: A Bilingual Approach
   Norbert Francis and Jon Reyhner
Languages in America: A Pluralist View
   Susan J. Dicker
Language, Power and Pedagogy: Bilingual Children in the Crossfire
   Jim Cummins
Language Use in Interlingual Families: A Japanese-English Sociolinguistic Study
   Masayo Yamamoto
Learners' Experiences of Immersion Education: Case Studies of French and Chinese
   Michèle de Courcy
Multicultural Children in the Early Years
   P. Woods, M. Boyle and N. Hubbard
Multicultural Child Care
   P. Vedder, E. Bouwer and T. Pels
The Native Speaker: Myth and Reality
   Alan Davies
Power, Prestige and Bilingualism: International Perspectives on Elite Bilingual Education
   Anne-Marie de Mejía
Reflections on Multiliterate Lives
   Diane Belcher and Ulla Connor (eds)
Working with Bilingual Children
   M.K. Verma, K.P. Corrigan and S. Firth (eds)
Young Bilingual Children in Nursery School
   Linda Thompson

Other Books of Interest
Beyond Boundaries: Language and Identity in Contemporary Europe
   Paul Gubbins and Mike Holt (eds)
The Care and Education of Young Bilinguals
   Colin Baker
Encyclopedia of Bilingualism and Bilingual Education
   Colin Baker and Sylvia Prys Jones
Understanding Deaf Culture: In Search of Deafhood
   Paddy Ladd

Please contact us for the latest book information:
Multilingual Matters, Frankfurt Lodge, Clevedon Hall,
Victoria Road, Clevedon, BS21 7HH, England
http://www.multilingual-matters.com

BILINGUAL EDUCATION AND BILINGUALISM 39
Series Editors: Nancy H. Hornberger and Colin Baker

Language Socialization in Bilingual and Multilingual Societies

Edited by
Robert Bayley and Sandra R. Schecter

MULTILINGUAL MATTERS LTD
Clevedon • Buffalo • Toronto • Sydney

Library of Congress Cataloging in Publication Data
Language Socialization in Bilingual and Multilingual Societies/Edited by Robert Bayley and
Sandra R. Schecter.
Bilingual Education and Bilingualism: 39
1. Sociolinguistics. 2. Socialization. 3. Bilingualism.
I. Bayley, Robert. II. Schecter, Sandra R. III. Series.
P40.5.S57 L36 2003
306.44–dc21   2002015684

British Library Cataloguing in Publication Data
A catalogue entry for this book is available from the British Library.

ISBN 1-85359-636-1 (hbk)
ISBN 1-85359-635-3 (pbk)

Multilingual Matters Ltd
UK: Frankfurt Lodge, Clevedon Hall, Victoria Road, Clevedon BS21 7HH.
USA: UTP, 2250 Military Road, Tonawanda, NY 14150, USA.
Canada: UTP, 5201 Dufferin Street, North York, Ontario M3H 5T8, Canada.
Australia: Footprint Books, PO Box 418, Church Point, NSW 2103, Australia.

Typeset by Wordworks Ltd.
Printed and bound in Great Britain by the Cromwell Press Ltd.

Contents

Contributors

Dwight Atkinson teaches in the Graduate School of Education, Temple University Japan. His research interests are in social and sociocognitive approaches to language and literacy, both theoretical and empirical.

Robert Bayley is Professor of Bicultural-Bilingual Studies at the University of Texas at San Antonio. He specializes in sociolinguistics and second language acquisition. Recent publications include *Sociolinguistic Variation in ASL* (Lucas *et al.*, 2001) and *Language as Cultural Practice* (Schecter & Bayley, 2002).

Jill Sinclair Bell is Professor of Education at York University, Toronto. She specializes in issues of adult literacy in multilingual contexts and in narrative research methodologies. Recent publications include *Literacy, Identity and Culture* (Bell, 1997) and *From the Classroom* (Turnbull *et al.*, 2002).

KimMarie Cole is Assistant Professor of English Education at the State University of New York at Fredonia. She teaches courses in literacy and language development as well as literacy and technology to future English teachers. Her most recent work appeared in *Urban Review* (Vavrus & Cole, 2002).

María T. de la Piedra is a Peruvian anthropologist and PhD candidate at the University of Texas, Austin. She specializes in educational anthropology, bilingual education, and literacy practices in bilingual communities.

Tara Goldstein works at the Ontario Institute for Studies in Education of the University of Toronto. Her teaching and research interests include schooling in multilingual communities and playwriting as critical ethnography. These interests come together in her first ethnographic play *Hong Kong, Canada,* which will be included in *Teaching and Learning in a Multilingual School Community* to be published by Lawrence Erlbaum in 2003.

Linda Harklau is Associate Professor in the Teaching Additional Languages Program at the University of Georgia. Her research focuses on English language learning and academic experiences of immigrant students in US high school and college settings. Recent work has appeared in *TESOL Quarterly* and the *Journal of Literacy Research*.

Agnes Weiyun He has published extensively in discourse linguistics and educational linguistics. She is the author of *Reconstructing Institutions* (He, 1998) and co-editor of *Talking and Testing* (Young & He, 1998). Her research has been funded by the Spencer Foundation and the National Academy of Education. She currently teaches at the State University of New York at Stony Brook.

Didi Khayatt is the author of *Lesbian Teachers: An Invisible Presence* (Khayatt, 1992) in addition to many refereed articles. She is a sociologist of education with interests in sexuality and feminist anti-racist pedagogy. She currently teaches at York University in Toronto.

Patricia Lamarre is Assistant Professor in the Faculty of Education of the University of Montreal. Using a "critical sociolinguistics" approach, her research focuses on the redefinition of the value of languages in Montreal, how the school system has reacted to the changing language context, and the efforts made by families to acquire and maintain more than one language.

Juliet Langman is Associate Professor of Bicultural–Bilingual Studies at the University of Texas at San Antonio. Her research interests focus on minority youth populations in multilingual settings, exploring the intersection between language use and identity, as well as language acquisition, language policy and planning, and language ideology.

Heather Lotherington is Associate Professor of Multilingual Education at York University, and co-editor of the *Canadian Modern Language Review*. She researches bilingual and multilingual education, particularly with regard to multiliteracies. Recent publications include *What's Bilingual Education All About? A Guide to Language Learning in Today's Schools* (Lotherington, 2000).

Aurolyn Luykx studied at the University of Florida at Gainesville and the University of Texas, Austin, winning the Council on Anthropology and Education's "Dissertation of the Year" award. She is author of *The Citizen Factory: Schooling and Cultural Production in Bolivia* (Luykx, 1999a). After several years of teaching and research in Bolivia, she is currently at the School of Educational Research, University of Miami.

Christopher McAll is Professor of Sociology and Director of the Research Programme on Racism and Discrimination at the University of Montreal. His research interests include social inequality and discrimination, the sociology of language, and the history of social thought. His most recent book (co-authored in French) is on poverty and prejudice: *Se libérer du regard* (McAll, *et al*. 2001).

Donna Patrick is Associate Professor in the Department of Applied Language Studies at Brock University. Her research addresses various issues related to minority languages (French and Inuktitut) and aboriginal peoples in Canada and minority languages in an international context. She is currently completing a book on language, politics, and social identity in an Inuit community.

Lucinda Pease-Alvarez is Associate Professor of Education at the University of California, Santa Cruz. She has worked with bilingual youngsters as a teacher and researcher in primary and secondary schools. Her research has focused on the bilingual language socialization of Mexican-descent children in home, school, and community settings. She is particularly interested in exploring how future educators' experiences working with youngsters outside of school contribute to their understanding about how teaching and learning can occur in schools and classrooms.

Gordon Pon is currently completing his doctorate in Education at York University in Toronto. His research interests include anti-racism education, globalization, Asian masculinities, Chinese indigenous knowledge, and the education of Chinese Canadians. He is a social worker who obtained his Master of Social Work degree from Carleton University, and currently works in child protection.

Harriett Romo is Associate Professor of Sociology at the University of Texas, San Antonio. She specializes in race and ethnic relations and the sociology of education, with a focus on Latino families and immigrant children.

Josefina Rossell Paredes is a doctoral student in the Faculty of Education of the University of Montreal. Her doctoral study examines the factors influencing language practices in Montreal schools. She recently participated in a major descriptive study on language use and the ethnic and linguistic composition of schools in Montreal.

Sylvie Roy is Assistant Professor in the Faculty of Education, Division of Teacher Preparation, at the University of Calgary, Alberta, Canada. She specializes in socio-linguistics and learning and teaching in a second language. Her recent publications include "La normalisation linguistique dans une entreprise: Le mot d'ordre mondial" in *The Canadian Modern Language Review* (Roy, 2000).

Sandra R. Schecter is Associate Professor of Education and Women's Studies at York University in Toronto, where she teaches courses in language pedagogy, communication, and research methods. An ethnolinguist, she has published on language socialization, language education, and language policy and planning.

Jane Zuengler is Professor in the Department of English, University of Wisconsin-Madison, and has teaching and research interests in sociocultural approaches to second language acquisition and use, with particular attention to classroom discourse. She recently co-edited a special issue of *Applied Linguistics*, which critically examines methods for microanalyzing classroom discourse (Zuengler & Mori, 2002).

Preface and Acknowledgments

Language Socialization in Bilingual and Multilingual Societies grew out of our joint research on family language use and children's bilingual development in California and Texas (Schecter & Bayley, 2002). Although our work extended over a number of years and focused on two distinct communities, we knew that a single research project could not capture the breadth and depth of language socialization research in bilingual and multilingual communities. At the same time, in our own work, we became increasingly concerned about the limits of language socialization theory as traditionally conceived (Schecter & Bayley, in press). We therefore decided to produce an edited volume that would explore language socialization from multiple theoretical perspectives in diverse bilingual and multilingual contexts. We were extremely gratified by the responses of many fine colleagues who agreed to join us in this enterprise. The result is a volume that explores language socialization from very early childhood through adulthood, not only in often-studied communities in Canada and the United States, but also in Australia, Bolivia, Egypt, India, and Slovakia. The global perspective gained by the inclusion of studies of communities representing every inhabited continent will, we hope, provide readers with an indication of the richness of the field as well as a guide for future work. The breadth of the collection, in particular, with chapters focusing on language socialization at different stages in the lifespan in well-known communities including Mexican-Americans in the United States and Francophones in Canada, as well as in communities that are less familiar to many readers, such as the Aymara in Bolivia or minority Hungarians in Slovakia, makes this volume a suitable text for upper-division and graduate courses in bilingualism, language education, second language acquisition, and socio-linguistics.

We thank all of the contributors for entrusting their work to us and for their good-will in responding to our editorial requests. We hope that *Language Socialization in Bilingual and Multilingual Societies* justifies their faith in our ability to bring out a coherent and timely collection that will prove useful to both students and scholars.

We acknowledge the usual assistance of our institutions in providing an appropriate home for academic activity, even for editing the work of others. We also thank Noe Gonzáles for assistance with the combined bibliography. We are grateful to Colin Baker and Nancy Hornberger for including this book in their series on Bilingual Education and Bilingualism. We are pleased to be in such good company. Special thanks to Tommi Grover, Ken Hall and the staff of Multilingual Matters for their care and attention in the production of this book. Finally, as always, we thank our respective families for their understanding, or tolerance, throughout the various stages of this odyssey.

Robert Bayley and Sandra R. Schecter

Introduction

Toward a Dynamic Model of Language Socialization

ROBERT BAYLEY AND SANDRA R. SCHECTER

Traditionally, language socialization research has focused on very young children acquiring their first language (e.g. Ochs, 1988; Ochs & Schieffelin, 1995; Schieffelin, 1990; Schieffelin & Ochs, 1986b) and on the relationships between culturally-specific patterns of language socialization and school achievement, particularly in the primary grades (e.g. Heath, 1982b, 1983; Michaels, 1986; Philips, 1983). In recent years, however, the study of language socialization has broadened to include how older children, adolescents, and adults acquire knowledge of the interpretative frameworks of their own and other cultures in which they must function (e.g. Eckert, 2000; Hoyle & Adger, 1998). Much of the more important inquiry in this tradition has focused on the dynamics of language socialization in bilingual and multilingual settings. This work attends closely to patterns of meaning suggested by the use of different linguistic codes in speech and literacy performances, as well as ideologies concerning the symbolic importance of different languages.

Among other topics, language socialization research in bilingual and multi-lingual settings has documented the difficulties of maintaining minority languages, whether Inuktitut in the far north of Quebec (Crago *et al.*, 1993), Taiap in rural Papua New Guinea (Kulick, 1992), or Spanish in cities in the United States (Schecter & Bayley, 1997, 2002; Vasquez *et al.*, 1994; Zentella, 1997). Research has examined children's developing competence in various speech and literacy events, such as teasing and other forms of verbal play (Eisenberg, 1986), reading Spanish language advertising flyers in Latino communities in the United States (Bayley *et al.*, 1996), and simultaneous translation (Pease-Alvarez & Vasquez, 1994). This line of research has also documented the wide range of linguistic resources available in bilingual and multilingual communities and the ways in which children, adolescents, and adults learn to choose among these resources for their symbolic value. Recent studies in bilingual and multilingual contexts have also examined language mixing in linguistically and ethnically diverse working class adolescent peer groups in Britain (Rampton, 1995), family and community roles in language socialization among the Aymara of Bolivia (Luykx, 1999b), and language socialization in the increasingly multilingual workplaces of Canada and the United States (Duff & Labrie, 2000; Goldstein, 1997b).

The chapters in this volume, selected to illustrate language socialization practices in a wide range of bilingual and multilingual contexts as well as among different age groups, contribute to this developing line of research. The volume brings together established and new scholarly voices to examine how children, adolescents, and adults in fluid bilingual and multilingual contexts are socialized by and through language into new domains of knowledge and cultural practice. Contexts range from Latino communities in the United States and Francophone communities in Canada to indigenous communities in both North and South America, minority Hungarians in Slovakia, lesbians in Egypt, and college students in southern India. Other chapters focus on diverse immigrant communities in Australia, Canada, and the United States. The book is organized into four main parts that address language socialization processes in the home, at school, in peer groups and communities, and in the workplace. Individual chapters focus on language socialization at different stages of childhood, adolescence, and adulthood. The essays address critical topics in the role of language in multilingual contexts: for example, the influence of parental patterns of language choice on indigenous language maintenance, socialization of immigrant students into academic subject matter discourse in secondary schools, the roles of speech and silence among Chinese immigrant students in Canada, parameters of "lesbian" identity in different language varieties, and differentiated talk in the workplace.

The chapters in Part 1 focus on the home and family, the traditional domain of language socialization research. Lucinda Pease-Alvarez draws on a rich body of data gathered in a seven-year study of language socialization in a Mexican-immigrant community in northern California. She documents the changing attitudes of parents representing different immigrant generations towards their children's bilingual language socialization, as well as the changing roles that Spanish and English play in family life. In the second chapter, Aurolyn Luykx examines Bolivian children's bilingual language socialization in Spanish and Aymara (one of the two main indigenous languages of the Andes) in the small community of Huatajata, located about two hours from the capital city of La Paz. Luykx pays special attention to the ways in which "the processes of language socialization both structure and are structured by gender roles and relations" (Chapter 2). She argues that by examining the relationship between gender and language socialization in bilingual communities, "we are addressing questions central to the human condition" (Chapter 2).

Chapter 3 moves from the broad description of parental attitudes toward and beliefs about bilingual socialization and the interplay of a dominant language, an indigenous language, and gender in children's socialization to a detailed examination of a single literacy event in a Mexican-immigrant family in south Texas.

María de la Piedra and Harriett Romo pay special attention to the important influence of siblings in their analysis of the ways in which language and literacy are socially constructed in a non-mainstream immigrant family. In the final chapter in this section, Patricia Lamarre and Josefina Rossell Paredes, drawing on Bourdieu's (1985, 1986) ideas of linguistic marketplaces, of language as a form of capital, and of "ethos" and "habitus," examine how young immigrant trilinguals in Montreal acquired their linguistic repertoires, how they use languages in their everyday lives, and how attitudes towards languages are constructed within immigrant families. Taken together, the chapters in this section, like the chapters in other sections, emphasize language socialization as an interactive process, in which those being socialized also act as agents rather than as mere passive initiates.

Part 2 focuses on language socialization at school. Unlike many of the earlier studies (e.g. Heath, 1983), however, four of the five chapters in this section focus on the experiences of adolescents and young adults. The section opens with Linda Harklau's detailed account of how four immigrant young people, representing different national origins and social class backgrounds, were socialized into the linguistic and cultural practices of a high school in western New York. Harklau explores how "texts, curricula, and face-to-face interactions served to maintain certain images ... of immigrant students" (Chapter 5) and the complexity of the communication patterns of multilingual adolescents. She found that immigrant students in the school were socialized through communicative practices that reflected simultaneously three different images: a color-blind representation, an idealized "Ellis Island" image, and an image of cognitive and linguistic deficiency. In Chapter 6, KimMarie Cole and Jane Zuengler continue the exploration of language socialization and adolescent identity formation, here within the context of a science class in an inner-city high school in the midwestern United States. On the basis of a remarkable corpus of longitudinal data, Cole and Zuengler examine how a select group of linguistically and ethnically diverse "Cyber Academy" students participating in a community-based science project, the Asthma Project, were positioned and positioned themselves as "good students," "real scientists," and "child laborers." In Chapter 7, Gordon Pon, Tara Goldstein, and Sandra Schecter examine the complex and seldom-studied issues of silence and speech in a majority Chinese urban high school in the Toronto area. Pon and his colleagues find that the immigrant Chinese at the school, mostly but not exclusively Cantonese speakers from Hong Kong, face "linguistic double binds." Their silence in class was perceived by Canadian-born students, both Chinese and non-Chinese, as a threat to the quality of their education because the immigrant Chinese were reluctant to contribute to class discussions or assume leadership roles in small group projects. The immigrant students, however, provided a different perspective on silence. Many seldom spoke, because they feared that their English would be ridiculed, while others maintained silence because they did not want to be perceived by members of their own group as "show offs." On a theoretical level, Pon *et al.* show how the ideology of Orientalism (Said, 1979) underpins assumptions about Asians as a "model minority" and offer a critique of the community-of-practice framework employed by Langman and Bell in their chapters in the later sections on language in peer groups (Part 3) and on communities and language in the workplace (Part 4).

The final two chapters in Part 2 concern language socialization in two different age groups and contexts: heritage language schools in the United States, and a college in India. Chapter 8, by Agnes Weiyun He, examines language socialization in four Chinese language heritage classrooms. A great deal of the earlier research on language socialization portrays a seamless process in which novices are conceived of as "passive, ready, and uniform recipients of socialization" (He, Chapter 8). By contrast, He concentrates on the crucial role of the novice (in this case the young children attending the heritage language classes) and their differential participation in activities designed to socialize them into particular linguistic and literacy practices such as the correct order of writing the strokes of Chinese characters. Much of the earlier research in language socialization also focused on how access or lack of access to standard English and other socially-dominant language varieties affected children's academic success in the early years of schooling. In Chapter 9, Dwight Atkinson extends this work to higher education. He examines the role of the acquisition and use of English in students' academic success in "All Souls College," a formerly elite English-medium institution in a predominantly Tamil-speaking area of southern India. Of particular interest in this chapter is Atkinson's analysis of the process of "dys-socialization" among local students who have been educated in Tamil, and hence are less proficient in English (the language of instruction) than are the traditional students drawn from a wide area. Atkinson shows how Tamil-educated students are developing social identities that militate against the acquisition of English and the consequent socialization into the traditional culture of the college.

Part 3 is devoted to four studies of language socialization in peer groups and communities. The chapters in this section cover a broad range of international contexts including Quebec, Slovakia, Australia, and Egypt. In Chapter 10, Donna Patrick explores language socialization and second (and third) language acquisition among the Inuit in the multilingual community of "Sandy Point" in Arctic Quebec, where both Cree and Inuktitut are spoken alongside English and French. Patrick shows how language attitudes, including notions of linguistic complexity and time required for acquisition, combine with patterns of language use to restrict language learning, particularly of third languages, even in a community where multilingualism is favorably viewed.

Questions of language and national and ethnic identity have come to the fore in the former socialist countries of Eastern Europe, particularly in the states that have emerged since the end of the Cold War. In Chapter 11, Juliet Langman examines Hungarian language socialization and identity formation among a group of young Hungarians in Slovakia. Using a community-of-practice framework (Lave, 1991; Lave & Wenger, 1991), Langman examines the formation of a Hungarian identity, centered on questions of language and preservation of cultural traditions, by members of the "Rock Crystal Dance Group" on the Hungarian/Slovak language border in eastern Slovakia. She shows not only how dance group members come to define themselves as Hungarian by creating a protected space for speaking Hungarian and by practicing traditional dance, but also how they distinguish themselves through negative identity practices from those they identify as "half Hungarians" (minority Hungarians who are becoming assimilated into Slovak culture and who no longer speak Hungarian).

Heather Lotherington (Chapter 12) continues the focus on language use and identity. Rather than studying an indigenous or long-established community, however, Lotherington examines the literacy practices of Cambodian and Vietnamese immigrant youth in "Springvale," a suburb of Melbourne, Australia that is home to a growing population of Southeast Asian immigrants. She illustrates the conflicting demands that non-European immigrant youth face in their efforts to forge a new Australian-Asian identity in a country that has only within the past generation allowed a substantial number of Asian immigrants to obtain an adequate Australian education. Finally, in the concluding chapter in this section, Didi Khayatt also explores the question of socialization into a new identity. Khayatt examines how one becomes socialized into a lesbian identity in a society in which the main language offers no word to describe that identity, at least not as it is commonly understood in Europe and North America.

The concluding three chapters concern language socialization in the workplace, the site where, as Christopher McAll observes (Chapter 14), most people spend most of their adult lives. McAll distinguishes between "language workers" (e.g. engineers, managers, salespeople) for whom language is central to work, and others (such as wood workers and metal workers) for whom the transformation of materials is central, and who often work in conditions that render sustained and frequent verbal interaction impossible. Drawing examples from his research on language use in the aerospace industry in Montreal, McAll shows how language difference remains a key instrument in maintaining inequality between speakers of a dominant language and speakers of a subordinate language over whom they exercise power. Thus, even in Montreal, where legislation has greatly expanded work opportunities for Francophones, McAll finds that English remains the dominant language of the engineering sector of the aerospace industry.

While McAll provides a broad view of the role of language in the workplace, in the following chapter Jill Bell focuses on a linguistically diverse group of unemployed workers participating in a job retraining program based at an Ontario community college. Like several other contributors, Bell adopts a community-of-practice approach and explores how individuals who have been socialized into one identity, that of worker, confront the challenge of acquiring a student identity in a situation in which both they and their instructors are viewed as marginal to the main purposes of the institution. Finally, Sylvie Roy examines the challenges faced by minority Francophone residents seeking employment in a bilingual call center in southern Ontario. Roy shows how the local vernacular French was regarded by management as insufficiently standard to satisfy the demands of the workplace. Thus, an ideology of language purity came to replace the community's earlier pride in the vernacular.

The chapters in this volume, with their focus on diverse communities, contexts, and age groups, provide illustrations of language socialization as a lifelong process in which those being socialized often, indeed normally, exhibit considerable agency. That is, socialization by and through language is not simply a process in which experts in a particular community pass on ways of understanding and acting in the world to novices. Rather, even young novices, as shown, for example, in He's chapter on language socialization in Chinese heritage schools, differ in what they draw from socialization activities. Indeed, the role of the novice is particularly important in the kinds of bilingual and multilingual contexts examined in this volume where, as Langman shows, for example, young people are defining themselves at least partially in opposition to older identities, or where, as in the chapters by Lotherington about Southeast Asian immigrant youth in Australia or by Khayatt on lesbians in Egypt, the identity being formed is not one that has previously been available.

In addition to illustrating language socialization as a process that occurs throughout the lifetime and in which those being socialized, particularly in contexts where more than one language is involved, also have opportunities for choice, many of the chapters gathered for this volume incorporate recent discourse about identity into a language socialization framework. As we have argued elsewhere (Schecter & Bayley, 2002), the bilingual persona in fluid societal and situational contexts may indeed have an ephemeral quality. In such environments, despite what official characterizations may imply, identity is not a fixed category and, as the chapters by Harklau, Cole and Zuengler, Atkinson, Lotherington, Bell, and others show, individuals choose among (and sometimes resist) the identities offered to them, and at times construct new identities when the circumstances in which they find themselves do not offer a desirable choice.

Finally, we suggest that the chapters in this volume, as well as recent research in bilingual and multilingual communities by scholars such as Kulick (1992), Norton (2000), and Zentella (1997), offer a more broadly representative picture of language socialization than studies that examine language socialization in contexts where only a single language is involved. As Luykx (Chapter 2) observes, in language socialization, as in other areas of language studies, monolingual contexts constitute the esoteric field. For most of the world, language socialization takes place in bilingual or multilingual settings that change across the lifespan. The focus on such settings, which is shared by all of the authors whose work is included here, will, we hope, contribute to the development of a more dynamic model of language socialization than heretofore available.

Part 1
Language Socialization at Home

Chapter 1

Transforming Perspectives on Bilingual Language Socialization[1]

LUCINDA PEASE-ALVAREZ

Recent accounts of immigrant parents' perspectives on their bilingual children's language education and socialization have been the subject of much discussion among those engaged in debates about the role that minority languages should play in schools and classrooms in the United States. By focusing on a restricted range of topics related to parental perspectives on language and schooling, recent research and media portrayals of parents' views about bilingual education provide us with a very narrow view of the way parents conceptualize language, bilingualism, and learning (Krashen, 1999). Moreover, these accounts, which tend to portray parental perspectives on bilingualism and bilingual education as monolithic and unvarying, contribute few insights into the processes implicated in the way these perspectives develop and change. Instead they are simply described as supporting or countering one side or another in national and state debates about bilingual education.

In contrast, researchers adopting a sociocultural approach to the study of language development have expanded our understanding of how the constitutive relationships among language, learning, and culture play out in the language socialization process. Building on traditions of scholarship that embed learning in the practical activities of communities (Heath, 1983, 1989; Lave & Wenger, 1991; Ochs, 1988; Rogoff, 1990;), scholars have shown how the different ways parents conceive of and participate in their children's language development both construct and reveal cultural practices and values. For example, Ochs (1988) and Heath (1989) have described how parental roles, dispositions, and identities are constructed and revealed through the everyday engagements that involve their children.

When considering the case of Mexican-descent families residing in the United

States, researchers who rely on sociocultural frameworks have contributed to our understanding of how parental perspectives on bilingual language socialization develop within the context of a complex and dynamic sociocultural ecology that comprises shifting cultural, institutional, and structural practices and circumstances. Perhaps not surprisingly, research has demonstrated that the language socialization practices of this group are varied, even in the case of those families committed to pursuing similar goals (Schecter & Bayley, 2002; Vasquez *et al.*, 1994). For example, Schecter and Bayley (2002) describe how historical and ecological variations in the experiences of Mexican-descent parents living in California and Texas help to explain the different ways in which they pursue their common goal of making sure that their children maintain Spanish.

Building on the lines of scholarship referred to above, the research reported here also contributes insights into ways that the thinking of Mexican-descent parents about languages, bilingualism, and learning relates to different aspects of their experience, including their histories, cultural practices, and social positioning. What distinguishes this account from others is the attention paid to the way parents' views change over time. The chapter, then, provides a perspective on bilingual language socialization that is often missing from other accounts.

Studying Parental Attitudes and Perspectives Over Time

This chapter is based on a seven-year study conducted from 1991 to 1998. The study investigated native language maintenance and shift toward English in a group of 63 Mexican-descent youngsters and their family members residing in Eastside (a pseudonym), California. To capture the way that generation and time spent in the United States affect bilingualism, parents were grouped according to increasing strength of family ties in this country. Based on a survey of all of the parents of third graders in the four Eastside schools, three groupings were identified:

(1)   Parents born in Mexico; immigrated at age 15 or older.
(2)   Parents born in Mexico; immigrated at age 10 or younger.
(3)   Parents born in the United States.

To assess the related phenomena of language maintenance and shift at a variety of levels, parents and their children from these different groups participated in interviews and activities designed to investigate their language proficiency, attitudes, and choices. The interviews included a variety of question formats to elicit information about parents' attitudes toward English, Spanish, bilingualism, and native language maintenance. Parents were also asked about their views concerning appropriate and inappropriate bilingual language practices and socialization strategies, their opinions regarding the role parents and schools should play in Latino youngsters' language socialization, and their expectations regarding what constituted appropriate or correct language practices and ability. Sixty-three parents, mostly mothers, participated in the first cycle of interviews in 1991 and 1992.

Table 1.1 Parents interviewed by immigration group

Immigration group	1991–92	1996–98
Parents born in Mexico; immigrated at age 15 or older	40	26
Parents born in Mexico; immigrated at age 10 or younger	13	6
Parents born in the United States	10	7
Total number of parents	63	39

Thirty-nine of the original group of 63 parents participated in the second cycle of interviews, which took place from 1996 to 1998. Table 1.1 shows the distribution of parents across the three immigration groups during the initial and later interviews.

The Community Context

Although Eastside is home to individuals from many ethnic backgrounds, people of Mexican descent are the majority. Most parent members of Mexican-descent Eastside families are from working class backgrounds with no more than a few years of grade school education, usually acquired in Mexico. While most parents in the sample worked in service-related jobs (e.g. gardeners, tree pruners, housekeepers), a handful of parents who had finished secondary school and, in some cases, at least a few years of college, had middle-income jobs (e.g. teachers, paralegals, computer technicians). Three families owned their own businesses – a marble works, a car repair shop, and a bakery.

Spanish is used throughout Eastside. It is widely used in the commercial sector by employees and patrons of stores and restaurants. Social service agencies, clinics, and some private businesses employ Spanish speakers as office and clerical workers who have the added responsibility of communicating with monolingual Spanish-speaking clients. In addition, the Catholic churches that most families attend conduct services in Spanish. During the course of the study (prior to the passage of Proposition 227), Spanish was also widely used by teachers and children in the four Eastside elementary schools, particularly in the early grades.[2] As is the case among many bilingual educators in the United States, the directors of bilingual education in the Eastside Elementary School District reasoned that their program enabled young children to establish the linguistic and academic foundation in their native language that would ultimately facilitate their acquisition of English and academic content in that language. Hence, most limited-English-proficient children enrolled in Eastside schools who were native Spanish speakers had access to native language instruction in at least kindergarten through second grade. By third grade, however, English had become the main language of the classroom.

Over the past 20 years, the use of Spanish by Eastsiders has been the subject of a great deal of criticism. Many European Americans who live in surrounding communities view Eastside as an enclave of monolingual Spanish speakers who are not interested in learning English or assimilating into the American mainstream. The press has repeatedly portrayed the linguistic circumstances of Eastsiders as a liability. Indeed, authors of several newspaper columns and articles attributed the low academic achievement of Eastside youngsters to their inability to speak English.

The Benefits of Bilingualism

The interviews revealed that parents held extremely positive opinions about English, Spanish, bilingualism, and native-language maintenance, and these views remained constant from 1991 to 1998. Thus, in the closed-response sections of both the earlier and later interviews, most parents' said that they regarded it as "important" or "very important" that their children's teachers and school principal know Spanish. Parents gave even stronger responses when asked how important it is that their children know Spanish, that they know English, and that they be bilingual. In both interview cycles, all the parents except two answered that they thought it "very important" for their children to know both languages and to be bilingual. In addition, when responding to open-ended questions, parents said that Spanish/English bilinguals should continue to use and develop their Spanish as they learn English. In elaborating upon these views, they commented that Spanish/English bilinguals enjoy economic and social benefits that are not available to monolinguals, including the greater likelihood of obtaining high-paying jobs in the United States and Mexico, communicating and interacting with a wide variety of people, and having access to knowledge sources both inside and outside their communities. Hence, similar to the findings reported by Lambert and Taylor (1987), the concept of bilingualism that seems to be most commonly upheld is one that emphasizes the importance of Spanish as well as English. Nevertheless, while parents appeared to endorse an additive view of bilingualism, they also revealed transformations in their thinking about children's bilingual language socialization. The following sections focus on the nature of these transformations.

Language Socialization and Identity: Oppositional Tensions and Orientations

The link between Spanish language and Mexicano/Chicano identity was a theme that characterized the majority of conversations with Eastside parents during both the earlier and the later interviews. Parents expressed this connection in a variety of ways. For most parents, regardless of immigration group, Spanish is a valued feature of their heritage that comes with being born in Mexico or having Mexican kin. Viewpoints that reflect strong relationships between Spanish language and Mexican identity are conveyed in the following excerpts from the interviews with both Mexican and US-born parents. When describing what it meant for Mexican-descent parents to have children who have lost their ability or desire to speak Spanish, parents from both groups told us that such a loss would imply a loss of the children's Mexican identity. For example, Ms Guarin, born in Mexico, commented:

> *Es una pena si pierden el español porque ya traes tus raíces en español o sea es tu idioma y perderlo, no aprovecharlo, no seguirlo, yo creo que no. Después yo creo que se van a lamentar. Es importante para ellos que sigan nuestras raíces, la cultura y que se sientan orgullosos de nosotros y de ellos porque ellos son mexicanos. No son nacidos aquí.*

> (It's a shame if they forget Spanish, because you carry your roots in Spanish and it's your language and to lose it, to not take advantage of it as you grow, I think not. Later I think they will regret it. It's important for them to continue their roots, the culture and that they feel proud of us and of themselves because they are Mexican. They aren't born here.)

Another mother, US-born Ms Duran, associated language loss with cultural loss. She commented: "In my experience when I've seen people who have lost their Spanish maybe their deep rooted values are still you know kind of Latino or whatever but their culture, like a lot of it is lost."

Yet, while much of parents' thinking about identity focuses on their heritage or family history, they also define themselves and others in ways that take into account the various structural forces and conditions affecting their lives in the United States. This was most apparent in the second cycle of interviews, during which the majority of respondents interpreted the passage of recent initiatives, including California's Proposition 187 and 209, as forms of discrimination directed against Latinos. During these interviews, parents across immigration backgrounds described ways in which discrimination and related differential perspectives on language status are implicated in the Spanish language socialization of children of Mexican-descent.[3] For example, when asked about a recent court case involving a judge who prohibited a Latina mother from using Spanish with her five-year-old daughter (a much-publicized and widely-discussed event in the Eastside community during the time of our second set of interviews), parents across immigration groups told us that the judge's decision emanated from racist views toward Latinos.

During both interview sessions, immigrant parents were highly critical of the decisions of parents of Mexican-descent to abandon the use of Spanish with their children, which they cited as the leading cause of language loss in their community, claiming that these decisions emanated from parents' desires to adopt English monolingual norms and Anglo values in an effort to improve their social status in this country. Ms Marti expanded upon this viewpoint when she told us that parents who no longer speak Spanish with their children are to blame for their children's loss of Spanish. She attributed their decision to what she described as the misguided belief that *"Ya son muy altos y no quieren hablar español porque ya son de aquí"* ("Now they are very high class and they don't want to speak Spanish because they are from here"). Similarly, Mrs Ramos argued that language loss occurs *"por causa de los papas"* ("because of parents") who no longer use the language with their children.

She chastises these parents, saying, "*Que no se te olvide que uno viene de raices, que uno es latino*" ("Don't forget that you have roots, that you are Latino"). Ms Cornelio conveyed similar sentiments, further arguing that all Spanish-speaking parents, even those who are married to non-Spanish speakers, are responsible for making sure that Spanish is used and learned in their homes:

> *Ahorita hay niños que sus papás son hispanos y no hablan nada de español. Es una verguenza porque si son hispanos por que no les hablan... . Yo conozco a muchos hombres en el trabajo y les digo, "Oiga señor su niña es española. Bárbaro. Enséñale. Algn da te lo va a agradecer." "No, pero su mamá no habla español." "Eso que importa."*

> (Now there are children whose parents are Hispanic and who don't speak any Spanish. It's a shame because if they are Hispanic why don't they speak to them (in Spanish). I know many men at work and I tell them, "Listen, mister, your daughter is Spanish. How shocking. Teach her. Some day she will thank you." "But her mother doesn't speak Spanish." "That doesn't matter.")

The juxtaposition of this prevailing view among immigrant parents with the views of US-born parents revealed both consistencies and discrepancies. Some parents who were born and/or raised in the United States since childhood mirrored the perspectives of their Mexican-born counterparts, describing Mexicans who abandoned their language and culture as having done so in order to enjoy the benefits that come with becoming or being American. For example, Ms Ochoa conveyed this viewpoint in the following description of her brother:

> He's a Mexican, *puro nopal*. But he's the kind of guy who drives a BMW. So he thinks he's white and he won't speak Spanish unless he has to his mother. You can tell he has a lot of problems with his culture. Like his name is Antonio. And you don't call him Antonio you call him Tony or Anthony. But not Antonio.

Ms Ochoa, along with the other parents born or raised in the United States since childhood, claimed that she was making sure that her children maintained or recovered Spanish as a means of preserving the children's Mexican identity. The efforts of these parents included using more Spanish in the home and/or seeking opportunities for their children to develop Spanish in educational settings (e.g. second and foreign language classes, exchange programs).

Yet several US-born parents described the difficulties they had experienced growing up in homes where their own parents insisted that they use Spanish. For example, when recounting her own childhood experiences living in a home where her father insisted that his children use Spanish, even in interactions that didn't include him, Ms Menez expressed resentment toward a practice that is supported by many Mexican-born parents. Although Ms Menez wants her two children to maintain their Spanish, she refuses to follow her father's example of insisting that Spanish be the exclusive language of the home. As she describes below, living in a home milieu in which children are obligated to use and maintain their language stifles growth:

There are a lot of families that want you to keep the Spanish. But you don't grow that way. I mean you're living here and you're bound to speak English and sometimes it hurts, I think, more than it helps to be obligated not to lose your culture and languages. Because then you start saying, you know, United States made me lose everything. Well, you decided to come here.

Like Ms Menez, Ms Duran, another US-born parent, also resented her parents' efforts to insist upon the use of Spanish in conversations with their children. She explained that her own decision to use English in her interactions at home with her parents and siblings grew out of her desire to resist her parents' wishes. In the following excerpt, she describes how renewed interest in Mexican culture and Chicano Power during her late teens and early twenties contributed to transformations in her own language-choice practices:

Yo no entendía las razones porque yo me sentía enojada de que mis padres me obliguen a aprenderlo. Pero luego cuando entre a la escuela intermedia y la secundaria el movimeiento chicano era muy fuerte. Yo recuerdo el orgullo de los afro-americanos y el orgullo del los chicanos. Era un clima político diferente. Así que yo creo que escuche a diferentes personas en la comunidad y reconocí que yo no debía avergonzarme de hablar español. Yo no sabía de donde venía y finalmente reconocí que tenía que venir de las escuelas. ¿Por qué es malo aprender chino? No lo es. ¿Por qué es malo aprender italiano? No lo es. ¿Por qué es malo aprender espanol? ¿De dónde viene esta actitud? Entonces me enfurecí, y con muchos de mis amigos tambien era lo mismo. Así que nos juntamos y fue como que regresamos a nuestra comunidad y comenzamos a ir a bailes mexicanos en la iglesia y ver películas mexicanas y cosas así. Fue como que nos sumergimos nuevamente en élla, y fue lindo. Y nos sentimos orgullosos y realizamos, "Ok nadie nos puede quitar ésto." Así que después de enojarse uno, uno regresa y hace lo que uno tiene que hacer para sentir la riqueza de nuestro idioma y la cultura nuevamente. Después uno está libre para escoger uno o el otro.

(I didn't understand why I felt mad at my parents who obligated me to learn Spanish. But later when I went to middle and secondary school, the Chicano movement was very strong. I remember the pride of the African-Americans and the pride of the Chicanos. It was a political climate that was different. I heard different people in the community and I realized that I shouldn't be ashamed of speaking Spanish. I didn't know where it came from and finally I realized that it had to come from the schools. Then I got mad. And with my friends it was the same. So we got together and returned to our community and began to go to Mexican dances at church and to see Mexican movies and things like that. We submerged ourselves once again in the culture and it was beautiful. And we felt proud and we realized, "Okay, no one is going to take this from us." So after one gets angry, one returns and does what one has to, so that once again, we feel the richness of our language and our culture.)

Contrary to opinions expressed by the majority of immigrant parents, a shift toward English language usage among second- and third-generation households does not necessarily symbolize the abandonment of Mexican identity. Ms Suarez, a US-born mother married to a man who is a fourth-generation Mexican-American and a monolingual English speaker, focused on the importance of her Mexican origins when describing her views about native-language maintenance and loss. Despite living in a household where family members use English almost exclusively in their dealings with one another, she feels that it is important that her children learn to speak and understand Spanish well "because that's their native origin. I think it is important that they maintain that." Yet, her discussion of how her monolingual English-speaking husband considers himself to be Mexican suggests an awareness that the preservation and maintenance of ethnic identity need not be tied to the maintenance and continued use of Spanish.[4] Thus, as indicated by Ms Suarez's remarks (as well as those of four other US-born parents of children who speak little or no Spanish), Spanish language usage is considered to be an important, though not essential, feature of cultural identity among those who have experienced a shift to English in their language-choice practices and proficiencies.

Roles, Responsibilities, and Relationships in the Language Socialization Process at Home: From Parental Obligation to Parental Overload

Work done in the Eastside community has portrayed the strength of parental influence on children's Spanish language development, particularly in the early years (Vasquez *et al.*, 1994). Interviews with immigrant and non-immigrant parents reinforce this view, and underscore the role that their use of Spanish plays in language maintenance. Conversely, language loss is attributed to parental decisions to abandon the use of Spanish with their children. Immigrant parents, in particular, reason that the shift toward greater use of English among parents and Spanish-speaking children is linked to the interest of the parents and the children in becoming American, which they view as a subtractive process entailing the abandonment of Mexican cultural traditions and identity.

In addition, parental views about their role as Spanish-language socialization agents emanate, at least in part, from their belief that parental influences are the most important to children's overall development. Ms Gamarra, Mr Cardona, and Ms Gutierrez believe that parents should bear the burden of responsibility when it comes to children's academic and intellectual development, including the maintenance and further development of their native languages. All three have adult-centered views of learning and teaching in which they direct the course of their children's development via lesson-like encounters that they claim to have made routine events in their homes (e.g. assigning extra homework and engaging children in recitation activities focused on a particular skill).

Although most parents said that they were key contributors to their children's and, in some cases, grandchildren's ethnolinguistic futures, several mothers discussed the difficulties associated with trying to make sure that their children continued to use and learn Spanish at home. As she implies in the following excerpt,

Ms Cardona feels her influence over her children's actions and development has diminished with age: *"No puedo decirla ya vaya atrás para la escuela [a estudiar español]. Ya es una mama. Y tiene la responsabilidad para su niña. La cosa es que no más ella haga el esfuerzo. No puedo decir mucho"* ("I can't tell her to go back to school [to study Spanish]. She's a mother now. She has the responsibility of her daughter. She has to make the effort. I can't tell her much").

Ms Duran conveyed a similar viewpoint when she spoke of the futility of forcing her child to use Spanish at home. From her vantage point, her daughter Frida must both want and decide to use and learn Spanish. Frida has responded to past efforts to enforce the use of the language at home by getting angry and refusing to use it – something that led to family tensions that Ms Duran felt were unhealthy.

Even Ms Oso, a US-born parent committed to the use of Spanish as a vehicle for language recovery, will not enforce the use of the language in her household despite her own decision to speak to her children exclusively in Spanish. In her discussion of the difficulties associated with enforcing a Spanish-only policy in the home, she brings up the challenges of maintaining a home that is conducive to the maintenance of Spanish. Instead, she holds the view that parents should develop ways to make the use of Spanish at home attractive or appealing to children, rather than an obligation:

> *Me ha tocado ver a algunas personas que ya no es una cosa importante si no que es una obligación. Qué les dicen a sus hijos "Tienes que hablar español." También así me tocó con la abuelita de mis hijos. Que ella les decía que cuando ella estaba que era mala educación hablar inglés delante de ella. Yo pienso que no debe ser obligación si no sólamente decirles que es importante por ellos mismos.*

> (I have seen some people for whom it [speaking Spanish at home] isn't important, but an obligation. What do they tell their children. "You have to speak Spanish." Also I had this experience with my children's grandmother. She told them that when she was around it was rude to speak English in front of her. I think that it shouldn't be an obligation if you can only tell them that it is important for their own good.)

During the 1996–98 interviews, several mothers spoke of how the economic challenges that they faced prevented them from taking active roles in their children's Spanish language socialization. For example, in her first interview in 1992, Ms Garrido shared her belief that she should be the primary language-socialization agent available to her children. While she felt teachers could offer some support, she considered herself to be the one adult ultimately responsible for making sure her five children continued to develop and maintain their Spanish. Subsequently, however, economic circumstances (in part due to the disappearance of her husband) had worsened, making it necessary for her to do two jobs outside the home. Although she described her efforts to further her children's Spanish language maintenance (trips to the library, purchase of Spanish language books), she was adamant that schools also needed to make sure that Latino children continued to develop and maintain Spanish. This was especially important, given that women like herself were no longer available to assume full-time care-giving roles.

Although the sentiments conveyed above may also be shared by the fathers of some of the youngsters, the mothers interviewed for this project felt that they were the ones most responsible for making sure that their children learned or recovered Spanish. This was particularly clear in the case of those households headed by a single mother or by a mother who was the only Spanish-speaking adult family member at home. (No households were headed by a single father.) Two complained that the task was difficult, given their heavy work demands. Ms Suarez, the only Spanish-speaking adult living in her household, describes how the need to work has hindered her efforts to help her children recover their Spanish:

> I think a lot of parents are working and I don't think they have the time to get their kids... It's a lot of work. And I have to say that first hand that I wish I could sit and spend a couple of hours a day because I'm sure I could teach them as well as the school could and you know that's so expensive. We don't have the time. You know we are living at such a fast paced life. Everything is so expensive, two working parents, you are constantly going, so you basically just let it go, and they start to lose it.

Ms Colon, who is married to a man she describes as a monolingual Spanish speaker, also clearly felt that it was her responsibility to make sure that her children "got their Spanish back," despite the fact that she feels more at ease using English in her conversations with them. During her first interview, she mentioned that she was relying mostly on English in her conversations with her children. But during the second interview she said that she was making an effort to use more Spanish with her younger children, saying that she had realized that it was up to her to change her language practices in order to ensure that her children would continue using and developing their Spanish. From her vantage point, her tendency to use English with her children had contributed to their loss of Spanish and to a rift in their relationship with their father, which she felt contributed to her daughter's decision to run away from home:

> Lisa lost communications with her father, with my husband ... I told her to start getting Spanish in high school, she did. She started getting it back. Before she would never talk with her father. She lost the relationship with him. We took her to counseling because she ran away from us and we had a lot of problems with her and all because she lost communication with her father. And ... I'm scared with Ariel [her younger son]. But now I am surprised Lisa and her father sit down. They talk. Lisa understands him and Lisa talks now. Before they didn't because Lisa couldn't talk to her father. It got better. Though her Spanish sounds terrible, she talks to him now. Ariel's Spanish is good but he doesn't think it is. He doesn't wanna bring it out. He doesn't think he knows enough to have a conversation with his father ... Lisa did the same thing and I'm scared that I'm gonna have the same lack of communication with Ariel.

Mothers may feel particularly compelled to play a pivotal role in their children's native language maintenance and development as a result of cultural expectations about their role in the socialization process. These expectations may exert a level of pressure on them that is not felt by fathers (Griffith & Schecter, 1998). While parents were not systematically asked to compare the child-raising responsibilities of mothers and fathers, we do know that gendered patterns of responsibility associated with child raising operate in the Eastside community (Vasquez *et al.*, 1994). Moreover, many mothers spoke of the difficulties they had making sure that their children were adequately cared for while they were at work, thereby conveying their understanding that they were their children's primary caretakers.[5]

Shifting Expectations about Schooling and Language

Despite the beliefs of parents that they should assume an important role in their children's native language socialization, most of the parents interviewed also felt that Spanish should play a role in some aspect of the schools' curricula. When making this point, some parents argued that life circumstances made it difficult for them to find time to teach their children Spanish, thereby revealing their own sense of obligation regarding who should take on the responsibility of supporting their children's Spanish language development. Ms Arana, a single mother and full-time machinist working a swing-shift schedule (from 3pm to 11pm) said that it was difficult for her to spend time with her children engaged in activities that she feels would support their development of Spanish, particularly literacy. Like many other parents, she reasoned that schools could take on some of this responsibility even if it took the form of a single hour-long class each day.

Quantitative findings from these interviews revealed some change over time in parents' views on this topic. In particular, a smaller percentage of parents in the 1996–98 interviews considered it important or very important for their children to have teachers and principals who spoke and understood Spanish than in the initial interviews in 1991–92. When responding to the question regarding which language, if any, they wished were emphasized in their children's schools, during the second interviews a larger percentage of parents favored English than during the initial interviews. Yet during both interviews, the majority of parents felt it was appropriate to initially place monolingual Spanish-speaking children in instructional settings where they could communicate with their teachers and receive at least some content-area instruction in a language they understood. When explaining this view, they cited two reasons: young children feel more comfortable at school when they can use their native language, and they are better able to engage with the academic curriculum.

Parents who had changed their opinions across interview sessions were asked to explain why during the second set of interviews they advocated a greater role for English in their children's schools than they had previously. Some parents explained their shift in views by telling us that Spanish need not occupy such an important role in their children's schooling and classrooms now since their children had learned enough English to be able to participate in an English-only or a primarily-English curriculum. Others said that it was time for teachers and schools to emphasize English because they were worried that their children had not learned enough English in previous grades to succeed in the English-medium curriculum that would be available to them once they reached middle and/or high school.

Still other parents had changed their views about bilingual education based on their children's experiences in bilingual classes. The most frequently-voiced concern focused on the teachers' lack of Spanish language ability. Several parents claimed that their children's teachers spoke *"un español mocho"* ("a broken Spanish") and were not proficient readers and writers of Spanish, citing the errors that teachers made in the notes they sent home, or the comments they wrote on children's papers. Ms Santos, a proponent of the district's bilingual education policy, raised this concern and its implications for students' academic achievement. She felt that teachers' inadequate Spanish language abilities contributed to the difficulties that children of Mexican descent were experiencing in Eastside schools. Ms Alponte reflected similar sentiments when she said that her children will never attain through bilingual education classes taught by Anglo teachers who are not proficient in Spanish the native levels of Spanish language proficiency that she values and wants for them. Consequently, she feels it makes more sense for these teachers to teach in English and to support the children's English language development – a goal more in line with what she perceives to be the teachers' own linguistic abilities.

Some parents also expressed the view that the bilingual classes in the Eastside district did not focus on the skills and subject matter that they felt constituted a strong academic program. When voicing their concerns, they made comparisons with the kind of education available in Mexico, and argued that the curriculum in Eastside schools was less rigorous than that found in Mexican schools or that Eastside teachers did not expect Mexican children to do well in school. Ms Ortiz, for example, said that, unlike schools in the western sector of the school district where the Latino population was less prevalent, Eastside schools are academically "lower" because "they are trying to concentrate on the English–Spanish part while they're not getting the math and the real other things." Mr Cardona and Ms Gamarra, the only two parents who described themselves as opponents of bilingual education, concurred with this line of reasoning. They took it a step further when they argued that bilingual education was racist because it was based on the assumption that Mexican or Latino children could not learn English.

Despite these shifts toward attaching a somewhat greater importance to English in the curriculum, in the later interviews a higher percentage of respondents than in the earlier interviews said that they wanted their children to receive at least some instruction in Spanish. A similar pattern emerged regarding parents' responses to whether or not they felt the school should play a role in preventing the loss of Spanish among Latino children. Several advocated the inclusion of special Spanish language classes in the curriculum as a means to further development of the language as well as to combat its loss. When describing these classes, parents referred to them as a dedicated period of time during the school day, usually no more than an hour, when teachers would focus on Spanish reading, writing, and/or grammar. Even parents opposed to bilingual education felt that their children as well as those of other Latinos should have access to Spanish language classes.

A Sociocultural Perspective on Parental Views

In contrast to recent media portrayals of parental views on bilingual education, research that draws on a sociocultural perspective on learning has yielded a complex and multifaceted account of bilingual language socialization. Because this view of learning acknowledges the complex dynamic that exists between social context and experience, it situates individuals' within a web of macro and micro practices and ecologies that constitute the materials that they use to construct, transform, and express their beliefs and understandings.

Conversations with parents revealed how changes in their everyday experiences, personal and collective histories, and structural forces and conditions converge and combine to define and shape their perspectives on their children's bilingualism and bilingual language socialization, thereby providing a better understanding of how changes in cultural practice and perspectives emerge. Not surprisingly, the interviews reveal that transformations in parents' perspectives on language accompany changes in their own lives and in the social contexts in which they live. For instance, upon their arrival in this country, immigrants draw on their past histories to interpret and construct new ways of participating in families and communities, a process that is reflected in their reference to Mexican cultural values and structural forces. As they experience life in US communities characterized by different institutional constraints and accompanying social relationships, some parents construct new dispositions toward language and learning. In some cases these transformations emerge through a negotiation of past histories and ongoing experiences. For example, over time the commitment of several parents to their Mexican heritage has been intensified through their experiences as members of subordinated groups in the United States. For some, language socialization practices that favor the continued use and maintenance of Spanish are interpreted as a means of resisting a social milieu that they feel disparages the Spanish language and Mexican culture.

Other transformations occurred across the generations in response to what parents themselves experienced in their homes growing up in Eastside or in other communities in the United States. Most noteworthy are reports by US-born parents of the frustration that they felt living in homes where their parents attempted to enforce Spanish-only policies. Interestingly, two of these individuals have decided not to follow the language socialization practices of their parents, citing a variety of reasons centered on their dissatisfaction with the ensuing family dynamics and relationships that they felt contributed to such a strictly enforced policy. In contrast, one parent is making deliberate efforts to use more Spanish with her children in order to enhance communication between her children and her monolingual Spanish-speaking husband.

The findings summarized here also provide insights into the way parents' perspectives on language and identity are transformed over time. As immigrants experience discrimination and come into contact with Latino youngsters who speak English as well as Spanish or who are monolingual English speakers, Spanish language socialization is interpreted as a means of countering threats to their children's Mexican identity. Yet with time, parents face pressures that make it difficult for them to maintain Spanish-speaking homes, as evidenced in the way that some working mothers, regardless of immigration background, interpret the difficulties they face in contributing to their children's native-language socialization. From their vantage point, the need to work outside the home has contributed to changes in language choice and socialization practices as well as possibly complicating and intensifying cultural expectations regarding their role in child-raising.

The struggles of parents with intercultural dilemmas have been a prominent theme throughout the study. These dilemmas center on the broad theme of making sure that what they hold to be features or symbols of their children's Mexican identity (including the use of Spanish in home settings) continue to play an important role in the lives of children who must accommodate to a new language and culture. Parents are particularly concerned about Latino children whom they perceive to have lost the ability or desire to speak Spanish, and they view them as having abandoned their culture and commitment to their families. Some are struggling to address conflicts that they are experiencing or have experienced at home over appropriate language practices and differences in the way they view the parent–child relationship. Issues that have begun to affect the way parents feel they can engage or interact with their children include the lack of time and resources at their disposal. Parents are also struggling with issues that pertain to their children's schooling. While most are glad that schools can be places where teachers and children use Spanish in instructional settings, they are concerned about the role that Spanish plays in their children's lives at schools. Many worry that Spanish is not given adequate attention across the grades. Others feel it has been overemphasized as a medium of instruction in schools. Still others worry about the quality of Spanish spoken by teachers.

Findings from these interviews and other data contribute to an interesting prognosis regarding the future of bilingualism among Eastside youth. The perspectives of immigrant parents regarding the importance of making sure that children use Spanish in their interactions with adults is corroborated by findings from their children's self-reports that they indeed do tend to use mostly Spanish when addressing their parents. Moreover, immigrant children, like their parents, have extremely positive views about bilingualism and Spanish language maintenance, including a commitment to making sure that it is a language that they will continue to use with their children once they are parents. However, during the course of this study, these children also reported an increase in the amount of English they used with siblings, friends, and teachers. If this tendency persists, it is quite likely that these youngsters, like those participants of second and third generation Mexican descent, will become members of households where English dominates, despite the generally positive beliefs held by parents and children about Spanish, bilingualism, and Mexican identity. Indeed, what may be the norm for this community is an intergenerational pattern of language shift occurring by the second generation with the added dimension of extremely favorable interrelated, though not necessarily causally connected, viewpoints toward Spanish, bilingualism, economic security, Mexican identity, and group solidarity.

Although the prognoses for the maintenance of Spanish across the generations may not be promising, especially given the current state of affairs in Eastside schools, findings from this study suggest that the aforementioned viewpoints and practices could be a jumping-off point for language revitalization efforts. This would mean developing venues in which these perspectives and practices are available to various educational stakeholders. At the very least this could entail tapping the viewpoints of families as a resource for educational programming. Better yet, would be concerted efforts on the part of schools, community agencies, and families to develop collaborative venues in which parents, children, teachers, and others work together to share, define and address educational goals, issues, and dilemmas. As some participants in similar kinds of educational collaborations have found, these venues can become spaces where individuals who hold a variety of viewpoints help one another draw upon their interpretive and intellectual resources to understand and address dilemmas in ways that contribute to the emergence of new understandings and practices (Ballinger, 1992; Matusov *et al.*, forthcoming; Schecter & Cummins, in press). However, such collaboration would most beneficially be of a respectable duration so that we can see how over time the lived experiences of parents and children become resources for change.

Notes

1. The research described in this chapter was supported by a major research grant awarded to the author and Kenji Hakuta by the Spencer Foundation. The author would like to thank the parents and children who participated in this study, as well as Carola Cabrejos and Melisa Cahnman who assisted in data collection and analysis. She would also like to acknowledge Kenji Hakuta for his contributions to the quantitative analysis and presentation of interview data.
2. In Spring, 1998, California votes passed Proposition 227 by a margin of 61% to 39%. The proposition mandates that children who are deemed to be of limited English proficiency be taught in classes where their instruction is delivered "overwhelmingly in English." Under special circumstances, parents may request waivers so that languages other than English are used to instruct their children.
3. In 1994, California voters passed Proposition 187, which has since that time been deemed unconstitutional. The initiative would have made it illegal for undocumented immigrants to obtain government services and attend public schools. Proposition 209, which passed in 1995, overturned affirmative action programs in the state.
4. As Keefe and Padilla (1987: 8) argue, ethnic identity among non-immigrant Mexican-descent individuals is strongly linked to processes other than language preservation, including the strengthening of kinship networks characterized by "extending local kin

networks incorporating other Mexican Americans through patterns of friendship associations and intermarriage." Interestingly, Mrs Suarez was one of only a few parents who told us that she wants her daughters to marry Latinos so that they maintain their Mexican culture.

5. Interestingly, we noted an increase in employment among mothers participating in both sets of interviews. Many immigrant women told us that this change in family employment patterns disrupted their family life. They told us that working outside the home was something that they or their mothers had not done prior to immigrating to the United States.

Chapter 2

Weaving Languages Together: Family Language Policy and Gender Socialization in Bilingual Aymara Households

AUROLYN LUYKX

A vestige of the cultural origins of modern linguistics is the fact that "Bilingual Studies" is still considered one of its sub-fields. An enormous amount of linguistic research comes out of the United States, a country where bilingualism is still widely perceived as deviant, a condition of immigrants and other disadvantaged minorities. But throughout the rest of the world (and increasingly within the United States itself), bilingualism is not the exception but the norm. Around two thirds of the world's population is bilingual. Monolinguals are concentrated among the most and least privileged of the planet (Baker & Prys Jones, 1998: vii), which partly accounts for their exaggerated visibility. The most privileged often constitute a social ideal, while the least privileged are usually perceived as a social problem, in need of attention from governments and researchers. This, and their subordinate status, means that disadvantaged populations are more often studied than the middle or upper classes are. Furthermore, those of the underprivileged who are not bilingual are often monolingual in a non-official or minority language, and aspire to bilingualism as a means of survival or social mobility; in that sense, their situation also falls under the purview of "bilingual studies." In short, the esoteric sub-field should really be, not "bilingual studies," but "monolingual studies." The theme of this volume, language socialization in bilingual and multilingual contexts, in fact describes the way in which *most* language socialization occurs.

Similarly, it would be a rare society indeed in which language socialization was not tightly linked to gender. Gender is a central organizing principle in every human society; inevitably, the processes of language socialization both structure and are structured by gender roles and relations. Thus, the relationship between gender and language socialization in bilingual contexts should not be seen as a rarified and exotic topic; by examining it, we are addressing questions that are central to the human condition.

The setting of this particular exploration is a Bolivian town inhabited by (mostly) bilingual speakers of Spanish and Aymara, an indigenous Andean language spoken by about one fourth of Bolivia's population of around 6.5 million (c.1992).[1] As is usually the case with indigenous languages, Aymara is the mother tongue of most of its speakers; it is rarely learned as a second language. A couple of generations ago, most rural Bolivians had little exposure to Spanish until they entered school. Nowadays, with increasing rural–urban contact and access to formal education, most Aymara adults are bilingual and can raise their own children bilingually, using both Aymara and Spanish in the home.[2]

Throughout Bolivia, language attitudes are changing as part of a more general resurgence of ethnic pride and indigenous demands for cultural, linguistic, and political recognition. These and other forces have contributed to Aymara's "legitimization." Whereas twenty years ago many Aymara speakers would deny knowledge of the language in order to distance themselves from the denigrated stereotype of the poor, uneducated *indio*, today many Aymara people openly take pride in the language. The Bolivian constitution (rewritten in 1993) explicitly recognizes cultural and linguistic diversity, and indigenous languages are now used in rural education, though their expansion into other official contexts has been noticeably slower.

Still, Aymara's status is nowhere near that of Spanish. Aymara parents are well aware of the social stigma attached to their language, and know that their children's chances for economic survival in the world beyond the home depend largely on their command of Spanish. For this reason, some Aymara parents attempt to speak mainly Spanish to their children, even though their own command of the language is shaky, thus giving rise to varieties of Spanish suffused with Aymara influences.

Increasingly, Aymara speech reveals influence from Spanish as well. Frequent use of Spanish loanwords is both a sign of prestige and a reflection of increased contact with urban products and institutions. As Canessa notes, "the Spanish language is seen not just as a means of access to metropolitan culture, but as a very important representation of that culture ..." (Canessa, 1997: 241, my translation). Furthermore, centuries of contact have given rise to Aymara variants that display strong grammatical, morphological and semantic influence from Spanish. In earlier decades, this phenomenon was linked to the presence of missionaries and *hacienda* owners who learned Aymara (incompletely) as a second language. Today, a regular presence within Aymara homes is the radio, where Aymara announcers often translate Spanish news briefs "on the fly," giving rise to a style of Aymara that is characterized by Spanish word order and numerous loanwords. In Aymara communities close to urban centers, and in the city of La Paz itself, this variety of

Aymara predominates, while more conservative dialects persist in areas less influenced by urban culture.

The town of Huatajata (*wa-ta-HA-ta*) lies along the shores of Lake Titicaca, about two hours from the capital city of La Paz, in the province of Omasuyos, heart of the Aymara culture area.[3] It is made up of seven smaller contiguous communities, each with about a thousand inhabitants. Though newspapers seldom reach Huatajata, there are numerous radio stations broadcasting in both Spanish and Aymara. Many homes also have television, which is exclusively in Spanish. Unlike more remote communities, Huatajata has two primary schools and a high school. Its inhabitants make their living farming, fishing, marketing, working as employees or lower-level professionals in La Paz, or some combination of these. Tourism is another source of income for those with small restaurants or powerboats. Following the general Andean pattern, *huatajateños* tend to diversify their family economy, deriving their income from several different sources. This, and the fact that many sell fish, wool, or agricultural produce in regional markets or in the city, means that they participate in a variety of linguistic contexts, using both languages, sometimes separately but often in combination.

Virtually all *huatajateños* speak Aymara, and around two thirds also speak Spanish. Aymara monolinguals are concentrated among those over fifty and under six years of age (Albó, 1995: 35, 85). As is often the case where educational and occupational opportunities are differentiated by sex, more men than women are bilingual. In situations where one language was historically the language of conquest, the greater frequency of bilingualism among males often reflects the conquerors' preference for dealing with the men of the conquered population, rather than with the women. This has certainly been a factor for the Aymara, and one that continued until recent years in contacts with government officials and non-governmental organizations. Even today, men's social networks are more likely to cross cultural/linguistic boundaries than are women's (Canessa, 1997: 235–36).

Different levels of Spanish fluency reflect where and when Spanish was acquired. Most Aymaras who are fluent bilinguals learned Spanish early in life, often in school – though, without continued regular exposure to Spanish, one or two years of school instruction are often forgotten. In earlier decades, rural girls seldom attended school, but among younger generations schooling, and therefore bilingualism, are less tightly tied to gender. Most *huatajateños* under forty, and virtually all children of school age, are bilingual.[4] It is less common for adults to achieve Spanish proficiency later in life. Market women who speak just enough Spanish to conduct their business may remain comfortably at this level of "situational fluency" throughout their adult lifetimes. Most environments that would provide opportunities for improving one's Spanish, such as work requiring contact with non-Aymara speakers, are closed to those who are not already fluent.

The speech data presented below were collected over a period of three months in 1987, as part of a broader research project analyzing the interrelationship of schooling, gender, and language use in Huatajata. During the fieldwork period, I lived mainly with one family and had contact with several others through participation in the normal social life of the community (marketing, religious events, etc.), and in more directly research-related tasks such as interviewing and classroom observation. My host family included five children of both sexes, between the ages of one and eleven, allowing observation of a range of speech interactions. While the father was an Aymara/Spanish bilingual who worked in the city, the mother was actually a Quechua/Spanish speaker who had learned Aymara as a third language[5] (her mother-in-law, a monolingual Aymara speaker, was also a frequent visitor to the home). Other community members commented approvingly to me on her fluency and the speed with which she had learned Aymara; certainly the pressure to do so would be great for anyone marrying into such a community. Though most of the data described below are from this particular family, observations of other families (and the fact that many of the speech patterns described below are common to both Aymara/Spanish and Quechua/Spanish bilinguals) led me to view them as typical of the community in general.

Parent–Child Interaction

The Aymara view the onset of speech as the threshold between babyhood and actual personhood. Young children acquiring the phonological, morphological, and grammatical rules of their mother tongue(s) also begin to learn the speech styles appropriate to their gender, observing and imitating the language habits of parents, grandparents, siblings, and others. As we shall see, many of these speech styles can be characterized by the ways in which they combine Spanish and Aymara elements.

In traditional agricultural communities, Aymara children usually accompany the parent of the same sex in their daily tasks; in Huatajata, many fathers worked in the city, so that boys (when not in school) were free to play outside in neighborhood groups. Girls had a much busier day, helping their mothers with the seemingly endless chores of cooking, washing, caring for younger siblings, and attending to livestock. Thus the peer group was a more important influence on boys' early linguistic socialization than on that of girls. Most of the following data on parent–child interaction refer to mothers rather than fathers, reflecting the fact that mothers in Huatajata spend more time around their children than fathers do.

Around adults, polite Aymara children are expected to listen rather than talk, though urban children are thought to be more talkative and even impertinent (Briggs, 1981: 107; United Nations, 1983: 62). Although children are expected to speak politely to adults at all times, parents often speak to children in a manner that would be considered rude if used with another adult. Use of Aymara imperative and remonstrative forms, without the "politive" suffixes normally used among adults, is common in parents' speech to children (as are Spanish imperatives), whereas use of the polite forms with children would be considered inappropriate (see Briggs, 1981: 111; Spedding, 1994: 39).

Bilingual Aymara parents often use a distinctive (Spanish) "baby talk" with infants, characterized by high pitch, childish pronunciation, and affectionate name-calling. This seems to be more frequent with girl babies, and includes such epithets as *coqueta* (flirt), *wawita* (little baby), *maricona* (sissy/crybaby) and *cochina* (dirty). The use of incongruous kin terms such as *mamita* (little mother), *papito* (little father), or *awila*/**awicha** (grandmother) with small children is also common.[6] Also, while the Spanish terms *chica/chiquita* (girl) and *chico/chiquito* (boy) carry a neutral or affectionate connotation, the analogous Aymara terms (**imilla** and **yuqalla**, respectively) are nearly always used to indicate disapproval or alarm.[7]

In my host household, the mother's commands to her children were almost always in Aymara, or combined a Spanish verb root with the Aymara imperative suffix. Commands or requests in Spanish seemed to be less effective, and were often followed up with **"Ratuki!"** ("quickly!"). Commands like *"Ahora!"* ("Right now!") and *"Deja!"* ("Leave that alone!") were followed by the Aymara equivalents if compliance was lagging. Scoldings were also usually in Aymara; on one occasion when this mother did rebuke her son in Spanish, she did it indirectly, addressing her complaints to me while the son stood by. In general, Aymara was the language of choice for expressing anger, among both parents and children. However, in the families I observed, it was mostly boys who talked back or argued with their parents; girls tended to avert their gaze and obey silently.

A child's gender did not seem to affect parents' choice of whether to use Spanish or Aymara, but did affect speech interaction in other ways. Boys' boisterous behavior was tolerated more than girls'; particularly during mealtimes, the oldest daughter in my host family was frequently reprimanded with "speak when you're spoken to," or similar comments. After punishment she was always silent, whereas her brothers generally made their displeasure known to all in the vicinity. Silly behavior or singing by boys usually met with parents' laughter or indifference, but in girls was often a cause for ridicule or reprimand. Apparently, gender-based norms on the use of different speech styles, and of silence, applied at an early age.

Though most children in Huatajata speak Spanish upon entering school, those preschool children I observed seemed to acquire Aymara first, though this process was often far from complete when they began to use some Spanish words. My host family's three-year-old daughter spoke almost completely in Aymara, though her parents and siblings were all bilingual; that is, they regularly used both languages productively and receptively. Nearly all the little girl's Spanish utterances were verbatim repetitions of utterances by parents, siblings, or the TV. Frequently (often when the TV was on) she would spontaneously pipe up with *"A todo bingo!"* (a slogan advertising the national lottery) or *"Tomará cerveza"* (from a beer commercial). She once overheard her father use the word *bastante*, and interrupted with "**Kunachi ukax bastantex?**" ("What's that, '*bastante*'?"). This drew laughter from the adults, causing her to repeat it several times. Adults frequently laughed at young children's use of Spanish; this sort of positive reinforcement no doubt influences Aymara children's use of Spanish during the early stages of language acquisition.

Even in homes with two bilingual parents, younger children tended to speak more Aymara than Spanish. Reasons for this can be traced to patterns of family life and language use. In many bilingual families, the husband worked in La Paz and was home only on weekends, which meant that he had less influence on children's speech. Aymara grandparents play a major role in the care of children, and older Aymara speakers are more likely to be monolingual. Nowadays, however, it is only in remote communities that children reach school age without *any* significant exposure to Spanish. Even children whose parents do not use Spanish at home soon pick it up from school-aged siblings and playmates.

In urban settings, older children of Aymara-speaking parents usually remain fluent in Aymara as they acquire Spanish. Younger ones may have a limited or passive knowledge of Aymara, owing to the influence of their school-aged (and increasingly Spanish-speaking) siblings. Also, as the older children progress through school and begin to use Spanish among themselves at home, the parents are likely to learn more Spanish as well – or at least feel more pressure to use it at home, however uncertainly, under the impression that this will help their children do well in school. Thus, by the time younger children enter school, Spanish plays a greater role in their home environment than it did for their older siblings. In this regard, it is notable that children are not just the objects of language socialization, but also its agents, influencing not only the speech of younger siblings but that of their parents as well. Many rural families move to urban centers to assure their children access to secondary education, or migrate to another region seasonally or permanently for economic reasons. Such moves present opportunities for adults to learn new linguistic varieties and registers as well. Clearly, home-language socialization is not a unidirectional process limited to early childhood, but a family network of mutual influences that shift and evolve in response to new situations, reflecting speakers' changing social roles and communicative needs.

Language and Play among Girls and Boys

The gender segregation characteristic of adult Aymara gatherings begins in childhood. Boys and girls play separately from an early age. Brothers and sisters may play together at home but, by school age, they learn that boys and girls constitute distinct social groups.[8] The settings for their play are also different: in Huatajata, boys spent most of their non-school time playing outside in groups ranging from three to more than a dozen. Girls, whose household labor was often in demand, had to stay within calling distance of their mothers, so most of their non-school time was spent at home. Even outside, their play groups seldom exceeded two or three members.

Boys also played very different types of games from girls. Boys tended towards competitive games with marbles or bottlecaps, or make-believe battles with toy pistols or karate moves. Their play was heavily influenced by television; figures such as Rambo and Bruce Lee were immensely popular with boys of all ages. Pick-up soccer games, as well as avid attention to televised soccer matches, were characteristically male activities (and, in the latter case, another occasion for the acquisition of a specialized Spanish register).

Aymara girls play a significant role in the care of younger siblings, and were observed to use Spanish with younger children even when these children did not yet use Spanish themselves. This was more often the case with reprimands (perhaps to emphasize the authority and "worldliness" of the older child), whereas the language of play at home was usually Aymara. Older children of both sexes sometimes used Spanish "baby talk" with younger siblings, demonstrating an ability to recognize different speech styles used by their parents and reproduce at least some of them in the appropriate circumstances.

The most striking characteristic of girls' play at home was how much it drew upon real-life situations – buying and selling, cooking, caring for children – often coinciding with the mother's participation in a similar activity.[9] However, girls' play was not restricted to acting out domestic chores (nor are the lives of Aymara women). I observed Aymara girls playing at marketing, which is a common activity among Aymara women, as well as driving a bus and selling ice cream, which are not. In all of these cases, the focus was on social interaction, rather than physical contest. The following rhyming exchange revealed the language socialization occurring between two sisters, ages seven and three, as they acted out marketing activities:

> "¿De dónde vienes?"   ("Where are you coming from?")
> "De Beni."   ("From Beni.")
> "¿A dónde vas?"   ("Where are you going to?")
> "A La Paz."   ("To La Paz.")

As mentioned earlier, the younger girl usually spoke Aymara; her occasional forays into Spanish were usually repetitions of utterances by family members or the television, or formulaic responses within games like this one. This rhyming game reflects the great amount of traveling that market women do, and is reminiscent of the typical Aymara greeting, **"Kawks saraskta?"** ("Where are you going?")

The above descriptions of Aymara children's play reveal their imitation of adult gender roles and their experimentation with adult speech styles: baby talk, the singsong of a bus driver calling out stops, or a market women bargaining for the best price. Also notable is the defiant or boastful speech of boys who, as men, will need to produce such speech or respond to it appropriately in order to become fully integrated members of male society.

Men's and Women's Speaking Roles at Home

Children learn to speak in particular ways, not only from the speech directed at them, but also from eavesdropping on conversations between parents and other adults. While quantitative analysis of conversational parameters (such as distribution of speaking time, interruption patterns, control of topic, etc.) would no doubt shed much light on how Aymara gender relations are manifested in language, little work of this sort has been done.

Still, some general patterns can be identified. Since social gatherings are loosely segregated by sex, most extended adult conversations, aside from those between family members, involve interlocutors of the same sex. Relaxed, attentive conversation with guests is seen as the husband's prerogative, since women at home must usually divide their attention between conversing, cooking, caring for children, and attending to other household tasks. The husband is seen as the desired conversationalist for special guests; the wife's role is to keep children and other disturbances from impinging on the conversation. Correspondingly, I had been in my host household for almost a week before the husband arrived home from his job in the city, questioned me about my fieldwork plans, gave his approval, and officially welcomed me to the household. Though I had been talking with his wife all week, this particular function was not hers to fulfill.

In the husband–wife interactions I observed, men took up considerably more of the speaking time than women did. Men's conversational dominance also extended to control of topic; in mixed conversations, a woman's attempt to supplement a male speaker's narrative would often be met by a hesitant, thoughtful look, as if the man were considering how this new information might fit into the discursive structure he was creating. After a pause he would often continue his original train of thought with no reference to the woman's intervention. This is reminiscent of Coates' observation that "[American men] do not feel they have to make a link with the previous speaker's contribution ... [they] are more likely to ignore what has been said before and to concentrate on making their own point" (Coates, 1986:152).

These conversational tendencies, like many other behaviors that could be characterized as sexist, were much more evident among younger men than among older ones, and seemed to reflect the speaker's degree of urban contact. Among older people without such contact, men did not noticeably dominate conversation, and conversation was nearly always in Aymara (the interactions described above took place in Spanish). As Briggs has noted, according to Aymara social norms, "it is expected that both men and women speak like **jaqi**.[10] Courtesy is not gender-specific" (Briggs, 1997: 183). Increased urban contact implies increased adoption of not only Spanish, but also the conversational and gender norms associated with monolingual Spanish speakers.

Code-Mixing and Code-Switching

Since most children in Huatajata grow up with at least one bilingual parent, mixing and switching between the two languages is common. Only rarely is this attributable to lack of fluency in one or the other language; rather, the fluid, creative use of intermediate and alternating codes constitutes a distinctive set of speech styles associated with a distinctive bilingual Aymara identity.

In the speech of *huatajateños*, Spanish and Aymara elements were often so tightly interwoven that it was hard to define utterances as "belonging" to either language. In the examples below, Aymara elements are in bold type:

"Apura**smaw**" ("you'd better hurry"):
apura- + */-sma/* deciderative + /-**wa**/ sentence suffix

"Deja**mcha**!" ("put that down"):
deja- + */-m/* imperative + /-**cha**/ sentence suffix

"Me asusta**xä**!"[11] ("it startled me"):
asusta- + */-**xa**/ sent. suffix + /-¨/ sent. suffix

Mixing also occurs in the opposite direction, with Spanish suffixes attached to Aymara roots:

"**Kumu**me" ("carry me [on a bicycle] "):
kumu- + /-*me*/ imperative, 1st pers. object

"**Anati**remos?" ("shall we play?"):
anati- + /-*remos*/ 1st pers. plural future

One might interpret the above forms as examples of borrowing, but several factors argue against this interpretation. Gumperz (1982: 66) defines borrowing as "the introduction of single words or short, frozen idiomatic phrases from one [speech] variety into another." While this also occurs between Aymara and Spanish, forms like those cited above are very productive, in that virtually any verb or noun stem from either language can be combined with suffixes from the other. Also, equivalent unmixed forms in both languages are also common, indicating that this sort of code-mixing is a stylistic choice and not simply a result of the displacement of Aymara elements by Spanish ones. Mixing at the word level – as in *"Bien* **tayxayaschiya**!" ("That's really cold!") and *"Pero* **jum** *primero* **sarnaqanim**!" ("But you go down first!") – was also common in *huatajateño* speech, as were more "traditional" forms of code-mixing and code-switching.[12]

Code-switching in children's speech is of particular interest for analyzing language socialization. Bilingual children not only learn which contexts are appropriate for the exclusive use of one language or another, but also learn how, when, and with whom one may mix or alternate codes. Even very young speakers exploit the social expectations around different languages for humorous purposes, like the three children I overheard laughing and singing a TV advertising jingle, incongruously substituting Aymara color terms for the Spanish ones. Metaphorical switching, especially for humorous or derisive ends, also transmits social expectations and values around different types of speech. The following example is from a young bilingual couple, joking about the Aymara interference in the speech of an old woman overheard exclaiming about a hurt finger:

"Mi riru, mi riru!"   "My finger, my finger!"
(Standard Spanish: *mi dedo*)

This sort of ridicule, though common in Bolivia, was observed only in small groups of fluent bilinguals; it would be considered quite rude in the presence of one whose speech displayed similar interference. Such joking, overheard by children, sends a clear message about the social prestige and public perception of those who attempt to use the dominant language despite a limited command of it.

Code-switching often marks in-group/out-group boundaries, including the boundary between men and women. Correspondingly, patterns of code-switching, as well as fluency in different codes, contributed to the marking of gender identities and roles in Huatajata. The following example occurred during a gathering of several men for an all-night vigil following the death of one man's young son. The children of the household were peripheral participants in the event, but were not expected to take an active part in conversation. Given the traditional, familial nature of the gathering, most of the men's conversation was in Aymara, but they switched into Spanish when conversation turned to the profusion of robberies in the capital. As speakers took turns recounting their encounters with thieves, the emphasis seemed to be on their shared status as men of the world, accustomed to the risks of city life since their work required that they spend much time there. However, the conversation shifted back to Aymara when the subject turned to drug addiction, highlighting the implicit feeling that this problem afflicted principally those *from* the city, and that rural people (i.e. Aymara speakers) did not take part in such behavior.

As Kramarae (1981: 91) has noted, and as this event shows, "speakers manipulate their speaking styles to emphasize or de-emphasize particular social identities." The switches described above indexed not only the particular topic at hand, but also the relationship of the speakers *as a social group* to those topics. Especially interesting in this case is that both Spanish and Aymara were alternately used to express solidarity within the same group of speakers, indeed within the same speech event. Speakers may have many things in common, and choose different codes depending on which criteria of group membership they wish to emphasize.

Nevertheless, there may not always be consensus around the use of different codes; rather, speech norms are negotiated in concrete speech events. These negotiations are usually implicit (employing gesture, tone, word choice, following or refusing to follow another's code-switch, etc.), but may erupt into explicit directives. At one point in the aforementioned event, one man began to talk in Spanish (perhaps for my benefit) about the beauty of the Aymara language and the "borrowed" status of Spanish as a language imposed by the *conquistadores*. Eventually another man shouted at him good-naturedly (in Aymara) to speak Aymara; the others murmured their assent, and certainly Aymara seemed more appropriate than Spanish for this intimate setting, with everyone drinking together in the aftermath of a family tragedy. The first speaker ceded the point and switched back to Aymara. One can interpret such moments, when the appropriateness of one or the other language to a particular situation is openly questioned, as evidence that language shift is occurring – as it undoubtedly is in this community.

In some bilingual communities, code-mixing and lexical borrowing are less frequent, or even absent. The presence or absence of these phenomena is determined not by structural factors in the languages involved (though these may play some role), but by the language habits and ideologies present in the speech community. In communities where code-mixing is considered unacceptable (or even impossible), children soon learn to keep their languages separate; in communities where code-mixing is essential to speakers' everyday interaction, children learn to employ it habitually and creatively as their elders do. Small children often mix languages, but can distinguish them from a very early age. If they continue to code-mix and code-switch as they grow older, this is due not to "confusion" between the two languages (as popular ideologies often assume), but to the speech norms of the community to which they belong. In other words, it is due not to individual cognitive factors but to social ones.

Men's and Women's Language Use in Public Contexts

By tagging along at the edges of adult society – in ritual gatherings, in meetings, at the market – children learn to use Spanish and Aymara, separately and in combination, in gender-appropriate ways. On formal occasions in Huatajata, men and women sat separately, and thus their conversation was also segregated. For example, at a pre-funeral gathering that I attended in the home of the deceased's brother and sister-in-law, the men sat speaking quietly in Aymara while the women cooked immense amounts of food in preparation for the funeral itself. During serious family or community events, Aymara is usually the language of choice, partly because these events include many older people, who tend to be monolingual in Aymara.

Ritual gatherings

At the funeral itself, several men made speeches in Aymara, and the school principal, a monolingual Spanish speaker, spoke briefly in Spanish (the deceased was a schoolteacher). Conversation among the mourners was in Aymara. Later, I was conversing with one of the speech makers, who by that time was fairly inebriated, when a woman sitting nearby called me over; she told me to leave the men to their drinking and come sit with the women. While heavy drinking was usual at such events, women did not partake to the degree that men did (in part because they were responsible for getting their men home), nor did they engage in the sometimes loud and belligerent, sometimes rambling and philosophical speech characteristic of men when they drank.

The gathering eventually moved indoors to an all-night vigil for the spirit of the deceased. The men sat in chairs on one side of the room; the women sat together on the floor. The men's conversation continued long into the night, alternating between Spanish and Aymara; the women were sleepy and quiet, saying little; children slept in the corners or in their mothers' laps. During this vigil, like the one described earlier, men expressed sympathy and intimacy by sharing alcohol, coca and conversation, while women's solidarity was marked by the sharing of food and silence.

Public meetings

One type of speech event that does not occur within the home, but is linked to others that do, is the public meeting. These interactions illustrate both the role of gender in linguistic socialization and the role of language in gender socialization. Though children do not participate actively at such events, they are often expected to listen closely and report back to their parents with near-verbatim accounts of the proceedings (Hardman, 1983). Briggs (1997: 183, my translation) notes that "one of the ways in which the Aymara recognize human conduct in speech is the correct use of inflectional verb suffixes that distinguish personal experience from reports based on what others have said." As children grow into their "human" status, they learn to use these suffixes properly. In reported speech, Aymara speakers usually quote directly rather than paraphrase (Briggs, 1997: 186; Stratford, 1989: 155–56), and children learn this skill as well by carrying out their "reporter" function.

The most frequent meetings were of the school parents' organization. Though directed by school personnel, these meetings differed from other school-related events in that they were carried out in Aymara (even though some school personnel did not speak Aymara), owing to the high number of Aymara monolinguals attending. School meetings usually involved long discussions over tedious bureaucratic issues, and were attended mainly by women; in contrast, meetings on issues of major concern to the entire community attracted more men.

One meeting, called to decide what kind of uniforms the students should have for physical education and for the upcoming Independence Day parade, and how much each family should contribute to hire a band, was moderated by the principal, who stood at the front accompanied by three teachers (all bilingual men). Women sat on the ground, some with their children, while the men sat or stood apart, against the wall of one of the school buildings. Female teachers (who were also native to the community) sat with the women, rather than with their male colleagues.

After a brief introduction by the principal, laying out the problems to be addressed, the floor was opened to suggestions and discussion. Subsequent participation by men and women revealed two distinct discourse styles. Nearly all talk directed towards the group as a whole was by men, who formally requested the floor and were recognized by the principal before speaking. The women talked among themselves in small groups, sometimes reacting to what a male speaker had said and sometimes talking while he was talking. Almost invariably, women directed their suggestions and criticisms to those in their immediate vicinity; only once or twice did a woman address the entire group, and on those occasions she did not ask or wait to be recognized, but simply started talking loudly enough to be heard by all. Despite this unorthodox manner of assuming the floor, women who did this were listened to attentively.

Occasionally, after simultaneous murmuring among the women, a man would take the floor to make a proposal. Only one issue (parade uniforms) was decided by a formal vote; the decision not to buy new physical education uniforms this year was reached after a period of simultaneous talk, without my at first realizing that it had been. Discussion of the quota for the band ended when a suggestion reiterated by the principal provoked no outcry from the group; lack of opposition constituted approval.

The speech of men and women in the meeting differed not only in the audience to whom it was directed and the manner of getting listeners' attention, but also in the registers employed. Most Aymara speakers use some Spanish borrowings, but these vary between men and women, and the distinction becomes sharper in formal contexts. In Huatajata, even women who spoke Spanish fluently usually limited Spanish borrowings to conjunctions (such as *pero* or *entonces*), or to verb and noun roots taking Aymara suffixes (**"uka** *kulur***ampi"** – "with that color"; "*iskwila***ru**" – "to the school"). In contrast, men incorporated entire Spanish phrases into longer Aymara utterances, especially qualifiers such as *"yo creo que"* ("I think that ...") or *"sin embargo"* ("nevertheless ..."). They often used Spanish to assume the floor (*"Una palabra, señor"* – "A word please, sir") or to preface their suggestions (*"Padres de familia, señores, con todo respeto"* – "Parents, gentlemen, with all due respect ...") before continuing in Aymara. These phrases served as code markers for a distinct Aymara speech register (observed also in church and the aforementioned funeral) associated with public discourse. Since women addressing the group invariably just started talking about the matter at hand, without asking to be recognized or introducing their statements in any way, they did not make use of these framing devices. Inasmuch as public discourse was a male domain, this register was distinctive of men's speech.

Local language ideologies were unambiguous about which kinds of public speech "counted." In my host family's home and elsewhere, I often heard (from women as well as men) that "women don't participate in meetings"; "the women don't want to talk, the men decide everything." These perceptions of who "participated" and "decided" reflected men's use of the recognized registers and channels for participation, more than the actual outcome of the meetings themselves. In the meetings observed, women spoke a great deal, but not to the men or the audience in general; rather, they discussed things among themselves in small groups. On one occasion, they easily voted down a proposal, supported by most of the men, that each family donate 2 *bolivianos* (about $1 US) to hire a band. Another time, when a suggestion on student uniforms was brought to a vote, the women laughed when mostly only men raised their hands; the suggestion was easily voted down in favor of a uniform that the women liked better. When there was no formal vote, women made their opinions known through collective murmurs or outcries at some suggestions, and tacit approval of others. Frequently a suggestion was discussed among small groups of women before a man would propose it formally. Either way, women usually decided the outcome by sheer force of numbers. Furthermore, several Aymara women (from communities besides Huatajata) have laughingly told me how men will put off a meeting or a decision with some pretext, when the real reason is that they need to discuss the issue with their wives at home. These "behind-the-scenes" procedures are not lost upon children, and form part of their learning on how different types of speech are distributed, and collective decisions made.

Another speech genre restricted to men in Huatajata was talk about the history and meaning of Aymara language and culture. As part of the cultural revitalization mentioned above, a politically conscious Aymara identity now requires being able not only to speak the language, but to speak knowledgeably *about* it. Several men expressed to me their disapproval of those whose Aymara speech was sprinkled with Spanish borrowings (though their own speech was seldom free of borrowings), or their theories on the origins of the Aymara language, the significance of Aymara culture, and similar topics. While I occasionally had conversations about Aymara language and culture with women, men were much quicker to adopt the "expert" role, and expounded at much greater length, the conversation often becoming a monologue. In contrast, when conversing with Aymara women, I never heard one talk for more than a minute or so without pausing to wait for a reply. This practice again reflects men's control over public speaking, in that only men adopted the role of cultural representatives educating someone outside the group.

Linguistic Repertoires of Aymara Men and Women

Clearly, in Huatajata there is a difference in the range of speech styles and genres available to each sex. Even women who were fluent bilinguals did not engage in the range of linguistic behavior that bilingual men did, and received particularly short shrift in those genres that are publicly valued and express collective sentiments. In sermons or speeches (even with an audience of one), men could speak with the weight of tradition or an institution behind their words; when a woman spoke, she spoke for herself alone.

Women's repertoire was also more limited in terms of the settings in which they spoke. In some settings, women seemed to choose silence, rather than have it imposed upon them. Men moderating public meetings sometimes urged the women to speak, with little success. The reasons why women choose not to assume certain discursive roles are undoubtedly linked to processes of gender socialization and childhood opportunities for verbal performance (see Luykx, 1989).

The above discussion should not obscure the fact that focusing on publicly valued speech may make women's linguistic repertoires appear more limited than they really are. Exploration of women's speech genres has lagged behind analysis of male genres, among indigenous groups even more than in the industrialized world. We should also remember that, in the Andes, non-verbal forms of symbolic representation (such as textiles), are semantically complex and structured in ways reminiscent of language, and are not only essential to children's socialization (usually but not exclusively girls' socialization) but are reflective of Aymara cosmology and social organization in general (see Arnold & Yapita, 2000).

The Long View: Language Socialization and Language Shift

The scenes described above may give the impression that Aymara is alive and well, thriving in the creative speech practices of bilinguals, in a stable if unequal relation with Spanish. This is only partly true. While Aymara is still widely used in the city of La Paz and surrounding rural areas, and continues to be transmitted to a sizable fraction of the younger generation, it is definitely losing ground to Spanish. Most Bolivians today are bilingual, but indigenous language monolingualism is declining, while Spanish monolingualism is on the rise (see Albó, 1995; Luykx, 1998). Longitudinally, we can imagine a "wave" of language shift moving from a period (some fifty years ago) when most Bolivians were monolingual Aymara or Quechua speakers, to a future in which monolingual Spanish speakers will form the majority. Currently, the crest of the wave is at the midpoint between these two extremes, but its direction is clear.

As if pressure from Spanish were not enough, Aymara is also losing ground to Quechua, as it probably has done since pre-Columbian times and certainly since the Spanish Conquest (see Albó, 1995: Calvet, 1998: 91–92). Aymara is declining in some areas where it has existed alongside Quechua for generations, but there is little data to indicate the historical depth of this shift. More recently, Quechua speakers have migrated to practically all parts of the country, sometimes in sufficient numbers to establish new Quechua speech communities in non-traditionally-Quechua areas. Simultaneously, smaller numbers of Aymara speakers have migrated into Quechua areas, where their language is not always well received (Bustamante, 2001: 110-111).[13]

Nearly fifty years ago, Weinreich (1953: 107) defined language shift as one language "yielding its functions to the other." In Bolivia, major state initiatives currently aim to expand indigenous languages into *new* contexts and functions, most notably school-related ones. While these efforts are laudable (though not without their own risks; see Luykx 1999b), it is the gradual displacement of Aymara by Spanish in functions that have traditionally been the former's stronghold (i.e. domestic ones) that may prove definitive for the future survival of the language. For this reason, it is necessary to expand our current conception of "language policy" to include not only the sphere of official state actions, but also decisions made at the community and family level. Such decisions are often implicit and unconscious, but they are no less crucial to determining the speed and direction of language shift. In this regard we may refer to *family language policy* as an important area for both research and activism.

Siguán and Mackey give an idea of the range of this concept:

> In any bilingual family it is easy to detect attitudes favorable to one or the other language, which generally reflect the attitudes existing in the social milieu to which the family belongs ... language attitudes become particularly clear at the moment of choosing the language in which the child will first learn to speak, and the order and time in which s/he will have contact with other languages. This choice may be the object of an explicit decision, which may imply changes in the linguistic behavior of the family and later influence the choice of school or type of instruction. That is, we may without exaggeration speak of a language policy of the family. (Siguán & Mackey 1986: 60–61, my translation)

Clearly, in order for Aymara to survive, it must continue to be transmitted to children in the home. But even when children are initially socialized in Aymara (accompanied or not by Spanish), speech patterns learned at home may be undermined when children begin to participate in other social contexts. Most families that have shifted from Aymara towards Spanish have done so over three or four generations (monolingual indigenous grandparents, bilingual parents, monolingual Spanish-speaking children). But this shift can occur within a single generation, particularly when the entrance into school is accompanied by strong prohibitions on the use of the mother tongue. Thus one encounters individuals who are practically monolingual in their *second* language (a condition often referred to as "subtractive bilingualism"). Even in less extreme situations, the predominance of Spanish in formal, institutional, and urban spaces (especially the school and the job market) grants a wealth of advantages to Spanish speakers, and exerts an inexorable pressure against the use of Aymara. As a result, many adults who grew up speaking Aymara choose to raise their own children in Spanish.

It is thus somewhat artificial to treat the home as an isolated sphere with regard to language socialization, given that wider social pressures penetrate the most intimate of domestic interactions. In the wake of modernization, parental norms and attitudes become less central to children's post-infancy language development. Defined by the dominant society as linguistically deficient, many indigenous parents place their hopes for their children's linguistic success in the school. Family language policy is often shaped in anticipation of the school's requirements. When it is, it may have negative consequences for the mother tongue; when it isn't, children's entrance into school is often traumatic. Even before entering school, Aymara children become aware of the association between school and Spanish, via older siblings' use of Spanish, their parents' switching from Aymara to Spanish to talk about the school, etc. We must therefore pay attention not only to family language policy per se, but to its articulation with the language policies of other spheres such as the school, the workplace, the neighborhood, and the media.

Conclusions

The examples explored in this chapter suggest various conclusions: programmatic, methodological, and theoretical. First, though the family is obviously not the only sphere implicated in minority language survival, efforts to preserve minority languages are doomed to failure if they do not take into account familial patterns of language choice (Fishman, 1991). Though most language planning resources are channeled toward higher-order spheres such as the school or the mass media, *"family language planning* is needed to ensure relatively stable and enduring bilingualism" (Baker, 2001: 93, emphasis in original).

At the same time, a dynamic view of language socialization shows that it is not limited to the family or to early childhood. Language competencies, choices, and ideologies change over a speaker's lifespan, reflecting changing social networks, pressures, and opportunities. Thus, while home language planning is essential to indigenous language maintenance, it is not by itself sufficient.

Methodologically, studies of language socialization must expand their focus not only beyond the home, but beyond the individual language learner as well. Home language socialization is not limited to everyday interactions between family members. Many other types of speech events (such as the funeral gatherings described above) also take place in the home, and family language interactions are directly or indirectly linked to many speech events (such as public meetings) that occur *outside* the home. Within these communicative networks, children participate in multiple roles and social configurations whose complexity surpasses the parent–child (or child–child) dyads that have traditionally been the focus of research (cf. Rogoff, 1990: 97–98).

It is also useful to view children's language socialization not as a one-way process, but as a dynamic network of mutual family influences. If parents shape children's speech behavior and attitudes, children's evolving competencies also influence parents' language choices; in the "language ecology" of the family, children are as much agents as objects. For this reason, socialization should be viewed in terms of "participation," rather than merely "transmission." As García notes in his study of Quechua children's socialization: "Understanding learning as participation frees us of the conventional notion of learning as the reception of 'knowledge' ... [and] helps us adequately situate the learner in sociocultural activities, recognizing his/her active role ... " (García, 2000: 52; my translation).

Similarly, Lave and Wenger (1991) conceive of learning as "legitimate peripheral participation," in which learners' socialization follows a path of gradually increasing participation in the discourses of particular communities of practice.[14] This relational view "focuses attention on ways in which [learning] is an evolving, continuously renewed set of relations" (Lave & Wenger 1991: 49–50), and shifts our gaze from bilingual children's internalization of a set of abstract grammatical rules and sociolinguistic norms, to how they *use* their languages in a diversity of interactions and negotiations with interlocutors whose own language socialization is also ongoing.

Finally, we have seen that, in terms of language use, a bilingual is not simply the sum of two monolinguals. Children growing up bilingually acquire, not two discrete systems, but an evolving linguistic repertoire that *draws upon* two systems. It includes not only their formal features (phonological, grammatical, semantic, pragmatic), but also conventions around how and when to combine them, the social meanings of different varieties and combinations of varieties, and local ideologies about all of these. As we come to realize how truly widespread these types of situations are, we may hope that more research will address the complexities of the language socialization of bilinguals, and its dialectical relationship with their socialization into particular gender, ethnic, national, and class identities.

Notes

1. Aymara is the second largest indigenous language in Bolivia, after Quechua, and is spoken in lesser numbers in Peru and Chile as well. Though child socialization among the Aymara has been less studied than among the Quechua, reflecting the latter's greater numbers and distribution throughout the continent, Aymara and Quechua peoples share many linguistic and cultural features. Some scholars (Libermann *et al.*, 1989; Urban, 1991) suggest that the two groups have melded to form a single cultural complex; thus the reader may find useful studies on primary socialization among Quechua populations (Romero, 1994; Franco & Ochoa, 1995; García, 2000; Rindstet, 2000).
2. Though reading and writing practices are an important part of home language socialization in many societies, this is not generally the case in rural indigenous Andean populations. This chapter therefore focuses exclusively on oral language.
3. The data presented here, collected in 1987, refer to one particular community (itself far from homogenous), and cannot be generalized to all Aymara communities. Throughout, I have tried to indicate which features analyzed are characteristic of Aymara cultural and speech patterns in general, and which are particular to Huatajata.
4. When these data were collected, children's fluency in Spanish was not associated with loss of Aymara in Huatajata, though this sort of subtractive bilingualism has been noted elsewhere.
5. I did not hear her use Quechua during the research period, except a few times at my request. There were no other Quechua speakers in Huatajata that I was aware of, and this woman had not attempted to pass her own first language on to her children.
6. Spanish words are in italics, Aymara words are in bold type; in some cases Spanish words are written to indicate an "aymarized" pronunciation.
7. In the city, these terms are sometimes used in a racist, disdainful way to refer to young indigenous adults, especially servants.
8. Miracle (1976: 252–256) describes several Aymara games played by both sexes, but I did not observe these in Huatajata.
9. Doll-play, which I never witnessed among boys, revealed some interesting features of the socialization of Aymara girls. Girls did not frequently initiate extensive role-playing with dolls; usually they would simply wrap up a doll and carry it around on their backs, as Aymara mothers (and sisters) do with babies. Nearly all role-playing involving dolls was initiated, not by little girls, but by *mothers*, and revolved around the social relations between mother, toddler, and "baby." See Luykx 1989: 42 for a more detailed description of such play.
10. Aymara for "person," but strongly implying social correctness and respect.
11. The diacritic ¨ indicates a long vowel, the /x/ a postvelar voiceless fricative. Stress is on the final syllable in the first set of examples, and on the penultimate syllable in the second set. For reasons of space, further phonological and semantic details are omitted here. Interested readers are referred to Hardman *et al.* (1988), Briggs (1993), and Cerrón-Palomino (2000).
12. "Traditional" in the sense of reflecting the classic features identified by Gumperz (1982), Hymes (1974b), Saville-Troike (1982) and others, such as switching at semantic or grammatical boundaries, to qualify an utterance, to highlight a particular topic or addressee, to mark in-group/out-group relationships, etc. For specific Aymara/Spanish examples, see Luykx 1989: 51–58.
13. Romero (1994: 80) mentions the "oppression" of Quechua by Aymara in a community inhabited mainly by native Quechua speakers, some of whom learn Aymara through contact with neighboring towns (and radio, since local Aymara programming greatly outweighs that in Quechua). However, this community is in the northern part of the (overwhelmingly Aymara) department of La Paz; in the country as a whole, the opposite situation is more common. In truly trilingual areas (Spanish/Quechua/Aymara),

Aymara often occupies an almost clandestine space, associated mainly with women and intimate, domestic contexts (L.E. López, personal communication).

14. Luykx (1999a) explores this theme with regard to bilingual Aymara students in a rural teachers' college, and the way their language use is linked to the creation of particular subjectivities – ethnic, gender, class, national and professional.

Chapter 3

Collaborative Literacy in a Mexican Immigrant Household: The Role of Sibling Mediators in the Socialization of Pre-School Learners[1]

MARÍA DE LA PIEDRA AND HARRIETT D. ROMO

This chapter focuses on a literacy event that occurred in the home of the Valdéz family, a Mexican immigrant household, involving a pre-literate, pre-verbal 18 month-old child. Our analysis of this literacy event addresses two main points: (1) the important influence of siblings in language socialization and literacy development, (2) the ways in which language and literacy are socially constructed in a non-mainstream immigrant family and community. This case study is part of a larger evaluation study of an Early Head Start program.[2] The definition of literacy used in this chapter is one of literacy as a cultural and social phenomenon. We explore the sociocultural contexts of a literacy event in which older siblings mediate the meaning of words through mutual knowledge, and play an important role in the language socialization of their younger sibling, Liliana (L).

We draw on theoretical frameworks presented by the "new literacy studies," which focus on cultural meanings and uses of local literacy practices (Baynham, 1993; Bloch, 1993; Camitta, 1993; Chirinos, 1997; Hornberger, 1997, 1998; Kulick & Stroud, 1993; Probst, 1993; Rockhill, 1993; Street, 1993, 1995) and the anthropological literature of "funds of knowledge" (Gonzales *et al.*, 1995; Moll *et al.*, 1993; Velez-Ibañez & Greenberg, 1992). The "funds of knowledge" literature emphasizes the role of social networks in the transmission, redefinition, and recreation of ways of knowing, and the significant role of culture in formal and informal education.

Vygotsky (1978, 1986) and Wertsch (1991, 1998) emphasized the importance of social conditions in understanding thinking and development, and viewed thinking as a characteristic not of the child alone but of the child-in-social-activities with others (Moll, 1990). Kreckel (1981) makes a distinction between common knowledge, which two or more people have in common as a result of being brought up under similar conditions such as culture, subculture, religion, and education, and shared knowledge, which is the negotiated common knowledge based on mutual interaction used for future interaction. Mutual knowledge refers to something that an individual holds to be true with great certainty – knowledge that the individual knows for sure that the other individual she is communicating with also knows for sure. Mutual knowledge is a basis for successful communication, and is key to the development of reading. For example, in the Valdéz family certain knowledge and beliefs may be unique to L and her sisters, since they share a separate set of world experiences from those of their mother. There is also the common background knowledge that the members of this particular family and members of this immigrant community assume to be held common by virtue of the fact that they have similar background or up-bringing (Lee, 2001).

Much of the traditional literature on language socialization has been conceptualized as a one-on-one, unidirectional process and has focused on the socialization process during adult caregiver–child communication. Studies of caregiver–child interactions in story reading and play have demonstrated the processes by which a young child learns not only to speak, but to speak and feel like a native speaker (Kanagy, 1999). Additionally most studies of child language acquisition have been conducted in mainstream families or mainstream classrooms where mothers talk to children using formulaic patterns or routines found in mainstream school settings. Heath (1982a) reminds us that the culture that children learn as they grow up is, in fact, ways of taking meaning from the environment around them. She emphasizes that the "ways of taking from books are as much a part of learned behavior as are ways of eating, sitting, playing games, and building houses" (reprinted in Schieffelin & Ochs, 1986b: 97). As parents interact with their children in the preschool years, they give them, through modeling and specific instruction, ways of taking from books that seem natural in numerous institutional settings such as schools, banks, post offices, businesses and government offices. Heath (1983) emphasized that each community's ways of taking from the printed word and using this knowledge are interdependent with the ways children learn to talk in their social interactions with caregivers.

Studies of language socialization in pre-school and elementary school classrooms have shown how teacher–student discourse in first and second language contexts socializes students to follow cultural norms of language interactions. However, recent studies of language socialization and cognition have found that peer interactions also serve as language socializing processes (Tudge, 1990). Cook (1999) demonstrated, for example, how peer presentations encouraged students to be active listeners and to provide reactions to peers while the teacher played a supportive, rather than an evaluative, role in the process. The impact of inter-actional routines on language socialization in a kindergarten setting was explored by Ruth Kanagy (1999). Analysis of naturalistic data from three classroom routines from several points in the year revealed incremental changes in the form, content, participant structure, and nonverbal behavior of teachers and students as learners moved from peripheral to autonomous participation. Through repetition and scaffolded help provided by teachers and peers, the children were socialized toward interactional competence. Language socialization studies show clearly that, whether in native or target contexts, language socialization and the acquisition of pragmatic competence require extended participation in culturally-mediated inter-actions. Empirical studies weave together new insights into the specific linguistic means used by caregivers (both parents and teachers) and peers in the socialization of interactional competence in children in home and school environments. This study contributes a unique perspective of how, in a non-mainstream, immigrant home, siblings help socialize young children to understand what it means to know a language.

In developing this chapter, we first present a review of studies of immigrant communities. Second, we include a transcription of a segment of a videotaped literacy event in the home of this immigrant family and use discourse analysis to show how the family members engage in "collective literacy" and how an older sibling uses mutual knowledge to mediate this literacy event for L. The findings demonstrate that siblings as well as adults act as literacy mediators to help young children participate in literacy events in the home. This interaction demonstrated the strong influence of siblings who may have mutual knowledge, outside of the experiences of adults, that can assist in the language socialization of a young child.

The Ideological Model of Literacy

Gathering evidence from an ethnography of middle class households and schools in the United States, Street (1995) argued that literacy is defined by middle class parents and schools within a framework of learning, teaching, and schooling – a process that Street and Street (1995) have called the "pedagogization of literacy." Street and Street (1995: 117) found that literacy practices within middle class house-hold contexts were similar to literacy practices found at school, and parents were concerned about socializing their children in ways legitimized by the school. Studies of immigrant families have suggested that researchers have conceptualized these domains in over-simplified ways, and perhaps the boundaries between family and community networks may not be as sharply delineated as in mainstream settings.

Ethnographies of "literacies" among immigrant populations (Baynham, 1993; Farr & Guerra, 1995; Rockhill, 1993; Weistein-Shr, 1993, 1994) and studies of indige-nous people in developing countries (Bloch, 1993; Chirinos, 1997; Hornberger 1988, 1997, 1998; Kulick & Stroud, 1993; Probst, 1993; Street 1984) have found that "local literacies" contest a hegemonic conception of literacy in diverse ways. These studies challenge the stigmatization of the "illiterate," who have been described as lacking cognitive abilities. They attempt to understand literacy in terms of concrete social practices and to theorize in terms of the ideologies in which different literacies are embedded (Bloch, 1993; Godenzzi, 1997; Hornberger, 1997, 1998; Hornberger & Hardman, 1994; Street, 1993; Street & Street, 1995).

Viewing literacies from the perspective of an ethnography of communication suggests that speaking (and reading and writing) are ways of communicating that are characteristic of a particular cultural group, and context is crucial to the interpretation of behavior and meaning (Hymes, 1974a; Farr & Guerra, 1995: 7; Hornberger & Hardman, 1994). These theories can be illustrated by the following review of three studies of literacies among immigrant populations.

Local Literacies

Literacy for immigrants learning a new culture becomes a valuable resource in the new context, one that is shared within the social network. Farr and Guerra (1995) focused on literacy practices among Mexican immigrant families in Chicago, and found that in the bilingual Mexicano community there were literacy practices in both English and Spanish that were linked to different domains of the lives of the families. The religious domain incorporated mainly literacy uses in Spanish. The researchers described two literacy events: *doctrina* (catechism) and the *levantamiento* (putting away the baby Jesus after Christmas)(Farr & Guerra, 1995: 15). Farr (1994) found that the extended social network, which is part of a way of living as Mexican immigrants, plays an important role in the literacy practices of the immigrants.

Weinstein-Shr (1993) studied the meanings and uses of literacy practices among Hmong immigrants in the United States. Like Farr and Guerra (1995), she focused on the relationship between literacy practices and other resources, such as kinship ties and the Hmong's native language literacy. She presents in-depth portraits of two Hmong men who used literacy in different ways depending on their own conceptions of their lives in Philadelphia. One of the men, Chou, wanted to assimilate as quickly as possible to the Philadelphia community. The second man, Pao Youa Lo, was not interested at all in learning English or becoming part of the larger Philadelphia community. Both men had positions of authority within their communities; however, these positions were defined by the host community standards and by traditional standards, respectively. Chou chose to live in a community where the majority of the Hmong held the same ideals towards assimilation. Chou used standard English literacy in order to reach his goals. He was a resource in English literacy for members of his community. His literacy enabled him to become a "cultural broker" among other Hmong members of his Church.

In contrast, Pao Youa Lo had poor English oral and written skills and did not really use them. Instead, he relied on alliances he had developed with the members of his clan. Pao used his native literacy skills to become informed about important events in his country and in the world, becoming a "community news keeper." The uses of literacy affected social relationships and created new roles (cultural broker and news keeper) for these two men within their local communities.

Baynham (1993) focused on "interpreters" and "mediators of literacy" to understand literacy practices among Moroccan immigrants in London. Baynham paid close attention to the *interactional context* of the literacy event in addition to ethnographic accounts and oral histories, where the "situatedness" of the interaction is important for Baynham's approach. From his perspective, literacy practices are a "joint construction" (Baynham, 1993: 301). Baynham compares "mediators of literacy" with "interpreters." Both include the participation of more than one person and the joint construction of the communicative (literacy) event. Mediators are not just passive participants of the event; they also interpret the meaning of the text. Baynham's research shows how communicative purposes can be achieved in situations where one or more participants lack the code knowledge needed to participate.

Baynham (1993: 309) found that an interaction that at first glance seemed like a fairly simple mix of the "oral" contains in fact some rather complex shifts and switches of footing in the ways that the text is related. For example, in order to explain the content of a letter from a government agency, the mediator of literacy switched mode from literate to oral, and also switched register from technical to non-technical. Baynham (1993: 313) argued that the mode and code-switchings are a result of living in a multilingual setting "where individuals and groups struggle to make texts speak and work for them, struggle to make and exchange meanings."

Each of these studies challenges the dominant belief that there is one "literacy" and that it is autonomous and isolated from social context. Contexts are mutually constructed, constantly shifting, situationally defined, and accomplished through the interactional work of participants (Erickson & Schultz, 1997). These studies provide conceptual and methodological tools to better understand the literacy practices found in the Valdéz family, a Mexican immigrant family in Texas.

Methodological Approach[3]

The participants in this study were a Mexican immigrant mother, Julia Valdéz (32 years old), and her five daughters: Juana (12), Ana (7), Milagros (5), L (18 months), and Melba (6 months). Pseudonyms have been used to protect the participants' identities. We met this family at Head Start activities and spoke with them several times before conducting this study. This family is one of several families who agreed to allow us to observe their child in their home and in the Early Head Start classroom. The data presented were gathered through fieldwork consisting of ten hours of participant observation, two 90-minute interviews with the mother about literacy meanings and uses, an interview with the oldest daughter, and videotapes and audio tapes of storytelling, songs, and natural interactions in the family's living room and front yard. In addition, approximately three hours of an afternoon with the family were videotaped. The interview with the mother included questions that could be part of a life history interview, as recommended by researchers of literacy among immigrant groups (Baynham, 1993; Weinstein-Shr, 1993, 1994). The interviews and videotaped literacy events were transcribed and analyzed in a search for the ways "mediators of literacy" participated in these literacy events. As mentioned above, "mediators of literacy" are participants of the literacy event who have literacy skills in the code being used. The mediators of literacy participate actively in the construction of the literacy event, not only reading or writing the message of the text, but also interpreting the meaning of it and constructing the social context in which it occurs. In this case study, adults and children became mediators of literacy when they helped L, who lacked knowledge of the written code (Spanish or English). By drawing upon "mutual knowledge," the older siblings were able to mediate L's participation in the literacy event and her understanding of the relationship between words and print.

The Valdéz Family

The Valdéz parents and the oldest daughter were born in Mexico, but the four youngest daughters were born in Texas. The main language spoken at home is Spanish. Some English is spoken among the children. The three oldest children are enrolled in public school. Two of them (the 5 year old and the 7 year old) attend a bilingual program at the local elementary school. The 18-month-old and 6-month-old children are enrolled in the Early Head Start program. The teachers talk to the youngest Valdéz children mostly in Spanish, although English is also used. The older daughter, Juana, attends middle school and takes all her courses in English. She said she felt more comfortable reading and writing in English than in Spanish. In oral language she felt comfortable in both languages. During our home visit the mother spoke mostly in Spanish but used words in English when she pointed to pictures during the literacy events (e.g. "fish," and "ice cream").

The family's rural, mobile-home community comprises mainly residents of Mexican origin. Juan, the father, works full time with a construction company. Julia has done a variety of jobs outside the home in the United States. She cleaned houses, worked at a factory, and presently works full time at the local high school cafeteria. Both parents finished high school in Mexico. Julia worked as a nurse and a literacy teacher in Mexico. They have been working to obtain residency papers for Julia and their oldest daughter. By May 1998 Julia had obtained permission to work in the United States, but she was still waiting for residency papers.

Literacy meanings

Julia explained that, as a child, she wanted to teach her father to read and write, but he did not see the need for learning literacy skills. He relied on his literate children as "literacy mediators." Since then, Julia has wanted to become a teacher.

She argued if a person is literate in a language, it does not matter if it is English or Spanish. She encouraged her friends to learn English literacy skills to meet basic needs in the United States. Thus, for Julia, literacy was not strictly related to getting a better education or becoming socially mobile. Her definition of literacy was not related to a "frame of schooling" as described by Street (1995). Literacy was necessary for survival. She used various strategies to improve her English abilities at home. For example, she and her daughters read the English captions that appeared on the TV screen as they watched programs.

Julia gave "consejos" (advice) about literacy to her children and friends through "storytelling," relating personal experiences that exemplified the messages she wanted to impart. Julia used her own schooling experience in Mexico to advise her daughters about homework and school projects. She gave advice to her friends who did not know how to read or write, and encouraged them to make an effort to learn because she considered literacy necessary to meet basic needs. The literacy meanings reported by Julia reflected the ways that she used literacy for everyday purposes.

Literacy uses

Julia and her family used literacy in many ways that are different from schooled literacy. Julia's literacy practices fit all the categories developed by Heath (1980: 128–129; 1983) in her study of a working-class, African-American community. We use these categories in this chapter, but suggest an additional category that emerged from the analyses of the data gathered from Julia's family. Julia and her family used literacy practices related to everyday needs, religious purposes and entertainment. There was a divide, which is not rigidly fixed, between English literacy and Spanish literacy. English literacy served primarily instrumental purposes and work-related tasks. Thus, English literacy was used primarily within the framework of US institutions, such as government agencies, the post office, the hospital, the schools, and diverse corporations. Spanish literacy was used primarily for religious, family, and educational domains. Spanish literacy also served to maintain connections with Mexican culture and institutions (writing letters and advising the children by telling them stories about schooling in Mexico).

Julia's family used one category of literacy practices that has not been described by Heath: *adaptations of schooled literacy.* Examples of adaptations of schooled literacy include family members reading from school notebooks, children pointing at the pictures in a book, and the family playing a word game. Materials used in these literacy events were books and notebooks from the US school, but the materials were not necessarily used as intended in the school context; the main purpose of these literacy events was not to practice reading or to read for new knowledge. Rather, the purpose was entertainment and distraction for the daughters. These literacy events occurred when the toddler was whining and crying for attention, and Julia started to "read" her a book. The daughters initiated the literacy events, asking their mother to read to them from the notebooks. Their informational questions served functionally as requests for their mother's attention. For example, a child asked, "Qué dice aquí?" (*"What does it say here?"*) and Julia turned her attention from household tasks to the child.

A school-adapted word game that we videotaped in the home was also played for the purpose of entertainment. The two oldest daughters (12 and 7 years old) started the game spontaneously. At the same time, the mother and the third daughter (5 years old) were involved in another literacy event, reading school materials. The mother at times involved the toddler in this activity by making explicit that the toddler was the addressee of the reading. At one point, the mother and the third daughter were drawn into the word game. The girls created different categories, such as "country or city," "name," "last name," "fruit," or "animal." One of the girls repeated the alphabet silently. When the other said *"basta!"* ("enough!"), the first girl had to identify the last letter of the alphabet she had repeated to herself. Both girls had to write words beginning with the letter. Afterwards they earned points for each word, and the one with more points won.

The game was clearly competitive and learned at school; however, in this literacy event the sisters helped one another and received help from the mother during the game. In this way, the daughter who was not literate (the 5-year-old) and the second oldest daughter (the 7-year-old), who did not have the same literacy skills as the oldest daughter, could participate in the game. The mother and the older siblings could be conceptualized as "mediators of literacy." This construct allows us to see that, in this household, children do not interact with print by themselves as much as they interact with print with the assistance of others.

The literacy event observed in this household and reported in this chapter is part of a much broader range of language practices in the family. Analyzing the interaction in detail helps us to recognize the sources of knowledge, beliefs and values that are integrated in family literacy practices, and the role of siblings as mediators in the socialization of younger children in language and literacy acquisition.

Mediators of literacy

When this family settled in the local host community, they brought with them literacy practices and meanings and uses of literacy from Mexico. During the interview, Julia recalled the ways she and her family used literacy in Mexico. Julia referred to oral and written language events as collective activities. When she gave examples of such practices, she referred to activities that involved two or more people. Usually the literacy event occurred within the framework of everyday life and entertainment. For example, Julia recalled that she had initiated learning to write her name. Her mother responded to her petition showing her letters from labels of food packages (such as *"maceca,"* a flour used to make tortillas).

Julia gave other examples of how she and her family used literacy in Mexico. She described reading the newspaper:

> ... *mis hermanos más grandes que yo, a ellos, para lo que les interesaba a ellos, para leer el*

periodico, los deportes sobre todo. Querían saber quien ganó o quien perdió. A nosotros, mi mamá a veces le gustaba que le leyera yo los chistes que venían alli, y a mi me gustaba a veces hacer el crucigrama, el juego de palabras. Y alli estabamos leyendo y buscando la respuesta tambien.

(... my older brothers needed literacy to read the newspaper, especially the sports section. They wanted to know who won or who lost. Sometimes my mother wanted me to read the comics to her, and I liked to do the crossword puzzles. And there we were, reading and looking for the correct answers.)

The literacy events we observed and taped in Julia's US home were also collective activities. These included reading the girls' school notebooks, reading books, pointing at pictures of the family and naming the relatives, reading words that appeared on the TV screen, the game played by Julia and her daughters, and storytelling. All of these literacy events involved at least two people.

In the eleven years this family has lived in the United States, family members have had contact with numerous institutions new to them that introduced new demands for literacy practices. Among others, the institutions included immigration and tax agencies, the children's schools, adult education classes, the telephone company, the post office, city services, and the hospital. Each institution required literacy practices that included a new language and different ways of doing things. Julia utilized her social networks and other resources to deal with these demands because she did not have the English skills to complete them alone. Literacy resources were shared among the members of the immigrant social networks. Within the context of the household, literacy resources were also shared, particularly among adults and children and among siblings.

Research has demonstrated that immigrants' social networks play an important role in survival and adaptation to the host community (Delgado-Gaitan, 1990; Farr, 1994; Fernandez Kelly, 1995). Social networks play a crucial role in the distribution of knowledge and literacy resources among the members of the network. When Julia first arrived in Texas and did not know English (spoken or written), she turned for help to various members of her social network. Julia's first friend, also a Mexican immigrant woman who had children in the same school that Juana attended, helped Julia get a phone installed, and a postal box. Julia also sought assistance from her daughters' teachers, who referred her to English classes at the community education center and helped her fill out forms in English. The staff of an immigration agency helped her acquire residency papers and a work permit. Her own English teachers in the Community Learning Center helped her. Members of this social network, established after Julia came to Texas, were clearly "mediators of literacy" as well as cultural and linguistic interpreters as described by Baynham (1993).

As noted by Baynham (1993), "mediators of literacy" actively interpret the meaning of the text. Mediators of literacy, by interpreting and communicating the text, include the cultural and institutional information missing in the text. Thus, mediators of literacy provide the cultural frames necessary to avoid misunderstandings. They might choose to use a frame that is already known by the participant who lacks the code knowledge to explain a text based on an unknown frame. In the next section we present an example of how siblings, as mediators of literacy, provide opportunities for the participant who lacks the code knowledge to actively participate in the literacy event and understand what is in print. This example demonstrates how mediators of literacy re-represent print in ways they believe the person lacking code knowledge would better understand. They use mutual knowledge to facilitate understanding and in doing so socialize the learner into language and literacy practices of the new context or situation.

Mmmmmm! Eating Ice Cream from the Book

The literacy events observed in Julia's household were among the children or among the children and the mother. In all, either the mother or the older sisters clearly acted as mediators of literacy. The older daughters and Julia constructed the meaning of the text, allowing the younger daughters who had little knowledge of the code to participate actively in the literacy event. In this sense the literacy events observed were "joint constructions" (Baynham, 1993: 301). Because of the young age of some participants, such as L, much of the active participation in the literacy event was conducted with gestures. Gestures functioned in this case as an accommodation to the toddler's frames of reference. Gestures, as well as the oral language, were transcribed (see Note 4 at the end of the chapter for the meanings of the symbols used in the transcriptions).

While this literacy event was occurring, another literacy event, the word game described earlier, was on-going. Before these events, the daughters had engaged in play activities (making a train, jumping on the bed, etc.). During this visit to the home, the girls also spent time kneeling in front of the sofa coloring pages of a Dinosaur coloring book placed on the cushions. The older daughters assisted the toddler, L, in the coloring and playing. Similar literacy events took place minutes before and after the literacy event presented here.

Literacy event

This literacy event took place in the living room of the home. The main participants were Julia (the mother), Milagros (5), and L (18-month-old toddler). Juana, the oldest sister, joined in in the middle of the interaction and participated by smiling and laughing at one point of the interaction, supporting the literacy event and contributing to its construction as a frame of entertainment. The baby (6 months old) was sleeping in an infant seat placed on the sofa. The mother sat on the sofa next to the baby during the literacy event. Milagros sat next to the mother. The three main participants formed a circle around one book, which became the focus of the interaction. Interestingly, the book was not arranged facing the reader, but was placed on the mother's lap directly facing Milagros. Thus, neither the mother nor the toddler could see the pictures of the book face-forward; both saw it from the side. In this case, it made sense to have the book in this arrangement. There was not just *one* reader, but four participants who were actively constructing the literacy event. The position of the book is meaningful to the literacy practices found in this household, which were predominantly collective literacy events.

The literacy event begins when the toddler (L) reached for a book that Juana (aged 12) was passing to Ana (aged 7). The sisters did not let her grab it and L started to cry, dropping herself to the floor, face down. The mother called L: "*Vente*" ("Come here"). After a couple of seconds of crying and being patted by Juana, L stood up and went toward the mother. At this moment Ana (7) put the book, which had been the motive of the struggle, on her mother's lap. Then the mother held the book to let L know that attention was directed to her, and that she was going to read the book to her: "*Ven L, ven. A ver qué quieres ver de este libro. Hm?*" ("Come L, come. Let's see what you want to see in this book. Hm?").

After this utterance, which signaled the beginning of the literacy event, L started to turn the pages of the book. Julia helped her, turning the pages or holding the pages that L had already turned. The mother pointed at a picture of a fish and said the word "fish" in English. At this time, Milagros (5) joined the mother and L, holding her school notebook. By looking at her mother and opening her book she indicated her desire to be read to also. Milagros said something inaudible; however, the mother immediately looked at Milagros, nodded, and said: "Hmm." At the same time L was turning the pages of the book. The following is a transcription of the interactions that illustrate how Milagros (Mi) and Julia (M) are mediators of literacy for L:

1 **Mi:**   PT and looking at notebook
2   Qué dice?/ [What does it say (here)]
3 **M:**   RD Mi's notebook
4   A (.)mi mamá./ [To my mother]
5 **Mi:**   PT at the book and >J
6   No/ aquí./ [No. Right here] ⇑>M
7 **M:**   Espérame [Wait]
8   Mother places the baby's bottle out of the reach of Milagros, in
             order to avoid spilling the bottle.[4]

At this point L was about to continue turning the pages, as she had while the last segment of interaction occurred. However, a picture of an ice-cream cone caught her attention and initiated the following interaction:

9 **L:**   PT at an ice cream picture in the book.
10   Mira. Ese **book**/ [Look at that book]
             -h/ Bah/ [here L seems to be saying "ball." During observa-
             tions of L at her household and at the daycare center she
             repeated that word "bah" continuously. Most of the time she
             related the word "bah" to indicate a real ball.]
11 **M:**   ∇⇓< L, PT at the picture
12   -h/ **Ice cream**/

At this point Milagros is doing what the mother told her to do, waiting. While she "waits" for a couple of seconds, she turns her face, looking at the baby on the sofa behind her. Milagros did not see the picture in the book, but she listened to the word "ice cream." This caught her attention and she immediately turned back to the group and looked at the book saying:

13 **Mi:**   Mmmmm.
14   ∇⇊ book. Makes gestures and sounds as if she were eating the
                 ice cream from the book.

Milagros' repetitive and exaggerated gestures did not represent the way ice cream is generally eaten (with a spoon or a cone). Eight times she placed her hand on the picture of the ice cream and then rapidly moved her hand toward her mouth, as if she were scooping ice cream into her mouth with her hands. These gestures represent a way of using a frame that is known by L to explain a frame that is not familiar to her. Milagros is mediating this literacy event by reshaping the abstract picture of an ice-cream cone into something familiar to L. The frame of reference of pretending to do something is familiar to L because she has learned that frame by playing with her older sisters. This play-acting is shared knowledge among the sisters. However, the idea that print can represent reality is a concept that L is learning at this point and that frame is less familiar. As will be seen later, the gestures facilitated L's understanding that the picture in the book represented food in the real world.

After the eighth time, looking at L, Milagros continued to use frames of reference that were familiar to the toddler. She said: "*rico!*" ("tasty"). Immediately looking at the picture, Milagros said: "Oh!" and began again pretending to eat the ice cream with scooping hand gestures. However, this time Milagros placed her hand on the page, then on her mouth, and moved her hand several times to her mouth, as if she were eating a lot of ice cream, making the gestures more exaggerated. At this point Milagros smiled and looked at the camera:

15 **Mi:**   ∇ camera smiling
16   Smiling ∇<⇊L
17   ∇>⇑M
18 **L:**   Δ<⇑M ((LF))
19   Makes gestures and sounds as if she were eating ice cream.
20 **M:**   ∇⇊<Mi ((LF))
21 **J:**   Smiling joins the group

In the above segment, the participants laughed with each other as if they were pretending to eat ice cream. At this point, L began to mimic the repetitive gestures that the older child had made (line 19). It is clear in the video that L progressively understands that the picture in the book represents something real. When she also pretends to scoop up the ice cream, she is sharing her older sister's knowledge. By repeating the gestures of the other participant in this interaction, L represents an action that persons do not do in text, but do demonstrate in the real world. The mother, realizing that L was repeating her sister's gestures, looked at Milagros and smiled, taking a sharp breath. This last breath represented joy and surprise and reinforced the participation of the toddler.

22 **M:**   **Ice cream**/
23 **L:**   PT book
24   ya ya ya/
25 **M:**   Mhm./ **Ice cream.**/

The last segment of the interaction is illustrative of how the mother interpreted L's "talk." It was impossible for non-family members to decipher what the toddler was saying. But the mother, who had participated in the shared practices of language within the family, interpreted the toddler's utterance as "ice cream" (line 25).

26 **Mi:**   ∇⇓ book. Makes gestures and sounds as if she were eating the
               ice cream from the book. This time Milagros scratched the ice
               cream two times before taking her hand to her mouth.

After this last sequence of gestures, Milagros indicated that she wanted her mother to read to her. She had held her book during the "ice cream" segment waiting for her mother to allocate her attention towards her. In order to get her mother's attention, Milagros intervened:

27 **Mi:**   Covers L's book with her notebook.
28.   Mira mami. [Look mom.]
29 **M:**   ∇⇓ Mi's notebook
30   Juana, quieres que te lo lea (ella)?/ [Do you want Juana to read
               it to you?]
31 **Mi:**   No
32 **L:**   PT at the refrigerator in the kitchen
33   ke/ ya ya, pa?
34   >⇑△ M
35   PT at the picture of the ice cream
36   ya/ya/

The last segment is important in the sense that it presents evidence that after the repetition of gestures by Milagros, repetition of the word "ice cream"by the mother, the interpretations of L's "talk" by the mother, and the step taken by L to treat the picture as something real, L was able to connect the picture of the ice cream with the ice cream in the refrigerator (lines 32–36). At the same time she seems to be trying to say something about the ice cream.

At this point Milagros claimed the attention of her mother and started to read to her from her notebook. After some seconds L tried to reclaim the mother's attention by calling her. She did not get attention after the first call (line 41); however, she did after the second call (line 52). This second call was made by L simultaneously with gestures of eating ice cream. That seemed to work in getting the mother's attention. At this point the mother asked her if the ice cream was cold and L seemed to respond, "Yeah, ice cream":

37 **Mi:**	∇>M	
	RD	
	Aueces?/ [Sometimes? reading 'aueses' instead of 'a veces']	
38 **M:**	∇<Mi. RD from Mi's book	
39	A/ veces/ [Sometimes]	
40 **Mi:**	te [reflexive, 2nd person singular]	
41 **M:**	te [reflexive, 2nd person singular]	
42 **L:**	PT to the picture of the ice cream	
43	Δ>⇑M Ma, ma, MA, MA <u>MA</u> (each ma is louder than the previous one)/	
44	Δ⇓ book PT at the picture of L's book	
	co/co/.	
45 **M:**	oh/ co/co/ ((LF))	
46 **L:**	co/co	
47 **Mi:**	∇⇓book, RD	
48	i?	
49 **M:**	RD∇⇓book	
50	te (.) impacientas [you loose your patience]	
51 **Mi:**	∇>M smiling, placing her head on her mother's shoulder	
52 **M:**	porque soy pequeño/ [because I am a child]	
53 **L:**	Δ>⇑M Making gestures of eating ice cream	
54	ma, ma, ma	
55 **M:**	Está frío? [Is it cold?]	
56 **L:**	∇⇓book PT at ice cream picture	
57	ya/aui [yeah, 'ice cream']	
58 **M:**	Uy! Está frío. [Oh! It's cold]	

In the literacy event presented, it is clear that the mother (M) and Milagros (Mi) were mediators of literacy for 18-month-old L. The interaction with print would not have been the same had L "read" the book by herself. Milagros looked at the picture and listened to her mother saying "ice cream." She interpreted the picture and the mother's words and constructed a way of telling her younger sister "ice cream" by drawing upon shared knowledge. She used frames of reference familiar to L, such as pretending to eat food and using the word *rico* (tasty). The smiles and laughing also communicated to L that the girls were pretending. L repeated the gestures and tried to say "ice cream" several times. The picture of the ice cream in the book was a big colorful ice-cream cone with many layers. It was very different from the ice cream that L regularly ate in her home, which came from a carton. However, because of the help of the mediators of literacy, L began to understand the meaning of the picture and could relate that picture to the ice cream in the refrigerator. In the end, the picture in the book, the mother's word "ice cream," and Milagros' uses of familiar frames of reference helped L to understand that the picture on the page represented ice cream. This experience contributed to L's acquisition of a new frame of reference in which print represents reality.

This example demonstrates that mediating literacy events not only involves shared knowledge of oral and written language, but also of non-verbal gestures, body movements, and patterns of interaction. This is particularly important when the participants are toddlers in the process of learning how to speak and understand print.

Interpretation of the Findings

In some households, particularly those of middle class families, children frequently engage in reading by themselves for periods of time. Solitary reading is also common in the Early Head Start classrooms that we observed. In contrast, all the activities observed and videotaped in this home were collectively constructed, and siblings as well as the mother played an important role in socializing the youngest children. Literacy practices as collective activities were congruent with the shared values and cultural practices found in this Mexican household, in the Mexican immigrant community, and in the literacy events the mother recalled in Mexico.

One of the principles that governed this family and allowed for organization of the household (five children and two working parents living in a very small space) was collective activity. Anthropological literature has identified reciprocal relationships that develop among relatives and friends in immigrant households and serve as sources of mutual aid. Vélez-Ibañez and Greenberg (1992) conducted research among Mexican families in the border region, and their findings suggest that children are born into a rich social context where they internalize social relationships that contain particular social expectations. The disposition to engage in generalized reciprocity orders social relationships, and children are socialized in these relationships. Frequent contacts among households, through formal and informal rituals, maintain and renovate social ties and also allow shared knowledge to flow. Based on the analyses of the literacy events we observed, we conclude that mediated literacy activities are a part of the funds of knowledge that are exchanged and transmitted among households engaged in reciprocal relationships. Knowledge, information, and cultural resources were shared among relatives and friends, among the members of the social networks, and among family members.

Within this household, mutual help was continuous. The older girls responded naturally when Julia instructed them to prepare the *mamila* (bottle), take care of younger siblings, or complete household tasks. Even L helped. The girls also helped one another. Juana watched L and shared the care of the infant with her mother. Mutual help and transmission of literacy resources clearly occurred during the literacy event presented above. Thus, there was a relationship between literacy practices and other social and cultural resources, such as social networks, common knowledge, and mutual help found in the local community.

Mediators of literacy are important in the literacy practices within this household. Older siblings and the mother helped the younger children participate in the literacy events. They adapted pedagogical literacy (school games, notebooks, etc.) to become shared play activities in the household. They provided familiar frames of meaning to help the younger children participate in literacy events, learn English vocabulary, and acquire an understanding of the relationship of print to reality. The older child looked for strategies in her communicative repertoire (such as gestures and pretend play), that interpreted the meaning of the ice-cream cone in ways familiar to the toddler. In all of these interactions, older siblings were active agents of socialization.

Understanding mediated literacy in this family contributes to a better understanding of the ways that literacy mediators help young children construct meaning and acquire knowledge. Older siblings provided known frames of reference for the toddler L that allowed her to participate in the literacy event. The mediators helped her construct meaning from the text and helped her learn a new word. This case study reveals how siblings as well as adults socialize young children to interactional competence through co-construction of meaning during participation in shared activities. Schieffelin and Ochs (1986b) demonstrate how socialization – the process by which children become competent members of their social group – begins at the first moment of social contact, and how language plays an important role in this process. This case study suggests that, besides the adult caretakers and teachers, there are many socializing agents who play an important role in helping young children learn to speak and to form the cognitive basis for literacy.

Socialization research has shown that children acquire sociocultural knowledge of their native language through participation in language-mediated activities in the home and community. This case study suggests that siblings are important mediators in this process. Scaffolded help provided by the mother and older sisters encouraged increasing autonomy in the toddler in initiating, participating in the literacy event, and in incorporating the meaning of words and linking text to real objects. A crucial ingredient for the successful participation of L in this literacy event was group collaboration and mutual knowledge. Through the provision of modeling and verbal and nonverbal cues, the older sibling socializes the younger child into interactional competence beyond her initial ability. In doing so, the sibling also conveys an implicit cultural message that success involves a specific set of shared skills that can be learned by observing carefully and following. By following the older sibling's lead and repeating her utterances and gestures, the young child gradually moved toward independent production of a word and meaning. The shared practices and common knowledge among these family members were sufficient to enable this preverbal child to achieve success within the structure of a family-mediated literacy event. The next step is for L to learn to apply these familiar routines to new situations outside her family.

Observing the ways in which this family participated in collective literacy events demonstrates how research on the experience of children and adults in families supports the educational achievement of children by encouraging family practices and shared knowledge as a crucial resource. Cultural and social values are continually expressed through social interaction. Among the members of this non-mainstream family, the boundaries between "family" and "community" networks may not be as sharply delineated as in mainstream settings. Language and literacy acquisition in this family context are clearly collaborative social processes involving more than one mediator located at different developmental levels. Nor are these processes unidirectional.

The examination of language and literacy interactions in immigrant, non-mainstream homes can furnish information about the variation in relationships between language and culture and what children are being taught about them. Since few studies of language socialization incorporate peer and sibling interactions, further research on how language and literacy are acquired in the social context of peer/sibling-mediated literacy events can shed light on this process of language and literacy acquisition.

Notes

1. We thank Elizabeth Keating for valuable advice on an earlier version of this chapter.
2. Early Head Start (EHS) is a federally-funded program that serves low-income families with children from zero to three years old. The EHS site of this study is administered by a community-based, non-profit organization that has administered Head Start programs since the 1960s, when Head Start was initially funded. This EHS program is one of seven such programs in Texas. The EHS provides, in collaboration with other programs, infant and toddler childcare, home visits, parenting sessions, parent–child activities, adult education and employment training for families that qualify. Four Family Advocates attend these families, providing weekly home visits. During these visits the Family Advocates provide information about social services and child development and check the needs that families may have. The EHS program is based on the belief that children's welfare depends on the family and community environment; thus its services integrate children, family and community. Families selected to participate have incomes below the federal poverty guidelines. Single mothers, families with special needs, or families taking steps towards self-sufficiency are given priority. The program facilitated our access to 75 families who participated in the evaluation study.
3. Over the past ten years Harriett Romo has collected data in the evaluation of several Head Start, Early Head Start, and Even Start literacy projects in this research community from approximately 200 families who participated in these projects. Working with these immigrant families has a special meaning for María de la Piedra. As an immigrant herself, she missed her country, her language, her friendships, and the conversations and family relationships she left behind. Working in the homes of these Spanish-speaking immigrants, seeing their children play, listening to the storytelling that goes on in the households, and the *consejos* (advice) parents gave to their children, made her feel close to home.
4. The following transcription conventions and abbreviations are used here and in subsequent examples:

Subjects:
Mother: M
Daughters:
J: 12
A: 7
Mi: 5
L: 18 months
Me: 6 months old

Context of interaction:
Family's living room.

Intonation:
((CR)) crying
((LF)) laughing

Audible breathing:
-h marks in-breath

Metatranscription marks:
( ) unclear reading, no hearing achieved
(cow) tentative reading

bold: English words.
[ ]: translation to English

Non-verbal transcription:
Present progressive used when the action and the utterance occurred simultaneously. Simple present used when action is prior or after utterance. Line above when action is prior, line below when action is subsequent. Same line when simultaneous.

Eye gaze:

< towards left

> towards right

∇ facing camera

Δ back of head to camera

⇑ Looks up

⇓ Looks down

Gestures:
PT: pointing
R: reaching
HD: holding
RD: reading

Chapter 4

Growing up Trilingual in Montreal: Perceptions of College Students

PATRICIA LAMARRE, IN COLLABORATION WITH JOSEFINA ROSSELL PAREDES

This chapter examines how young trilinguals who have grown up in Montreal acquired their linguistic repertoires and how they use languages in their everyday lives. We also examine how they perceive their multilingualism, and how attitudes towards languages are constructed within the family. We draw on Bourdieu's theoretical framework (more specifically, his notions of linguistic marketplaces, of language as a form of capital, and of "ethos" or "habitus") since this framework provides effective and powerful analytical tools to help us understand how individual language behavior is related to specific linguistic "markets." As census data reveal, language behavior in Montreal has changed quite radically as the status of French as a *lingua franca* has improved. Data from interviews with trilingual students provides information on how this period of transformation is experienced within the families of newcomers, and how multilingualism as a form of capital is perceived by this new generation of Montrealers.

Research on Language Socialization

In the mid-eighties, Schiefflin and Ochs (1986a) proposed that we think of language socialization as having two dimensions. Pulling together different theories on language, they argued that children are *socialized to use languages* (Heath, 1983), but that they are also *socialized through language* – acquiring cognitive skills (Vygotsky, 1978), as well as knowledge or ethnotheories about the world they live in (Sapir, 1949; Whorf, 1941). They further proposed that these two dimensions are intricately related. Much of the research conducted in the area of language socialization has been faithful to this definition, examining the acquisition of language and literacy as related to the construction of social and cultural identity. Relying primarily on ethnographic research methods and an interactionist approach, work in this area reveals how caregivers provide explicit instruction in activity/event speech behavior (socialization to language) and how interactants see their own and others' social position (socialization through language).

As a field of study, language socialization has progressed quickly, providing much rich detail on what goes on in homes and, to a somewhat lesser extent in schools, commonly considered the two most important sites of language socialization. There are, however, weaknesses within what we know. A first weakness is that research, while generally ethnographic, tends to be limited to one or two sites and to take place within a relatively short timespan. A further weakness in existing research is that, while situations are defined by interactants, in keeping with interactionist or ethno-methodological approaches, analysis fails to take into account that definitions of situations are rarely neutral or innocent. As Bourdieu (1985) proposes, all social practices are "interested," even if individuals are unaware of their interests, and even when the stakes are not material. In our opinion, Bourdieu's theory of constructive structuralism offers powerful analytical tools for interpreting ethnographic data on language socialization, since it considers how existing structures guide and constrain practices at the same time as it recognizes how individuals (through their capacities for thought, reflection, and action) construct social and cultural phenomenon. Providing the interface between subjective experience, individual strategies, and structural "determinants" is Bourdieu's notion of "habitus," a concept that lies at the heart of his theory of social class reproduction (Bourdieu, 1985). It is through habitus that families adopt cultural values (including expectations and attitudes towards the capital owned by the family) which are largely related to social class position. It is also through habitus that adjustment to social change can be examined, since it is through habitus that individuals and families interpret the world around them, define their attitudes and strategies, and make decisions.

In this chapter, we draw on Bourdieu to understand Montreal as a city with a recently transformed linguistic market and to examine how families adjust to changes within this specific linguistic market and attribute value to language as a form of capital.

Montreal: From Anglo-dominant to Bilingual City

Because of recent efforts to make French a majority language in the province, Quebec offers an interesting situation in which to study how communities, united around language and shared social and cultural interests, bring about social change. What at one level can be understood as the reversal of a "language shift situation" (Fishman, 1991) can be understood at another level as the mobilization of a linguistic minority to improve its collective position in society and insure its continued existence as a community. In other words, Quebec provides a strong example of the relationship between language and social and cultural reproduction. It also provides an opportunity to observe how linguistic markets are transformed and how, within these markets, individuals adjust to the reallocation of value to linguistic resources.

In Quebec, the French-speaking population has always been the demographic majority, although Anglo-Quebecers occupied the position of majority or dominant group in the sociological sense (Canada, 1969). In the sixties, these power relations were clearly reflected in language practices in Montreal, where it was far more likely to find bilingual Francophones[1] than Anglophones (Gendron, 1972) and where it was also more likely for newcomers to the province to learn English, the language of social and economic power, rather than French. By the seventies, Francophones moved to change this situation, and the adoption of Bill 101, Quebec's language policy (Quebec, 1977), is often referred to as the turning point in intergroup and language relations.

Over the past twenty-five years, efforts to improve the status of French have been quite successful, and a steady and rapid increase in French language skills is evident among immigrants and their children, as well as among Anglophones. While French has gained considerable ground, this has not been to the detriment of English/French bilingualism. Montreal has always been the Canadian city with the highest rate of individual bilingualism. Interestingly, it is also the city with the highest percentage of trilinguals in Canada, and quite possibly in North America, a phenomenon that has gone relatively unnoticed until recently.

Multilingualism in Montreal: Demographic Data

In Quebec, the number of people who speak a first language other than French or English is on the rise, presently representing 10% of the population (Marmen & Corbeil, 1999) – most of whom live in Montreal. Like other major urban centers, ethnic and linguistic diversity is now a trait of Montreal. However, what makes Montreal different from other Canadian cities is the extremely high rate of trilingualism among its allophone population. Census data for 1996 reveals that 46.8% of Quebec allophones speak both official languages, in comparison with 5.4% in the rest of Canada. In other words, trilingualism[2] is nine times higher in Quebec than it is in the rest of Canada (Marmen & Corbeil, 1999).

If we take a brief look at statistics since the seventies and the adoption of Bill 101, dramatic change in language behavior is quite evident and goes a long way in explaining the high rate of trilingualism. It is much more likely today than twenty or thirty years ago that an Allophone will speak French. In effect, between 1971 and 1991 the number of allophones with French skills increased from 47% to 69%. On the other hand, the percentage of allophones who speak English has remained relatively stable, dropping very slightly from 69% to 68%. It is this stability with respect to English skills, combined with an increase in French language skills, that has contributed to the rate of trilingualism among allophones, more specifically, in Montreal, going from 33.4% to 44% between 1971 and 1996 (Marmen & Corbeil, 1999). The trend is clearly upward, and if we look at younger allophones the rate of trilingualism is 67.6%.

It seems that, regardless of the headway made in making French the "lingua franca," Montreal remains a city in which English/French bilingualism remains valuable. Drawing on concepts put forward by Bourdieu (1977, 1982a), census data can be interpreted as indicative of a particular "linguistic market"– one that has been vastly transformed by language policy to improve the status of French (and of French speakers), but nevertheless, a linguistic market in which the importance of English within the North American and global contexts cannot be ignored. If the value of French language skills has been enhanced through language policy, French/English bilingualism as a form of capital has also been affected. Bilingualism is no longer of value primarily to French speakers, but has become valuable to all speakers, including newcomers.

Although Montreal offers an unusual opportunity to study multilingualism, there has been relatively little research on the topic (Lamarre, 2000). Questions of language transfer and of the use of French in public interactions have largely dominated research on language practices. Much less is known about the use of many languages in the home, in social networks, and in public spaces. Given the lack of information, this study was undertaken as a first exploratory phase on which to build a larger research program.

Investigating Multilingualism in Montreal

As a first phase of a broader research agenda, we expected that interviews with trilingual college students would provide insights on which to build more in-depth ethnographic work. We chose this age group for a number of reasons. First, students who are in college now represent the first generation to have grown up in the wake of Bill 101, in a period of radical change in linguistic behavior. In effect, they are often referred to as "the children of Bill 101." Second, students of college age could talk to us about how they acquired their linguistic repertoires at home and school while the experience was still relatively recent. We could also learn about how, as young adults, they use languages across sites: in the home, in their neighborhoods, in their ethnic communities, with friends at school and in informal settings, and within their first forays into the work force. As argued in the introduction to this chapter, we contend that to understand how multilingualism is acquired in Montreal, we need to look at language socialization experiences across sites and over longer periods of time.

In the spring of 2000, we conducted open-ended interviews with multilingual students enrolled in Montreal's college system, called *cegeps*.[3] We chose to interview students from a variety of ethnolinguistic backgrounds rather than from a specific language community. By doing this, we hoped to understand how immigrants and the children of immigrants perceive, and are adjusting to, the changing linguistic marketplace of Montreal, rather than to examine how a specific community has adjusted to change.

We conducted in-depth interviews with six male and four female students. All of the interviewees spoke a minority language as a first language and had learned English and French while growing up. Their age ranged from 18 to 20, except for one 24 year old student, Charry, who immigrated to Canada at the age of 17 and spent a few years in an adult education program learning French before enrolling in *cegep*. Five interviewees were Canadian-born, four immigrated to Quebec when they were adolescents, and one did so when she was a small child.[4]

The parents of all of the participants were foreign-born, and spoke a first language other than English or French. At present, some parents speak both official languages (French and English), while a smaller number speak English, but not French. Many of the parents, however, have more than one "non-official" language[5] in their repertoire – either because of intermarriage or because of the multi-lingualism present in their countries of origin. Parents' occupations vary from clerk to cook to businessman. Almost all of the parents, however, have a college or university education.

The first backgrounds of the participants covered a wide range of languages, reflecting some of the current diversity of immigration to Quebec: Tagalog, Portuguese, Fanti, Italian, Spanish, Punjabi, Cantonese, and Arabic. When interviewees were asked to rate their skills in these languages, it became evident that they did not consider themselves "equilingual," since none of them felt that they spoke all their languages equally well. Some participants gave themselves quite high ratings in all of their languages, while others felt that their writing skills in some languages were lacking. Two students rated their skills in their first language, both oral and written, very negatively.

Findings

Acquiring a multilingual repertoire

One of our goals was to get a sense of how multilingual repertoires are acquired by young allophones growing up in Montreal. In this respect, interviews clearly point toward a multisite process of language acquisition in which the home is the most important site for the development of first language skills, and the school is the most important site for the acquisition of a first "official" language and also, to a lesser degree, the second "official" language. The relationship between language acquisition and specific sites, however, does not fall into any tidy category.

Pre-migratory experience of multilingualism

Not all of the participants were born in Canada. For these students from Third World countries, bilingualism and multilingualism are not new experiences.

Rather, in their countries of origin, many participants experienced societal bilingualism and situations of diglossia in which the language of the home was not the language of schooling. Furthermore, in many Third World countries, ex-colonial languages, often English, may still occupy an important place in the school curriculum. These young people arrive in Montreal with a complex linguistic repertoire, and with a heightened sense of the different value of languages and how this difference is related to social power and status.

Meena's trajectory provides a good example of a pre-migratory experience of multilingualism. Meena immigrated to Quebec from India when she was seven. Her first language is Punjabi, and this was the language spoken with her family and relatives and in her village. Schooling, however, was in Hindi, which was also the language used in formal situations and for speaking with strangers. English was taught from the early years on, so that, by the time Meena migrated to Quebec, her language repertoire was already trilingual. Furthermore, she had already acquired an awareness of the status of languages. More specifically, the prestige accorded English in India seems to play a part in the way she experiences having to learn French in Quebec and how she perceives the status of French.

Multilingualism in the home

A very strong impression to emerge from the interviews is that the complexity and diversity of language practices in the home in modern cities is not to be underestimated. What is also very clear is that, for these trilingual students, the home is the most important site when it comes to learning the first language. This said, in very few homes is the first language the only language used. In almost all of the homes described, some combination of the first language and English and/or French is in use.

It came as no surprise that some families are much more committed to the maintenance of the first language, insisting on its use in the home, while others are less strict in this respect. In some families, parents felt strongly that children must be literate in their first language, and helped them to develop reading and writing skills. Other families felt that developing oral skills in the minority language was sufficient and perceived the minority language as something that is primarily useful for maintaining ties with relatives and with traditions and culture, but not of great value on the job market.

For some participants, the home is in itself a "linguistically complex" environment, since they are the children of mixed marriages. Daniel's home provides a good example of the complexity of some households. Canadian-born Daniel has four languages. Both of his parents are immigrants, his mother from Venezuela and his father from Italy. In Daniel's home, Italian is the stronger language since the family has strong ties with Montreal's Italian community and, when he was small, his Italian grandparents lived with the family. Daniel has no Spanish-speaking relatives in Montreal, and his mother has no connections with the Hispanic community. The family does, however, visit relatives in Venezuela on a regular basis. Nevertheless, according to Daniel, his mother has "become Italian." She speaks the language very fluently and, when her sons were growing up, she spoke to them in Italian. With her younger daughter, however, she speaks mostly Spanish. More recently, she has taken to using English when talking to her sons. Daniel's father, also quadri-lingual, is very keen on multilingualism and has tried different strategies inside the home to help his children develop a multilingual repertoire – such as using one language a week or a system of rotating languages at mealtimes. As Daniel and his brothers have grown up, however, it has become increasingly common to use English in the home. While Daniel's description of language use in the home was definitely one of the more complex narratives we heard, he was not the only student to describe a "linguistically complex" home.

The interviews also revealed that language use in the home is not stable, and many interviewees report changes over time. Specific events seem to spark changes in language practices in the home. For example, a change in language use can be brought about by the presence of elderly relatives, as when a grandparent, who speaks little English or French, moves in with a family. It can also come about when grandparents pass away and the need to use a minority language diminishes. To return to Daniel's family, when he and his siblings were small, their home was very Italian, because both his Italian grandparents lived with the family. After their death, using Italian became something that his father had to insist upon and try to encourage by developing rules for language use in the home, rules that appear to have often been left by the wayside.

Some families talk more than others about the value of languages and of multilingualism. Quite a few participants said that they would get tired of hearing parents harp on about the importance of learning languages, but they also said that, as they got older, they realized how right their parents were and they are glad that their parents insisted on first-language maintenance. For all the interviewees, the home was described as the site where the first language was most important, in terms of both actual use and symbolic value.

Primary and secondary schooling

Schools are clearly major sites in language socialization, and play a very important role in the integration of newcomers into existing "official language communities." As institutional settings, they have a historical *raison d'être* and are very obviously tied to the reproduction of "official language communities" in Quebec. Regardless of the diversity of the student population that attends a school, in Quebec a school is either a French site or an English one. The school they go to appears to affect the friendship networks that students develop. Those who had attended a French school were more likely to have French-speaking friends in their network, and vice versa.

Schooling also affects the languages spoken in the home. More specifically, siblings who once talked to each other in their first language when they were small, often switch to the language of schooling as they grow up. Again, let us use Daniel as an example. Before starting school, Daniel spoke Italian to his brothers and sisters but, once he was of school age, he switched to English, and English remains the siblings' main language of communication. Schooling plays a major role in creating an intergenerational dynamic of language use within a family. Siblings who once spoke to each other in their first language switch to or use more frequently the language of schooling. With their parents or other older relatives, however, they are more likely to use their first language – in some instances to facilitate communication, but also as a sign of respect.

Ethnic community

Most of the participants attend some church-related or community-related activities. For some families, however, ties to a community are less formal, and take place through large family gatherings and informal friendship networks among the parents' generation. When we asked about the languages they used with members of their community and/or with relatives, many interviewees distinguished according to the age of the person being spoken to. Many insisted that speaking their first language to older members of their community was a sign of respect, but that among their own age group they practice trilingual code-switching. Within the community, a further divide can be found: the period of settlement in Quebec. For example, participants whose families settled in Montreal prior to Bill 101, while trilingual, are often stronger in English than in French. Sandra, whose family arrived in Quebec from Portugal "post Bill 101," talked to us about how she had trouble communicating with her cousins when she was small because she spoke no English and their French skills were still rudimentary. Now, however, Sandra says she uses all three languages with cousins of her own age.

Some families' ties to their country of origin are still very strong and they return, either occasionally or frequently, to visit relatives. For some, this is perceived as a way of keeping the minority language alive, while other families simply see this as a visit, without paying much attention to whether it helps develop language skills.

In the cegep

When interviewed, participants were enrolled in an English language *cegep*. In this setting, they claim to use English all the time and insist that the *cegep* is an "English place." When this type of statement was probed, however, it became evident that they also frequently use other languages, and code-switch. Nevertheless, students seem somewhat less likely to draw on their multilingual repertoires in the *cegep* than in more neutral settings (such as a friend's house or a shopping center). Interestingly, use of French seems to be more common than minority languages within the *cegep*. Students say that they will easily switch to French to talk to friends, or to help out a student from the French high school system who is learning English, and also if they are "stuck for a word in English." Apparently, using French in an English *cegep* is not considered offensive to anyone, since English/French bilingualism is taken for granted among their age group: "everyone can understand what you are saying." Using a mother tongue can be considered offensive for the opposite reason: not everyone understands, so it is "not polite." Among friends who understand the minority tongue, it is acceptable to switch to that language, but participants claim that, if another person who doesn't speak the language joins a grouping, they switch back to English. Some said that they felt most comfortable using their first language in an ethnic association clubroom and consciously switch to English when they leave the club. Most insisted, however, that there were no ill-feelings toward the use of languages other than English in the *cegep*, as long as languages were not used to exclude others.

When asked about extra-curricular activities, students reported a strong use of English and the occasional use of French and almost never the use of other languages. For example, one student reported being a member of the United Nations Club, in which everything was done in either English or French, adding ironically, "no ethnics there."

With friends

Interviewees were asked a number of questions about the use of languages with their friends. They were also asked to provide information on the language backgrounds of their three best friends and to indicate what language they used when speaking to each of them. A diversity of practices immediately became apparent. Respondents generally describe their friendship networks as multicultural and multilingual. With some friends, they speak their first language and code-switch to English or French; with others, they use English or French or both. Code-switching is described as common, and young people generally take pride in their ability to move from one language to another. From their descriptions of language practices with friends outside the *cegep*, informal settings seem more likely than the more institutional setting of the *cegep* to encourage code-switching and the use of a first language.

In the workplace

Most of the interviewees have part-time jobs, and it is in the workplace that they say they use their French skills the most frequently, whether to talk to their boss, to other employees or to customers. For many, it is also in the workplace that they are most likely to come into contact with Francophone Montrealers. Even though French is used more frequently at work than in other sites, the workplace is described by almost all students as bilingual. Generally speaking, they are far less likely to use their first language skills in this setting.

In summary, the interviews point to a relationship between site and language practices. Interestingly, when we asked what determined the choice of a language in a given interaction, participants insisted it was the language skills of the person they were talking to. Under closer scrutiny, this does not seem to be the case. While all languages might be used in all sites, sites seem to be associated with a particular type of predominant language practice: the home with the first language, the school with the language of schooling, and the work place with English/French bilingualism. Friendship networks seem to be where students do the most code-switching, perhaps because they feel freed both from the restraints of family efforts to develop a first language and from the pressure to use the language of schooling in educational institutions.

Multilingualism as Choice or as Consequence

One of the other topics we wanted to explore with trilinguals was how multilingualism was experienced and perceived within families of newcomers to Montreal. Looking across the narratives, we found that the experience of multilingualism could be categorized into two main trends. From the interviews, it became clear that there were families who made very deliberate efforts to develop a multilingual repertoire, making thought-out decisions about the use of languages in the home, and choosing practices that contribute to the development of the family's first language, as well as other languages. Other families took a more passive role, and acquire the languages required by circumstances. Families who had deliberate strategies for language maintenance in the home often talked to their children about the importance of languages. It seems that these families stress not only the economic value of languages within the local market, but the value of languages as a form of social and cultural capital, with a conversion value in other markets. In other words, parents express explicitly an ethos or habitus around language learning and language as a form of capital, and they teach this to children. Furthermore, these families were more likely to use what we call "educational strategies." They had thought out how to use educational programs and the school system to develop a multilingual repertoire. In essence, they saw themselves as in charge of their multilingualism, and were active players in its acquisition. Sandra's description of language use and language attitudes within her family serves as a good example of multilingualism experienced as choice.

Multilingualism as choice

Sandra, 18 years old at the time of the interview, was born in Canada of Portuguese parents, both of whom were born in Portugal. Her father received a university education in Montreal and currently works as an engineer. He is trilingual, but uses mostly French at work. He understands English, but is not comfortable speaking it. Sandra's mother has a college education, works as a receptionist, and has four languages in her repertoire. She uses all four languages at work. When we asked Sandra about her first language, she was very clear that it is Portuguese. When she was small, Portuguese was the only language in her home. This was something her father has always felt very strongly about, since he feared that his children would lose their mother tongue. To this day, Sandra speaks only Portuguese with her parents.

Because Sandra was going to attend a French school, her parents chose to send her to French language daycare to prepare her for schooling. She then went to a French elementary school, where she was the only immigrant. At school, she used French all the time with the other children. After school, she mostly played with her cousins. Sandra said that at that time she had trouble communicating with her cousins, who spoke much more English than French. Their parents had migrated to Quebec earlier, and English was the language that their family had adopted. Since Sandra spoke no English at this point in time, they communicated in French, even though her cousins' skills were limited.

Since her parents were committed to developing Sandra's skills in Portuguese, they enrolled her in a heritage language program when she was in elementary school. The program was run on Saturdays from 8 a.m. to 2 p.m. Although the initial decision to attend this program was her parents', in the eleven years that she has been in the program, Sandra has never once questioned her enrollment. She feels that heritage language programs have contributed significantly to her written skills in Portuguese, and that she has a good background in Portuguese literature.

Even though Sandra had been in an ESL program since grade four,[6] she considers that she first really started learning English in grade six, when her parents enrolled her in a six-month intensive ESL program offered in French language schools – the equivalent of a mini-immersion program. She says that, prior to this program, she couldn't understand her mother when she spoke in English to her cousins or other relatives. Thanks to this mini-immersion program in English, when Sandra moved into high school, she was able to attend an enriched English program.

Sandra emphasized the diversity of her French-language high school, as compared to her elementary school. It was described as a much more multicultural environment. Accordingly, her use of languages became more complex: with monolingual students, she spoke only French, with other friends from other backgrounds, she used French, English, and Spanish, a language that she appears to have picked up quite easily during this period.

Sandra's French skills are very good and, when she graduated from high school, she applied to both French and English language *cegeps* and was accepted by both. She chose an English language program because she wanted to improve her English skills – the language she considered her weakest. She intends to continue her education in an English language university.

At present, Sandra says that she uses Portuguese to speak to her older relatives. With her cousins, she uses English, now that she can speak it. They switch to Portuguese if there are any older relatives around. With her two brothers, who are still in French primary school, she speaks French most of the time. She has always used Portuguese with her father, and almost always with her mother, though recently she has started to use English. Sandra still goes to Portuguese church and participates in a Portuguese youth group. In these activities, she says she uses all three languages with the younger members of her community, and Portuguese with older members.

When we asked Sandra about the languages that people need to live in Montreal, she was very clear that they needed both French and English. She insists that the importance of languages depends on the context in which they are considered: "since, like, ok, we are in a, in a French province in an English country, whatever, but I think that we have to be able to ... Everybody should be able to speak French and English. It's just, it's basic." Sandra very clearly considers her multilingual repertoire of value within a global market.

Sandra feels fine with the prospect of working in more than one language and believes that she has the skills to do this, including the written skills. She also feels strongly that her multilingualism is an asset and feels sorry for people who speak only one language:

> I have to say that I feel proud ... It's true because ... I see some people who ... they only know French and nothing else and I'm sad, you know. Its kind of sad, cause they can't ... I don't know. I think it [multilingualism] is a great treasure.

Sandra evaluates her skills in all of her languages highly, and feels confident that she can work in any of her languages. She socializes with people from many backgrounds and seems completely at ease moving from one world to another. When asked if she felt that learning languages was important to her family, Sandra answered:

> Yeah ... Well, my reference is my father. When he came here, he was like twenty-five years old and he knew no word of English, no word of French. And he only spoke Portuguese and he came and like he started learning French and he studied and like now he's an engineer now. But he studied here and uh, it did lots of changes. Like if he hadn't learned French, he wouldn't have the job he has now.

As Sandra's trajectory reveals, her parents have taken every available opportunity to help their daughter develop or acquire languages, both at home and in school. Sandra has adopted the same outlook, and now makes her own decisions based on the continuing development of her multilingual repertoire. In other words, she seems to have adopted the habitus or ethos of her parents with respect to languages, and describes them as valuable forms of capital.

Multilingualism as consequence

Not all multilingual youths or families appear to feel this degree of control over their language experiences. For some, multilingualism appears to be experienced more as a "consequence" of where they have lived and of the immigration process than as a choice. Jo's trajectory is a case in point.

Jo, 20 years old at the time of the interview, was born in Ghana, as were both his parents. He moved to Quebec at the age of 15. His premigratory experience of language was multilingual. When he arrived in Quebec, he was already trilingual, and has since learned French.

Jo's first language is Fanti, but he says that, in Ghana, among his family and neighbors, Fanti was heavily laden with English words (such as TV and fridge), for which there were no Fanti equivalents. Jo emphasized the importance of English in Ghana, and how it is used as a lingua franca between speakers of different African languages. Furthermore, in Ghana, English is also the language of schooling, which remains very much under the influence of the British educational system. When Jo started attending school, his parents began speaking to him in English, thinking that this practice would help him to succeed at school. As a child in Ghana, he used only Fanti with his grandmother, who could not speak English, but with most of his relatives he spoke a mixture of Fanti and English. Jo has never gone back to Ghana. He speaks of Fanti as the language of a "small people," only worth knowing within Ghana and even there, as subordinate to English. For Jo, the status of English has been clear since childhood.

When he was 15, Jo's family migrated to Montreal. Jo's father is university educated, but currently works as a machinist. His mother has a high school education and works in a factory. Both parents spoke Fanti, Ga (another local language), and English before arriving in Montreal and have yet to learn French. When Jo enrolled in the school system, he was "put in a welcoming class" in a French-language high school. In the first year at the school, he had no friends because he could speak no French. After school, he would just go home:

> I just went home 'cause like, I just had to learn French so like ... I was always learning French 'cause if you can't speak the language, you can't speak with anyone ... cause the other kids they all speak French. And they don't speak English. So what are you going to say to them ... so you just go home.

After a year and a half in the "welcome" program, he "was moved" into the regular high school program in a different building. He liked the high school, partly because of the diversity of kids from different countries. He made a lot of friends at this point and hung out with them after school. With these friends, he sometimes spoke in English and, with those who could speak no English, he spoke in French. He has some friends from Ghana and says that he found this very important when he first started living in Montreal, but less so as time went by. Jo graduated from high school two years after integrating into the regular program. He chose an English language *cegep* and feels that his level of French would not have allowed him to follow a program in a French language *cegep*. He feels little attachment to Fanti or Ga, and is not concerned with maintaining his skills in these languages. His concerns are with improving his English and French, languages that he feels are required for living in Montreal.

At home, Jo has two younger sisters who are enrolled in French school. With his sisters, he speaks mostly French. With his parents, he currently speaks a mixture of Fanti, English, and some French. Jo's parents feel that you need to have languages to succeed, and the languages they consider important are French and English. In the past, they bought him workbooks to help him learn English and French.

Jo claims to use mostly English in his everyday life. He sometimes uses French to watch TV or listen to the radio, to talk to neighbors or when he is shopping. He considers his English skills to be stronger than his French skills, and also stronger than his skills in Fanti:

> There is only two that I want to improve, which is French and English, 'cause like everywhere you go ... English is the dominant, like everywhere you go, like they speak it everywhere and French ... you have to be able to speak French to be ... to get advantage of it. Let's say you are looking for a job and speak only English, it's hard. You have to speak French, too, or other languages. Spanish or English.

He plans to improve his French skills in the coming years, but will attend an English-language university.

In Jo's case, the experience of acquiring a multilingual repertoire has been a relatively passive one, a consequence of circumstances and of immigration, rather than of active decision-making. The terms he uses to talk about his experience are in effect passive: he was *put into* a welcoming class and then *moved into* a regular program. He talks about languages in terms of what is needed to succeed, but not in terms of what he has that is to his advantage.

This contrast in the way multilingualism is experienced by families was striking across the interviews. Some respondents revealed that, regardless of their pre-migratory experience, the status of their first languages, and their current multilingual practices, their families strongly value multilingualism. Others recognize the economic need for languages, but without seeing multilingualism as something in their control. Respondents like Jo, who have experienced multilingualism as a consequence seem to have spent little time thinking about languages and, in their families, the importance of language is not part of a verbally expressed ethos. In the families where multilingualism is experienced more actively, students say that their parents talked about languages frequently, some say *ad nauseam*, and that they were taught to see multilingualism as a social and economic advantage and as an important resource to be drawn upon.

Language as Capital, Language as Identity

While the experience of multilingualism seemed to fall into two divergent categories, all the young people we interviewed considered languages as an individual resource and, generally speaking, they associated languages with advantages. A few talked about the difficulties of building a multilingual repertoire, considering the development of written skills in many languages as particularly challenging. Despite difficulties, there was a good deal of consensus that being multilingual was better than being monolingual:

> Some people who, they only know French and nothing else. And I'm sad, you know. It's kind of sad because they can't ... I think it's a great treasure, like, to have many (languages).

Distinctions were made, however, with respect to the different languages in their repertoire. All of the respondents very clearly expressed their awareness of the value of English/French bilingualism in Montreal, especially with regard to the work world: As Jo put it: "To be able to work in Montreal, you have to be able to know the two languages." While bilingualism held the highest value in terms of capital, French was seen as the dominant language within Montreal. We heard statements to the effect that: "First, I think you need to learn French. And then to learn some English. In Montreal, it's not as important as French." For those of us who grew up in Quebec in the sixties, statements to this effect are surprising, and represent a major shift in attitude.

Students were extremely prompt to nuance the status and value of languages according to context. If French is important in Montreal, it is less important as soon as one thinks of the larger Canadian, North American, or global context. As one student put it:

> ... (languages) are all important in different situations ... in different places ... so I don't know if one is more important than the others. It's depending on the circumstances. French is important because I live here. If I didn't live here, I don't know if I would have learned French. But because I live here, it's important.

In the interviews, this type of statement was perhaps the most revealing of sensitivity to linguistic markets and the specificity of markets.

If multilingualism was perceived as important within a global market, English was clearly recognized as the most important language within the international context and within North America. At the international level, interviewees perceive English as the most likely of their language skills to have a conversion value regardless of context.

When it came to their first languages, some young people, such as Sandra and Daniel who speak Spanish as well as English and French, felt their languages were economically valuable in many countries. Others felt that their first language had value only within their country of origin. Charry, for example, described Tagalog as "useful for Filipinos, just for Filipinos. It's not like English that you can use anywhere in the world."

Regardless of their economic value, first languages were almost always associated with an attachment to identity, loyalty to family, and membership in a community. Being able to speak their first language was sometimes perceived as a requirement for membership in their ethnic communities in Montreal and, for many, for acceptance in their countries of origin. They are often described as something vital in communicating with relatives and as a prerequisite "to fit in." For others, it is not so much a question of fitting in, as a sense of who you are. Harminder had this to say:

> Even though I may not be Punjabi, because I was not born there, but I still have to remember where my parents come from and I have to remember what culture I came from. If I lost Punjabi, I would lose part of myself, because it is who I am ... It's not like, if you don't know Punjabi, you're out ... It's not that.

One final aspect of multilingualism that was explored in the interviews was respondents' sense of identity as multilinguals. Generally speaking, they expressed a positive attitude toward their identity as multilinguals, which they describe as complex and ambiguous. Daniel, whose home background was admittedly more complex than most, had this to say:

> You are one person spread four ways, as opposed to one person that's concentrated in one direction ... I think I am like an empty space. I don't know... I don't call myself Italian. I don't say I'm Spanish, 'cause I'm both and I realize... I have some characteristics of one and of the other. And of the English culture, since I've grown up ... and with the French people and everything. I'm just like one big clay. I'm like you see blue clay and red clay and white clay, you know. I'm just one big ball of clay. No identity to it, not yet at least. They haven't characterized us yet. Maybe put us a name or something. Well, I guess in having many different identities ... you produce ... you come out as one identity.

Many students said they liked being able to move from one world to another, being able to relate to people from different cultural and linguistic backgrounds. Although not clearly expressed as such, multilingual youths often describe themselves as though they had more than one passport, and were able to move across boundaries in Montreal, whereas others who are monolingual are perceived as constrained by these boundaries.

Finally, when asked to define themselves in terms of ethnic, national, or linguistic identity, many stated that, in terms of nationality or citizenship, they felt Canadian, but in terms of ethnicity, they referred to their country of origin or that of their parents. Most described themselves as hyphenated Canadians. Sandra explained how this hyphenated identity is constructed: "I'm Portuguese because of my parents, but I'm Canadian because I was born right here." From these self-descriptions, it would appear that ethnic, national, and racial traits are more likely to be brought up in terms of multiple identity, than linguistic ones, regardless of the tendency in Quebec to think of intergroup relations in terms of language (Anglophone, Francophone, allophone). Only Meena defined her identity as closely related to her linguistic traits:

> I'm a multilingual person. I'm a multiculturalist. I just feel ok, I learned the languages and I know a little bit about the cultures, that's all I mean. It's not like I know only about Indian culture. I know about other people's cultures.

Conclusions

From interviewees' descriptions of their everyday activities emerges a portrait of a city in which multilingualism pervades all aspects of their lives. The young people we interviewed came from homes where more than one language was spoken. They describe their neighborhoods as places where many languages are heard and in which they use many languages, switching from French to English to their mother tongue as they walk down the streets, talk to friends and neighbors, and shop. Many have large family and community networks that they describe as multilingual and in which code-switching appears to be common. Interestingly, within ethnic communities, a generational divide exists, often determining the use of English or French. This divide corresponds to the adoption of Bill 101.

When it came to the institutional setting of the *cegep*, the young people we talked to were adamant that the *cegep* was an "English place." They were also quick to qualify this comment, talking about the multiculturalism of the student population who come "from everywhere and speak many languages," often adding that diversity in the student population made them feel comfortable. Most said they hung out with friends from varied ethnic and linguistic backgrounds, whether in the *cegep* or after classes in more informal settings. A few have a network of friends from the same ethnic and linguistic background: while others reject this type of network, describing it as confining and artificial. A few respondents talked of their need, during their first years in Quebec, for a network of friends with the same background, but said that now they feel most comfortable in "multicultural" groups rather than in monoethnic ones.

When the young people described Montreal, they talked of a "big city," a cosmopolitan and multilingual city, where speaking many languages is a plus. However, they also spoke of Montreal as a place where English and French are necessities – for getting a job, but also for being able to talk to "everyone," and as a form of social capital. While French was perceived as the most important language in Quebec, English/French bilingualism was perceived as the most valuable type of linguistic capital. Often respondents said they felt sorry for monolinguals, whom they saw not only as at a disadvantage in the workforce, but also as constrained by only one world view, one way of looking at things, as compared to multilinguals who could see things through many different cultures. Most interviewees described their multilingualism as something valuable and useful, an advantage, "a kind of treasure." None felt that the disadvantages of being multilingual outweighed the advantages.

From descriptions of how interviewees use languages in their everyday lives, a first impression to emerge is that many languages are used in all sorts of situations and settings and that, in interactions, it the other person's language skills that determines the choice of one language over another. When we look further, however, what emerges is that sites do affect the choice of language. For example, work sites are almost always described as bilingual, whereas in *cegeps*, it is expected that the common language will be English. But this statement needs to be nuanced. Sites are not monolingual, but they can be associated with the predominance of one or more languages. Furthermore, some languages are more likely than others to be used across sites. More specifically, all the students we interviewed claimed that they used English everywhere – in their homes, in public places, for leisure activities, and at work. French, however, was also used in almost all sites and in many different leisure activities, such as shopping, watching TV, and reading the newspaper. Minority languages were less likely to be used across sites and three students claimed that they never or very rarely use their first language outside of the home.

What this broad portrait of Montreal reveals is a city that has been significantly transformed by language reform, as evidenced by the importance all of the interviewees accorded French. But what also emerges is a portrait of a city where English/French bilingualism is alive and well and perceived as useful and valuable. In effect, these narratives of growing up in Montreal add flesh to trends already revealed in the census data presented earlier.

From these narratives, however, also emerges a portrait of a city currently in the process of being transformed by the diversity of its inhabitants. While English/French bilingualism is necessary for full participation in the life of the city, Montreal is also a place where multilingualism is a fact of life for an important proportion of the population, and where multilingualism is considered a valuable resource. In essence, if Montreal can be understood as a linguistic market deliberately transformed through language policy, it is also a market transformed through more subtle internal and external processes – the settlement of immigrants and the changing status of languages provoked by globalization.

Interestingly, while all the interviewees perceived languages as capital, they were able to nuance this statement, allocating different amounts of value to each language within their repertoire and determining value according to specific contexts. In other words, multilingualism might be valuable, but how valuable is determined by the status of the languages within a given repertoire, and the linguistic markets in which languages drawn upon.

It was also seen that families experience multilingualism quite differently. For some families, multilingualism is experienced as a consequence and an individual's role within its acquisition as passive. These families also seem to take a passive role with regard to the linguistic market in which they live. They talk about languages as resources that are needed within a market, but rarely about resources that are owned and can be used to advantage within a market. Other families, living within the same contextual constraints and opportunities, perceive multilingualism as a choice or an opportunity, something they have active control over. They see family members as owners of resources that can be deployed to advantage. These divergent ways of looking at multilingualism reinforce Bourdieu's notion that families have an ethos toward their own resources, an ethos that affects how family members will use these resources to maintain or improve their position in a society.

As a final comment, we would like to underline that this account is exploratory, and relies on interview techniques. Although further research is needed to examine the findings in greater depth, findings clearly point to the need for a multi-site approach if we are to understand language socialization and language practices in Montreal. It also seems clear that, given that Montreal (as a "language contact" context) makes apparent what is often hidden in situations where one language dominates, research on the language perceptions and practices of the "children of Bill 101" (the children of immigrants to Montreal) can provide a rare opportunity to understand the relationship between language perceptions and practices and specific language markets.

Notes

1. In Quebec, the term allophone is used to refer to speakers of languages other than French or English. French speakers are referred to as Francophones, and English speakers as Anglophones.
2. In this chapter, trilingualism is defined as knowledge of Canada's two official languages and another language. Here, we discuss only the trilingualism of people whose first language is neither French nor English.
3. In general, interviews lasted just over an hour, with some lasting an hour and a half when the person being interviewed spoke more than three languages. Interviews were completely transcribed. Each interview was analyzed in the first instance as a case study and then responses across topic areas were compared. Finally, we looked at all the interviews with an eye for broad commonalities of experience.
4. In Quebec, while language of schooling at the primary and secondary level is legally determined, there are no restrictions at the post-secondary level. We feel that it is important to emphasize that the data we collected are from students who have chosen an English *cegep* over a French one. Roughly half had attended French-language schools. Their presence in English-language *cegeps* is not surprising, since statistics reveal that just over half of all allophone students are in English *cegeps*. Since the experience and attitudes of these students might differ from those of students who have chosen to go to college in French, we are presently conducting interviews with students enrolled in a French-language *cegep*. At a later date, we will be able to examine how their experiences and attitudes differ.
5. In Canada, two languages have "official status," English and French. Other languages can be referred to as non-official languages.
6. In Quebec, ESL refers to a second language program offered to all students in French language schools. It does not refer to language programs for immigrants who are in the process of integrating into a community.

Part 2

Language Socialization at School

Chapter 5

Representational Practices and Multi-modal Communication in US High Schools: Implications for Adolescent Immigrants

LINDA HARKLAU

The educational system has always played a major role in the socialization of newcomers in immigrant-receiving countries such as the United States. In fact, public secondary schools were established in part because of the perceived need to socialize and "Americanize" a large number of immigrants at the turn of the twentieth century (see, for example, Olneck, 1995). In light of the increasingly prominent role that language is seen to play in constructing the social world, it may be argued that all socialization is language socialization. Nevertheless, research on language socialization and research on immigrant socialization in schools have generally remained separate scholarly spheres with little conceptual overlap. In recent years, the notion of language socialization has broadened, going beyond its origins in the analysis of young children's initial stages of first language acquisition and into consideration of the sociocultural and linguistic realms of multilingual adolescents and adults. There is a growing convergence between language socialization perspectives and notions of how adolescent immigrant identities are shaped in schools. In this chapter, I contribute to this conceptual synthesis by suggesting ways in which the acknowledged role of secondary schooling as an arena for immigrant socialization can be integrated with a language socialization perspective. I explore the dynamics through which one particular group of immigrants was socialized into the linguistic and academic cultural practices of a US secondary school, exploring two major themes. First I examine how texts, curricula, and face-to-face interactions served to maintain certain images or representations of immigrant students at the school. Next, I describe the multimodality of high school classroom communication and the complexity of the communicative worlds of multilingual adolescents.

This chapter draws from year-long case studies taking an ethnographic (Green & Bloome, 1996; Merriam, 1998: 34) or "ethnographic style" approach (Lea & Street, 1998). The intent of this study was to examine the perspectives of linguistic minority students on the "cultures of knowledge" of high school and college and literacy practices associated with each. The first half of the study, which is the focus of this chapter, took place in an ethnically diverse urban high school in western New York from January to June 1994. Participants included four female students from ethnolinguistic backgrounds that were representative of the community in which the study took place: Aeyfer was a Turkish-American from a working class background; Claudia was a Vietnamese-American from a low-income background; Penny was a middle class Vietnamese-American from a Chinese ethnic background; Hanh was a middle class Vietnamese-American.

As is typical in qualitative case study methodology, the study is based on three forms of data: audiotaped and transcribed interviews, observations and field notes in classrooms, and written documents from case study students and their teachers.[1] In keeping with the post-structuralist approach taken here, I do not claim to have uncovered a social reality independent of my own perceptions and interpretations. Rather, I see the descriptions here, and any social science descriptions, as inevitably intertwined with participants' and my own social positioning and constantly shifting senses of the social world in which we operate.

Below, I first show how students positioned themselves and were positioned socially through representational practices, describing three main images of immigrants prevalent within the school – a "colorblind" representation, a representation invoking Ellis Island mythology about immigration in US society, and a representation of bilinguals as linguistically and cognitively deficient. Next, I consider the implications of multimodal classroom communicative practices for processes of adolescent socialization.

Socialization through Representational Practices

Historians and sociologists have long viewed educational institutions as one of the primary sites through which individuals are socialized to take particular societal roles (Oakes, 1985; Olneck, 1995). That is especially true in the United States, where universal access to free public education has been seen explicitly as a tool to instill in newcomers the habits, norms, and values deemed desirable for their participation in American society (Olneck, 1995; Tollefson, 1989). The basic goals and structure of secondary schooling in particular were originally instituted at the turn of the twentieth century as a means of socializing and "Americanizing" the large influx of immigrants of the time into the beliefs and behaviors deemed necessary for civic participation in American society. A second purpose was to socialize these new-comers to fill their expected roles in the lowest rungs of the economy as agricultural and industrial workers (Oakes, 1985; Tollefson, 1989). From their very inception, then, US secondary schools have been a key site or "arena" (Olneck, 1995) for conveying messages to immigrant students about their social identities.

Post-structuralist perspectives, like social constructivist approaches to language socialization (see, for example, Ochs, 1993), do not view societal messages about immigrant ethnicity, identity, and school achievement as imposed deterministically. Rather, they view the target of socialization as constantly moving, dynamic and multiple. From this perspective, societal messages about identity or "discourses" (Foucault, 1983, 1995/1979) exist in fluid and reciprocal relationships with commu-nicative practices in individual schools and classrooms. Through texts, visuals, curricula, and face-to-face interactions among teachers and students, these discourses both shape and are shaped by the way immigrants view themselves and others (see, for example, Davidson, 1996; McKay & Wong, 1996). From a post-structuralist perspective, discourses about immigrant student identities are also seen as diffuse. They are not unitary but multiple, not consistent but conflicting. They are also inherently unstable, shifting constantly through every interaction with other individuals, with text, and with visual imagery.

At the same time, we tend to have the feeling that what it means to be "bilingual" or an "immigrant" or an "ESOL [English as a second/other language] student" is stable and self-evident in any given place or time. To explain this apparent contradiction, we might draw upon the notion of "representation." While it has varying definitions (see, for example, Hall, 1997; hooks, 1992; Weedon, 1997), at its core the notion of representation suggests that we make sense of the social world and the discourses that are chaotic and constantly in flux by imposing contrasting categories or representations. Within the representations we create (e.g. "ESOL student" or "non-native speaker of English") we tend to homogenize, focusing on similarity and neglecting variation. Furthermore, because social life takes place in unequal relations of power (e.g. between teachers and students, between native speakers and non-native speakers, between majority and minority), the exercise of representation is not neutral. Rather, the representations of some prevail over those of others. In terms of immigrants and other language minority students, this means that the exercise of power may impose "internal colonization" (Olivas, 1986) whereby multilingual students come to see themselves as the dominant monolin-gual group perceives them. Post-structuralist views resist the portrayal of any single individual or group as responsible for producing domination and inequali-ties. Instead, systematic patterns of immigrant socialization can be seen as produced through individual interactions with people, texts, and visuals that constantly reassert group interests and desires (Luke, 1995; Ryan, 1991). At the same time, that is not to say that individuals have no effect. Rather, all teachers and students have agency and constantly act to resist or reshape the representations to which they are subject. In all, then, there is a good deal of overlap between post-structuralist notions of socialization and recent views of language socialization. Both go beyond a conceptualization of a unilinear process of induction of children, adolescents, and adults towards relatively fixed domains of knowledge and cultural practice towards a view of socialization processes that are complex, dynamic, and reciprocal. The notion of representation contributes to this view by emphasizing the inherent linkage between local socialization practices and broader historical, social, and political contexts.

US secondary schools, with their explicit institutional mission of socialization, are arguably a key site of representational practices. In this particular institutional context, most or all of the classroom experiences of multilingual students' took place in "mainstream" or content area courses where the vast majority of students and teachers were American-born English monolinguals. Two of the four case study students (Claudia and Aeyfer) were not enrolled in ESOL at all in their senior year. For several years, none of the four had spent more than one of their six class periods per day in ESOL. One consequence of this common practice of integrating bilingual students into classrooms with a monolingual majority is that bilingual student status is marked. It renders students subject to socialization practices and social positionings that are predicated on assumptions and beliefs about their salient identities as ethnic minorities, as immigrants, and as non-native speakers of English. In this particular context, the positioning of students as English language learners among monolingual speakers of English appeared to have important ramifications both for broad processes of identity formation and for the language and literacy practices into which they were socialized. Below, I describe three major examples of representations of immigrant identity in the high school experiences of the case study students: a "colorblind" view in which ethnic difference was leveled or over-looked, an "othered" view of immigrants as both ennobled and exotic, and a representation of bilingual students as linguistically and cognitively deficient.

Colorblind representation

As in many other urban classrooms across the United States, these high school students and educators encountered diversity as a daily fact of life. Black–white differences were perhaps most salient in this particular setting. African-Americans formed the majority of the student body, but most of teachers were white. There was also considerable heterogeneity in socioeconomic status within and among ethnic groups at the school. At one level, the subject of diversity was dealt with matter of factly in the daily life of the high school. "Hallway multiculturalism" (Hoffman, 1996) was evident; for example, posters along the corridors featured successful sports and media figures, predominantly African-American, proclaiming the value of education, and exhorting students to finish high school. Curricula in the students' classrooms were clearly influenced by the US educational system's drive to incorporate multicultural themes. One English teacher's final exam, for example, drew upon short stories and poetry from Native -American, Asian-American, and African-American authors. Another English teacher showed the movie, *Good-bye Miss Fourth of July* which Penny reported was about "a girl who from Greek [*sic*] and she came to a small town in Virginia. And she fought for prejudice and racism." Hanh's psychology course at the school included a lesson on "Multicultural Social Skills." A handout from the class identified skills such as "Seeks mutual enrichment by creating multiple opportunities for interaction." and "Avoids insensitive and offensive remarks about others who are different from oneself." In the same course, the teacher identified multiculturalism as one of the key issues in the dynamics of group interaction.

While the subject of student diversity was not actively avoided, the public face-to-face discourse of the educators and students in these classrooms seemed to construct diversity as something "out there" to be addressed through the curriculum. Rarely was it linked to specific attributes or experiences of specific students or teachers. In the forum of classroom discussion, many educators at the high school seemed to subscribe to what Schofield (1986) has described as a "colorblind perspective," believing that ethnic and racial backgrounds of students should be irrelevant and that to acknowledge them explicitly was discriminatory. For example, this perspective seemed to be at work when Claudia gained US citizenship and in the process changed her name from her given Vietnamese name to what she considered to be a more "American" name. One teacher dealt with this change by simply walking into class one day and calling her Claudia. No explanation was given to the class, and I looked on as classmates exchanged puzzled looks and muttered, "Claudia?!" Still, the teacher and perhaps Claudia herself evidently felt that it was inappropriate to address this very noticeable aspect of Claudia's ethnic and immigrant identity explicitly in the classroom. Schofield and other scholars (see, for example, Hoffman, 1996; hooks, 1992; Sleeter, 1993) have critiqued the colorblind perspective, noting that it is apolitical and can obscure issues of majority–minority power relations in the classroom and in society. At the same time, however, the colorblind perspective allowed the ESOL students in this study a social space to construct public classroom identities that were seemingly unmarked.

"Ellis Island" immigrant representation

While these immigrant students may have wished in some ways to blend into the crowd and to be considered indistinguishable from other students, at the same time it was clear that their status as immigrants was salient to their peers. This was indicated, for example, by the harassment that the students had endured from classmates in their initial years in the United States. Claudia wrote about encounters with bullies who victimized the newly arrived with racial slurs. Aeyfer described her first years of school in the United States as an ordeal, observing that she was so afraid of the children who made fun of her that she had wanted to drop out of school.

While the colorblind perspective may have predominated in class discussions, the interactions of the case study students with their teachers through written modalities tended to emphasize a representation of themselves as aligned with an "Ellis Island" myth of the immigrant experience prevalent in US societal discourses. The Ellis Island myth portrays immigration as an ennobling process in which individuals leave their family, friends, and the customs of their homelands under adverse circumstances to come to the United States. Upon arrival, they persevere through a financially and psychologically difficult period of adjustment. Through hard work, they earn the American dream of upward social mobility and prosperity. Case study students frequently drew upon their own experiences to align themselves with the representation of immigrant hardship and striving. For example, when the students were asked to "give an account of an event that actually happened or that you imagined," Claudia wrote about one particular encounter in elementary school with a bully who told her to go back to her country and threatened to "beat the hell" out of her. When asked to propose and describe the celebration of a new "special holiday," Claudia wrote about the celebration of Vietnamese New Year. In response to a prompt asking her to write a "how-to" instructional essay, Claudia responded with an essay entitled "How to come to America," in which she chronicled her departure from Vietnam and her arrival in western New York. Another composition offered a fictional description of an emotional reunion with her extended family in Vietnam. In fact, while a small number of Claudia's compositions took on more prosaic topics (e.g. a tongue-in-cheek letter to her grandmother thanking her for an odd gift, and an essay describing the perks and special events she looked forward to as a senior at the high school), most of the essays she wrote took on some aspect of her experience as an immigrant.

Not only did the students take opportunities to write stories about themselves as immigrants, but their teachers also selected reading assignments that provided models for exactly these sorts of immigrant stories. These included stories about leaving their homelands, stories about trauma and hardships they had endured in relocating to the United States, and stories about customs in their "other" cultures. For example, Penny's English teacher asked the class to read the book, *Journey to America*, which Penny described as being about a Jewish family fleeing Germany during the Second World War. Teachers and students thus mutually invoked the Ellis Island immigrant representation, largely through written communication. Through these immigrant stories, students and their teachers mutually worked to reinforce students' alignment with the Ellis Island representation of immigrants and associated moral standing as individuals who valued education as a vehicle for self-advancement. At the same time, the invocation of this representation also served to position teachers reciprocally in the favorable role of moral leaders and agents of opportunity. Claudia, for example, wrote "Education is always the first thing for me to do before anything else." She also wrote:

> In four years I like all of my teachers. I think they do a very good job teaching me not only the subjects that they're supposed to teach, but they also teach me how to live in the real world after graduation and not to be prejudiced at people because they are not the same color.

Likewise, Aeyfer wrote to her teacher, "I think the solution for discrimination is education." Hanh's English teacher even explicitly solicited these sorts of opinions from students by asking them to write about their attitudes towards school. In response, Hanh wrote, "School is my partner. It helps me a lot. I depend my future goals on it." She added with a slight edge, "I will never getting tired (but I will get bored sometimes) of going to school." On occasion, this sentiment of persevering immigrants merged with an Asian "model minority" stereotype, such as when Hanh's psychology teacher related his impression that Asian immigrants are highly motivated.

The representation of immigrants as morally upright individuals who particularly valued education was also reinforced through their classroom behavior. They showed open affection for some of their teachers, such as when Aeyfer put her arm around her computer teacher's shoulder as she introduced her to me. They attended class more regularly than their American-born classmates. In classes, they appeared diligent and attentive. For example, teachers reported approvingly that Hanh and Penny regularly finished their work before the native speakers in their classes. Teachers in response tended to laud the immigrant students in their classes, speaking of them with admiration and affection. One English teacher, for example, referred to Penny with an affectionate diminutive as "my little Penny" and commented, "She's a real sweetheart. I really like her." Teachers may have not realized that the behavior of the case study students did not mean that they viewed teachers any less critically than American-born students did, only that they did not share these opinions with them. Aeyfer said of her math class, for example, "I can't say nothing to no teacher. I don't want to do nothing in there, so I just sit there and try to learn."

Teachers' enthusiasm for immigrant stories provided further incentives for students to continue the cycle of creating such stories. Hanh, Claudia, and Aeyfer's English teacher, for example, assigned autobiography projects to which students unsurprisingly responded with immigrant stories. When asked about the autobiographies, the instructor reported, "Oh, those are WONDERFUL! Absolutely WONDERFUL!" and "They're turning in really neat stuff. These are beautiful." A veteran teacher of almost 25 years whom one would not expect to be easily impressed, he nonetheless seemed to accept enthusiastically and even encourage students to formulate this representation of themselves. Given this reaction, students jumped in to portray themselves as immigrants and as cultural and linguistic others even when they were not explicitly asked to. Note, for example, that many of the examples of Claudia's essays described earlier were written in response to prompts that did not explicitly elicit this sort of narrative. In some cases, in fact, Claudia wrote an essay that was off topic in order to produce one of these stories.

Ironically, the "other" cultures that students evoked and wrote about to their teachers were by their very nature hybridized. For example, Aeyfer noted how living in the United States had caused her to think differently about her past in Turkey:

> From the day I put my feet in America I have learned a lot of things about life. One of them is to respect your own people and country. When I was in Turkey, I always wanted to go out of Turkey and never remember it again. But America helped me change the way I think. Over the four years I realized that my people and my country are very important to me. If I have a chance to go back, I will never despise them again.

Having grown to adulthood in the United States, these students conjured cultures that were idealized precisely because of their distance in space and time. As a result, the "other" cultures jointly constructed by students and their teachers in essays like Aeyfer's were actually syncretic and hybrid. In other words, the case study students and the cultural identities they wrote about were as much a product of their life in the United States as they were of the cultures of their families or their native countries. As Hanh once told me, she did not consider herself entirely Vietnamese or American, but "half."

There is no doubt that some of the case study students had experienced severe hardships. It was also clear that the students used compositions as a vehicle to explore heartfelt sentiments such as pride in their heritage or their sense of anomie living in the United States. In some ways, the representation of Ellis Island immigrants seemed to cast these students in a positive light at the school, positioning them as hard workers who persevered and overcame adversity, gaining upward social mobility through education. Nevertheless, the representation also potentially encouraged teachers and the students themselves to think of immigrants in essentialized ways, as perpetual foreigners who were primarily exemplars of ethnolinguistic identities and only secondarily individuals. Students had been subjected to this representation so persistently that they had, in some ways, succumbed to internal colonization and had come to see themselves as perpetual newcomers, excluding the possibility of multiple affiliations or identities. For example, even in the process of becoming American citizens, and even after five to ten years in the United States, they tended to refer only to their natal land as "my country." More telling, perhaps, is an observation of Penny's in her final essay for a high school English class. When asked to compare the main characters in two stories they had read in class, *Stranger in a Strange Land* (Heinlein, 1961) and *Crickets* (Butler, 1992), Penny wrote that, "These two characters both came from the different places. Micheal was came from Mars, and Ted came from Vietnam." After years of representing herself as a cultural "other," Penny evidently had come to see her status as a Vietnamese immigrant as so foreign that it was tantamount to being from another planet.

Linguistic deficit representation

In a predominantly monolingual society in which one single standard target English is assumed to exist, the case study students were also subject to a third representation in which bilingualism was implicitly associated with linguistic or even cognitive deficit. For example, because the ability to produce standard English is often regarded as a relatively transparent window to thought processes, some teachers took students' perseverance and hard work in school to be a possible indication of a lack of innate ability. One English teacher, for example, pointed out that none of the case study students had been in "regents" (advanced level) courses in English, and observed that "The ABSTRACT quality [in writing] sort of separates – I think theoretically what really separates non-regents from regents is that ability to do that other type of thinking." The same teacher wondered:

> I don't know now, because they are so motivated, and we have also gotten away from even this kind of thinking – I don't know how *intelligent* they are. And that is also real – largely discounted now, but it's also a real fact. If they were literate in English, let's say – how good could they be? Again, they'll be successful because they are very *motivated*, but I have no idea of what their natural ability is.

Other teachers' attitudes also reflected ambivalence about students' multilingualism. Penny's English teacher, for example, asserted that the immigrant students she had taught had difficulty writing analytically, while at the same time vehemently noting, "They're NOT slow! They're not stupid!"

Often multilingualism of other students seemed to be regarded not as a resource, but rather as a "problem" (Ruíz, 1984), and their proficiency in two or three languages was reduced to a deficit in one. Very few social spaces were made in the life of the school in which they might demonstrate their full linguistic talents and resources as multilinguals. Only the ESOL teacher seemed to make regular opportunities for students to use other languages, such as developing multilingual hallway direction signs and writing bilingual poetry. During the study, only one other student or teacher, a friend of Hanh's, who asked her to teach him Vietnamese, expressed any interest in or appreciation for the linguistic resources of the case study students in languages other than English. In contrast, the case study students and their families clearly valued multilingualism. Aeyfer, for example, intended to capitalize upon her proficiency in both Turkish and English to develop a career in the tourism industry. She also told me that her family had hired tutors to teach them to read the Quran in Arabic. Likewise, Penny's mother had hired a tutor to develop Penny's literacy in her native Cantonese. Measured only against monolingual native speaker norms for language use, these students' linguistic resources in other languages were rendered invisible at the school, and the students were perceived only as struggling to overcome a deficit in English.

As in the British school context described by Leung, Harris, and Rampton (1997), there is a widespread assumption in the societal and educational discourses of the United States that there exists an undifferentiated Standard English target for second language learners. This assumption did not account for the presence of non-standard or vernacular Englishes – either contact dialects by immigrants, or African-American vernacular English used in informal contexts by many of the case study students' peers. For example, this assumption was evidenced by one of the English teachers who contended that:

> One of these problems in an urban school like this ... is for the most part they never hear English spoken. They speak their own languages at home and here, if you ever walked down the halls, you'd just DIE! ... So they never even hear correct pronunciation, even.

In sum, immigrant students in this particular US high school setting were socialized in and through communicative practices that simultaneously forwarded at least three coexisting representations of what it means to be an immigrant. These representations – a "colorblind" representation, a representation of immigrants as exemplars of Ellis Island American mythology about immigration, and a representation of immigrants as linguistically and cognitively deficient – can be viewed as forms of language socialization, since they were constantly reinvoked and reshaped through students' interactions with teachers and texts. They can also simultaneously be viewed in terms of broader sociocultural forces or discourses about immigration and about multilingualism in US society and educational institutions. In all, then, the notion of representations points out the significant linkage between processes of language socialization and bilingual adolescent identity formation in school settings.

Socialization in and through Multimodal Classroom Communicative Practices

A second potentially generative area of integration of the conceptual frameworks of language socialization and adolescent immigrant socialization in schools lies in the examination of classroom literacy and other semiotic practices. While a substantial body of literature has developed on language socialization in classrooms (see, for example, Cazden, 1988; Cazden *et al.*, 1972; Cook-Gumperz, 1986; Goldenberg & Patthey-Chavez, 1995; Green & Wallat, 1981; Gutierrez, 1995; Heath, 1983; Tharp & Gallimore, 1988; Tharp, 1989), considerably more of this work has taken place at the elementary than at the secondary level (Faltis, 1993). Communicative practices in secondary classrooms such as the US mainstream high school classrooms featured in this study are qualitatively different than those in classrooms with younger children. Bilingual adolescents are schooled in contexts in which students are assumed to have undergone almost a decade of socialization into school-based English language and literacy practices. As a result, teachers and students tend to presume an expanded set of shared communicative resources. In particular, reading and writing permeate every aspect of students' schooling and language learning experiences in higher grades. In US secondary school classrooms, for example, Alvermann and Moore (1996) report that some 60% of high school classroom activities incorporate reading in some form. Likewise, almost half of high school classroom time reportedly involves writing activities in some way (Applebee, 1981). Moreover, unlike young children, bilingual students who are educated in US high school classrooms may bring a considerable degree of literacy in languages other than English, and therefore come to the classroom with prior socialization into school-based literate practices.

This sociolinguistic and semiotic environment has several implications for the joint processes of adolescent bilingual language socialization and socialization into what it means to "do school" in a US high school. One is that language minority students work with a complex orchestration of spoken, written, and visual modalities. In the classrooms of the case study students, for example, students were explicitly socialized into the coordination of note-taking practices with teacher lecture, writing on an overhead projector or the board, and handouts. As part of their ongoing socialization into note-taking practices, teachers often marked these note-taking sessions with explicit routines. For example, Penny reported that her high school physics teacher required that students take notes from textbook readings, which he reviewed and graded. The same teacher handed out packets of incomplete notes for each unit and instructed students to fill in the blanks during his lectures and demonstrations. Likewise, in an observation of Hanh's physics class, the teacher opened a lecture and demonstration in his class by instructing the class to "Take out a sheet of paper," and then gave the class explicit cues about what to put in their notes, such as "Write that down," "Draw that," and "You should have three drawings now." In these classrooms, students were expected to simultaneously attend to and process aural and visual cues coming from the teacher's face-to-face communication, textual sources in their notes and on the board, and visuals coming from teacher drawings or overhead charts. Similarly, Zuengler, Ford, and Fassnacht (1998) describe how a teacher and students tightly coordinated face-to-face interaction in reference to a textual image on an overhead projection screen. Goldman (1997) also describes the integration of face-to-face and textual means of communication in middle school student group projects as members jointly select, interpret, and synthesize texts. In all, then, adolescent bilingual students must learn to work with communicative practices that entail constant coordination and orchestration of multiple modalities. The notion of "multiliteracies" proposed by the New London Group (Cope & Kalantzis, 2000) embodies this view, suggesting that computers and other technological advances will make multimodal communication ever more prevalent.

Another implication of the multimodality of the classroom worlds of American bilingual adolescents is that, as Alvermann and Moore (1996) point out, there are many possible routes to socialization, communication, and learning. For example, adolescent and adult bilingual learners have multiple options for the modality through which they communicate in the classroom. Incipient bilinguals still actively engaged in the protracted process of school-based academic language learning might prefer to work through texts than through spoken interaction, because the texts are reviewable while teacher and peer talk is not. Furthermore, the social organization of many secondary classrooms provides more opportunities for students to engage in extended interactions with their instructors through texts than through classroom talk. With up to 30 students in a classroom, for example, the overall opportunities of the case study students to get the floor to speak were fairly limited. In addition, studies of classroom activities and language use in US secondary classrooms (Alvermann & Moore, 1996; Applebee, 1981; Nystrand, 1997) have shown that teachers tend to hold the floor in classroom discussions and allot students opportunities only for short responses to questions. Written exchanges between case study students and their teachers (e.g. student essays and teacher feedback) thus provided students with opportunities for interaction and socialization that were as significant as those provided by face-to-face classroom interactions. In addition, the presence of multiple communicative modalities creates the possibility for simultaneous and even conflicting forms of socialization to be taking place simultaneously through different modes of communication. For example, as related above, while a "colorblind" representation of case study students predominated in face-to-face classroom discussions, an Ellis Island representation of immigrants predominated in students' written exchanges with their teachers.

Language socialization and immigrant adolescent socialization perspectives clearly intersect in the study of communicative modalities associated with ability grouping. It has long been noted that different language practices are associated with differentiation of learning in US high school "tracks" (e.g. vocational or honors tracks) (Harklau, 1994; Medina, 1988; Mehan *et al.*, 1994; Oakes *et al.*, 1992). As Gutierrez (1995) and Goldenberg and Patthey-Chavez (1995) point out, students in higher tracks are socialized into the integration and manipulation of multiple communicative modalities and ways of interacting with academic content in ways that anticipate college-level communicative practices. Socialization into these practices thus simultaneously instantiates college-bound status in these students. In case study students' high track classes, such as Hanh's Advanced Placement calculus class, literate and oral modes of presentation were coordinated, and literate modes of presentation such as texts were utilized to concentrate and extend the amount of academic context conveyed to students outside of the classroom. Students were therefore socialized into considerable autonomous interaction with texts outside of the bounds of the classroom. Hanh reported that her calculus teacher expected students to read the text and do problem sets outside of classroom time. Hanh's class sessions were spent in teacher lectures and demonstrations that paralleled and coordinated with, but did not replace, students' out-of-class interactions with the text. Talking about her homework assignments from her text, Hanh noted, "If you want to do good in math, then you do it."

In lower track classes, on the other hand, students are socialized into different manipulations and combinations of communicative modalities that mark them as remedial or non-college bound. For example, in case study students' low track classes, most communication about subject matter took place within classroom time under direct teacher supervision. Oral and written modes of presentation were often used redundantly to present the same information. In Aeyfer's math class, for example, the students were allotted ten minutes of class time to work individually on a review sheet before the teacher reviewed the same material orally with the class. Classes such as Penny's low track English classes sometimes combined aural and textual modes through reading a text aloud. Penny's teacher paused at the end of each paragraph to provide interpretation and commentary that Penny described as consisting of "what happened, you know, which part and what happened. And if we have any questions, like which part we don't understand, we can ask her." The redundancy of these activities and their boundedness in the classroom put significant limitations on the amount of academic content covered. On one occasion, for example, Hanh noted that it had taken her English class two days to cover a two page reading. Penny's senior English class spent nearly two months of class time on their final research papers as they looked up sources, read them in class, drafted text in class, and conferenced with the teacher about their drafts. The configuration of these students' low track high school communicative practices mirror findings in a large scale study of low track middle and secondary school English classrooms (Nystrand *et al.*, 1997: 50).

In all then, processes of language socialization and US bilingual adolescent identity formation take place in classroom settings marked by a complex orchestration of oral/aural, textual, and visual communicative resources. The multimodal nature of communication provides bilingual students with a wider array of classroom communicative options (such as speaking vs. writing) than are available to younger children. At the same time, it makes it possible for multiple and perhaps even conflicting forms of socialization to take place simultaneously through different modalities. Finally, configurations of communicative practices in US high school classrooms are profoundly interconnected with processes of differential language socialization and adolescent immigrant identity socialization. Students in different tracks learn to deploy and manipulate communicative resources in different ways, and in the process come to be seen and see themselves as possessing differential academic and social futures.

Implications

The notion of representational practices developed here has implications for the socialization of bilingual adolescents into schooling paths and ultimate educational and occupational futures. The representations described have origins and effects that were simultaneously both positive and negative. In some ways, for example, the image of case study students as striving immigrants clearly seemed advantageous in that they were viewed more favorably than their English monolingual peers. At the same time, however, this representation required students and teachers to constantly reinvoke and reinforce students' status as linguistic and cultural others. Likewise, while the colorblind perspective provided case study students with a social space where they were undifferentiated from American-born peers, at the same time it also failed to provide them with any means to explore the xenophobia and discrimination they had encountered. Some would argue that any representations or collective images of students are ignorant or misguided, and argue for their elimination. However, from the perspective advanced here, representations or images of immigrant identity are only partially the creation of individuals. Rather, representations are to some extent an inevitable artifact of human meaning-making processes, and are generated in the context of institutional and societal discourses (Hall, 1997). Attempts at their total elimination may simply result in different, but equally reified, forms of categorization (Hoffman, 1996; McCarthy, 1993).

At the same time, however, individuals have agency and the ability to work against institutional and societal discourses, and to question the deleterious effects of representations. For example, while the representation of immigrants as persevering and noble is one that societal discourses make easily available to us, we nevertheless can work against that representation and question what Wong (1992) has termed the "pathologizing" of immigrant experience. Educators and students can, for example, explore the potential creativity and liberation as well as the anomie that come with multiple linguistic and cultural affiliations (Spack, 1997b). Likewise, we can work against societal and institutional discourses that make an idealized representation of the monolingual native speaker (see, for example, Pennycook, 1994: 176). In a world where multilingualism tends to be the norm and where dialects and indigenized versions of English are proliferating, the implicit measurement of all language performance against that prescriptivist ideal is increasingly untenable. Like the British secondary school described by Rampton (1995), the experiences of multilingual students at this US urban high school points out just how problematic the notion of "native speaker" can be in terms of student identity formation and instructional paradigms. Moreover, as a result of globalization and increasing ease of world-wide computer and satellite communication, the New London Group (Cope & Kalantzis, 2000) contends that language learners do not need to learn a single "correct" language as much as they need to learn how to negotiate the multiple and varying visual, iconic, linguistic, and textual environments they are likely to encounter. In these environments, immigrant students' multilingualism is clearly a resource, and not a problem.

The multimodal nature of communicative practices among bilingual adolescents and adults has yet to be fully explored, and may have significant implications for how we investigate socialization processes in the classroom. The experiences of our case study students suggest some possible lines of investigation. The notion that language socialization takes place as much through textual and visual modalities as it does through face-to-face interaction implies a need to give balanced and integrated research attention to the various semiotic resources through which socialization processes occur, and to render holistically the real-time orchestration of face-to-face, visual, and textual modalities in classroom communication (Zuengler *et al.*, 1998). Further work might also explore how multiple and simultaneous representations are constructed in and aligned with various communicative practices such as whole classroom interaction, student writing, and texts, and furthermore how representations forwarded in one mode may reinforce, mitigate, conflict with, or subvert representations prevalent in another mode. In addition, because school-based written interactions by their very nature can take place remote from the classroom itself, naturalistic work on language socialization processes in adolescents and adults might adopt methodologies utilized in much of the recent work on second language writing (see, for example, Leki, 1995, 1999; Leki & Carson, 1994;

Prior, 1995; Spack, 1997a). This work has relied on a range of investigative forms such as interviews and written documents to track literate communicative activity occurring both in and outside of the classroom, supplementing the observation and recording of the modes of face-to-face classroom communication that have thus far predominated in language socialization studies.

Notes

1. See Harklau (2001) for a detailed discussion of the study's methodology.

Chapter 6

Engaging in an Authentic Science Project: Appropriating, Resisting, and Denying "Scientific" Identities

KIMMARIE COLE AND JANE ZUENGLER

The study of identities and their formation continues to raise important questions for researchers and educators. In many cases, learners experience the same instructional methods and do the same homework, yet their educational outcomes can vary greatly. Their conduct in class, their handwriting on the page, the clothes they wear leave us wondering "who is this?" The increased interest in the notion of identity has provided us with new language and analytic tools to further our investigation. We contend that it is this identity work, the negotiation of and struggle for different selves (Weedon, 1987), that serves as the primary explanation for what went on in a classroom science project that is the focus of this chapter. Through understanding identity and its positioning, we come to see why a curricular project, designed to engage students in the scientific process and offer them a positive experience from curricular and science reform standards, actually worked to alienate most students from the process and create a divisive atmosphere in the classroom.

The primary framework within which we examine identity is that of language socialization. This perspective embeds language and its use in the midst of social activities, and offers important insights into the links between local moments of interaction and the broader "cultural" events in which this language use is situated. A language socialization perspective emphasizes the relationships formed in interaction by new members of any community. It provides a way to consider how *talk* works both as a method and as a means to communicate and transmit the activities, values, and beliefs of a group. As Ochs writes:

A basic underlying tenet of language socialization is that language must be studied not only as a symbolic system that encodes local social and cultural structures, but also as a tool for establishing (i.e. maintaining, creating) social and psychological realities. Both the symbolic and tool-like properties are exploited in the process of language socialization. (Ochs, 1988: 210)

These properties of language socialization have most often been used in the study of small children with their primary care-givers (Schieffelin & Ochs, 1986b), where the traits and values of a given cultural group are described through the social practices engaged in by the participants. A secondary activity is to then compare one group with another, for example, showing the differences in clarification sequences between Samoan and white middle class caregivers (Ochs, 1988). The "identity" often presumed in this work is that of a "native speaker" in a singular home or primary culture.

The insights made available by adopting a language socialization framework extend beyond this initial, domestic setting to "secondary" socialization settings as well since these symbolic and tool-like features of language are also used in creating and maintaining social structures. Willett (1995), for example, showed how second language learners are socialized into primary schools, while Baquedano-Lopez (1999) provided a language socialization account of young children in a church school setting. In these studies, too, there was an emphasis on a primary identity being socialized, that of elementary school student or member of a collective organization. This work allows us to see how language forms correspond with the values, beliefs, and practices of a particular group and how novices can come to adopt them in interaction.

This central premise of language socialization – that it is through language that social structures and roles are made visible and available – is present for older students as well, although work in this area has, to this point, been more limited. Poole (1992) demonstrated how previous socialization to classroom participation structures affected students in adult ESL classes. More recent research (Duff, 1996; Duff & Early, 1999) has expanded the focus by examining mainstream secondary school classes as important sites for language socialization. Our chapter joins this direction in paying special attention to the ways in which classroom identities are socialized, with important consequences for student learning.

Schools are significant sites of "secondary" socialization. Students join to varying degrees, transform, and/or resist socialization into any given classroom or school community as they proceed through the institution. In these settings, identity becomes an important area of discussion, since identities are social constructions. Taking a language socialization perspective "allows us to examine the building of multiple yet perfectly compatible identities – identities that are subtle and perhaps have no label, blended identities, even blurred identities" (Ochs, 1993: 298). This perspective also allows us to see when these identities are in conflict. Members in communities learn the "ways of being" that are accepted and acceptable. In schools, the individual classroom can be considered to be a community (see Duff, 1996; Duff & Early, 1999) with specific practices (Toohey, 2000).

In their participation in classroom communities, students display particular identities and subsequently experience the outcomes of their actions. Members can be ratified on some occasions and sanctioned on others. By the time they are adolescents, individuals are no longer novices to schooling – most have some "student identity" they can use, though they are required to renegotiate the ways that identity can be enacted in the different classes they enter. Since they participate in multiple communities, adolescents are also people with other identities in play, some of which reinforce their school and classroom identities, while others are points of conflict. Indeed, central to our analysis is the complex interplay that occurs where these different identities meet one another in the science classroom.

Language Socialization in a Multilingual, Multi-ethnic, Urban High School

We are engaged in a five-year longitudinal study of language socialization in one multilingual, multi-ethnic, urban high school in "Center City." Our research team was in the school twice weekly from the fall of 1996 through the spring of 2000. We videotaped and took field notes in science and social studies classes, conducted interviews with the teachers, and had periodic focus groups with the students. After observing widely in all the school's programs and divisions, we began to follow a group of 9th graders in the fall of 1997. Although the groups did not remain completely intact, owing to shifts in programs, drop outs, and scheduling changes, we were able to follow many of those same students through the completion of their junior year advanced classes.

The setting

"Jefferson" High School is located in a large metropolitan area we have named Center City. It is a city that in the past few decades has experienced many of the same demographic and cultural changes as other urban areas in the United States. In 1977, for example, 53% of the students in the city's public schools were white, but as of 1997, white students made up only about 20% of the city's public school student body (Rummler, 1997). Currently, 61% of the students in Center City's public schools are African-American, 12% Hispanic-American, and 5% Asian-American. There has also been an increase in recent years in the number of students in Center City who qualify for the Federal free lunch program, with 81% of the children in primary school now eligible for the program compared with 69% of primary school students in 1993–94 (Borsuk, 1998).

The school is on the south side of Center City in an area that has undergone a profound demographic shift in recent years. The south side was once a stronghold of the city's Eastern European community, but today it is populated largely by Hispanic, Lao, and Hmong residents. More than 50% of Center City's Hispanic population live in the neighborhoods around Jefferson High, and this has led to a change in the composition of the student body at the school (Guskin, 1992). Current enrollment figures for Jefferson High School indicate that 60% of the students are Hispanic, 20% are African-American, 10% are white, 8% are Asian, and 2% are Native American. These numbers differ from the overall statistics for the district, but common to both Jefferson High school and the district-wide enrollment is the relatively high number of "minorities" and the high degree of poverty. More than 75% of the students at the school qualify for the Federal free and reduced-price lunch program. Moreover, between 76% and 99% of the students live in single-parent families (School Context Form, December 5, 1996). Some lawmakers, including the state's governor, have threatened a state takeover of the Center City School District if test scores and attendance do not improve. They cite statistics showing that third graders in Center City are reading at levels far below the average for the state, that attendance is at 85%, and that the dropout rate is 14% (Jones & Williams, 1998). Jefferson High has a "no show rate" of approximately 15%, an attendance rate in the upper 70% range, and a drop-out rate of 30%. The enrollment situation at the school this year has led to concerns among school administrators that the budget will be cut unless the attendance reports show a higher rate of enrollment.

The economic and political environment outside the classroom has an impact on the content and organization of the curriculum at Jefferson High School. In a community with high unemployment and few dual-parent households, it is not surprising that the curriculum emphasizes work readiness in most of the school-within-a-school "families." The family concept is the cornerstone of Jefferson High's School to Work (STW) program. The organization of the academic programs at Jefferson High School is based on the five STW families: Allied Health, Arts, Cyber Academy, Engineering, and Urban Planning.

The Cyber Academy and its students

The Cyber Academy students were heavily recruited to this program to begin school in the fall of 1997. The Cyber Academy itself was a new program in the school and was the pet project of the principal, who felt that the school needed to address district concerns about the low performance of students in the school. By starting a rigorous, college-prep program, he hoped to raise the positive profile of the school. The principal took an active role in finding students and encouraging their participation in the program, promising them support and resources. According to information circulated to the teachers and other staff, the Cyber Academy curriculum "employs the latest technology to obtain instant information, connects with the world's resources and produces quality demonstrations of acquired knowledge (the school's *Weekly Bulletin*, February 2–6, 1998). Each family had a vocational component linked to its academic offerings. For the Cyber Academy, regarded by most students and teachers as the "elite" family for college-bound students, "vocational" courses were in computer technology.

The incoming Cyber Academy students were among the strongest in their middle schools and were required to enter the program with a minimum grade point average (GPA) of 3.5 (on a 4-point scale). Of the 30 students in the Cyber Academy, 21 were young women and 9 were young men. Like the demographics of the school, this group represented considerable diversity, both linguistic and ethnic. Their numbers, though, contrasted sharply with those of the broader school population and yet they are not precisely like those of the district as a whole either. Sixty-seven percent of them were African-American, 20% were Latino, 10% were Asian, and the rest were white. Many were bilingual. While most of the Asian and Hispanic students lived near the school and recognized it as a part of their local neighborhood and community, most of the other students lived in different parts of the city and were bussed into the neighborhood to participate in the Cyber Academy. These students had attended a range of middle schools, from foreign language magnet schools to programs for the gifted and talented. A number of them also attended "regular" middle schools within the school district.

While the students in this group were quite strong academically, the positioning of the school as a troubled, urban school within a troubled district was well known to all. They talked about their "ghetto" school and were aware that it was one of the two "dumping ground" schools in the district. The Cyber Academy was instituted to serve as a magnet throughout the city and draw good students, in much the way Devine (1996) talks about magnet schools in New York City. The students in this program were aware of their privileged status within Jefferson High School, although some resisted the "college bound" and professional aspirations that were assumed for them. These "Cyber kids" considered their academic competition to be the students in other magnet programs throughout the city, something that we did not realize initially, but which came to be important to our understanding of the Asthma Project.

The Cyber students' teacher and her biology classroom

As mentioned earlier, the Jefferson High principal took an active part in building the Cyber Academy. He asked highly respected, experienced teachers to work with the Cyber students. Mrs Belmontes was one such teacher. A veteran teacher at Jefferson High School, Mrs Belmontes had been teaching science for more than 20 years. She regularly attended teacher in-service programs and meetings, looking for new techniques and innovative ways of working with students. Her classroom walls were covered with student projects and models, and she actively invited others into her classroom to show what her students were working on. A native speaker of Colombian Spanish, Mrs Belmontes served as the Chair of the school's bilingual program and was originally a member of the Bilingual Engineering family. At the request of the principal, she undertook science with the Cyber Academy students as well when that program opened in the fall of 1997. The academic orientation of the program and her participation in it underlined her commitment to high level instruction and a willingness to accept challenges in her personal development. Another signal of her professionalism was Mrs Belmontes' enthusiastic agreement to allow our research team into her Freshman Biology Class with the Cyber Academy students. Their accelerated curriculum placed them in biology in their first year, rather than in the introductory integrated science class that other freshmen in the school take.

One focus of Mrs Belmontes' continued development as a teacher was her search for "real science" experiences for her students. For several years, the science program at Jefferson High had maintained an informal collaboration with a neighborhood health clinic. Students at Jefferson worked with elementary school students on health issues with the support of the clinic. When the clinic expressed an interest in involving the students as investigators for this "Asthma Project," Mrs Belmontes accepted it as a way for her students to get involved in a meaningful project that linked the science concepts presented in her classroom with a problem that was of increasing importance in their urban community. The plan was for the students to construct a survey that would be used in data gathering in their high school and at least one other high school in the city. When the survey results were in, the students would tabulate them, working with spreadsheets and doing some statistical analyses with the assistance of their math teacher. Ultimately, they would present the results to the clinic staff and work with them to disseminate the results to the community.

Identity work in the Asthma Project

In telling the story of the Asthma Project, we will be foregrounding the identities that were negotiated in the discourse we observed in the class. As we watched and listened, there emerged four identities which, at varying times, students shared, actively constructed, or resisted:

(1) the "good student" versus "not good enough student" identity;
(2) the "scientist-researcher" identity;
(3) the ghetto or poor performance "Jefferson High School" identity; and
(4) the "child laborer" identity.

Classroom participants drew on these identities at different points over the course of the project. Some of them appeared almost immediately and became threads that wove through the work done by the students and teacher; others were not made visible until later stages in the process.

The good student

One of the earliest identities to emerge as salient for members of this classroom community was the "good student" versus the "not good enough student." As part of the initial training for the work the whole class would do, a team of students would leave the classroom to seek special training in survey design at a workshop held outside the school. In that workshop, they would join other students from another school. These students were to return to the classroom and use their new skills to train their classmates so that the survey they constructed was a sound one that would yield useful results. As students heard their first introduction to the project, Mrs Belmontes highlighted the fact that only some would be chosen to receive special training. And who would get chosen? Mrs Belmontes, who had the power to choose, announced that these would be only the "super good" students, that is, those who had already demonstrated to her the values and behaviors it took to be "good" in her class, and who showed a continuing desire to maintain that identity [a key to the transcription symbols can be found in the Appendix]:

Mrs B:	Okay. All right now I'm going to tell you this. I'm going to select five or six of you okay. I already spoke to some of your teachers. On the nineteenth (.) five or six of you will be selected by me to go to the education center. Okay and this (.) know you're going to be put with some real top notch kids from Tech. Wh- wh- which are taking advanced pla- placement science class. Okay. they're working on the same thing we are. We want to find information about asthma in the south side. I have good news for you. some other guy has found out about our research and our and he wants to uh include some information with some school in the north side. Because um they want to know if it's uh related to ethnic group or other things. But the don't let that kind of blemish your brain. Okay what uh what I what we want to do is find out as much as we have about we can about asthma. We are going to design a survey that tells us certain things. And we are going to be working with those five people. Now those five people that I select are going to get extra points. You know why. So those that are are super good and want to get an "A" they're going to work well.
?FS:	I'm going to.
Mrs B:	Because those people are going to have to come and train the rest of the class. So I have to pick like good ones. Okay.
Ariel:	Me.
Mrs B:	((throws kisses))
?Students:	((Laughter))
Mrs B:	Modesty is in your vocabulary right.

2SC32Belmontes (from February 11, 1998)

As we see, those who get chosen as "super good" students not only receive special training outside, but are rewarded locally in their classroom with extra points. In this light, it is not surprising to see some students bid for ratification of their good student identity. The teacher's laughing response acknowledges this bid. Since the teacher indexes the good student identity with previous class activity, students can almost instantly place themselves and their past results. Indeed, one student who has consistently been in the lower performing group in terms of grades, classroom participation, and behavior lobbies the teacher after class, making the case that it shouldn't just be the students with 'As' who get to participate.

Within the week, the five "super good" students are chosen, and the remainder learn through the selection process that they are the "not so good." Of those who "stay behind" while the others go for training, Mrs Belmontes further constructs the tracking of the students into "good" and "not so good." Regularly in the days between the introduction to and the onset of the project, the teacher refers to those who will go and the work that will be done in class by those who "stay behind." Though she clearly states that all the work makes an important contribution to the final outcomes of their survey process, the amount of class time and attention that the departing group receives indicates that those students and their expected subsequent contributions are special. Their selection for training opportunity awarded the five chosen students access to external professional and scientific communities as well, and provided them with enhanced status within their classroom. However, contrary to what was originally planned, the five did not end up training the others in their class. Instead, they were given special tasks – preparing a web page, planning and presenting the project at a district-wide "Technofest" – which often took them out of the classroom into the computer lab, and positioned them, regularly, as separate and special in Mrs Belmontes' class. The good student identity was not limited to the original chosen group, however. With each part of the Asthma Project, there were opportunities for most students to enact a good student self. This and other identities were neither static nor closed.

The scientist-researcher

Another identity at play during the Asthma Project was that of scientist or scientist-as-researcher. Throughout the year, the students had been working with the ideas of biology and what biologists do. They had been trained and drilled in the scientific method and had practiced labs and activities that required its application. The scientists they had read about and watched in videos inhabited this scientific identity in meaningful and action-oriented ways. Until the start of the Asthma Project, whenever the students and teacher discussed their taking on this identity, it was at most a hypothetical situation. "Pretend you are scientists. What would you do?" During the Asthma Project, however, this identity was constructed and functioned in several different ways. Regularly when the teacher was setting up an activity – whether it was Mrs Belmontes or the master science teacher who occasionally stepped in – she reminded the students that they were engaged in scientific research. An example of this occurred when Mrs Belmontes asked the students to take specific survey questions and turn them into hypotheses:

Mrs B: But *then*, what we're going to do, I, I don't think we should have too many changes after that, but then what we're going to *do* is, we're going to go back. And that's one of the things that we're going to, we're going to *hypothesize*. You're going to sit there and predict. Well who do you think, before we do the survey, what do you think, uh, the outcome is going to be. Do you think, uh, these kind of people get more asthma, what are your projections as far as males and females, we're going to take each of the questions and we're going to predict what do you think the results of the survey are going to be. Because in effect that's what scientists do they make predictions what they

think the answer might be and then you *actually* do uhm, the
accounting of this, and see if your prediction was right or wrong.
                                    2SC41Belmontes (April 20, 1998)

Another reminder to the students that they were scientific researchers came
when the master science teacher, who took over the teaching of some of the activities, prepared the students for giving out the survey:

Mrs Graham: This is so *rich* a survey, that people not just across this town,
                  but across this nation are interested in your data. Because it's so
                  rich in teaching statistics and understanding statistics, and
                  applying it to something really meaningful for our community.
                  So it's an important survey and urge your friends who, if when
                  they take it on Wednesday, to *answer* honestly, because this *is*
                  real research, not just what's your favorite soda research.
                                    2SC41Belmontes (from May 18, 1998)

As we see, the teachers, in providing accounts for the activities, were reminding
the students that they were engaged in doing scientific research. As such, they were
offering the identity of the scientist-researcher. However, as these examples show,
there were other messages often folded into the discourse that complicated the
notion of what it meant to the students to do scientific research. Though they might
be reminded that they were doing science, the students frequently heard about
scientists in the third person, rather than hearing "you and I" or "we" as scientists.
For example, in the transcript, Mrs Belmontes says of scientists: "*they* make predictions what *they* think the answer might be." She reserves the "you" of the students to
refer to their "accounting" of what was predicted. This pronoun use corresponds
with Wortham (1994), who found that in their use of indexicals, teachers do
positioning work and show how they see themselves and their interlocutors, not
only in their roles as teachers and students, but also as people in the world. As we
observed on multiple occasions, the use of "they" for scientists and "you" or "we"
for the class served to signal a divide between them, a message that there may be not
be easy access to being a real scientist doing real research.

Through the project students were also learning that research involves other
people. Some of them, including the Department of Natural Resources (DNR)
specialists, the statistics teacher from the other school, and the staff at the clinic,
were unseen presences who evaluated their work, made them revise, set deadlines,
and eagerly waited to get their research results. This was a message to the students
that, though they were doing scientific research, it was often dependent on and
deferential to those others "out there" beyond their classroom. As we will see,
students' recognition of this fact led to their reframing and resisting this identity.

The scientist-researcher identity functioned in the classroom in one more way
that was not positive for the students. As the project continued over several months,
students began to display boredom and frustration from the tedium of activities
involving sorting and tallying of results from the surveys. In an effort to appease
them, Mrs Belmontes would invoke science, and the nature of scientific research, as

a means of defending the activities (and their tedium). As a defensive ploy, Mrs Belmontes was heard to say, "Research is not always exciting. There's also the groundwork. This is part of the groundwork." On another day, recognizing that she knows the project has dragged on, she says, "Real science doesn't happen in little packets"; a little later she says, "Real science takes a long time."

The attitude of class members about inhabiting the scientist identity is best exemplified by the following. One day, Mrs Belmontes cheerfully informed the students that the DNR would hire some of them over the summer as "apprentices" to continue the research begun in class. Although many of the students worked during the summer and were looking for jobs, this proposition met with no uptake.

The ghetto school

Earlier, while describing the sociocultural contexts within which this class was embedded, we mentioned that there was a widely held belief that Jefferson High School was a poor, ghetto school. This understanding shaped the third student identity we see in the discourse during the Asthma Project. Unlike the good versus bad student sorting that went on in the biology class, taking on the "ghetto" self was a way in which students and teacher alike could show solidarity with one another. When the asthma survey was reported in the city newspaper, only the other school involved in the project was mentioned, even though it was Jefferson High that was spearheading the survey. In almost every instance when Jefferson High School *was* mentioned in the city newspaper, the high school and its environs were highlighted as poor-performing, crime infested, dangerous, and poor. While the Cyber Academy students did not all live in the neighborhood, their affiliation with the school was one that was often denigrated by others. In the introduction to the project that was provided earlier, it was mentioned that the students from the other high school in the project, "Tech," were referred to as top-notch and involved in AP courses – that is, were constructed as higher status.

In some ways the checks imposed by others on the "scientists" at Jefferson were a way that the external context positioned the students and Mrs Belmontes within this ghetto identity. This positioning had links to the fourth identity that was foregrounded in the discourse of the students and teacher, the child laborer.

The child laborer

While five students were given the opportunity to receive special training and engage in special, stimulating tasks part of the time, for most if not all of the biology students, the Asthma Project activities largely came to be mechanically-oriented – sorting and tallying of responses to survey questions. These were teacher-directed and tended to emphasize timeliness and correct form over the substance of the survey. Students often displayed no clear engagement in what they were directed to complete:

Mrs B: Even if you have to, some of you have your sheets, uhm, and I don't mind if you pair up by twos? You know if you pair up by twos? A-but you each have to, just for purposes of sharing the questionnaire. But you have to each do your own questions. So. You do the ones that have to do with o:ne? Pay attention and write it down, 'cause you're going to forget. You're number one, part A. And you (xxx), go get me paper from down there, (xxx) the TV, and give everybody a sheet. OK. One. Part A, one. And it's parts two, two, three, four, part B, one. Part B, write it down. Part B one. Part B two. Part B three. Part B four. Part B: six. Oh five.

?FS:	[((singing, unintelligible))
Vanessa:	[Where is five?
Pauline:	(xxx) five. (There is no five).
Vanessa:	(That's what I said).
Mrs B:	And then C, you're doing C one.
	[C one and its parts=
Vanessa:	[What?
Mrs B:	=so you will do like o:ne, OK? So you predict on exercise what they're going to say under yes and no. And and the part they said yes, how many. OK? [And if they say how-
Melissa:	[Hmm
Mrs B:	[which how many times (xxx). OK.
Melissa:	[Miss Belmontes, (only) four parts (xxx)=
Mrs B:	=You-you're-that's OK.=
Melissa:	=It's only four parts in here (xxx).
Mrs Be:	No honey=
Melissa:	You take the part (xxx)
Mrs B:	No [Part page three:, you're doing this question.
?FS:	[(xxxxxxxxxxx what you're doing xxxxxxxxxxxx) Four.
Mrs B:	You just do that one.

(2SC46Belmontes, from May 13, 1998)

Though the survey questions had originally been written by the students, they were subjected to multiple and major revisions by others (teachers, DNR officials, clinicians) who were evaluating them, setting deadlines, in short, taking ownership of their work. As students undertook what were largely tallying and tabulating tasks, subject to deadlines, expectations, and evaluations of others, they began displaying a resistance to the work they were laboring to complete. Thus emerged students' reframing of the identity to one they called "child laborer." In this excerpt, for example, when Mrs Belmontes mentioned that there was a possibility of displaying the findings of their study on the local clinic's web page, rather than being excited about the "publication and dissemination possibilities" that most scientists strive for, the students emphasize that others will use their work and should pay for the privilege.

Mrs B:	Our fellow colleagues, they want to present (.) as a matter of fact, (.) the clinic said they want to use the (.) web page to connect to

	the clinic. but then [there are also- there are a couple more things that need to be (.) in it. ok?
Shavonne:	[just use our stuff.
Melissa:	[tell them they've got to pay us for it.
Shavonne:	(xxx)(the sa:me). Just use our stuff.
?Fs:	Let's get a patent.:
?Fs:	labor.
Miguel:	labor,
Ss:	((laughing))
?Fs:	twenty five
	[(xxx)
?Fs:	[child labor.
Mrs B:	[((lau[ghing))
Herlinda:	[twenty five?
?Fs:	[a minute. Ss
	((laughing))
?Fs:	She said twenty five dollars a minute.
Mrs B:	Anyway, u:h
Shavonne:	You've got to pay to use stuff on the internet, they should pay us for using our stuff.
?Fs:	Yeah, (.) they should.

2SC45Belmontes (from May 11, 1998)

In this and in later classes, students actively reframed the scientist-researcher identity toward one that more accurately reflected their experience on the project. And their choice for reframing it shows their interpretation of the research process as an enterprise, with them filling the bottom rung – illegitimately so, according to the student who proclaims it "child labor." As productive workers, they sought compensation from those who wanted to benefit from them and their ideas, and requested payment or protection through getting a patent.

Synthesis

While there were undoubtedly many identities that were rarely foregrounded over the course of this unit, we have posited that there were four widely discussed identities that were salient for the students who participated in the Asthma Project. But what are the implications of recognizing these multiple identities at play in the classroom? Centrally, language socialization is a process by which people become members of communities. Within communities, different members have access to and use different identities. It is through language that people are made aware of the possible identities within any given community, and ultimately it is also through language that they are socialized to accept or resist those identities.

Our study of the Asthma Project reveals that multiple identities are present, constructed, or resisted in the classroom, and that these identities can be foregrounded or backgrounded in the moment-to-moment interactions of any class period. For example, when the students worked with their own written survey questions and formed their own hypotheses predicting the survey outcomes, their scientist identity was foregrounded. When, in her next breath, Mrs Belmontes required them to work on a particular combination of questions that would be of interest to the clinic, she positioned them as "child laborers" and reminded them that to be "good students" they needed to comply with this work within the strict deadline she imposed. Wortham's (1994) work on participant examples similarly reveals multiple positionings in a single classroom discussion. Wortham shows that classroom teachers can convey beliefs about students' moral selves as well as about their class position in society, all while discussing the content of a piece of literature. The examples of multiple identities in our work and that of Wortham's lead to questions about the interplay of these different identities functioning together.

Though the four identities that were foregrounded in the classroom discourse were distinct from one another, they had some shared or overlapping features. Neatness and timeliness, for example, were as crucial to the work of the "child laborers" as to the work of the "good students." It is possible that the interplay of features resonated strongly with another identity that was certainly present and available to members of the classroom community – that is, a general "student" identity. However, this is not simply a fifth identity, to be added to the four we have reported on. Instead, it is an identity available for the students, at the time, place, and setting in which they undertook the Asthma Project. As an identity that both predates and shares aspects with the other identities, this "student" identity may be one that the students readily adopt when there is no investment (to use Peirce's 1995 term) or compelling reason to appropriate the others. In other words, it may function as a kind of default identity. However, we are not implying that this general student identity is a simple one. Indeed, it is complex and tied to other identities (such as being "Cyber Academy students") that students have access to.

When discussing the language socialization process, in addition to talking about what identities community members may be engaging with, there is the question of *how* that process occurs. Language socialization presumes an expert/novice model for the transmission and negotiation of information. In Rogoff's (1990) terms, there is the need for guided participation in the process of joining a community. If we consider the identities at play in the Asthma Project as being enacted, tested, and ratified in the social activities of the classroom community, we must look for the ways in which those identities were being modeled for the students.

Like the multiple identities that could be foregrounded in a single context, there were multiple sources of guided participation. While several experts were available to some students on a limited basis (namely, for the five who attended training outside the school), all the students came into regular contact with the classroom teacher, Mrs Belmontes. Their source of expertise for this project was the same person who was responsible for taking attendance and calculating their grades. Her insistence that their work be neat and turned in on time was arguably guidance in the development of both a "scientist" and a "good student" identity. However, the multiple demands placed on them in the course of completing each part of the Asthma Project may have restricted the students' ability or interest in considering, or even seeing, the different identities as viable options.

The way in which this project unfolded also meant that Mrs Belmontes' expertise was called into question and potentially negated at different points in the process. For example, when Mrs Graham, the science resource teacher, was in class, she physically and discursively was positioned as the "knower." Mrs Belmontes became her assistant, though both women had received the same training in tabulating the results of the questionnaires. At another stage in the process of getting the surveys ready, Mrs Belmontes was asked to turn them over to the district office for translation, even though she had already translated the questions once. Thus, her position as Spanish-language expert was institutionally destabilized. After a newsletter article written by Mrs Belmontes was published instead in Mrs Graham's name, Mrs Belmontes read the article to her class and repeatedly referred to the ways that others took credit for her work. Thus, Mrs Belmontes' positioning as expert was undermined on more than one occasion, adding to students' confusion about the nature of her expertise.

Even if the students had been clear about Mrs Belmontes' position in the project, guided participation is a process that, in classrooms, takes place within other institutionally-imposed deadlines and boundaries. In the case of the Asthma Project, these deadlines may have hindered students' apprenticeship into the "scientist" identity. Because of the demands placed on the project by the clinic, the DNR, the Techno-Fest deadlines and the academic school year, participants were always under a "time crunch" for the next part of the project. Instead of being able to focus on participants' developing skills and encouraging their appropriation of the "scientist" identity, Mrs Belmontes and the students were required to "labor" more and more quickly in order to finish. While there might have been ways to build in greater guidance and exploration for individual students or the group as a whole, those options were not obvious to participants at the time. In terms of trying on "possible selves" and in terms of the skills and developing knowledge that were part of the Asthma Project, the constraints on the project and the ways they played out in this classroom context left the engaged "scientist" identity, in effect, on the shelf.

Conclusion

The work that we have reported on both extends and complicates the conception of language socialization in schools and classrooms. One outcome of our study is the recognition that expert guidance in the socialization process may be multiple, conflicting, and contested – in short, more nuanced and potentially problematic than most previous research on language socialization acknowledges. Like other "authentic" science curricula, the Asthma Project grew into an effort involving a number of people and agencies beyond Ms. Belmontes and her class. As a consequence, Mrs Belmontes not only was repositioned as one among many guides, but came to have her expertise threatened and increasingly diminished as the Project unfolded. Bringing, as she did, her frustrations about this situation into the class, she may have conveyed a solidarity with the students; however, at the same time her positioning as the expert guide was increasingly problematic.

This study's findings also inform our understandings of students' involvement in the socialization process. A tenet of language socialization theory is that, rather than simply internalizing experts' norms and values, novices are involved in a reciprocal process, one in which they actively co-construct their socialization (Jacoby & Ochs, 1995; Ochs, 1991; Ochs, 1993). And, as Jacoby and Ochs (1995) clarify, co-construction does not imply agreement; people also co-construct disagreement and resistance. Such a conception portrays novices as having and making socialization choices, as actively participating in the process. Our findings show that at the local level, within the classroom interactions, students actively negotiated multiple identities. However, the socialization choices that novices actively co-construct locally may have ramifications in the broader community beyond the classroom, and may lead to a positioning of the novice that could be fundamentally different from what has been co-constructed locally. An example concerns the lack of positive response to Mrs Belmontes' enthusiastic announce-ment about summer job opportunities as science apprentices. Indeed, the summer apprenticeships may have involved a lot of the tedious, mechanical tasks that students were resisting. However, such apprenticeships might also have provided students with guidance from experts in the actual fields of science rather than the hybrid they received in the classroom. They would have been likely to encounter advanced science opportunities and seen other facets of the "scientist identity" than those they had experienced. Like the schoolboys in Willis' (1981) study whose rejec-tion of schooled identities reproduced the social conditions that proved problem-atic, these students may have rejected experiences that could have changed their perspectives about science. From their local experiences, this resistance was a logical choice; but its outcome could be seen as "laziness," "lack of ability," or an "unwillingness to get involved" – all traits that reinforce the ghetto identity that was so real within this school and for its students.

If the report of our experience seems negative, it certainly came to be that way for almost everyone in the classroom during the course of the Asthma Project. When Mrs Belmontes laid out the idea of the project and first engaged the students in conversation about it, there were many who were interested (or at least appeared to be). Students vied for the opportunity to join the group participating in the training; many vigorously explored ideas about why more people in their community didn't know about asthma. Gradually, the negative talk one often hears in classrooms about assignments became louder and more pointed. There were more challenges to the teacher's authority. While they were engaged in their "child labor" tasks, there was increasing noise among students, and "off task" talk replaced discussions of asthma, its symptoms, causes and cures. Because of the longitudinal nature of our study, we have heard students two years later complain about the Asthma Project and its effects. Notwithstanding, an ironic outcome is that the state legislature, four months after these students left the biology class, awarded the students, teacher, and school a commendation for their fine work.

Appendix: Transcription conventions used in this project

Transcription conventions for this project are modified from Atkinson and Heritage (1984) and correspond to the following guidelines.

[	overlapping talk
=	latched utterances
(1)	timed silence in seconds
(.)	micro pause
(....)	longer pause, not timed
tra:nscribe	stretched sound
tra::nscribe	longer stretched sound
transcribe.	falling final intonation
transcribe,	falling but continuing intonation
transcribe?	rising final intonation
transcribe-	abrupt cutoff
transcribe	emphasis
TRANSCRIBE	louder talk
transcribe	softer talk
.hhh	inbreath
hhh.	outbreath
(xxxx)	unintelligible talk
(transcript)	transcriber's best guess of talk
((waving hands))	transcriber's note about nonverbal activities or classroom activity observed on video

Chapter 7
Interrupted by Silences: The Contemporary Education of Hong-Kong-born Chinese Canadians

GORDON PON, TARA GOLDSTEIN AND SANDRA R. SCHECTER

> To understand what silence says requires many things including transcendence of our Eurocentric context and its assumptions about other cultures and silence ... the Eurocentric view of silence conceives silence as weakness and also uses it for oppressing people. (Gerrard & Javed, 1994: 65)

In this chapter we explore issues of speech and silence in a twelfth grade class in an urban secondary school in which Chinese-Canadian students constitute the majority population. We describe how pedagogical strategies that are intended to promote English speech in the English-medium classroom are interrupted by the silences of the Hong-Kong-born Chinese students enrolled in the class. These interruptions render a site intended for learning a locus of linguistic and racial tension, as the silences of immigrant Chinese students are considered burdensome and are resented by some Canadian-born non-Chinese, and even Chinese, youth. These youth regard the silences of their Hong-Kong-born Chinese classmates as indices of lack of agency and/or intellectual deficit, and ultimately as a threat to their own ability to secure a good quality public school education. Using students' perspectives as a heuristic, we elucidate the linguistic double binds faced by many Chinese students in North American mainstream schools, and go on to suggest how the silences of Chinese students might productively be understood differently.

Popular Conceptions of Speech and Silence

The quote that introduces this chapter alludes to the popular constructions of speech and silence in Western societies. Indeed, especially in institutional settings such as schools, speech is generally associated with positive attributes, such as assertiveness, agency, and intelligence. In contrast, silence is associated with passivity, powerlessness, and lack of presence (Cheung, 1993; Hogue, 1996; Wong, 1993).

King-Kok Cheung (1993) noted that North American attitudes toward Asian (North) American silence are implicated in nineteenth century discourses on civilization such as Orientalism, a constellation of beliefs that constructed the East as the antithesis of the West. In his seminal book, *Orientalism*, Edward Said (1979) described how Western intellectuals imagined the geography and history of the "Orient" as the cultural polarity of the "Occident." According to Said, the Orient was reified as a mythical and exotic geopolitical entity, a place where events and practices of a perverse, cruel, and ignorant nature were thought to occur.

Orientalist discourses, especially as they related to dimensions of speech and silence, have often served to ensnare Asians living in the diaspora in a double bind. These discourses have associated Asian silence with suspicious activity on the one hand and deferential behavior on the other. Thus, the quiet Asian has been viewed as devious, shrewd, and inscrutable – at times even feared, as evidenced in nineteenth century discourses on the "Yellow Peril" (see Pon, 1996). Alternatively, the quiet Asian has been regarded as timid, docile, submissive, and obedient, to many, a "model minority" (Lee, 1996).[1] Moreover, the model minority construct has been deployed to silence other racial minority groups who challenged systemic and structural forms of racism and class oppression in Western liberal democracies (Lee, 1996; Lowe, 1996; Ong, 1999; Pon, 2000). Thus, Asian silence and its associated acquiescent behaviors have been held up as elements of a code deserving of emulation by other putatively less deserving minority groups.

McKay and Wong (1996) argued that in America's multiethnic and multilingual schools, racialized dynamics influenced by Orientalist and colonialist discourses find daily expression. One such expression is the belief that English-speaking ability is not only predictive of academic success, but also an index of cognitive maturity and overall personal worthiness. Conversely, immigrant status and limited English proficiency are often associated with states of deficiency and backwardness (McKay & Wong, 1996). However, notwithstanding the struggles faced by many Asian North American students, especially those who have recently immigrated, little research has attended to issues of race and racism in relation to the schooling of this group. We offer two reasons to explain this oversight. First, the prevalent belief that as model minorities Asians are superlative students who excel at school operates to position Asian North Americans outside of, and marginal to, debates about educational equity and race. Second, historically North American narratives of racialized divisions have been cast within the paradigm of the black/white encounter (Lee, 1996; Omi & Takagi, 1996), a hegemonic model which contributes to the erasure of Asians from discourses about the role of race in social reproduction.

Recently, some researchers and educators have used the term "reluctant talker" to describe some Chinese North American and Australian students (see, for example, Cummins *et al.*, 1998). Although intended as a descriptive tool through which to address an important issue related to educational access, this term reinforces the prevalent stereotypical belief that Chinese students are quiet, docile, and reticent. It also reinforces Eurocentric constructions of speech and silence in that (English) speech is equated with participation in class activities and engagement in the academic curriculum, while silence is equated with an absence of participation and a lack of motivation with regard to school activities.

The Empirical Study of Speech and Silence

Our study of issues of speech and silence in a Grade 12 classroom is part of a larger, four-year (1998–2001) ethnographic project that examined the language uses of linguistic minority students attending a large high school in the Greater Toronto area. The main goal of the larger project was to explore effective strategies in preparing immigrant students to negotiate instruction in an unfamiliar language. The study that is the object of this chapter was guided by the following research questions, refined over the course of ethnographic observation:

(1) How are the roles and functions of speech and silence understood by different individuals and/or groups who are stakeholders in the class?
(2) How might alternative understandings of silence be helpful to educators and students in negotiating the linguistic, racial, and pedagogic tensions in multilingual, multiethnic, and multiracial classrooms?

Before continuing, we would comment that, in considering our research methodology and its relation to possible interpretations of findings, we were overwhelmed by the absence of attention paid in the scholarly literature to the role and significance of silence and silences. This lacuna is all the more striking given the methodology indicated by our research agenda – close ethnographic observation inevitably requires a relatively large commitment to transcription. While most socio- and ethno-linguists would probably concede that transcription is a painstaking task, and that decisions about what to transcribe are never theory-neutral (see, for example, Kerswill & Wright, 1990; Nolan & Kerswill, 1990), scholarly analyses of conversational data do not reveal an attentiveness to the representation of silences that are complementary to that shown to spoken discourse. Specifically, researchers in language socialization often find it useful to provide in their transcriptions information about the prosodic (intonational) and morphophonemic qualities of the spoken discourse that they observe. Where judged relevant to interpretations, they also provide information about primary (and sometimes secondary) stress patterns and indicate emphatic stress by marking vowel elongations and volume increases. They document the abrupt cutting off of sounds, and mark points in running discourse at which an utterance in progress is joined by another "interrupting" utterance. However, short of noting the absence of speech in timed sequences (through conventions used to mark a "pause" and/or a "long pause"), similar attention has not been given by researchers to the interrupting function of silence – the very notion, it would seem, an oxymoron, as in most popular representations (but see Tannen & Saville-Troike, 1985).

Cheung (1993) argued that understanding Asian North American silences must involve a fundamental re-shifting of Western interpretations of speech and silence. She also cautioned that verbal and non-verbal assertion should not be viewed in hierarchical and binary terms. In addition, Cheung took issue with a singular mono-lithic concept of silence, proposing instead different modes, or tonalities. She identi-fied five separate, potentially overlapping, modes or tonalities of silences: (1) stoic, (2) protective, (3) attentive, (4) inhibitive, and (5) oppressive. An *attentive silence* reveals acute listening, empathy, and sensitivity to the subtlest signals from a speaker. *Oppressive silence* can be manifested in forms of racism that arise at the confluence of social policy and inter-group hatred. For example, laws that forbade Chinese people living in Canada to give testimony in court (see Chan, 1983) can be seen as instigating an oppressive silence. A *stoic* modality is revealed in the quiet suffering exhibited by Asian immigrants such as the *Issei* in Joy Kogawa's (1981) novel, *Obasan*. Cheung viewed *inhibitive silence* as the mode that has proved most debilitating for North American Asians. We will discuss this silence in detail below, especially as it intersects with the notion of the "reluctant talker." Cheung emphasized that all modes of silences can be enabling or debilitating depending on individuals' situations and circumstances.[2]

Silence and Speech in a Grade Twelve English Class

Northside Secondary School is located in a middle to upper-middle class neigh-borhood in the Greater Toronto area.[3] Chinese students make up the majority (67%) of the student population. In Hong Kong, Northside is regarded as a highly repu-table public school with a strong academic program. Most students who attend Northside anticipate pursuing a university-level education upon graduation; and the school offers most courses at the Advanced level, with a few at the General or Basic levels. Eighty-six percent of the students at Northside are immigrants to Canada, the majority of these from Hong Kong. The five leading primary languages spoken by students at Northside are English (38%), Cantonese (35%), Mandarin (6%), Farsi/Persian (5%), and Korean (4%). Although English is the language of instruction, everyday student life at the school unfolds in several languages. The languages most commonly heard spoken in the hallways, cafeteria, and classrooms are English and Cantonese.

In anticipation of students wanting to use languages other than English at school, Northside teachers have experimented with and developed a variety of pedagog-ical strategies designed to elicit English speech, a practice that teachers associate with students' academic success. In the Grade 12 Advanced English class that we observed over a period of three months, the teacher, Mrs Yee, planned several strategic pedagogical interventions to encourage the use of English by all students. Given that her class consisted primarily of Chinese students, many of whom were not native speakers of English and several of whom had been in Canada for less than two years, based upon past experiences Mrs Yee expected that many students would be "quiet." She also anticipated that many would want to use their mother tongue in class. Accordingly, she established an English-only policy and organized the formation of racially and linguistically mixed small groups to encourage low-English-proficiency students to "practice" speaking English and communicate with more proficient students. Notwithstanding these efforts, silence figured prominently in the classroom performances of the majority of the Hong-Kong-born Chinese students. We observed that many Chinese students spoke very little – some not at all – during whole-class discussions and in small group work. Moreover, many of the Chinese students never raised their hands to volunteer responses, offer commentary, or pose questions. (In truth, we saw how their behaviors could evoke the image of the "reluctant talker" about which we earlier expressed reservation.) In this manner, the reluctance on the part of the Chinese students to speak English in Mrs Yee's class disrupted the teacher's pedagogic agenda.

In addition, Mrs Yee's insistence on the formation of racially and linguistically-mixed working groups incited racial tensions between Hong-Kong-born Chinese, Canadian-born Chinese, and non-Chinese students. In the group work sessions that we observed, the Hong-Kong-born Chinese students spoke little, while the Canadian-born Chinese and non-Chinese students assumed leadership roles in their attempts to elicit verbal participation from the quieter Chinese students. In debriefings with non-Chinese students, many reported that they found the Chinese students' reticence to speak burdensome in that they, the native speakers of English, were required to assume more than their fair share of the conversational load (see Tannen, 1984). Many also felt that this dynamic ultimately threatened the quality of their education in that they were being deprived of the opportunity to develop critical, integrative thinking skills through oral discussion and debate. The following is an excerpt from a conversation with Mina, a Canadian-born woman of Indo-Caribbean ancestry:

> Okay, I say my part but like there's no like other stimuli from any other person in the class. They just sit there, you know what I mean? There's nothing there to like you know conflict with. In my other classes, I have other people [who] will say things, will disagree with me, will give me – in this class I have nothing. Everyone in that class just sits there like this. They're really quiet, they don't do nothing like you know what I mean. In other classes, I have other people that are on the same level in the same way as I am, so I have something to conflict with me. Seriously, I don't think half of those people in that class should be in a Grade 12 Advanced class. That's honestly what I'm saying. They shouldn't, they can't speak proper English.[4]

Mina's comments illustrate the inter-group tensions that permeated the dynamics of this class. Specifically, they show how the silences of the Hong-Kong-born Chinese students were equated with lack of engagement, passivity, and their failure to work at grade level. In addition, Mina's views about her Chinese classmates' inabilities to speak "proper English," and her association of their non-native speaker status with cognitive and emotional immaturity, evoke the colonialist and racialist discourses referenced earlier by McKay and Wong (1996). As well, Mina's Eurocentric reverence for voice and her longing for "conflict" informed her disparagement of the ways in which some of her Chinese classmates interacted in class.

Mina's understanding of the participation styles of her Chinese peers underscores the pervasive influence of the Orientalist perspective in broader societal discourses (Kondo, 1997; Said, 1979). We find clear evidence of this perspective in the following excerpt from Mina's response to our probe concerning why it might be that many of her Chinese classmates are quiet:

> I have no clue. In most of my other classes people are just loud and most of my classes are more mixed. In this class there are more Orientals and Orientals I find to be quieter people like you know maybe that's why. I have no clue why but like everyone in that class is like really quiet.

We noted earlier that implicated in the racial and linguistic tensions of the class are concerns on the part of some of the non-Chinese students that they are required to assume a disproportionately large share of the conversational burden in class. In the following excerpt, Marilyn, a white Canadian-born young woman, reveals her frustration with having to assume responsibility for doing most, if not all, of the talking in her small linguistically and racially mixed group:

> I feel like I'm just there to teach them and then – and I'm not really learning anything, I'm not getting anything out of it. Whereas if I was working with someone at the same level then we could put in our ideas and it's not going to be just my ideas. And then the outcome will be like – we'd probably get better marks, I think because when we're doing presentations and stuff its not just one person or two people's idea out of a group of five.

In the linguistic and racial tensions in this English-medium classroom we see a conflation of two problems. First, the invocation of discourses that pathologize the quiet "Oriental" students was clearly at play. Thus, the "reluctance" to talk on the part of some Chinese students functioned to affirm, in the minds of non-Chinese students, dominant negative stereotypes of Asians. At the same time, the very real, material pressure placed on students by family members and teachers to achieve high grades and excel academically weighed heavily on the minds of Marilyn and Mina, as it did on those of many Northside students. For this reason, negative reactions to attributes or behaviors associated with Asians became more strident when these behaviors were perceived to put at jeopardy the collective marks of the group.

The comments of Mina and Marilyn also point us to the conclusion that Mrs Yee's well-intentioned pedagogical strategy involving mixed groups was undermined by the force of these two problematic conditions – group stereotyping, and community and peer pressure on students to obtain high grades. Thus, contrary to her most sincere wishes, the participant structures around which Mrs Yee organized her curricular delivery actually contributed to disenabling positive race relations and exacerbating tensions in her classroom (see Philips, 1972).

Unfortunately, Mina, Marilyn, and other non-Chinese students were unable to grasp the complex social and political forces that shaped the interactional patterns of the Hong-Kong-born Chinese students. These dynamics engendered linguistic double binds that invariably trapped linguistic minority students into debilitating silences. However, as we elucidate presently, contrary to Mina's reductionist inference, these discursive patterns were attributable to the knowledge base of the non-native speaking, immigrant student, and had little to do with the category "Oriental" (Gumperz, 1997; Irvine, 1987).

Immigrant students' linguistic double binds

Using Cheung's (1993) framework, we want to argue that there are alternative ways to understand the silences that proved so irksome to non-Chinese and Canadian-born Chinese students and so challenging for teachers at Northside. Some of the Chinese students in Mrs Yee's class attributed their silence to their self-consciousness about their level of English proficiency and their fears that their English pronunciation would become an object of ridicule. Thus, Chinese students responded with an *inhibitive silence*. Evidence for this interpretation was provided by Cathy, a Hong-Kong-born Chinese Canadian who was enrolled in Mrs Yee's English class:

> They're embarrassing of the English. They can't speak. They scared that people will laugh at them, because I try that – I'm in that stage before – right? So I know how they think and how they feel.

Alternatively, other Hong-Kong-born Chinese students explained that they often chose to remain silent in class for fear that answering questions and speaking in English would be perceived by members of their social group as "showing off." Asked why it was that native Cantonese-speakers rarely addressed their peers in English, Victor volunteered:

> For the Hong Kong people, right, we will, we will rarely use English to speak to each other except that [for those] people is born in here or have been here for a long time. If that is not the case, right, we will speak Cantonese because if we, like, talk English with them, right, they do think you are really, like, showing off your skill in English.

Similarly, when Victor was queried about why he did not volunteer to answer questions in class, he responded:

> When I wanted to answer some questions, I was thinking about, "If I answer," right? "What will other Cantonese student or students from Hong Kong think

of me?" If I ... like they may be thinking about [how] I am showing off my knowledge. I mean, yeah, I know the questions right? I know it, that's good, I can keep it in my heart. But then, if I put my hand up and then say, "Sir, I understand" and then answer the questions, right? They [Hong-Kong-born Chinese students] will, they may think I am showing off. So it's really hard.

Following Cheung, the type of silence described by Victor may be considered both *inhibitive* and *attentive*. The attentiveness of Victor to the reactions of his Hong-Kong-born Chinese peers is evidenced in his worry that if he speaks in English he will be disparaged for "showing off." This attentive silence, however, traps Victor in a linguistic double bind. Indeed, he is caught in a "lose-lose" situation. On the one hand, if he does not perform in English he stands to jeopardize his grade and incur the censure of his non-Chinese and some of his Canadian-born Chinese classmates. On the other hand, if he uses English, he stands to attract negative reactions from his Hong-Kong-born Chinese peers. This interpretation also accounts for the negative reactions on the part of the majority of Hong-Kong-born Chinese students toward their English-speaking Chinese student peers, and elucidates the friendship formations that are at stake in these racial identity politics. When we probed Charles, a Hong-Kong-born Chinese student at Northside, about how his Cantonese-speaking friends would react if he spoke to them in English, he responded without hesitation: "They'd think I'm whitewashed."

In our research at Northside, we found that Hong-Kong-born Chinese youth sometimes referred to Chinese peers who do not speak Cantonese as *juk-sing*, a pejorative term also used to describe Canadian-born Chinese persons. Following Yee (1993), the term literally means the nodes in bamboo that obstruct the flow of water. The epithet alludes to the manner in which Canadian-born Chinese youth are perceived to be in a void, virtual non-entities – neither fully Chinese, nor fully Canadian.[5] Arguably, the inhibitive and attentive silences in Victor's self-described class behavior are linked to the identity politics at Northside and, specifically, to his desire to avoid being considered *juk-sing*.

Another linguistic double bind can be associated with the wish on the part of Canadian-born Chinese and non-Chinese students' for Chinese-dialect speech to be "whispered" rather than spoken openly in public areas such as school hallways, classrooms, and the cafeteria. In the following excerpt, Tony, a Chinese student who was born in China but came to Canada at a very young age, expresses this position bluntly:

Cantonese [speakers] tend to shout out – that annoys me. We don't [English speakers] shout ... . Many Chinese shout and the Cantonese accent – it always has the long tail, a stretched out sound – it annoys me.

However, the expressed preference for non-English speech to be spoken quietly and thus relegated to the private domain of intimate conversation placed many Hong-Kong-born Chinese students at Northside in a double bind that served to reinforce an image of Chinese students as "reluctant talkers." If Hong-Kong-born students were perceived to speak loudly in Chinese, they opened themselves up to possible censure from some non-Chinese and Canadian-born Chinese students; yet, when speaking in English, they were often considered inaudible and were regularly exhorted by teachers and peers to "speak louder." In sum, while recorded observed decibel levels did not correlate with such perceptions, overall Hong-Kong-born Chinese students were considered by other group members to speak too loudly in Cantonese and too softly in English.

Tony's impatience upon hearing "loud" Cantonese reinforces the disenabling dimensions of the double binds that trap Hong-Kong-born Chinese students into silence. On the one hand, Chinese students who chose to speak English stood to lose important friendships among their Hong-Kong-born peers; on the other, if they chose to speak Cantonese, they were perceived by other students to be behaving in an irritating and intrusive manner. These tensions placed immigrant students in a stressful situation, in that they were caught between a Cantonese youth culture that valued loyalty toward the heritage culture and humility in reference to the majority language, and a Eurocentric culture that valued the animated use of English.

Tony's sentiments may further represent the systemic disparagement of "other" peoples, cultures, and languages that is part of the legacy of the universalizing project of colonial expansion (Gilman, 1986; Gilroy, 1993; Goldberg, 1993). In particular, the writings of Asian North American authors (for example, Hogue, 1996; Kim, 1982; Kingston, 1978; Wong, 1993) contain critiques of the ways in which North American society and schools have served to exclude and categorize Asian people as "other." These racist practices have colluded to produce – especially among North-American-born Chinese youth – an ambivalence toward their "Chineseness," including a reluctance to endorse the maintenance and use of the heritage language (Hwang, 1990; Kingston, 1978; Ma, 1998). As noted earlier, this ambivalence is linked to dominant Western perspectives on speech and silence. It is also linked to the valorization of the use of the societally dominant language and the concomitant devaluation of the use of other, less prestigious, minority languages. Since at Northside High School student speech in languages other than English was not seen to be indicative of student agency or even to occupy a legitimate space in the public arena, we were not surprised by Tony's admission that, in the years since immigrating to Canada, he had become "not that good in Mandarin anymore."

The Interactional Bases of Northside High School Classes

We have shown how Hong-Kong-born Chinese Canadian students at Northside are continually engaged in a negotiation of linguistic double binds. These predicaments invariably contribute to a reticence on the part of many Chinese students to speak English. The consequent silences of many Chinese students engender resentment from non-Chinese and some Canadian-born Chinese classmates who associate these behaviors with a compromised educational experience and the risk of low grades. We have argued that these sentiments arise from the interaction of stereotypes associated with colonialist and Orientalist discourses and the prevalence of a Eurocentric valorization of speech, and from the pressures placed on students to excel academically.

Before we turn our attentions to how alternate understandings of silence and speech may help teachers work with students to negotiate linguistic and racial tensions in multilingual and multiracial classrooms, we want to consider the language socialization issues raised by this study's findings. We do so, not only because we find the theoretical problematic compelling, but also because we cannot entertain pedagogical responses without carefully examining the socio-demographic context in which the formal education of Northside High School students takes place.

Recent years have witnessed the evolution of Toronto's urban status from that of metropolis to one of cosmopolis. The recent demographic history of the city reveals patterns of mobility and flux that reflect waves of transnational migration and an overlapping trend of ongoing, continuous transportation of people across national and local boundaries. The language practices of those who inhabit this dense urban landscape are diverse and varied.

Recently, a considerable amount of attention has been devoted by scholars in the social sciences to the applicability of a *community of practice* (CofP) framework to the understanding of language socialization in groups (see, for example, Eckert, 2000; Holmes & Meyerhoff, 1999; Lave & Wenger, 1991). Following Wenger (1998: 72–73), communities of practice exhibit three main characteristics. The first is *mutual engagement*, that is, participants' engagement in relationships and actions whose meanings they negotiate with one another. The second is that a community of practice involves *a joint enterprise*. This pre-condition does not necessarily entail a uniform understanding of the roles of participants, but it does involve a commitment on their parts to mutual accountability and to making what they are there to do "real and livable" (Wenger, 1998: 79). Third, a community of practice entails *a shared repertoire*. Again, this characteristic does not imply that there is necessarily an agreement on the common resources to be used, but it does entail communal acknowledgment of the need for coordinating perspectives to arrive at a determination of what these resources should be.

While we acknowledge the usefulness of this concept for the understanding of different types of organizational and informal group practices, our analysis of the discursive practices of students and teachers at Northside High School engenders in us a reticence to endorse this characterization with reference to our own research setting. We arrive at this conclusion, not because we found considerable variability in the discursive practices of students and teachers – indeed, variability and diversity are integrated in the definition of speech communities (Bayley, 2002; Labov, 1972; Patrick, 2002) – but rather because the setting did not meet all three preconditions for CofP status. Our observations do not provide evidence that participants, whether willing or reluctant (see Bell, this volume), have agreed to negotiate the expectations that they hold for their academic experience or the participation formats and discourse styles through which they will cooperate to achieve their goals. To the contrary, not unlike Labov's (1972) islanders,[6] as Victor's assertions attest, the speech practices of Hong Kong-born Chinese students at Northside can be explained in large part by the fact that they seek to set themselves apart from their non-Chinese and Canadian-born Chinese peers. Thus, their primary business is not to negotiate participation in a community where members work toward a commonly sanctioned goal, but rather to develop abilities to employ the discourse strategies that are necessary conditions for access to the social relationships and support that being a member of a group of Chinese immigrant learners provides.

While the situation that we have studied is not, in our view, best served theoretically by a CofP model, it lends itself readily to Gumperz' (1997) notion of *social network*, where power relationships that obtain among institutional members (this factor is related, of course, to dynamics within the wider society) determine the types of association available to the constitutive population, or a subset thereof. Once persons are defined (by themselves or others) as members of certain groups, relevant knowledge is acquired and reinforced in the course of socialization processes that rest in large part on informal peer contacts within an institutionalized setting with (formal and informal) rules for engagement. That these various interactional scripts, and the goals that motivate them, are weighted differentially in the linguistic marketplace (if we might borrow a phrase from Bourdieu, 1982a), where values are assigned to diverse discursive practices, comes as no surprise to those who hold that "an integrated view of the role of language in identity construction acknowledges the relevance of ideological and power relations" (Schecter & Bayley, 1997: 514).

On Negotiating Speech and Silence in the Urban Classroom

There are two applied questions that arise directly from this study's findings:

(1) What kinds of pedagogical adaptations would enable Hong Kong-born Chinese students to negotiate their linguistic double binds productively?
(2) What kinds of curricular interventions or strategies could alleviate the intergroup tensions that arise from the stereotypes and pressures that frame the educational experiences of non-native-speaking Chinese students?

We first emphasize that the Northside teachers who have been reflecting on and working with the set of problems we have uncovered in this research have much to contribute to pedagogical responses to the interactional dilemmas confronting Northside students. We see in the following interview excerpt that Mrs Yee captures an important dimension of the problem from the perspective of the Hong Kong-born Chinese students:

> Silence is a signal for lack of trust. It also means insecurity, that I don't feel good about my English. I want to hide it, I don't want to hear it, I don't want to be picked on. It requires a lot of courage for me to say something in a language in which I know I have an accent, in which I know that I may not be able to use the

right word. I may use it wrong and people may laugh at me. I am not going to show you something that I am not good at.

Speaking in the first person as an immigrant student, Mrs Yee demonstrates an understanding that helping students to negotiate the roles of speech and silence in the classroom will entail a process of deconstructing myths and stereotypes around "accents" and non-native varieties of English – stereotypes that have been internalized by immigrant as well as by mainstream students. Mrs Yee has found that during whole group instruction one effective strategy for working with a response of "dead silence" to a teacher elicitation is to invite the student to discuss the question with a partner for a few minutes. The teacher moves on with her lesson, and finds that when she returns to the same question after a short time, the "silent" student is able to answer with greater ease and less self-consciousness than would be the case if the teacher had pressed for an immediate response.

Mr Dunn, an English teacher who, like Mrs Yee, has worked with mixed linguistic and racial groups, agrees that modifying participation sequences for teacher–student interaction during whole group instruction is a more beneficial strategy than either insisting on a response from a "silent" student or "just saying, 'You don't know, we'll go to someone else.'" "'Cause if you just sort of come off and call on someone else," the teacher explains, "then they look bad." Mr Dunn prefers to return later to reticent students: "It's okay to say if you don't know right now. You can think about it and we'll come back and look at your response later. [I] give them that option." In response to inhibitive silences that emerge in group work, Mr Dunn favors the following strategy:

> I ... have them prepare something, maybe even show it to me ahead of time. "Show me what you are going to give your group today." So that they have something to contribute and they know that it's okay.

Encouraging students to prepare texts (that will be vetted by their teacher) to bring to their group meetings provides immigrant learners with a significant measure of control over their learning process. They have choice as to the mode of participation (see Harklau, this volume), and the opportunity to show their work to teachers or to helpful classmates before the group meets reduces the likelihood that learners who are self-conscious about their English-speaking abilities will lose face by showing their peers work about which they are not confident. At the same time, in providing remaining group members with expected input into class assignments, non-native-speaking immigrant students demonstrate to their peers that they are indeed willing to carry their load.

For our part, we want to endorse pedagogical strategies and interventions that sanction and encourage the use of the mother tongue. In addition to facilitating the understanding of academic content, such practices help to foster important social relationships among immigrant students that can be linked to social integration and academic success. To illustrate, Cantonese-speaking students enrolled in a summer math course at Northside were able to use Cantonese in their instructional and social interactions with classmates. Friends helped one another to decode and complete homework assignments, elicit the teacher's attention when assistance was needed, and negotiate grades on weekly quizzes and tests (Goldstein, 1997a). In addition, the friendships that developed in Cantonese over the summer months provided immigrant students with social relationships to which they could turn for support in the regular school year.

Beyond compensatory strategies, as part of normal classroom practice we encourage individual and small group activities that enable rather than restrict the use of languages other than English. For example, where sufficient numbers of speakers exist, we see no reason why students cannot from time to time, or for a circumscribed period, work in same-mother-tongue groups to negotiate class assignments. While non-native-speaking students may thus forfeit some opportunities to practice English, they will gain opportunities to negotiate academic content in ways that are empowering and that might better prepare them for the kind of interaction, debate, and even "conflict" that students like Mina desire and that is valued in North American classrooms. In addition, using bilingual and multilingual materials in class would help to foster the development of empathy on the part of mainstream students who have not been required to learn academic content in a non-native language. For example, teachers may want to experiment with a bilingual math module, where all students complete the same computations on the same worksheets, with English equivalents for numerals in unfamiliar scripts provided in translation keys (see Schecter & Cummins, in press).

Finally, the issues raised in this chapter and elsewhere can provide the basis for critical classroom discussions on language awareness that aim to foster in students the development of analytic thinking around issues of language, power, and racism. Some excellent work in this area has been undertaken by American linguist Rosina Lippi-Green. In her book, *English with an Accent: Language, Ideology and Discrimination in the United States* (Lippi-Green, 1997), she discusses ways in which linguistic discrimination manifests itself in the classroom, the court, the media, and corporate culture. Of particular interest are her examinations of how the notions of "non-accent" and "standard language" are used to maintain and justify social order, and how language ideology based on myths and stereotypes influences students in classrooms.

Such pedagogical responses to linguistic and racial tensions in multilingual and multiracial classrooms require teachers and students to work with and through immigrant students' feelings of embarrassment, frustration, and anger. They ask teachers to engage with the question of whether it is fair practice to consistently privilege some interactional styles and formats over others. At the same time, by providing options as to mode and venue, they call on linguistic minority students to assume responsibility for taking an active role in the learning of the group. And they place monolingual English-speaking students who are not accustomed to sharing their social space with people who speak other languages in the virtual reality of discomfort associated with incomplete, partial understandings that comprise the lived experiences of non-native speakers. In this manner, these approaches bring all stakeholders face to face with the marginalizing legacy of colonialism. From this sorry place we can all move forward toward a more responsible pedagogy.

Notes

1. The "model minority" stereotype is part of a larger discourse that emerged in the 1960s in the United States, championing the educational and occupational success of Chinese North Americans (Lee, 1996; Maclear, 1994; McKay & Wong, 1996). This group was cast in contradistinction to African Americans, who at the time were mobilizing to effect vigorous demands for civil rights. The implication was that the "trouble-making" minorities should model themselves after Chinese American's hard work ethic, strong family unity, and willingness to assimilate (Lee, 1996; McKay & Wong, 1996). Critics of the stereotype noted that it promoted the idea that Asian North Americans have overcome historical barriers such as poverty and racism and now constitute a uniformly affluent and successful group. The flip of this stereotype is the belief that Chinese people are quiet, overly passive, nerdy, conformist, willing to assimilate, and exceptional students, particularly in the maths and sciences (Wong, 1993).
2. For this reason, Cheung warned against the romanticization or eroticizing of silences. For example, she noted the desire among some Asian North American parents to protect their children from harsh histories of racism. Cheung maintained that, while this variety of silence can enable children when they are young, as they get older it can infantilize them through an enforced innocence (Cheung, 1993).
3. To preserve the anonymity of the study's respondents, we have used pseudonyms for the high school as well as for the students and teachers associated with interview excerpts.
4. The interview excerpts that appear in this chapter are transcribed in conventional prose.
5. According to Yee, the term is conceptually analogous to "banana," another pejorative term used by Chinese people to refer to one who is considered "yellow on the outside but white on the inside."
6. In this early study, Labov accounted for changes in the speech on the island of Martha's Vineyard by showing that islanders had an interest in setting themselves apart from the summer tourist stock.

Chapter 8

Novices and Their Speech Roles in Chinese Heritage Language Classes

AGNES WEIYUN HE

The Role of the Novice in Language Socialization

As outlined by Ochs and Schieffelin (Ochs, 1990, 1996; Ochs & Schieffelin, 1984; Schieffelin & Ochs, 1986a, 1986b, 1996), *language socialization*, a linguistic anthropological model of the intricate connection between linguistic development and cultural development, has a two-faceted concern:

(1) how novices (e.g. children, second language learners) are socialized to be competent members in the target culture through language use;
(2) how novices are socialized to use language.[1]

Given such formulation, with "novices" being the grammatical subject of some passive voice construction, it is perhaps not entirely surprising that research drawing upon this model tends to emphasize the efforts made by the experts (e.g. mothers, other caregivers, teachers) to socialize the novices (e.g. children, students). Less visible are the reactions and responses of the novices. Consequently, the process of socialization is often characterized as smooth and seamless, and novices are often presumed to be passive, ready, and uniform recipients of socialization.

Yet we know that in any kind of social action and interaction, including language socialization, there exist clashes of ideas, goals, dispositions, expectations, and norms of interaction between the experts and the novices (Chaiklin & Lave, 1993; Erickson & Schultz, 1982; He & Keating, 1991; Jacoby & Gonzales, 1991; Latour, 1987). For socialization to take place, the expert and the novice need to negotiate their differences through interaction. Even in idealized cases where the expert and the novice share the same goals, expectations and norms of behavior, socialization cannot be accomplished without the co-construction of the novice, since any constitution of action, activity, identity, emotion, ideology or other culturally meaningful reality is inherently a joint achievement by all the participants (Jacoby & Ochs, 1995).

Further, novices vary in their manner and degree of participation in socialization activities. They may be centrally involved in these activities, or remain peripheral (Lave & Wenger, 1991). They may learn by actually doing what experts do or by simply observing experts do what they do (Rogoff, 1990). Novices also differ in what and how much they take from socialization activities, depending on their individual goals, orientations, and circumstances. For example, He (1998) showed that the same academic advice may be taken by various student counselees to bear upon a wide range of different issues, including university courses, grade point average, future career, and relationships with professors.

This chapter emphasizes the indispensable and important role of the novice by highlighting the dialectical, interactional perspective within language socialization. Drawing from four Chinese heritage language classrooms in the United States, it focuses on the construction of varied speech roles of novices – the students – and their associated values, responsibilities, and obligations. It further examines students' reactions and responses to these constructions. This chapter also compares the findings with available research on participation frameworks in mainstream English-speaking classrooms, and draws implications for Chinese-American students in bilingual, bicultural contexts of school, home, and community.

Research Context

Participants and settings

The research presented in this chapter was set in four classrooms in two Chinese Heritage Language schools where evening or weekend Chinese language classes are offered for the children of professionals who come from China or Taiwan. These children were either born in the United States or immigrated with their parents at a very young age. Most of them attend mainstream English-speaking schools on weekdays. While many are bilingual in spoken Chinese and English, some are already English-dominant, and few have opportunities to learn how to read and write in Chinese. Parents send their children to these schools to acquire literacy in the heritage language. As researchers have long noted, combining elements from family, community, and school, heritage language schools function as important vehicles for ethnic minority children to acquire heritage language skills and cultural values (Bradunas & Topping, 1988; Cummins, 1992; Fishman, 1966; Wang, 1996).[2]

Analytic framework

As the primary object of our inquiry will be speech roles, our analysis can be illuminated by Goffman's (1981: 128) concept of "footing," which refers to the "alignment we take up to ourselves and the others present as expressed in the way we manage the production and reception of an utterance." In his model of communication, Goffman outlines varying forms and degrees of participation in social interaction, and breaks down the roles of speaking and hearing into specific "footings." With regard to the production of utterances, speakers may take up various footings in relation to their own remarks. By employing different "production formats" (Goffman, 1981: 145), they may convey distinctions between the (1) animator, (2) author, and (3) principal of what is said. The "animator" is the person who produces the utterance. The "author" is the person who originates the beliefs and sentiments, and composes the utterances through which they are expressed. And the "principal" is the person whose viewpoint or position is being expressed in and through the utterance.

With regard to the reception of utterances, the recipient of an utterance may also assume (or be assigned by the speaker) various "participation statuses" (Goffman, 1981: 137). The recipient may have the official status of a "ratified participant" in an interaction. In this case s/he may either be "addressed" (as in a two-party conversation) or "unaddressed" (as in a multiparty-conversation where at each given moment only the participant may receive the speaker's visual attention, while the others are included in the interaction, but are not directly addressed). The recipient may also not be an official, ratified participant in the interaction, but may have access to the interaction as a "bystander" in two different ways. S/he may be an "eavesdropper," purposely and maybe secretively listening in on conversations, or an "overhearer," unintentionally and inadvertently hearing the conversation. A speaker may purposely design his/her talk in order to be heard by someone who is not officially participating in the interaction, in which case the otherwise "unintended overhearer" becomes an "intended overhearer." Figure 8.1 makes the above explanations more transparent.

In what follows, I will use Goffman's model as guidance to discuss the ways in which the students' roles in classroom interaction are constructed, socialized, and responded to. My main objective is to examine the kinds of opportunities that are afforded students to participate in classroom activities, the ways in which these opportunities are created or denied, and the ways in which these opportunities are taken up or rejected by students.

Socializing Production Formats

Students become speakers in these classrooms for a number of reasons and in a number of different ways. Below are several illustrations, selected because the interactional organization (and consequently, one might argue, the cultural organization) therein differs from the canonical dyadic pattern.

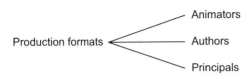

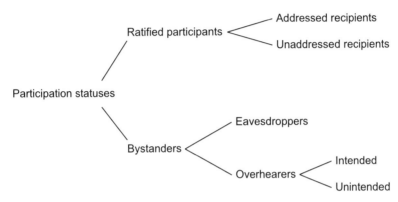

Figure 8.1 Goffman's model of communication

Student as co-animator/author

Teachers often invite students to complete their utterances collaboratively. Specifically, the teacher takes a pause in her utterance before a recognizable intonational, syntactic, or pragmatic completion (Ford & Thompson, 1996), elongates the last syllable, and uses rising intonation. In so doing, she invites and coordinates completion of her utterance by the class as a whole, as in (1). Grammatical glosses can be found in Appendix C, and transcription symbols in Appendix B.

(1) (TZCDL:952) "yi na"
((Tz and Ss are learning the strokes for the character "tian" (sky); "heng," "pie" and "na" are names for various strokes.))

1 **Tz:**   hao,   kan laoshi ((faces blackboard))
           good   look teacher
           Good, look at me.

2   tian (.3) yi   heng   zai   yi   heng
        sky   one "heng" then   one   "heng"
        Sky. One "heng" and then another "heng."

3   ranhou yi   pie   zai::: ((turns and looks at Ss))
        then   one "pie"   then
        Then one "pie" followed by

4　　　　(.2)

5　**Tz:**　yi::: ((shifts gaze from Ss to blackboard and back to Ss))
　　　　one

6　**Ss:**　na:
　　　　"na"

7　**Tz:**　yi　na (.)　hao.
　　　　One "na"　good.
　　　　One "na." Good.

Here, toward the end of her description of the strokes for "tian," the teacher lengthens the conjunction ("zai," line 3) prior to the last stroke "na" and gives visual attention to the class. When she does not receive any student uptake (line 4), she supplies an increment to her own turn ("yi," line 5) in the same manner as she delivered "zai" (line 3). At this point the students in choral response name the last missing stroke in the character (line 6), thus completing Tz's description. Tz subsequently affirms the students' contribution (line 7).

The practice of using incomplete turn-constructional-units in structuring subsequent student participation is similar to what is described by Lerner (1995). Lerner examined English-speaking instructional contexts involving Spanish-dominant, bilingual third grade students. He reported using incomplete turn-constructional-units as one way (along with other strategies such as word search) to invite recipients' response and thus to serve as an instructional resource. Through the "scaffold" (Cazden, 1988: 101–102) provided by the incomplete turn-constructional-units, the teacher creates and presents an opportunity for the students to partake in the formulation of the learning material, thereby assigning some authorship (and thus ownership) to the students. On all occasions observed, the students appeared to respond well to such opportunities.

Student as constructed-author/principal

Tannen (1986: 312) argues that what is commonly referred to as direct or indirect speech is in fact "constructed dialogue," "a means by which experience surpasses story to become drama." Some "quotations" are in fact dialogue that was never spoken, as in:

You can't say, "Well Daddy I didn't HEAR you." (Tannen, 1986: 313)

However, it does not matter whether the actual utterance was ever made or not; the point is that this or similar utterances could have been made. The accuracy with regard to specificity (e.g. who actually said what to whom when) is rendered unimportant or irrelevant in view of the general plausibility of the utterance and of the phenomenon.

Similarly, teachers sometimes "quote" an indefinite student as a means to foster discussion. Consider example (2).

(2) (TCCDL:952) "Mr Dongguo"
((Tc is telling Ss the story of Mr Dongguo, a country gentleman, whose name has become the synonym of extreme benevolence in Chinese.))

1 **Tc:->**   you   tongxue wen   e
      exist   student   ask   ASP
      Some student has asked

2   mayi   wenshenme bu   neng cai?
      ant   why   NEG   can   trample
      Why can't we step on ants?

3   Dongguo   xianshen   jiu   shi   zheyang
      Dongguo   gentleman   CONJ   COP   this way
      Mr Dongguo was just like this

4   lian   mayi dou   bu   cai
      even   ant   CONJ NEG   trample
      He wouldn't even step on ants

5   dui   shenme dongxi dou   hen   renci
      toward   any   thing   CONJ very   benevolent
      He was very benevolent toward everything.

Viewing the transcript for the entire lesson, no prior student utterance as reported by **Tc** (lines 1–2) was available. The point of constructing an utterance and attributing it to some indefinite student is to enable further description of Mr Dongguo as being extremely benevolent (lines 3–5). Perhaps not surprisingly, as is the case in casual conversation as described by Tannen (1986), no one in the class questioned the validity of Tc's report. The students appeared to acquiesce in the teacher's construction of their role as author or principal.

Student as revoiced author/principal

Many researchers subscribe to the notion that the "teacher initiation, student response, teacher evaluation" (IRE) sequence is the most common discourse pattern in the classroom (see, for example, Cazden, 1988; Mehan, 1979). This pattern, or its alternative IRF (F for feedback) proposed by Sinclair and Coulthard (1975), clearly does not account for variations in participation frameworks in the classroom, nor does it specify what sorts of constructions/configurations are possible in each slot – a topic beyond the scope of the present chapter. Nonetheless, the IRE construct is valuable in drawing our attention to what happens subsequent to the student's speaking turn. Besides evaluations such as "Okay," "Right," or "Good," the teacher (and sometimes peer students) may provide a number of different uptakes to students' utterances.

Another study more directly relevant to our present discussion is that by O'Conner and Michaels (1993) on the role that the teacher's revoicing plays in shaping participation structures in sixth grade classrooms. In that study, the authors showed a pattern in which (a) the teacher draws further inference from the student's utterance and (b) the student has the right and an interactional opportunity to challenge or affirm the teacher's inference. They provide the following example:

Steven: ... um/but if she/kept her/um/sugar/
And used that/
And then/look her/thing of ten to twenty-two
And just picked another number/like half way/
Like Allison said/
And then just made that her concentrate//

Lynne: So then, you don't agree with Sarita that if she/
Picks a number halfway between/
That that's not really making her first concentrate either//
(O'Conner and Michaels 1993: 322)

In this case, they argue, Lynne, the teacher, is creating a participant framework in which (a) she uses the opportunity to draw inference from Steven's utterance, (b) Steven has the right to validate her inference and to take on a position himself with respect to the learning task at hand, and (c) Steven has been positioned in opposition to Sarita in the discussion of the relative merits of two different proposals.

Our findings contrast sharply with O'Conner and Michaels' example. In (3), the teacher re-presents *as her own speech* the student's utterance either verbatim or with mild modification. In so doing, the student's voice is obscured, blurred, and blended with that of the teacher and of the textbook. Not only does the student not have an opportunity to affirm and challenge the teacher's re-presentation, the student may not even recognize that the teacher's utterance originated from her very own.

(3) (TCCDL:952) "Mr Dongguo"
((This segment is taken from the same context as segment (2).))

1 **Tc:**   dongguo   xianshen (.2) zhege uh   dayi   shi   sheme?
Dongguo   gentleman   this   PRT   meaning COP Q
What is the meaning of (the story of) Mr Dongguo?

2 **G4:**   wo juede ta hen   haoxin.
I   think   he very   good-heart.
I think he is very kind.

3 **Tc:** ta hen (.3) renci   >dui   bu   dui<?
      he very   benevolent correct NEG   correct
      He is very benevolent right?

4   ((Tc turns away from class to begin to write on the blackboard))

5 **G4:** bu (.2) ta   tai   haoxin   le.
      NEG   he   too   good-heart   PRT
      No, he is too kind.

6   ((Apparently G4 does not understand the word "renci," benevolent.))

7 **B2:** Wo   shuo   ta   tai BEN   le!
      I   say   he   too stupid PRT
      I say he is too stupid!

8   ((Tc turns back to face the class))

9 **Tc:** shuo ta tai haoxin dui   ma?
      say he too kind   correct Q
      Is it right to say he is too kind?

10   ((Tc looks at the entire class; no Ss uptake))

11 **Tc:** zai   kankan dayi   shi   sheme.
      again   see   meaning COP Q
      Look again to see what the meaning (of the story) is.

12   ((Tc again turns around to write on the blackboard))

When asked what the meaning of the story is, G4 replies with what she thinks (line 2). Tc rephrases G4's response by substituting "haoxin" (kind) with "renci" (benevolent) (line 3), the exact descriptor used in the textbook. Tc also attaches to her utterance a discourse marker "dui bu dui." In this context, this serves to move the discourse forward rather than to elicit the students' response (Chen & He, 2001), as she breaks her eye contact with the students and is about to start a new activity of writing on the board (line 4). In so doing, she does not mention G4 as the original source for claiming "good-hearted"; neither is the affinity of "good-hearted" to "benevolent" recognized. Consequently, owing to her limited vocabulary, G4 does not realize that Tc is rephrasing her own (G4) speech; instead, she takes Tc to be making a different proposal and thus issues a disagreement ("no, he is too kind," line 5).

At this point, a second and a different opinion is voiced by another student, B2 ("I think he is too stupid," line 7). Instead of overtly negating this view, Tc appropriates part of the student's utterance ("shou ta tai ..." ["say he is too ..."], line 9); she then deletes the grammatical subject of "saying," replaces "stupid" with "kind," a synonym to "benevolent," a descriptor originally proposed by G4 (line 2), and turns the utterance into a question (line 9). In other words, B2's contribution is here syntactically transformed and semantically deleted. Hence Tc has in effect obscured the roles of both G4 and B2 as authors and animators.

If O'Conner and Michaels' (1993) interactional model is one of triangulation involving two students representing two different views and the teacher who acts as a mediator, our pattern here is one in which the teacher makes sure that classroom interaction remains between two parties: the teacher and the class. Schematically, the interactional sequence looks like the following:

Teacher: question/command$_1$ addressed to whole class
Student 1:   answer/response$_1$
                      → (subject) + predication$_1$
Teacher: re-presentation of answer/response$_1$
                      → null subject + (modified) predication$_1$
                      tagged question/command$_2$ addressed to whole class
Student 2:   answer/response$_2$
Teacher: re-presentation of answer/response$_1$ or answer/response$_2$
                      tagged question/command$_3$ addressed to whole class

Although the students' full reaction to the teacher's appropriation of their speech may not be readily observable (from verbal behavior) in the case of (3), there was a sense of frustration after Tc asked the class to look at the text again to find the "right" meaning. In the following 4–5 minutes, the students appeared to be lost or not as interested as they were before; no student volunteered to speak again. In an effort to move the lesson forward, Tc eventually gave the students the "official" answer from the textbook.

Student as unratified animator/author

Finally, in this section, I consider instances in which the student initiates interaction but his/her speakership is not ratified by the teacher, who in effect sequentially deletes the student's utterance. Consider (4).

(4) (TWATL:934) "iron bridges"

1 **Tw:** Hao xianzai women lai   kan   "qiao"
              ok   now   we   come look at "bridge"
              Okay now let's look at the character "qiao" (bridge)

2   (.4)

3 **B2:** Wo   zhidao >wo zhidao< mu::: qiao
              I   know   I   know   wood bridge
              I know I know wood bridges

4   (.2)

5 **B2:->** >You mei   you< you mei   you tie   qiao?
       exist NEG exist exist NEG exist iron bridge?
       Are there are there iron bridges?

6 **Tw:->** Qiao ah q-i-ao qiao >   gen   wo   nian<
                        with   me   read
       Qiao ah q-i-ao qiao read after me

In this instance, in the context of Tw's discussion of the phonetic spelling (*pinyin*) of "qiao" (bridge), B2 mentions that he is aware of a certain type of bridge (line 3) and asks the teacher whether there are other types (line 5). Tw however directly proceeds to teach the *pinyin* of "qiao" as if B2's digression never existed. In other words, in Tw's uptake, there is no marking for disjunction in interaction; Tw has sequentially deleted B2's initiation of topic. In so doing, Tw effectively stopped B2's digression, and the class focus on the *pinyin* of "qiao" was sustained.

Elsewhere (He, in press), sequential deletions of this sort are discussed in relation to the teacher's disciplining practices. Instances like (4) indicate that sequential organization of talk provides the teachers with an effective means of showing students what not to do. In other words, disciplining inappropriate verbal behavior can be accomplished not merely by what is said (e.g. "Don't talk now."), but also by the interactional structure of what is said (e.g. ignoring what the child is saying). The students in question appear to respond to this particular type of disciplining practice with compliance. What is sequentially deleted by the teacher is not likely to be brought up again, at least not in the short space of observable interaction. Whether the interactional behavior (not the actual utterances) perceived by the teacher as problematic is curbed in the long term, however, remains a separate issue.

To sum up, we can see that, besides the canonical identity of the "speaker," students in the Chinese heritage language classes studied here are positioned into varied speaking roles with varying degrees and forms of participation and legitimacy in classroom interaction. They may be cast as co-authors through joint completion of the teacher's speaking turns, as in example (1), as is the case with bilingual classes documented elsewhere. Or, much as happens in ordinary conversation, they may be cast as constructed-authors for the convenience of the teacher, as in (2). Or, their speech may be appropriated by the teacher and their authorship diminished, as in (3), in contrast to revoicing practices found in mainstream English-speaking classrooms. Or, their speakership may be rendered illegitimate and their speaking turns sequentially deleted, as in (4). To these various roles and positions, the students' immediate reactions may be positive, as in (1), acquiescent, as in (2), disinterested, as in (3), or compliant, as in (4).

Socializing Participation Statuses

I now turn to the role of the students in the reception of teachers' utterances. Just as speakership takes various forms, so hearership varies considerably from the canonical officially addressed, fully participating recipiency. An unspoken but underlying rule in the classroom is that everyone should participate fully and actively, whether or not addressed by the teacher. Premised on this assumption, the teacher uses her privileged position as the always-legitimate-speaker to variously target her talk either to the entire class, or to a subgroup in the class, or to an individual student.

Addressing the bystander

As mentioned above, by virtue of the fact that interaction takes place during classroom activities, no students, at least in principle, should ever be bystanders. In the event that they become bystanders, as in example (5), something is considered wrong, and must be corrected.

(5) (TWATL:931) "pay attention"
((In the middle of a class, several students, especially B5, appear tired or bored. They are sitting sideways, kicking their legs, and not paying attention to Tw.))

1 **Tw:**	A,	baba	mama	hua	le	hen	DA	de	liqi
	PRT	father	mother	spend	PERT	very	big	POS	effort

Ah, your parents spent lots of efforts

2	cong	HEN	YUAN	de	difang ba	nimen song lai >	shi	bu	shi<?
	from	very	far	POS	place PTP	you send COMP	right	NEG	right

Sending you here from distant places, right?

3   (.5)

4 **Tw:**	Hai	zai	waitou	deng	zhe	nimen
	even	at	outside	wait	DUR	you

They are even waiting for you outside

5	ruguo	nimen	meiyou haohao xuexi	meiyou	dedao eh:::
	if	you	NEG well study	NEG	gain

If you do not study hard, and learn something, eh:::

6	meiyou dedao	dongxi	de	hua, (.2) a
	NEG gain	thing	PRT	case PRT

If you don't get anything

7	na	jiu	bu	heSUAN	le
	then	CONJ	NEG	worthwhile	PRT

Then it is not worthwhile

8   (.4) ((Ss turn their heads and look around the classroom))

9 **Tw:**	A,	suoyi (.2)	women YIDING	yao	zuo hao:::
	PRT	therefore	we surely	should	sit well

Ah, so, we must sit well.

10   ((B5 stops kicking and turns to face Tw))

As discussed elsewhere (He, 2000), this example is illustrative of the three-phased, morally and practically embedded directives (Orientation-Evaluation-Directive) that teachers often use to discipline wrong behavior. In this case Teacher Wang uses the opportunity of asking her students to sit well to inculcate the idea that children should be filial, that is, show gratitude to their parents by meeting their expectations. Here I would like to highlight that the teacher remedies the problematic situation of some students not paying attention by attempting to alter their participation statuses from that of inattentive overhearer to that of officially addressed (and thus, hopefully, fully participating) recipient.

Notice Tw's use of "you" in this talk. In lines 1–4, the talk appears to be addressed to the entire class, although clearly some students are not paying attention and may or may not be listening to Tw. In lines 5–6, "you" has a narrower referential scope, as the actions described there specifically refer to what a few students (i.e. B5 and others) were currently doing. In spite of their non-participating, inattentive stance and status, the teacher addresses B5 and a couple of others as "you," thus positioning them in the role of the addressed-recipients and obligating them to return to full participation in classroom activities. The effort to include B5 and others and to keep them fully engaged culminates in line 9 when Tw uses the inclusive "we" in addressing the entire class as a whole and the problematic students in particular.

Most of the students in this class appear to understand that Tw's talk is targeted at someone other than themselves (as evidenced by their head movement in line 8). The bystanders, B5 in particular, also appear to understand Tw's talk as a directive to correct their behavior, and they swiftly comply with Tw's command. In other words, Tw's socialization effort here is met with understanding and cooperation.

Not-addressing the ratified participants

Conversely, an individual student may appear to be the addressed recipient in form, but in function is being used as a conduit for the teacher to engage the whole class in interaction. In other words, the teacher may appear to design her talk in such a way that only one individual student is cast as a ratified participant and the rest of the students seem to be left out of the interaction.

(6) (TSCDL:951) "a pair of hands"
((Ss are learning how to write the character "pair" in "a pair of hands"))

1 **Ts:->**   Xinxin, ni   shang lai   xie   xie   kan
             Xinxin, you come   COMP write write see
             Xinxin, you come up here and see if you can write

2   (.4)

3 **B2:**   wo wangji   le
          I   forget   ASP
          I have forgotten (how to write the character)

4 **Ts:**   na   ni   lai ((to G1))
          CONJ you come
          Then you come and try.

5   ((G1 writes on the board))

6 **Ts:->** Xinxin, zhe ge   zi   dui   ma? ((looking at board))
          Xinxin, this MSR character correct Q
          Xinxin, is this character correct?

7   (.4)

8 **Ts:**   Xinxin, dui   bu   dui   a? ((looking at whole class))
          Xinxin, correct NEG correct Q
          Xinxin, is it correct or not

9   (.4)

10 **Ts:**   a?
          Q
          Ah?

11 **Ss:**   Dui:::=
          correct

12 **B2:->** =°wo shuo le   bu   zhidao°=
          I   say   ASP NEG know
          I said I don't know.

13 **Ts:**   Dui,   hen   hao ((to G1))
          correct very good
          It's correct. Good job.

In this segment, Ts appears to be making several attempts to engage B2. She first selects him to write on the blackboard (line 1), and then repeatedly asks him to evaluate another student's performance (lines 6 and 8). Noteworthy is that, when B2 does not respond to the teacher's question (line 7), Ts continues addressing B2 by name while shifting visual attention to the whole class (line 8). When there is no uptake by anyone (line 9), Ts further pursues a response, this time without specifying her audience (line 10). Ts's effort finally produced two results: the class gave the teacher a choral response (line 11), and B2 murmured a complaint (line 12). Arguments can be made here that in line 8, despite the fact that B2 is addressed in form, Ts in fact designs her talk to be heard and responded to by the entire class. At least four pieces of evidence may support this claim: First, Ts shifted her visual attention to the whole class (line 8). Second, the entire class, though not addressed, eventually understood Ts to be directing her talk to them, and responded to her (line 11). Third, B2, the addressed recipient, found the attention to him somewhat objectionable (line 12). And finally, Ts provided uptake to the choral response by the class (line 13), but did not attend to B2's reaction.

Unlike in (5), where everyone seemed to understand and go along with the teacher's agenda, in (6), the contradiction between Ts's verbal and visual attention created some difficulties for the other participants. The whole class did not immediately recognize that they were in fact the targeted recipients (as evidenced by the pause in line 9 and Ts's further pursuit in line 10); and B2 apparently failed to see the purpose of Ts' continuous verbal attention to him (line 12).

In brief, the ways in which the individual student in these classes is assigned the role of the hearer may be more complicated than one might initially expect. Given that a common disciplinary problem is that not all students participate in classroom activities all the time, teachers may design their talk in a way that helps ensure that everyone remains an official, full participant in class, as in example (5). On the other hand, based on the assumption that everyone should pay attention to the teacher all the time, teachers may elect to address only some individual student(s) while still expecting the whole class to assume the role of ratified participants, as in (6).

Regrettably, there is no comparable literature on classroom discourse in this regard. Our discussion may, however, benefit from accounts by Ochs and Schieffelin (1995) of the cultural organization of talk to children. The researchers outlined two major types of cultural tendencies:

(1) talking to children as preferred addressees, as in middle class families in many Western societies;
(2) talking to children as overhearers, as in African-American working families (Heath, 1983), or more traditional communities such as West Samoa (Ochs, 1988) and the Kaluli of Papua New Guinea (Schieffelin, 1990).

With regard to (1), children are expected to be conversational partners from a very young age. However, in the case of (2), children are expected to be engaged in verbal interaction with adults only when they are considered to have mastered how to talk.

The implication of the work of Ochs and Schieffelin (1995) for what has been observed is, then, that teachers set up varying expectations of the students either by addressing them directly or by sometimes seeming to assign them the role of the overhearer. When students are addressed recipients, their participation in class activities is expected/required immediately, as in (5). When they are framed as overhearers, their participation is still expected, but at a later point, as when the addressed recipient fails to meet his interactional requirements – as in (6).

Summary and Discussion

In this chapter I have looked at the varied speech roles in which students are positioned in four Chinese heritage language classrooms. By focusing on how speech roles are organized, negotiated, and accomplished, we get a glimpse of the social and cultural organization of interaction in these Chinese heritage language classrooms, especially as it differs from mainstream English-speaking classrooms. From the various speaking and hearing roles and statuses described, we may infer that in this setting a competent student is one who is flexible with the shifting and/or multiple speech roles that s/he is expected to assume, and who is adaptable to the responsibilities and obligations associated with these roles. Thus, the socialization functions of classroom interactions entail practice in talking collaboratively and cooperatively, exploiting the metaphorical function of speakership, appropriating or relinquishing authorship, withholding talk on a given moment, and listening between the lines and responding accordingly.

Our analysis of students' speech roles in Chinese heritage classes may be especially valuable in understanding the language socialization of children in linguistically and culturally heterogeneous communities in the US. (Admittedly, in our analysis, it is sometimes not easy to tease apart that which is culture-specific from that which is classroom-specific, for reason of insufficient comparable data.) The body of research guided by the theoretical model of language socialization has focused largely on the impact of culture on the acquisition of one particular language, whether it is the first language (Goodwin, 1990; Heath, 1983; Ochs, 1988; Schieffelin, 1990), heritage language (Chen & He, in press; He, 2000, 2001), or second/foreign language (Kanagy, 1999; Ohta, 1999; Poole, 1992). Research has barely begun to attend to socialization of more than one language and one culture in linguistically and culturally heterogeneous communities (Duff, 2000; Kulick, 1992; Schieffelin, 1994). When we have comparable cross-sectional studies of speech roles in other settings, we will have a better sense of :

(1) whether speech roles are constructed differently in Chinese heritage language classes;
(2) what difficulties these students may encounter (or what advantages they may enjoy) when they are exposed to multiple modes of socialization and multiple systems of values and patterns of discourse;
(3) the implications the above might have for the learning of a first language, heritage language, foreign or second language.

In addition, in an effort to remedy the situation where researchers all too often tend to focus exclusively on the "experts" in the socialization process, this chapter has focused on the speech roles of the novices/students, and documented in some detail their reactions and responses. The result is to remind us that language socialization, to the extent that it can be observed in micro-interactional details, is not a unidirectional process. Students and teachers may have different expectations, which in turn can bring about frustration or puzzlement. Even in seemingly smooth cases, students' collaboration, cooperation, and coordination on a moment-to-moment basis are required for socialization activities to be meaningful and successful.

This chapter has also shown that novices may not be constitute a homogeneous group. Different students may participate differentially in classroom socialization activities, and the same students may participate to different degrees in different socialization activities. For example, some students may remain full, participating recipients whether addressed by the teacher or not, while others are merely tangentially and accidentally involved. Furthermore, the students' participation may be volunteered or invited or revised. I venture that part of the reason that researchers have tended to neglect "novices" in language socialization studies is that the reactions and responses of novices are not always immediately observable. For example, although a student may start or stop speaking as directed by the teacher, whether or not s/he has fully comprehended, absorbed, and appreciated the cultural values underpinning the speech practices in which s/he participates will remain unknown until we find out how s/he behaves in other similar contexts. In order to more fully assess the role of the novice and the impact of socialization, future longitudinal studies are needed to complement the approach presented in this chapter.

Notes

1. Research reported in this chapter was made possible by a grant from the Spencer Foundation ("Language socialization of Chinese American children," Principal Investigator: Agnes Weiyun He) and by a National Academy of Education/Spencer Postdoctoral Fellowship. I am grateful to both the Spencer Foundation and the NAE for their support. The views expressed are exclusively my own.
2. The corpus includes: 30 hours of audio- and video-recorded class meetings involving four teachers in four different classes, and a total of 35 children (aged 4.5 to 9 years); classroom observations; and interviews with parents, teachers and school administrators. A sketch of the four classrooms can be found in Appendix A.

Appendix A: The four classrooms

Classroom 1

This was a higher-middle level (*bin ban*) class in a range of four proficiency level classes offered in City A, a metropolitan city in southeast US. The students consisted of 4 girls and 9 boys, aged between 4.5 and 8 years. Classes met from 1:30–3:30pm (with a 10-minute break at 2:30), on Sundays, on the top (18th) floor of a university apartment building. A total of 10 hours of lessons in this setting were audio taped.

The instructor was Teacher Wang (Tw), a 45-year-old female with a bachelor's degree from China in philosophy. Prior to coming to the US, she had taught in elementary school and middle schools, as well as in universities in Beijing and its vicinities. She spoke little English.

Classroom 2

Eight hours of class meetings provided the database for Classroom 2, which was beginning-level Chinese, the lowest of the three levels (*xiao ban*) offered in City C, a university town in mid-west US. There were 2 boys and 1 girl in this class, aged between 5 and 6. Classes met from 6:15–7:50pm on Tuesdays, on the university campus.

Teacher Zhang (Tz), the instructor, was a 33-year-old female, who had recently received a master's degree in educational psychology in China, where she had taught adult students. She was frustrated by the lack of appropriate textbooks for overseas Chinese children, and was very interested in learning (new) ways of teaching children.

Classroom 3

Six hours of video- and audio-recorded class meetings provided the database for Classroom 3, which was intermediate level Chinese, the middle of the three levels (*zhong ban*) offered in the same school as Classroom 2. There were 5 girls and 2 boys in this class, aged between 5 and 9. Classes met at the same time in the same building as Classroom 2.

Teacher Shen (Ts), the instructor, was a 27-year-old female, a native of Taiwan, who had recently received a master's degree in accounting in the US. She had been teaching in this capacity for two years.

Classroom 4

Six hours of video- and audio-recorded class meetings provided the database for Classroom 4, which was advanced level Chinese, the highest of the three levels (*da ban*) offered in the same setting as Classrooms 2 and 3. There were 8 girls and 4 or 5 boys in this class, aged between 5 and 9. Classes met at the same time in the same building as Classrooms 2 and 3.

Teacher Chao (Tc), the instructor, was a 28-year-old female, a native of Taiwan, who had been in the US for 6 years and was taking some computer courses in a local community college. She had experience teaching in a similar Chinese language school in another state and had been teaching in this particular school for 2 months. Table 8.1 summarizes the above, while Table 8.2 shows the arrangement of the four classrooms.

Table 8.1 Data and subjects

Classroom	Teacher/Origin of teacher	Number/ age of students	Class level	Hours/ forms of data
1	Wang (Tw)/ mainland China	13/4.5–8	Intermediate	10/audio
2	Zhang (Tz)/ mainland China	3/5–6	Elementary	8/audio+video
3	Shen (Ts)/ Taiwan	7/5–9	Intermediate	6/audio+video
4	Chao (Tc)/ Taiwan	12/5–9	Advanced	6/audio+video

Table 8.2 Arrangement of the four classrooms

Classroom 1	Classroom 2
blackboard Teacher Wang l o n g d e s k B1 B2 B3 B4 G1 G2 B5 l o n g d e s k B6 B7 G3 B8 G4 B9 (AWH*)	*blackboard* Teacher Shen G1 G2 B1 B2 G3 G4 G5 (AWH)
Classroom 3	Classroom 4
blackboard Teacher Zhang G B1 B2 (AWH)	*blackboard* Teacher Chao G1 G2 G3 G4 B1 B2 G5 G6 G7 B3 B4 G8 B5** (AWH)

 * AWH indicates where the researcher was seated.
** B5 did not attend class meetings regularly.

Appendix B: Transcription symbols

CAPS	emphasis, signaled by pitch or volume
.	falling intonation
,	falling-rising intonation
°	quiet speech
[ ]	overlapped talk
-	cut-off
=	latched talk
:	prolonged sound or syllable
(0.0)	silences roughly in seconds and tenths of seconds (measured more according to the relative speech rate of the interaction than to the actual clock time)
(.)	short, untimed pauses of one tenth of a second or less

( )	undecipherable or doubtful hearing
(( ))	additional observation
T:	at the beginning of a stretch of talk, identifies the speaker; T is for teacher, G for girl, B for boy, Ss for whole class.
< >	slow speech
> <	fast speech
->	a speaking turn of analytical focus

Appendix C: Grammatical gloss

COMP	directional or resultative complement of verb
CONJ	conjunction
COP	copula
DUR	durative aspect marker
EMP	emphatic marker
LOC	locative marker
MSR	measure
NEG	negative marker
PERT	perfective aspect marker
POS	possessive
PRT	sentence, vocative or nominal subordinative particle
PTP	pre-transitive preposition
Q	question marker

Chapter 9

Language Socialization and Dys-socialization in a South Indian College

DWIGHT ATKINSON

For Pierre Bourdieu (1986), *cultural capital* is a form of historically accumulated social advantage, as reflected or embodied in such objectified social facts as prestige accents, educational ability and qualifications, skill in competitive examinations, knowledge of high art and culture, and, most simply if inexactly, "merit" and "cultivation." Although strictly speaking non-economic, cultural capital derives its value from its scarcity, and from its potential if indirect convertibility into economic power. Like other forms of capital, it tends to be disproportionately concentrated in the hands of a relative minority, and to favor its own reproduction and further accumulation by that minority. And, crucially for Bourdieu, cultural capital is largely reproduced and accumulated through its implicit but early-initiated transmission across generations.

At a different level of specificity – but by no means dissimilarly – a major focus of language socialization research (e.g. Heath, 1983; Hymes, 1972; Schieffelin & Ochs, 1986b) has been on how varying patterns of primary language socialization affect the later academic achievement of children from different social groups. Heath (1982b, 1983), for example, demonstrated that the early exposure of US middle class city-dwelling children to (among other things) question-rich interactions with caregivers, the breaking down of complex behaviors into learnable component parts, and particular approaches to recounting past events contributed substantially to their higher levels of primary school success. At the same time, Heath found that children from two social groups that did not emphasize such behaviors (urban working class African-Americans and rural working class Anglo-Americans) were seriously disadvantaged in their later schooling. Research by other linguists and anthropologists (e.g. Cochran-Smith, 1984; Gee, 1996; Michaels, 1981, 1986; Philips, 1983; Scollon & Scollon, 1981) has further established the finding that high levels of continuity between early home and school language use are closely related to subsequent academic achievement.

In this chapter, I examine an additional but quite different context in which language socialization appears to affect academic success – the learning and use of English in a formerly elite English-medium college in South India. Like other long-established tertiary institutions in India (e.g. Atkinson, 1999b), over the past two decades the college has experienced a substantial change in the social backgrounds of its students, and concomitantly in their sociolinguistic attributes and dispositions. This case differs markedly from those in the language socialization literature cited above in that:

(1)   the language being socialized – English – is a second/additional language for almost all those involved;
(2)   the type of language socialization at issue is therefore of a later, non-primary nature; and
(3)   an opposing process of language *dys-socialization* also appears to be taking place – in other words, some students appear to be developing and having reinforced social identities that militate *against* the acquisition of English.

However, these differences should not divert attention from a crucial similarity between this case and the others cited so far – that cultural capital is actively being (re)produced and accumulated through language socialization in each of these contexts, and, by the same token, denied where such socialization is not occurring.

Conceptual Background: Language Socialization, Power, and Identity

As already indicated, a concern with differential access to social goods – based, at least indirectly, on the notion of *power* – has always played a role in language socialization research. In what can be regarded as one of its originating statements, for example, Hymes (1972) called for investigation into the linguistic realities and sociolinguistic values that disadvantage minority children in US schools. At the same time, however, the concept of power as related specifically to language ability and use has received most of its theoretical development: (1) in the years since language socialization was first conceptualized and developed; and (2) in areas of research for the most part only indirectly connected to it (e.g. Bourdieu, 1991; Fairclough, 1989; but see Gee, 1996). For these reasons, it is probably fair to say that the two areas of language research have yet to settle into an entirely comfortable relationship (see Atkinson, 1999a; de Castell & Walker, 1991).

One concept with potential for lessening this gap may be that of the language learner/user's social *identity* (e.g. Norton & Toohey, 2002; Peirce, 1995). Norton (1997: 417) defines identity in terms of the ways "people understand their relationship to the world, how that relationship is constructed across time and space, and how people understand their possibilities for the future." Power is central to this definition, since the relationships between speakers and hearers are "rarely equal." In the terms, once again, of Bourdieu (1977: 652, cited in Norton & Toohey, 2002), "[S]peech always owes a major part of its value to the value of the person who utters it," and people have differential "rights to speech" and "power to impose reception." As we shall see presently, this includes the ways and degrees to which different kinds of students integrate the notion of "English speaker" into their ever-developing identities, and how they are or are not permitted to do so by others.

Empirical Background: English in India, Higher Education in India

English in India[1]

In origin a wholly alien imposition, the English language plays a variety of complexly interwoven roles in modern Indian society. First, as an "associate national language" English is a major language of central government administration, the courts, interstate and international commerce, and in fact all "higher level jobs in both the public and private sectors" (Sood, 1995: 173). Also, since postcolonial India is a pastiche of ethnic groups and languages, English serves as an important "link language" (Schiffman, 1996) – a major medium of interethnic and inter-regional communication. Especially relevant in the present context, English is also the official medium of instruction in the majority of Indian colleges and universities (Jayaram, 1997), as well as in many primary and secondary schools. As with other Indian social institutions, this situation obviously reflects the British origins of the current educational set-up, but it also acknowledges the contemporary dominance of English in the promulgation of new knowledge – or, in Indian terms, as a "library language." Most importantly, however, from a social point of view, English acts as a crucial marker of the traditionally-educated versus the uneducated classes in India, with social power and prestige flowing disproportionately to those who speak it fluently and "correctly" (Agnihotri & Khanna, 1995).

While the foregoing describes the main roles of English in India generally, local factors also prevail in different parts of the country. In the southeastern-most state of Tamil Nadu, where the research project reported on here is in progress, a central government decision in the mid-1960s to make a North Indian Indo-Aryan language, Hindi, the pre-eminent national language of India culminated in anti-Hindi riots in which a number of people died. It was principally for this reason that English was retained as an associate national language – as preferable in government and other institutions to the more immediately objectionable Hindi. Even today relatively few in South India know Hindi, and its official national language status remains a contentious issue in the region. As a result, where Hindi assumes the role of *de facto* second language for most Indians who don't speak it as a mother tongue, South Indians typically prefer English.[2]

Higher education in India

As a direct result of colonialism, the history and current state of higher education in India are intimately bound up with the notion of English education. Although indigenous institutions of advanced learning certainly predated the colonial period, by the mid-nineteenth century, India's imperial rulers were busy advancing a policy of English university education for a small Indian elite, whose role it was to help them to govern the masses (e.g. Basu, 1989; Kachru, 1994). It was increasingly believed, as well, that an English education based on the great literary works of Britain would play a pivotal "trickle-down" role in freeing the native population from the shackles of Hindu myth, ritual, casteism, and superstition, replacing them with more useful, rational, and moral – basically Christian – knowledge and religion (Vishwanathan, 1989).

While the religious purpose of English education in India may have waned from the mid-nineteenth century onward (Vishwanathan, 1989), most of its other features held true. These included:

(1)   a strong emphasis on memorization and examinations;
(2)   the inculcation of abstract, "liberal" (typically literary) knowledge;
(3)   devotion to educating a tiny elite; and
(4)   primary emphasis on the colonizer's language as medium of instruction.

Yet while the middle two of these attributes have undergone substantial change in the late twentieth century, the first and last, though widely debated, have not (Kachru, 1994). The current situation is discussed in the following paragraphs.

In repudiation of its formerly elitist aims, Indian higher education has undergone a mind-boggling and largely haphazard expansion in recent history, such that the total number of students grew from 174,000 in 1950 to 4,611,000 in 1990, and continues to grow apace (Jayaram, 1997). In one sense, this expansion of opportunity undoubtedly represents a marked improvement. Driven substantially by perhaps the world's most aggressive affirmative action policies, it has led to a situation in which percentages of college students from traditionally uneducated sections of Indian society, such as the Scheduled Castes (i.e. the former "untouchables," now commonly called *Dalits*), are beginning to approach their proportional representation in the population at large (Jayaram, 1997). This fact, however, masks continued dramatic variation in the nature and quality of higher education, as well as resulting employment outcomes (Jayaram, 1993).

In terms of its earlier "liberal," literary focus, Indian higher education has in recent years developed engineering and professional education as its most attractive options, although competition to enter well-reputed programs in these fields remains intense. Current Indian contributions to the computer and Internet revolution suggest that this trend will also continue in the future, most clearly as regards engineering and business. In the present educational climate, the liberal arts and sciences therefore represent significantly less attractive choices for many students, with arts bringing up the rear.

Despite its modest successes, contemporary Indian higher education is often portrayed by its observers as in a state of crisis, based substantially on the following factors (see Jayaram, 1997; Naik, 1982):

(1) continued reliance on a dysfunctional colonial system of education, to the degree that abstract and irrelevant knowledge is still being inculcated, with resulting low student motivation;
(2) the closely related problem of a memorization- and exam-based curriculum;
(3) the overproduction and subsequent unemployment of educated individuals[3];
(4) administrative inefficiency and corruption; and
(5) the role of a non-indigenous language (English) as the predominant medium of instruction.

English Language Socialization and Dys-socialization in an Indian College Context

The college

Located near a large metropolitan area in Tamil Nadu, All Souls College (ASC, a pseudonym) was originally established as a comprehensive school by British missionaries in the mid-1800s. Specializing in English education, it developed into a full-fledged college in the second half of the century. While the gradual process of faculty indigenization began in the late 1800s, the British missionaries remained in charge of the college into the early 1960s. Since its founding, the college has held a distinguished place in Indian society as one of its earliest and historically most elite institutions of higher (Western) education, and several of India's leading figures have been educated there.

Recent changes in ASC's student population[4]

There have been fundamental changes in the nature of ASC's student body in recent years. Up until about 20 years ago, the college was overwhelmingly attended by students from the upper rungs of Indian society – students who had English as part of their cultural capital. For the small number who did not, total immersion in the English-speaking environment of ASC (until that time a predominantly residential college with a residential hall system based on British models) provided a rich and by all accounts effective environment in which to acquire the language. Over the past two decades, however, heightened social consciousness, strong governmental affirmative action policies aimed at equalizing educational opportunity, a much-expanded range of institutions for higher education seekers to select from, and the lessening popularity of the liberal arts and sciences have brought about major changes in the student body. For example, approximately 33% of the 2,653 students enrolled in 1999–2000 had graduated from or done most of their schooling in Tamil-medium secondary schools, and 75% of students now commute locally from off-campus, while the remaining 25% dwell on-campus in one of four residential halls. Currently, although English continues to be the official and primary medium of instruction, the language most commonly used among ASC students themselves is Tamil.

Student groups on campus

On campus, students can be identified as falling into various groups, although such identification is not always obvious or straightforward. As alluded to above, one way of categorizing students is according to whether they reside on-campus or off-campus – the terms "hall residents" and "day scholars" are frequently used by students and faculty to mark the distinction. But this apparently mundane difference carries social significance, in that it correlates more or less closely with differences in socioeconomic status, family educational history, caste/community affiliation, and knowledge of English.

More specifically, hall residents tend to come from more affluent backgrounds, to have had English-medium schooling (especially in "public," "matriculation," or "convent" schools), and to have parents who are also college-educated. Day scholars, on the other hand, tend to come from two different kinds of social backgrounds:

(1) one substantially shared with the majority of hall residents, except that these day scholars tend to hail from the nearby metropolitan area; and
(2) one substantially different from that of most hall residents, in that these students tend to be poorer, to hail from the local towns and villages surrounding ASC, to have had most or all of their schooling in Tamil, and to be first-generation college-goers.

Much of this latter group comes from low-caste backgrounds – from either scheduled or "backward" castes, both of which are currently supported by preferential admission policies and government scholarships. In what follows, I refer to the hall residents and primarily city-dwelling day scholars as "traditional (ASC) students," and the primarily local day scholars as "non-traditional (ASC) students."[5]

Although it was often difficult from my perspective to identify students from these two groups – at least without hearing them use English (for which see below) – traditional students and faculty members told me that differences were often clearly perceptible. Besides using skin color as a rough guide, they mentioned different clothing styles, relations between the sexes, choice of major subject, and tastes in popular culture (especially music and films) as identifying factors. All of these differences were in the direction of more "Westernized" behavior for the traditional students, and more local culture-based behavior for the non-traditional students. Differences in the area of popular culture were especially salient – most of the traditional students I knew strongly favored Western (typically American) movies and music, and I heard far more Western pop music than other varieties in my two-month stay in one of the men's residence halls. In contrast, non-traditional students were substantially more interested in Indian (especially Tamil) cinema and music.

The clearest marker of difference between traditional and non-traditional students, however, concerned their use and command of English. Traditional students tended to speak English comfortably and "correctly," while non-traditional students did not; in fact, some did not speak it at all. Although I did not seek to analyze it in a strict way, the English spoken by traditional students also tended to be linguistically more influenced by "Western" cosmopolitan models: it seemed to be significantly less indigenized and significantly more comprehensible (at least initially) to my American ear (see Kachru, 1994, for the various features and levels of intelligibility of different varieties of Indian English).

Traditional ASC students tended to regard the dilution of the college's elite status – and therefore some part of their own socioeducational status – as due largely to the democratizing of the student population. As recorded in my fieldnotes, for example, one traditional student told me that current and former non-traditional students, whom he simply equated at this point with day scholars:

> weren't really ASC students, and he wasn't happy they were going around saying they were ASC graduates – that they've really changed the complexion of the college. Guys from off-campus "were not noblemen" – you could say that only about the [hall] residents. If an [alumnus] or someone who knew about colleges around here met a recent ASC graduate and asked them which hall they were in ... and the student said he was from off-campus, then they might think you're not a real ASCian. (FN2: 17)

Alluded to in this student's comments was an oft-mentioned and important concept in the identity of at least *some* ASC students – "Noblemen of ASC." By all accounts this was the public label given to ASC students when it was an elite (and more dominantly male) institution – as here, hall residents frequently mentioned it when comparing themselves to their non-traditional counterparts.[6]

Likewise, ASC alumni also indicated a primarily negative view of changes in the student population. In conversations with older alumni – some of whom were visiting the campus again after many years – they invariably remarked on the lower quality of the institution, often focusing on the degraded state of students' English language skills. One current hall resident also reported to me that he had once been asked by an older alumni, "What are all these black faces?" in reference to the said-to-be darker complexions of the non-traditional students.

As might be imagined, non-traditional students saw their presence at ASC in rather different terms than traditional students did. While some mentioned the strong policies and support of the (especially state) government as the main reason that people like themselves were now attending ASC, others saw the opening up of the college to different kinds of students as a continuation of a tradition of tolerance and anti-casteism – part of the Christian message in India since colonial times. One non-traditional (and non-Christian) student even wrote and produced a school-wide drama to this effect, enacting scenes from the college's early history in which its British founders took strong stands against exclusivity and caste discrimination.

At least some non-traditional students displayed awareness of the widely-held opinion that the quality of education at the college had declined sharply as a result of their inclusion in the student body. According to one such student:

> There's opinion like this, no? After the local people entered in the college, the shape of the college, the standard of the college have been decreased or something like that – that sort of opinion. And I have also heard that sort of opinion – even my friend have been uttering. In another sense, we can feel that noblemens [*sic*] out of ASC has decreased.[7] (SI8: 6)

More generally, however, non-traditional students chose to look at the changes in more positive terms, i.e. the wider social and economic representation of students who now attended. Most did not mention the idea of falling standards.

Significantly, non-traditional students sometimes expressed their own special take on the notion of "Noblemen of ASC," as seen briefly in the previous interview excerpt. The same student also gave a detailed description of the attributes of the ideal ASC nobleman, including fluent and correct English, the ability to "dress right – suit, coat, and tie," a somewhat elevated social and economic background, and a Christian-oriented concern to "serve people ... making them culturally good." At the same time, he appraised the traditional ASC students' *actual* – as opposed to ideal – behavior in rather damning (if not completely consistent) terms:

> But after attending this college, I could see the behavior of people [i.e. traditional students] over here [is] much worser than the ordinary people – ordinary in the sense [of] the simple people living around. There's not much change between the behavior – the personal behavior between the people and the hall students ... These people here are also doing the same thing, no? But then soon they'll tell 'em we're noblemen of ASC and something like that. And when I entered into this college, that's one thing I could find – I couldn't find any difference between the people living here (within) ASC [who] was calling themselves nobleman [*sic*], and people who are living outside the campus. (SI8: 4)

In regard to the bad behavior mentioned here, this student referred particularly to both traditional students and "ordinary people" consuming alcohol – not a widely accepted social practice across much of South Indian society.

Faculty attitudes toward the changing student population and their English language abilities

Faculty members, virtually all of whom were ASC graduates as well (mostly from the college's elite era), also saw it as a greatly changed place in the last two decades. Commonly noted in this regard were the substantially less elevated social backgrounds of many of the students and, correlatively, the falling standard of students' English language skills. As characterized by one professor:

> See a long time ago, along these corridors and on campus, students hardly ever used to speak in the regional language.... . But of late that seems to be the norm rather than English. So we realize, yeah, a change has taken place these past 10 or 15 years, and there was more of an elitist crowd in this college – this was one of the elitist colleges in India. And so the composition of students has changed

down the years. And I've been around for the past 25 years, so I know what's happening here. Students I think now come more from a rural background – no longer the city crowd coming from public schools and so on. And many of them now come from a Tamil-medium background. Whether it is from standard 1 to 12 they have only studied everything in Tamil, and only one paper [i.e. course] as English. So those students are obviously going to find it a problem when everything is taught in English. So I think that is what we're increasingly facing these days. (FI2: 3)

Other changes commonly noted by faculty members were that the curriculum had become substantially more exam-oriented, that students seemed less motivated, and that the syllabus for compulsory English language classes, although still literature-based, had been made considerably less challenging.[8] Also mentioned was the fact that candidates for admission these days found ASC a much less desirable choice than previously – that they now "come in [to the college] because they have very few options left" (FI6: 1).

Regarding these changes in the student population, the issue of their effects on student motivation, in particular, was highlighted. Professors viewed the current crop of students as basically unmotivated to learn at the college level – as interested largely or only in obtaining a degree. This was mentioned especially in connection with the learning of English, and was in a general way corroborated in the course of extensive observations of compulsory English language classes, at least for male students from non-traditional backgrounds. These students rarely brought their textbooks to class (if they had them at all), which made it impossible for them to follow what was going on in the (highly text-based) classroom. They were also frequently observed sleeping, chatting, or completing unrelated written assignments in the course of their compulsory English classes – almost invariably they sat at the back of classrooms, while female students sat at the front (see Shamim, 1996) and seemed generally more attentive.

Changes in the student body were rarely portrayed by faculty members in a positive light, although many seemed resigned to the current state of affairs. Some saw the lack of motivation as, in part, a response to the students not getting into institutions or majors that they had set their sights on. A second reason given was that students were too busy enjoying the nonacademic aspects of college life, especially after having to study hard in high school under a highly competitive college entrance system.

As regards, specifically, changing abilities in and motivations to study English, several professors indicated that students increasingly did not see English as important in their lives and future careers. This was partly because those from the "reserved" categories (i.e. caste/religious groups receiving preferential treatment under government affirmative action policies) did not need English proficiency in order to obtain government jobs upon graduating. Further, the state government's strong advocacy of the use of Tamil in government institutions (see also note 2) was viewed as a demotivating factor. Three additional factors mentioned were that:

(1)   grades from compulsory English classes were not counted in the final determination of students' overall collegiate performance;
(2)   faculty teaching compulsory English classes were themselves merely "going through the motions" (FI2: 5), given the large class sizes, low motivation, and mixed abilities of their students; and
(3)   non-traditional students often had severe "inferiority complexes" *vis-à-vis* others in regard to English that effectively prevented them from acquiring it. This last factor is explored in more detail in the following section.

"Inferiority complexes" and resistance of non-traditional ASC students

Nearly all faculty members, and many students, mentioned that non-traditional students often exhibited strong feelings of inferiority *vis-à-vis* traditional students. This factor was said to broadly influence the former's college experience, and especially their ability to acquire English. According to one professor:

> Generally, affluence and English go together [in India], so when a student comes from a very poor background, he has a wrong notion that only those who are affluent, only those who are rich are capable of acquiring English: "Whatever I try, whatever I struggle, I don't think I'll ever succeed in acquiring English," because English seems to be a kind of exclusive endowment for the rich and affluent... . Certain students coming from certain castes feel that English is not their privilege. They always shrink – they do not open up at all. Their confidence level is very low, they'll never participate, they don't have an opinion of their own. That self-identity is alien to them – an opinion of their own they never try to gain. Then they look at somebody who gets up and then articulates so freely and so confidently – they further shrink. They get into a shell. (FI8: 7) [9]

Explanations by faculty members for what they commonly called an "inferiority complex" included non-traditional students' earlier lack of exposure to English in the home and school, their fear of revealing themselves as non-English speakers in the classroom, and – as seen in the above excerpt – their generally low social and economic status and the internalized feelings of inadequacy that accompany it. This was seen to be especially true for students from stigmatized social groups, such as Dalits:

> The complex is mainly because of the social background that they come out of, specially the Dalit students. They've developed a kind of complex which is always working within them, all the time telling them you're a Dalit, you can't master English, you can't come up in life. So they unconsciously develop a kind of complex – inferiority complex. As a result of which they feel themselves always that they can't do this or can't do that. Especially with regard to English – they always tell themselves that they can't learn English. (FI7: 4)

Occasionally, faculty members related this attitude to its seeming formal opposite – the strongly held notion in Indian society that being an English speaker (and most powerfully and desirably by far a speaker of "correct" English) is an index of intellectual and perhaps moral superiority:

> [W]e tend to feel that it is elitist [sic] to speak English, and a person who makes a mistake in English is necessarily inferior – I think that's the basic problem here. So we don't approach [the teaching of English] from the perspective of the person who needs to know English and I think that's a terrible thing. We classify students as intelligent or unintelligent according to their knowledge of the language, which I think is absolutely crazy. And it's bad enough that the British did it when they were here – it's terrible we should continue to do the same thing. (FI3: 7)

In fact, faculty members frequently referred to students with a command of English as "intelligent," "bright," or "good" – and, occasionally, to those without as "bad" – students. Even professors who did so, however, seemed to have a kind of "double vision" (see Bhabha, 1994) regarding the connection between superior status and English, since there was widespread agreement that the linkage was a direct result of the colonial experience – a "colonial hangover" in the words of several.

The non-traditional students themselves strongly associated this "inferiority complex" with their lack of proficiency in English. As recorded in fieldnotes, one such student told me "that students [from his background] felt hopeless and scared about learning English, especially when others spoke it so well" (FN2: 12). Another amplified on this theme in an interview:

> There is some sort of low feeling, shyness, inferiority complex in our minds. We fear to speak in English with other departments' students – it is hard to get to know one another. We make friends only in the Tamil Department. It is completely impossible to make friends with the other students. There again comes the question of language and communication – the only possible word with which we can go about is "Excuse me." (SI6: 16, translated from Tamil)

This student's major department, Tamil Literature, was said by several of its other majors to be particularly looked down upon. A second student from this department, who was being interviewed together with the first, immediately followed the previous comments by saying:

> ASC is not a Tamil [-medium?] institution. The only way we can learn English is during the General [i.e. compulsory] English class. Tamil Literature itself has been looked down upon – not only the department but also the students. So our contacts with other departments are really poor. (SI6: 16, translated from Tamil)

However, even non-traditional students who had managed to acquire a fair amount of English, and who were majoring in higher-status subjects, expressed feelings of inferiority. Thus, a recent graduate of a highly regarded department whose father was a manual worker on campus stated:

Student: But they [i.e. non-traditional students] wouldn't participate in other [extra-curricular] programs which used English. I never – even myself, yeah myself. One of the reasons [was that] I didn't interested in that. One more thing – just sort of feeling very somewhat inferior competence there. Go in there and simply blank (speaking) without knowing.

Dwight: So you're suggesting that the inferiority complex is widely shared among, widely felt among students who don't feel comfortable in English?

Student: Yeah that's there. Even myself, yeah. Even now I'm not comfortable with moving [with] people with other departments and this sort of all cultural, and (that's one more thing) that is people simply shouting, dancing, singing – another thing. (SI8: 3)

At the same time, non-traditional students also expressed resistance to being made to feel inferior. Immediately continuing the foregoing interview excerpt, for instance, I asked (in reference to the "shouting, dancing, singing" statement):

Dwight: You don't like that? Or that seems odd? Tell me your – respond to that.

Student: Yeah that sort of, see, cultural domination. See your people always would – even [residence] halls they would put [on] some sort of pop songs and every evening they will except test days, right? Every day they will put [on] that pop songs only in English, no Tamil singing... . That is the name of ASC: English (come from ASC), and English something the culture of the western culture the same. (SI8: 3)

Several other students also expressed resistance to outside domination – in some cases citing the importance of protecting their Tamil language and identity. Thus, one second-year Tamil Literature student stated:

I'm not interested in English the first year – I want to talk only in Tamil. Because we have language problem in our country, Tamil Nadu, so I don't like to speak English ... .We want to save our language, Tamil, so I hate the other language ... I'm not the enemy for English, not only English – Hindi, Telugu, Malayalam in my country. I want to save my language. (SI7: 2)

Faculty members likewise saw relatively strong resistance to English and associated "traditional" practices in the behavior of non-traditional students. One termed it a "repulsion ... like a prejudice" (FI6: 8), which he described in terms of how non-traditional students typically react when he enters their compulsory English classroom on the first day of classes: "See the moment I walk in, I have a barrier already built. I'm an ENGLISH teacher, with a proficiency in English. That is something that they not just fear, but they are repulsed from." (FI6: 2)

This same professor indicated that he regarded at least the male non-traditional students in his compulsory English classes as so overwhelmed by these feelings that their presence in the classroom was due merely to strict attendance requirements: "I'm not talking about the guys – the guys are useless. Sorry for that. I mean, they all come in because they need to be there" (FI6: 2). Though perhaps extreme, such comments suggest that the low-level non-conforming behavior I repeatedly observed among non-traditional male students in compulsory English classes can also be seen as strategies of resistance, no matter how inchoate or unconscious (Canagarajah, 1993; Willis, 1977).

English Language Socialization and English Language Teaching at ASC

Traditional studies of language socialization tend to closely follow children in intensive interactions with caregivers, siblings, and peers – most typically in or around the home environment (e.g. Schieffelin & Ochs, 1986a). Somewhat less usually, socialization research (e.g. Heath, 1982b; Michaels, 1981, 1986) has followed children into the primary school classroom, examining how ways in which they learn (or don't learn) in that setting relate to their home-based socialization.

Studies of later school/non-primary language socialization, on the other hand, must often take different approaches, and will often feature different kinds of data. If the current study had focused on the (no doubt often early-initiated) English language socialization of *traditional* ASC students, it might have been able to take a closer, more traditional approach. Even without doing so, however, there exist accounts of what early socialization to English for such students may be like. Canagarajah (2001: 1–2), for example, evocatively describes his early experience with English in a Sri Lankan Tamil context that cannot be so different from that of many traditional students at ASC:

> While we were seated under the mango trees outside our house on a warm breezy afternoon in Jaffna chatting in Tamil, my dad suddenly whispers something in English to my mother and they both sneak into the room inside, letting me play with the maid. They would emerge a couple of hours later seeming tired and exhausted, leaving me curious as to what they had uttered in English earlier. There are other occasions when we'll be talking about some wayward relatives, when my parents would switch to English to discuss some unpleasant episodes that shouldn't be understood by a four year-old like me. Or, while planning my upcoming birthday party, they would quickly switch to English to talk about a gift or invitee they like to keep hidden from me. These early experiences would leave a lasting impression on me of English as a language of secrecy, power, and mystery; a language owned by others, not belonging to me... . Many weeks and months later I would continue to put one and one together, understand with the help of context, guess the meaning, til I gradually began to break the code. Thus, even before I started attending school, I grew into some rudimentary levels of proficiency in English... . It was exhilarating to join the exclusive club of bilinguals. (Canagarajah, 2001)

Such accounts can be contrasted with the widely reported scenario for non-traditional students at colleges like ASC – no appreciable use of English in the family, poor or minimal instruction in English as a foreign language at the secondary level, and the gradual build-up of complexes and "repulsions" as participants in a postcolonial education system (and a society at large as well) where one is still substantially defined by one's expertise in the ex-colonial language.[10]

In situations like these, a heavy burden falls on the English language teacher and the English language curriculum, especially at the tertiary level in colleges such as ASC – the only place where adequate resources have even a chance of being allocated to the formidable task at hand. Many of the faculty members I met at ASC lamented that it was an *impossible* burden – that it was "too little too late" at the college level to do much about the English language skills of these students. Others, however, told of students who had entered the college with minimal English skills, only to leave – by dint of hard work – as advanced, sophisticated speakers of English.

Granted, stories of low-status individuals transcending their early socialization experiences through personal effort often have the ideological function of legitimizing the current social structure – of placing the onus of failure on the deficient (often "lazy") students as representatives of their social groups. If one takes the view that modern education in India and elsewhere has the primary purpose of reproducing a highly inequitable social structure (e.g. Bourdieu, 1982b; Scrase, 1993), then such a conclusion would be unsurprising. But I prefer for present purposes to distinguish what is *likely* from what is *possible* in educational settings – to look up at the horizon, not down at our feet. What therefore can be done to aid such students in finding a way out of the dilemma they find themselves in – the dilemma of being caught in an educational system that increasingly offers them access without allowing them attainment, at least as regards a primary marker of the "educated" person in India, English?

Obviously, there is no simple solution. Some glimmers of hope, however, do exist, and they should be the starting point. First, English language teaching at ASC has not always proceeded along the lines it does today – a primarily literature-based syllabus and curriculum, taught in a large-class, lecture format. In the recent past there in fact existed a "streaming" approach to English language teaching whereby students with differing proficiencies were placed in different classes and taught according to different syllabi (see also Atkinson, 1999b). Within the faculty there is general assent that this approach had modest success, even if the potential it held for a new kind of discrimination (giving the same academic credit for disparate levels of academic attainment) brought about its demise in its original form.

A second suggestive line of practical inquiry concerns the recent emphasis in educational research on "communities of practice" (Lave & Wenger, 1991; Wenger, 1998), whereby all learning is seen as meaningful participation in social activity, often under the guidance of a more experienced social member. Such courses as "English for Journalism"(already seen at ASC as future alternatives to the literature-based curriculum) would seem to fit naturally in this framework, as would also forms of peer-based and non-classroom-based experiential learning (e.g. Atkinson, 1997). This approach seeks to capitalize on the idea that learning is a natural and ongoing condition – that progressive adaptation to one's (ever-changing) local environment is the ultimate strategy of human survival, and, therefore, that learning as social activity *is what defines human beings as human beings.* In terms of language socialization theory, this approach buttresses the idea that learning/ socialization does not stop at some determinate endpoint, but rather continues across the lifespan, aiding as it does the fitness of the organism in the sociocognitive world.

Clearly, the availability and non-availability of English has a powerful influence on the present (and probably future) identities of non-traditional students at places such as ASC. Efforts to make this language accessible to a greater range of individuals-in-society (and a fortiori in a world where this language is in some senses taking on even greater significance) will have a profound effect on the future shape of human societies in general. If equality is to be anything other than an ideal concept, efforts must be made to circumvent the current stranglehold that some social groups have on social resources or cultural capital such as English – at base to make ecologically effective socialization a *common* resource and a *common* good.

Notes

1. It must be admitted that the account of the role of English in present-day India that I give here is basically the "received" version. Tripathi (1992: 7) presents an alternative view, which can be read alongside this one or in its place.
2. In a recent, massive "state-of-the-nation" poll conducted by ORG-MARG pollsters for the weekly news magazine *India Today* (1997), 30% of respondents from the "South" reported understanding Hindi, as compared with 94% nationally. Interestingly, this is approximately the same proportion of Southerners opting for Hindi (31%) in response to the question, "Do you think there should be one language across the nation?" The percentage of Indians who reported understanding English nationally was also 31% (no regional breakdown was given for this last statistic). These statistics, it should be noted, are substantially higher than those more commonly cited in the literature on the percentages of Indians who know English and Hindi. It would be remiss not to mention here strong sentiments and political actions in Tamil Nadu toward replacing English (at least in its official functions) with Tamil. Tamil has for several years been the main language of government in the state, and in 1999 the State Government decreed Tamil to be the sole legal medium of instruction in primary and secondary education, to be phased in over a period of five years. There continues to be widespread debate and disagreement over this declaration, which is currently tied up in the courts.
3. Unemployment among college-educated individuals in India in 1985 was found by Jayaram (1993) to be at or very near the 22% level across Arts, Science, and Commerce graduates. Among other social problems, involvement in armed revolutionary groups attempting to overthrow the government (such as the People's War Group and the Tamil Nadu Liberation Army) is sometimes attributed in the media to the overproduction of educated youths (e.g. *New Indian Express-Chennai*, 2000a; 2000b).
4. The following description should be considered a progress report, since the investigation from which it emanates is ongoing. It is based on data collected during two periods of residence on the ASC campus: August–December 1999 and August–December 2000. Data collected during this period include 74 pages of fieldnotes; 36 interviews with students, faculty, and others connected to the college; 75 hours of classroom observations; and various other kinds of data. This investigation extends earlier work carried out in another part of India (Atkinson, 1999b) and supported by the Spencer Foundation. For 1999–2000

the current project was supported by a postdoctoral fellowship from the National Academy of Education (US).

5. It is freely acknowledged that this distinction is rather rough, notional, and liable to exception. Christian students, for example, were one large group that often seemed to cross-cut these categories, in that many of them came from college-educated families and were English-speaking, but may have had low-caste origins and possibly roots in the local community. Despite such exceptions, however, the distinction made here between traditional and non-traditional ASC students was widely accepted and actively used by students and faculty members alike.

6. The use of male personal pronouns and male gender-marked language when talking about ASC students was a common phenomenon among the students and faculty I encountered. I do not yet know if this is a local phenomenon (related to the past history of ASC as an exclusively male college, and its current history as a majority-male institution) or whether masculine forms in gender-sensitive reference may be the unmarked choice in Indian English.

7. The verbatim excerpts of interview data featured in this paper are transcribed in regular prose with the exception of the following special transcription conventions:
    • continuous capital letters = emphatic stress on the word or phrase capitalized
    • enclosing parentheses = transcriber doubt (i.e. words that couldn't be heard clearly)
    The data excerpts are identified using the following abbreviations: FI = Faculty Interview; SI = Student Interview; FN = Fieldnotes; CO = Classroom Observations; and WA = Written Artifacts. The number immediately following one of these abbreviations (e.g. CO4: 3) gives the code number of the interview/fieldnotes/observation, while the number to the right of the following colon indicates the page number of the data excerpt in the text/transcript cited. It should also be mentioned here that interview excerpts have been edited for the sake of presentation for language features that would have made them more difficult to read and understand – i.e. dysfluencies, hesitations, listener feedback, and pauses. Bracketed words have also occasionally been added for the same purpose.

8. All undergraduate students are required to take four semesters of English language classes.

9. Bourdieu (1984: 414–415) comments on freely expressed personal opinion as a form of socialized educational endowment, i.e. cultural capital.

10. In both the current study and earlier work done in another part of India (Atkinson, 1999b), for example, non-traditional college students consistently reported no appreciable exposure to English in home or school environments beyond English language classes, which they generally saw as grossly inadequate and poorly taught. These findings are widely supported by the existing literature on English teaching in India (e.g. Agnihotri & Khanna, 1995).

Part 3
Language Socialization in Communities and Peer Groups

Chapter 10

Language Socialization and Second Language Acquisition in a Multilingual Arctic Quebec Community

DONNA PATRICK

Arctic Quebec, the vast region in the northern part of Canada's largest province, is inhabited by about 8000 Inuit and 500 non-Native residents, who refer to this region as Nunavik.[1] Here, 98.6% of Inuit continue to use their language, Inuktitut, into adulthood, giving Nunavik one of the highest indigenous language retention rates in North America. At the same time, Inuktitut/English bilingualism, and to a lesser extent Inuktitut/French bilingualism, is on the rise, given the perceived importance of these languages in the northern political economy. Despite the relatively high rate of bilingualism, however, language socialization and second language acquisition are not simple matters for Inuktitut-, French- and English-speakers in this region.

In this chapter I explore second (and third) language acquisition among adolescents and adults in Great Whale River,[2] my name for a multilingual community where two indigenous languages, Cree and Inuktitut, are spoken alongside French and English. I focus on the attitudes of community members toward language learning, and relate these attitudes to my own observations of language use in intercultural settings in this community. More specifically, I focus on how attitudes toward the learning of French and Inuktitut as third languages operate in conjunction with patterns of language choice in community settings to place constraints on language learning. That is, language attitudes, which include conceptions of linguistic complexity and difficulty and the amount of time required for third language acquisition, operate alongside patterns of language use to restrict language learning, even though many people here consider multilingualism to be desirable.

Previous research on language socialization in Nunavik has focused on the cultural aspects of language use and language acquisition in the home and in the school (Crago, 1992; Crago *et al.*, 1997). Studies of Inuktitut socialization in monolingual Inuit homes reveal specific patterns of language use between caregivers and children, including the exclusion of young children from adult conversations, the frequent use of imperatives, and the infrequent use of questions (specifically questions to which the caregiver already knows the answer, and which are quite common in non-Native middle class families). Although these traditional Inuit discourse patterns are now changing among younger Inuit mothers who are influenced by Western school-based discursive practices (see Crago *et al.*, 1993), the language socialization and behavior of Inuit children, and their interaction with adults, are markedly different from non-Native middle class norms. Many of the children's interactions in the home settings studied by Crago and her associates took place between siblings and peers, rather than with adults.

The cultural patterns of language use observed in Inuit homes have been compared with school-based discursive practices, where non-Native teachers favor teacher-centered classrooms in which children interact directly with the teacher and are publicly evaluated for their performances. Children must learn to initiate these performances, either by raising their hands or by being called upon to perform on demand (Crago & Allen, 1999: 252–253). Of course, the cultural mismatch in discursive styles poses pedagogical challenges for second-language teachers and pupils, who both need to be socialized into new ways of interacting.

Research has also addressed the issue of language socialization in bilingual Nunavik homes in which a non-Native (often a French/English bilingual) father is raising a family with an Inuk (usually Inuktitut/English bilingual) mother. The investigation among these families of attitudes and decisions related to language use in the home reveals various levels of English-language dominance in the home. Despite the relatively frequent use of English in these bilingual (and sometimes trilingual) homes, almost all the children acquire Inuktitut, which (we might assume) arises from their exposure to the language not only from their mothers, but elsewhere in the community – particularly among peers, and eventually at school.

While home and classroom language practices give us one part of the picture of second and third language acquisition, other community settings offer further areas for investigation. Interactional practices and language attitudes that arise in institutional, recreational, and work-related settings are important for our understanding of the complex processes of language socialization among adolescents and adults. While individual motivation and personalities may play a role in these processes, they may not be as salient as social factors in settings where language use has become politicized in the struggle for cultural identity and economic control. This analytical turn towards community practices, the role of language in constructing identity and indexing ethnicity, and the wider sociocultural, political, and economic values of particular languages for particular speakers, is crucial for understanding how children, adolescents, and adults acquire languages and are socialized into particular linguistic communities.

Seen from a broad historical perspective, second language learning and socialization in this community are influenced by imbalances in the political, economic, and social relations of speakers of Inuktitut and speakers of the dominant Euro-Canadian languages, French and English. The three languages have been associated with different forms of political control and different economic and cultural practices; and all three have come to hold different symbolic, cultural, economic, and political values and meanings for different speakers in the region.

At the micro-level of face-to-face interaction, everyday linguistic and cultural practices construct group boundaries and ethnolinguistic identities. Ethnic groups and social categories are formed through processes of exclusion, accommodation, and the regulation of group boundaries, which allow speakers access to valued linguistic resources in this multilingual region. As regards language learning, it is precisely such large-scale political economic processes, coupled with the processes of social group formation and identification, that have shaped language policy, linguistic interaction, and language learning in the community.

An examination of the ethnic make-up of the 1200 residents of Great Whale River reveals that about 100 of them are non-Native, and that half of the remaining 1100 residents are Inuit and the other half Cree. Among the Inuit, with whom this chapter will be most concerned, almost everyone born after 1950 speaks English as a second language, the result of the introduction of English schooling by the Federal Government in 1958. Almost all non-Native community members (the majority of whom have French as a first language) are bilingual in French and English; most members of this group have come here for work. Overall, Great Whale River is a heterogeneous community, composed of people with different backgrounds and interests. Nevertheless, these people form distinct and well-defined ethnic groups, which are linked through social networks in which language choice plays a key role in producing and reproducing intergroup boundaries.

In Nunavik, modernization, and the increased contact with Southern Canada and the high rate of bilingualism that are the result of this, have led some to worry about the state of the language and the potential influence of English on the structure and vitality of Inuktitut (Dorais, 1997; Taylor *et al.*, 1993). However, despite this social reality, historical and political circumstances, together with the rules that operate to construct social networks and group identities, have served to promote the use of both French and Inuktitut in certain community contexts.

Great Whale River is a unique community in Nunavik, in that four languages are used in everyday situations. It needs, then, to be understood as a particular locale, shaped by its own set of historical and ecological circumstances, and in this respect distinct from other Northern communities. In Great Whale River, almost everyone is bilingual or trilingual: that is, most Inuit speak English and/or French in addition to Inuktitut. A relatively high proportion of Inuit elders are fluent in Cree as well as Inuktitut; and the majority of Francophones (Québécois), Anglophones (English Canadians), and allophones (those whose first language is neither French nor

English) are bilingual in French and English. An understanding of this multilingualism – and in particular, the mechanisms and constraints involved in language learning in community contexts – is crucial for an understanding of language learning in this community. As we shall see, despite the desire of many non-Native residents to learn Inuktitut and of many Inuit to learn French, these forms of multilingualism are socio-linguistically constrained in workplace, home, and recreational settings.

The discussion that follows draws on interview and observational data gathered over a 14-month period of ethnographic fieldwork conducted in 1993–94. I shall be drawing on 22 interviews conducted during this time with Inuit and non-Inuit adults in either English or French, and on my own observations and linguistic inter-actions in the community.

The first part of the discussion concerns the historical, political, and economic importance of these three languages for community members. The second part concerns the importance of social networks and language use in the community, and will include examples of sociolinguistic constraints on language choice and thus on second- or third-language learning in the community.

Historical Overview: Politics and Language in Nunavik

In Nunavik, the competition between French, English, and Inuktitut in the symbolic, sociopolitical, and economic realms is best understood by examining the colonial history of the region (see Patrick 1994, 1998 for further discussion). The formation of the Hudson's Bay Company in 1670 and the subsequent establishment of trading posts and missionary settlements led to the introduction of English in the region, and to years of Inuit resistance throughout the eighteenth and early nine-teenth centuries. Eventually the Inuit hunting economy was coopted into the world capitalist system through the fur trade (Wolf, 1982). In the 1950s, the introduction of wage labor presented a new shift in the local political economy. The introduction of English-language schooling coincided with the Inuit adopting a sedentary way of life and the introduction of a cash economy, in which Inuit were often hired to construct and maintain the community infrastructure and military or other govern-ment buildings. Great Whale River was the site of an army base constructed in 1955 as part of the American-sponsored DEW Line (Distant Early Warning radar system), which spanned the Canadian Arctic. Thus, for more than three centuries, various linguistic and cultural practices and European material goods have been integral to Inuit society.

The 1960s saw the rise of Quebec interests in the region and of the role of French as a language of state, business, and administration. Subsequent economic inter-ests, in the form of hydroelectric development on Cree and Inuit territory, marked the beginning of Inuit political mobilization in the 1970s and eventually led in 1975 to the signing of a landmark land claims settlement, the James Bay and Northern Quebec Agreement (JBNQA). As a result of the JBNQA, Inuit regional government and economic organizations were formed, with the common goal of giving Inuit more control over their territory. The creation of Nunavik as a political entity has resulted in the current language policy and practices, which legitimize the region's three languages in education, government publications, and services.

In Arctic Quebec, each language group vying for power has sought a different way to legitimize its right to dominate the territory. English-language speakers tend to justify the role of English in the region in terms of its historical significance and its national and international role in communication – including communication with other aboriginal peoples. English is the language of globalization and of international markets, and holds a hegemonic cultural, political, and economic position, as well as being one of the official languages of the federal state. Inuit are Canadian citizens, and federal institutions continue to exist in Nunavik, where Inuit educated in English deal with federal government offices and such matters as taxation in English. The historical role of English and its current role nationally and internationally insure its dominance in the territory.

French is the dominant language of the Quebec state, and has become the dominant language of the provincial bureaucracy. Technically, Quebec has had the right to govern the territory since 1912, when the province's borders were extended to include the area known as Nouveau-Québec. But the real dominance of French in Great Whale River and in the region more generally began in the 1960s, with a shift from federal to provincial jurisdiction over such areas as education, health care, and policing. This, and the concomitant rise in the numbers of Québécois workers and the size of the local managerial class, made the competition between French and English in Great Whale River more salient. This competition was particularly visible in the school system – which, for a short period during the transfer of services, involved both federal and provincial government participation, leading to a duplication in services, and making control of the school system a key issue. Although French language instruction was not popular at first, Inuktitut language programs implemented by the Quebec-controlled school board were (see Patrick & Shearwood, 1999). The provincial takeover of the school system has thus had a great impact on the structure of education in Arctic Quebec.

Inuit claims to power and their lobbying for the use of Inuktitut as an official language within this Arctic territory stem from the fact that they have inhabited this region for centuries, and had not ceded it before signing the JBNQA. In accordance with the Agreement, a number of institutions and governing bodies accountable to the Inuit population of Nunavik have been established, and in these Inuktitut plays a key symbolic and practical role. Thus, Inuktitut has become not only a language used in schools and governing bodies, but also a necessary symbol in defining an institution as Inuit and in claiming political power for the population.

The existence of three language groups and of the claims of each to legitimacy and power in Nunavik has had consequences for institutional language use in Inuit communities. Schools use Inuktitut as the sole medium of instruction until grade 3, after which children enter either the French stream or the English stream and are taught Inuktitut as a subject. The school administration attempts to maintain a balance between the three languages at both local and regional administrative levels. Other key institutions such as the nursing station and the courthouse operate through translators to provide services in French, English, and Inuktitut. Most services in Great Whale River – including postal and telephone (including telephone directory) services, local government offices, and airline ticket sales services – are offered in all three languages, plus Cree. The only institution that has not really needed a strategy to cope with French is the Anglican Church, which for over a century has locally incorporated Inuktitut and Cree into its services and English structure.

Despite the competition and the historical imbalance of political and economic power associated with Inuktitut, English, and French, all are perceived as crucial to the Inuit goals of modernization, self-sufficiency, and autonomy within the Canadian nation-state. All three languages are also crucial in the construction of group identities. Social groups, including Inuit, French, and Anglo-Canadian, are fluid social categories that are constructed in part by language practices – between members of the same social or ethnic group or between members of different groups. The following section will draw on interview and ethnographic data to exemplify these points, and to elaborate on some of the constraints on language choice in the community that affect the acquisition of these languages by Inuit adults and youth.

Language Use in Great Whale River

Great Whale River has three distinct communities, formed through historical patterns of settlement and through the borders created by the JBNQA. More specifically, the land was divided into Inuit and Cree territories, with the non-Native settlement (housing some of the Anglophones and almost all of the Francophones) straddling both territories and separated from the respective Native communities by an old airstrip that was part of an army base built in the 1950s. These geographical divisions between ethnic groups play a role in language use inasmuch as members of each community share the same geographical space, and communicate frequently and easily with one another.

In sociolinguistic research, network analysis has often been used in urban contexts to examine the closeness of members of a particular group or the amount of interaction between people in working- or middle-class communities (Labov, 1972; Milroy, 1987). Networks between speakers can be weak or strong depending on who is interacting with whom. Thus a relationship between a store clerk and a customer would constitute a "weaker" link than one between friends, family members, or neighbors, who might exchange support, advice, and information. These latter, "stronger" types of networks operate as systems of exchange to form close-knit communities, where language use serves a strong solidarity function (Milroy & Wei, 1995: 138).

In Great Whale River, "social networks" are important in the analysis of language use, since strong social ties between speakers constrain language use in everyday, informal contexts (Gal, 1979; Gumperz, 1982; Milroy, 1987). As Milroy and Wei (1995: 139) observe, "close-knit social networks consisting mainly of strong ties seem to have a particular capacity to maintain and even enforce local conventions and norms – including linguistic norms." In other words, social interaction within close-knit networks constrains linguistic and social behavior and operates to favor the use of one language variety over another.

In close-knit social networks based on ethnicity, language to some extent defines the group and is an important element in constructing social identities and boundaries. The language used by those of the same ethnic group has an interactive role in producing and reproducing group cohesion and solidarity. In Great Whale River, when two people with the same first language meet, they will almost invariably speak in that language, even if they share a second (or third) language. That is, two Inuktitut speakers will speak Inuktitut and two Francophones will speak French, even if each also speaks English. This pattern of language use cuts across contexts, including settings and participants, and across network types, whether work-, friendship-, or family-related, and despite the historical dominance of English and its use in intercultural communication.

Since English is spoken to some degree by almost everyone in the community, it functions as a lingua franca between speakers of different languages. The wide distribution of English is, as noted earlier, a legacy of the English-language schools set up for Inuit and Cree by the Federal Government in 1958. It is also the second language of the educated Native elite, who have pursued their studies in Southern high schools, colleges, and universities, and among the Francophone managers and government employees, who need English for their work in the North. In Great Whale River, English is currently the language used in settings where people from all four language groups congregate, such as the gymnasium, where signs, schedules, and the like are written in English.

While English is the language used between speakers of different ethnic groups, French and Inuktitut are both widely spoken among Québécois and Inuit, respectively. However, because of the rather rigid patterns of language choice between group members, very little French is spoken outside of the non-Native sector and very little Inuktitut is used by non-Inuit in the community. This is the case despite the importance of French in various workplaces, including provincial government offices, the police station, and local construction sites, and also the desire of many Inuit to learn French and the desire of members of the non-Native community to learn Inuktitut. In the next section I investigate these attitudes towards language learning, and address the question why learning a third language can be difficult for Inuit and non-Inuit in Great Whale River.

Attitudes towards language learning

In Great Whale River, choices regarding which language to speak and which second language to learn are not random or insignificant, given the relations between ethnic groups and the history of language politics in Quebec and Canada

(Arnopoulos & Clift, 1984; Heller, 1999; Levine, 1989). While the desire to obtain (better-paying) work governs some language learning, an equally strong motivation is the symbolic role that language plays in forging friendships, leveling barriers between groups, and constructing social identities. Language practices thus constitute highly valued symbolic resources in an environment that is often politically charged. However, the wish to learn a second or third language, whether for material or symbolic reasons, is not the most important criterion in language learning. This can be seen from interviews with non-Native speakers of French and English who wish to learn Inuktitut, and with Inuit who wish to learn English and French; these interviews offer us a view of the social complexity of language learning in this northern community.

Learning English

In Great Whale River, fewer than 15% of the non-Native population speak English as their first language, yet English has the highest number of speakers in the community. Some speakers are more fluent than others, yet everyone (except for a small number of Inuit and Cree elders) uses some form of English in intercultural encounters. These encounters take place daily at the three stores, the school, the post office, the gymnasium, the skating arena, and the nursing station. This means that there are many opportunities in community settings for non-English speakers to learn and practice English.

In addition to the obvious reasons for learning English (to communicate with others locally, nationally, and globally, and to increase employment possibilities) there are some less obvious reasons, which are related to group membership and social identity.

One of these concerns the use of English as a status symbol, representing a form of knowledge acquired in school and used to construct emerging Inuit youth identities and peer groups. In other words, English becomes an attractive language for young people who are turning increasingly to North American popular culture – even if its actual use in peer group interaction is very limited.

I once observed an example of such English use in peer groups while I was working as an adult education instructor in a northern Nunavik community. I was approached by a young woman in her early twenties, who had dropped out of school at a young age, and now wanted desperately to improve her English. One day she told me why: the friends with whom she had grown up and who were now her classmates in adult education would use English words and phrases when they were together, and in doing so excluded her from their group. Even though this exclusion might not have been intentional, it nevertheless had the effect of limiting her ability to participate in their conversations. This caused her a great deal of frustration – which could be overcome, she felt, only if she studied English. In this case, then, English was used in the negotiation of power within peer groups. However, the fact that English was chosen as the language of exclusion strongly suggests that it had another role to play: orienting younger Inuktitut speakers towards Euro-Canadian culture, perhaps as a result of television and other forms of North American influence.

Learning and speaking English can also be linked to identity in other ways. English is an integral part of Northern Canada's colonial history, and for centuries held a dominant position (as the language of traders, missionaries, and bureaucrats) in the Inuit cultural and economic practices that characterized this period of contact. One woman whom I interviewed identified speaking English as a second language with being Inuk. When I asked her why this was, she replied: "Since I'm Inuk, English is my second language. The English came here and they wanted us to learn how to speak English. I really want to understand very much English." She then added: "I have nothing against French; if I ever need a translator my son will translate for me." (Enrolling one's children in the French stream at school, as we shall see, is a common strategy for dealing with the more recent rise of French in the community and the province.)

In sum, English is tied to local identities, and is – at least to some degree – also identified as a language of Inuit youth culture. For many Inuit, then, knowing English and Inuktitut is sufficient for their communicative purposes in the community. As one Inuk man noted: "When I communicate with the Cree, for example, or the French, the communication is in English, and that's no problem, everybody seems to speak English."

Learning French

Yet, for many Inuit, knowing French is also desirable, and many would like to learn the language for social and work-related reasons, having seen an increasing need to learn French over the past twenty or thirty years. This desire distinguishes them from the Anglophones in Great Whale River, who are either French speakers already (having learned the language before moving to this community), or are not French speakers and have little desire to learn the language, being mostly from outside of Quebec (either from other Canadian provinces or from the United States) and able to live and work comfortably in English.

Unlike the latter group of Anglophones, however, the Inuit of Great Whale River claim this region as their ancestral home, and they have witnessed a sharp increase in French-language government offices and small businesses in their communities. They are also exposed to French through travel to southern French-speaking centers for services, sports events, and higher education. In response to this French reality, the Inuit-run Kativik School Board offers a choice between English- and French-language schooling in the fourth year of school, when a child is about nine years old and has completed grades K, 1, and 2 in Inuktitut. In addition, some Inuit have attended the adult French language courses offered in the community. Nevertheless, many of the Inuit who have been educated in English at the federal day schools are not actively learning French. There is thus a discrepancy in Great Whale River between the relatively large number of people who clearly see and express both a need and a desire to learn French, and the rather small number of people who are actually engaged in language learning.

There are many reasons why many adult Inuit see knowledge of French as a necessity even when they have not made learning the language a priority. During my interviews with members of this group, it became clear that the new political and economic reality of Nunavik is situated within the larger French-speaking Quebec State, and that there are forms of French dominance in government agencies and French symbolic domination in institutional practices. When asked, many Inuit said that they would like to learn French because of its position in the wider province, even though its importance is still secondary to Inuktitut and English more locally. As one council employee noted, Inuktitut is the primary language in Nunavik, although French is still a language he would like to learn: "We live in Quebec and the second language here is French on top of English. So, I think it has a lot of importance."

In order to obtain provincial health or social services, including provincial government information, government pensions, welfare, driver's licenses, and the like, it certainly does help to speak French. These services can be obtained in English, but it can take more time if the offices are in smaller Francophone communities with limited bilingual staff (which generally serve the North). This is emphasized in the following excerpts from interviews with Inuit council employees and an Anglophone resident, respectively:

> Even if you don't need it in your community, you may need French when you are down south. I was really stuck once, it turned out that the doctor didn't speak English and I didn't know how to communicate. Not only with the doctors, I was lost too in the city. You going around with nobody being able to understand you, I wouldn't want that feeling for my children, not a bit. (Female Inuk Municipal Council employee)

> ... we have problems with government documents, provincial documents. For example, old age pension, welfare, these things they send the forms in French. In my case I get some documents in French as well... Same thing with the driver's license, it's all in French; there's some rules and regulations on the back. (Male Inuk Municipal Council employee)

> ... you can get English services over the phone, but it's hard, you have to wait a long time. Like some days, I've gone through days before I've been able to get through for English services ... . Like I do people's income tax returns, because the Inuit have to pay income tax, So when it comes to income tax time, they're usually missing a lot of information [receipts for their family allowance, pension slips, etc.]. And to try and get that information is really hard ... (Female non-Native resident)

Another reason for valuing French is that it is used in the workplace, especially in positions that involve dealing with provincial agencies and departments and with employees from southern Quebec. Many Inuit and Anglophones can cite occasions when they have had to deal with a monolingual French speaker, or when some aspect of their work involved written French:

> I never learned French. It was important in my working areas, because I have to speak to people who only know French sometimes for the telephone .... Even now they ask me "parlez-vous français?" and I have to say no. Even though I understand that, but ... I don't know French. (Female Inuk Municipal Council employee)

Despite the prevalence of French in these situations, however, very few non-French speakers are actually trying to learn the language in Great Whale River, as I have already noted. One reason for not pursuing French courses is a simple lack of time. As one woman noted:

> I thought of it, but it takes too much of my time. I'd rather be pursuing traditional sewing than to take the time to learn French, and be at home afterward, especially if I'm [a single parent] it's very hard. (Female Inuk Municipal Council employee)

Other reasons include the view of many Inuit that knowing two languages is sufficient, and that learning a third should not be necessary if one can manage without it. What is more, language requirements – in particular, relatively high levels of proficiency in second or third languages – serve as gate-keeping mechanisms for employment and promotion in certain workplaces. Therefore, the external incentives to learn French are quite high, yet mastering the language is seen as an almost unrealizable goal, given the time needed to invest in classes, and the developing of strategies in the workplaces to 'get by' with translations and help from Francophone employees. These points are alluded to in the following excerpt from a provincial government employee, who has sought out French language training:

> ... this job that I have is nothing but French, with some translation and stuff, I'm able to do this. My co-workers here don't speak French [but] they all ... they can do the job. You get a little training, you get the hang of it and you can do the job ... I've been trying hard to learn French. I even took a six-week immersion course this year, but it's not enough. Like I already have two languages [Inuktitut and English], putting in a third one, you know it's kind of hard. (Male Inuk Québec Government employee)

Whatever the reasons expressed for not pursuing language training in French, it is clear that the non-French-speakers in Great Whale River are coping in the workplace, in the wider community, and in the province as a whole. This is largely because of the strategies that they have adopted to cope with the presence of French. One strategy has been to hire a fluent French speaker (the husband of an Inuk woman in the community) to work in the municipal council office; this employee is thus able to deal with any government forms or documents that are sent to the community in French. Another strategy is for a family to enrol one child in the French stream at school, in order to have an Inuktitut/French translator in the family.

Although studying French at school is the most obvious way to learn the language, practising French outside the classroom is not easy, despite the large number of Francophones in Great Whale River. Language practices and patterns of intercultural communication in the community constrain the use of French because of the tradition of using English with those of different ethnic backgrounds, even when both interlocutors speak French. This has the effect of leaving French language learners with few opportunities to practice in community situations.

This point is highlighted in the cross-linguistic situations to be described in the next section, which I observed during the course of my fieldwork. One situation involves a French language teacher and a child with whom she was not familiar, another involves students of French and non-French-speaking interlocutors and bystanders, and a third involves routine language patterns in a provincially-run institution. These situations demonstrate not only how established patterns of English language use constrain the use of French (even by Inuit children studying French at school), but also how language is used to construct ethnic groups and social identities and to negotiate relations of power and solidarity.

Social constraints on language choice between Inuit and Francophones

Constraints on language choice, which arise from considerations of who is speaking to whom, in what context, and with what bystanders present, result in particular patterns of behavior with particular consequences. The nature of these constraints was brought home to me during an interview with Maryse, a Francophone woman who had been working in Great Whale River for more than five years. When I asked her whether Inuit high school students used French in the community, she responded, *"Non, jamais"* ("No, never"). The interview continued as follows:

D: *Est-ce qu'ils parlent français avec toi?*
(Do they speak French with you?)

M: *Pas beaucoup. Mais, moi quand je sais qu'ils étudient en français, je vais leur parler en français. Et c'est drôle que tu dis ça, parce que la fille à Maggie, elle étudie en français et mardi passé j'ai joué au badminton avec, et je sais qu'elle et Eva étudient en français, puis à un moment on jouait et elle m'a posé des questions en anglais. Elle sait que moi je parle français, elle sait que je sais qu'elle étudie en français... mais moi je dis que c'est correct ça. Il faut leur laisser leur temps, mais moi j'ai répondu en français. Mais si elle n'est pas confortable, même si je pousse, je pousse, mais je pense que c'est à developper une bonne relation quand elle sera plus géniale avec moi, peut-être elle va parler français avec moi.*

(Not a lot. But, when I know that they are studying in French, I talk to them in French. It's funny that you mention that, because Maggie's daughter, she's studying in French and last Tuesday I was playing badminton with her, and I know that she and Eva are studying in French, and then, while we were playing, she asked me some questions in English. She knows that I speak

French, she knows that I know that she is studying in French... but I say, well, that's alright. You have to give them time, but I answered in French. But if she isn't comfortable, even when I push and push, but I think that a good relationship with her has to be developed and when she is more friendly with me, then perhaps she'll speak French with me.)

Maryse then described how she continued to speak French with Maggie's daughter. She noted how other Francophones often used English with Inuit whom they did not realize were studying in French. Maryse, however, made an effort to use French, and continued to describe her approach to interacting with Maggie's daughter:

M: *Mais quelque fois comme quand j'étais avec elle, elle me posait des questions en anglais. Je vais répondre en français et des fois je vais dire les choses et elle ne comprenait pas, quand elle ne comprenait pas, j'utilisais quelques mots en anglais, puis là, je revenais en français. Mais elle, elle ne me parlait pas en français. Mais je dis c'est correct si elle ne le fait pas tout de suite.*
(But sometimes when I am with her, she asks me questions in English. I respond in French, and sometimes I say things that she doesn't understand. When she doesn't understand, I use some English words, and then, I switch back to French. But she doesn't speak to me in French. But I say to myself, it's okay if she doesn't do it right away.)

Maryse had developed a pattern of using French with people who were just beginning to learn French or who were second language speakers like myself. I had witnessed her speaking French slowly and clearly, waiting patiently for responses, and continuing conversations with adult Inuit and Cree who were taking beginning language courses. But, as she remarked, she was one of the few Francophones who insisted on using French in public places with Inuit French-language students, even though they often replied to her in English.

In examining the case of Maggie's daughter using English instead of French, one could speculate that she was simply shy about using a language that she had not mastered, or that the Inuit community was simply not yet prepared to embrace a third language for daily interaction. However, closer examination of the contexts in which these interactions take place and the participants in these interactions suggests a more complex explanation.

I myself witnessed a similar cross-linguistic interaction one evening at the gymnasium, after I noticed three Inuit teenagers conversing in Inuktitut as they gathered up their belongings. I recognized two of them from school: one from the French senior high school class and one from the English class. A Francophone teacher in the next badminton court greeted the student who studied in French with *"Salut Anna! Comment ça va?,"* to which Anna replied, *"Bien."* Anna then quickly returned to speaking in Inuktitut to her friends, and did not continue the conversation in French. Again the reason might be shyness or unfamiliarity with the teacher, but it was also clear that she was more interested in speaking Inuktitut than French, and probably did not want to exclude her friends by using a language that they did not understand. In effect, Anna choose solidarity (with her friends) over French language practice with a relative stranger, perhaps because the social cost of speaking French was simply too high. In the intercultural situation described above, involving Maryse and Maggie's daughter, similar sociolinguistic processes might have been at play, which determined a choice of English or Inuktitut over French, and thus of solidarity over the ability to use a language of power and possible exclusion of friends.

One final example of an intercultural interaction in Great Whale River that reflects the complexities of language choice in this community is one between an Inuk boy, William, who was studying in French and a Francophone nurse at the nursing station. Although William was in the French stream at school, the nurses had no way of knowing this. (As it happens, it is impossible for nursing staff to know whether a child is studying in French or English unless they have already obtained this information elsewhere. My own observations suggested that even a child studying in French will not always say so when asked directly in French, and that even school teachers sometimes have difficulty keeping track of the children in the English stream and the children in the French stream.) So, although the Inuit interpreters greeted William and engaged him in a brief conversation in Inuktitut, he was treated by the nurses in English without the benefit of Inuktitut translation, which is reserved for older Inuit. It was unclear, however, how much he really understood of what the nurse who was treating him said (although his ability to comprehend was admittedly not crucial, given his age). In this situation, however, it was clear that English was the language of interaction with the nurses – that it was English, rather than Inuktitut or French, that healthcare providers used when dealing with Inuit, even when both the healthcare provider and the client actually spoke French. These institutionalized patterns of English-language use between non-Natives and younger Inuit (that is, those attending school) limit the use of French even in settings where one might expect otherwise.

The use of English instead of French with Inuit appears well-intentioned: by using English, Francophones are seeking to include Inuit students, patients, clients, and others, and to avoid negative reactions, such as being seen as rude or secretive. It is also perhaps a tacit recognition on the part of some Francophones that the position of French in the communicative hierarchy is still unstable in this particular settlement, where English is so prevalent. These assumptions are based, in part, on the recognition of Francophones in the settlement that English is the second language of most Inuit, and on the expectation of these Francophones that younger Inuit, in particular, will be able to understand English whether or not they are actually studying in English. Unfortunately, such patterns of language use may also have serious repercussions for students of French who want to master the language, since they severely restrict the opportunities that such learners have to use French outside the classroom.

These patterns of institutional language use – of Francophones using English with Inuit youth, often not knowing whether these youth are studying in French or

English – serve to reproduce the ethnic boundaries that define this community. English, as the language of intercultural communication, is used in settings where one might reasonably expect French to be used. Given the shifting political economy of Nunavik and the importance of French in this process, this situation is of increasing concern to many members of the Inuit community. Learning a community language is not as straightforward as one might think, as we shall see in the attempts of non-Native speakers to learn Inuktitut.

Learning Inuktitut

Historically, it was not unusual for European traders and missionaries to learn Inuktitut when they came to Arctic Quebec in order to facilitate their work there. In the late twentieth century, however, knowing French and English seems to be sufficient for the majority of the non-Native population, since most of the Inuit and Cree whom they encounter in Great Whale River are able to communicate in English. Nevertheless, some of the people whom I interviewed had indeed been trying to learn Inuktitut. In this section, I shall describe three such cases: those of two Francophone men and one Anglophone woman who had expressed interest and been actively involving in learning Inuktitut.

One Francophone man, J., who was married to an Inuk woman, was motivated to speak the language in order to integrate himself more fully into the community. In the excerpt below, he cites the complexity of the language and the fact that it is not Indo-European as the sources of his difficulties:

J: (laughter) The language is sooo hard – I try, I really try. And my wife is Inuk, obviously, and our children are Inuit too, but I would rather say, it is easier for me now, my son is three years old, and I am at his level, so every word he picks up, I pick [it] up too. I learn a lot from children, but the language itself is really hard, you cannot use any English or French background ... . (Male non-Native government employee)

What is crucial in these remarks is not that the language is so difficult to learn, but that the language of communication between J. and his wife is English. During the time of my fieldwork, there were six mixed marriages in Great Whale River, with Francophone men married to Inuit women. In all cases, English was almost always used between husband and wife, although mothers often spoke to their children in Inuktitut, and fathers sometimes spoke to them in French. Thus, despite being married to an Inuk, and the dominance of Inuktitut in the community and in Inuit family life, very few non-Natives who lived in Native households spoke Inuktitut.

The other Francophone man learning Inuktitut was the manager of a Quebec government utility who had to deal with Inuit employees in northern communities. He cited a different reason for his language-learning difficulties: a lack of courses and of good course materials that could aid him in his learning. The Francophone manager was, in fact, highly motivated to learn Inuktitut, given his position as an outsider in a position of power and the symbolic value of speaking Inuktitut in helping to level the boundary between him and his Inuit employees. But this had not been enough:

> I'm trying to learn Inuktitut, it could be very interesting for me, because up the coast and everything it's better when you know a few words for the people I meet. And I got the same thing, I've got a course with cassette and videocassette from [the school board], and I find it very hard to follow.
> There should be a course at night, like it's a big village. Because I talked with a lot of people and [we just want] the basic and the vocabulary like what is a door, an office. (Male non-Native manager)

What is interesting here is that this learner has obviously had contact with Inuit and Inuktitut on a regular basis, yet has still been unable to pick up "a few words of Inuktitut" that he could use with the people he meets. He has tried self-instruction through materials produced by the school board but, like others I interviewed, he wishes to take a course in order to gain real access to the language. These two points – the complexity of the language and the lack of accessible language learning materials and courses – were echoed by other non-Native residents. However, other sociolinguistic constraints are at play here that clearly do not promote successful language learning.

My third and final example of a non-Native resident trying to learn Inuktitut is Susan, a Protestant missionary from Western Canada who had been learning Inuktitut in Nunavik over a number of years. Most of her ability to speak the language, however, derived from her earlier work in a more northern Inuit community where she had been able to work with a private tutor and to gain more practice in everyday conversation. Both of these possibilities were severely restricted in Great Whale River:

> People use a lot more English here. It's so much easier to get by in English, with people my own age. Even some of the elders speak a little bit of English, which wasn't so in the other communities. In the other communities, anybody over 50 probably didn't speak a word of English, and here there are some who at least understand a bit. And the kids speak a lot more English here as well. And they tend to want to try their English on you, as an English-speaking person. And I find that when kids can speak some English, I'll talk to them in Inuktitut, and they'll answer me in English. And that's really frustrating, because I'm trying to practice my Inuktitut and they're trying to practice their English. And the young people especially do this ....

Susan continues by talking about her difficulties in finding a tutor and the necessity of learning the language on her own. She notes some of the contexts in which it is more acceptable for her to speak Inuktitut: on the land, while ice-fishing, hiking, or picking berries:

> The Inuit and Cree are more apt to talk Inuktitut or Cree out on the land, espe-

cially if you're in a group, if you're in a group, it's really good for language, because they talk to each other all the time, and they might talk to you in English, but you can listen to them speaking to each other and you can enter into the conversation. It's much easier to use Inuktitut when you're in a group than when you are one-on-one.

These observations were corroborated by my own experience of ice-fishing with Inuit during a community fishing derby: during this time, I was never addressed in English by Inuit. This may have been an extension of a sociolinguistic rule that traditional activities, such as hunting and other community recreational events, are conducted in Inuktitut. In short, context, domain, and social network play a significant role in language choice and in appropriate language use in Great Whale River. As we have seen with French language use, particular contexts lead to particular language choices, which can lessen the opportunities for second or third language learning.

Conclusion

In this chapter we have seen how historical events, social processes, and the wider political economy have led to the valuing of particular language varieties in an Arctic Quebec community. However, despite the desire and motivation of some members of this community to become trilingual, language learning can be a difficult process for Native and non-Native residents alike.

In face-to-face interaction, particular language varieties index ethnicity and serve to construct identities. Thus, despite the motivation of certain residents to learn other languages in order to gain access to desirable jobs and other material and symbolic resources, constraints on language use in the community severely limit language practice and thus language learning. In contrast to the plentiful opportunities to use English, opportunities for non-Inuit and non-Francophones to use Inuktitut and French, respectively, in community encounters are highly limited.

A systematic examination at the micro-level of interaction within particular social networks can greatly aid our understanding of the process of second and third language learning in particular communities, as I hope that I have shown.

Notes

1. I would like to thank the people of Great Whale River, the Katvik School Board, and the Social Sciences and Humanities Research Council of Canada for making this research possible.
2. In this chapter, I use the name Great Whale River for the community. It is also known as Kuujjuarapik in Inuktitut, Whapmaguostui in Cree, and Poste-de-la-Baleine in French.

Chapter 11

Growing a *Bányavirág* (Rock Crystal) on Barren Soil: Forming a Hungarian Identity in Eastern Slovakia through Joint (Inter)action

JULIET LANGMAN

Language Socialization in Young Adulthood

Processes of language socialization have traditionally been explored from the perspective of young children developing the knowledge they need to become fully functioning "adult" members of a particular society. Language socialization from this perspective outlines a developmental process by means of which children learn to become adults by speaking like adults, in a society whose rules, norms and values are pre-determined (Schieffelin & Ochs, 1986b). Ochs (1986: 3) defines the process of socialization: "through their participation in social interactions, children come to internalize and gain performance competence in ... sociocultural [*sic*] defined contexts ... ."

More recent work extends the view of language socialization in two ways. The first is the extension of language socialization as a process that extends across the life span. Adolescence, in this extension, takes on a particular importance as the period at which individuals in modern societies find themselves at the intersection between childhood and adulthood, the period during which social identity forma-tion becomes central. Eckert (2000: 15–16) points out that the value of studying adolescents rests in the fact that "the elaboration of adolescent social practices stems from the need to create a viable alternative to adulthood, making adolescent life both short and intense – a social hothouse."[1] Adolescence is, moreover, the period during which the formation of social identity becomes central.

The second extension of the socialization concept entails a shift from seeing socialization as a developmental process to one that sees socialization as practice. From this perspective, individuals engage in the practice of identity in age-appropriate ways throughout their lives, in response to the social environment in which they find themselves. An adolescent's practice, for example, is not simply a training ground for eventual adult participation in a community, but is also a practice in its own right, as individuals (at all ages) act as they are, and become who they are, within a social context that is relevant to the individual. In essence, this second perspective suggests that language socialization is not simply a developmental process leading to adulthood, but rather a component of what it means to be human, namely to be a member of a group. No one but an adolescent can be a fully socialized well-functioning member of certain adolescent groups. Eckert (1996, 2000) suggests that we come to view socialization in a way that merges developmental with mature-state models. This social-practice view of (language) socialization allows for a more fluid and multi-faceted conception of socialization and the social identit(ies) associated with it.[2]

An additional consequence of a practice view of (language) socialization is that the norms and values of society, or of a given group to which one is being socialized, are not fixed. Rather, these norms and values are in a constant state of negotiation, as individuals define themselves with respect to other individuals as well as to social institutions and, in turn, define those institutions. Levine and Moreland (1991: 266) suggest that "[d]uring socialization, the group attempts to change the individual so that he or she can contribute more to the achievement of group goals, whereas the individual attempts to change the group so that it can better satisfy his or her personal needs." In a social practice view of language socialization, the central unit of analysis is the community of practice (CofP) defined as:

> An aggregate of people who come together around mutual engagement in an endeavor. Ways of doing things, ways of talking, beliefs, values, power relations – in short, practices – emerge in the course of this mutual endeavor. As a social construct, a CofP is different from the traditional community, primarily because it is defined simultaneously by its membership and by the practice in which that membership engages. (Eckert & McConnell-Ginet, 1992: 464)

The construct of the community of practice stems from a theory of learning that sees learning "as a social phenomenon constituted in the experienced lived-in world" (Lave, 1991: 64). Learning consists of the development of "knowledgeable skills" that in turn are the basis for the development of an identity related to the mastery of those skills (Lave, 1991; Lave & Wenger, 1991). In fact, "learning and a sense of identity are inseparable" (Lave & Wenger, 1991: 115). Socialization entails practicing activities that are relevant to the group (at whatever level of proficiency the individual has), and through that practice developing an identity within the community, be it as a novice, an expert, or a central or peripheral member.

In seeing socialization as practice, individuals become agents of socialization (Eckert 2000).[3] An individual practices an identity with reference to a wide variety of communities of practice, ranging from a school group to a community group, a church group or a family. In such practice, dimensions of identity related to various social categories such as ethnicity, class, and gender are practiced and negotiated in specific social settings. Yet, and importantly, at various times in an individual's life, a particular community of practice becomes central to that individual's identity practice. Within the context of the suburban high school in the United States, Eckert (2000) outlines two central identities associated with two central communities of practice, "the jocks" and "the burnouts," as well as a third group, "the in-betweens." These groups are at one and the same time local sites of identity practice for adolescents, and a reflection of central social groupings within US society. In her study, Eckert (2000) points to *class* as the focal social categorization around which local identities are practiced.

In East Central Europe, arguably prior to the vast social changes since the late 1980s and early 1990s, and certainly subsequent to that, the most relevant social categorization is ethnic or national group.[4] The tremendous growth of expressions of nationalism and the conception of the state as co-terminous with the nation in many East Central European countries provides evidence for this claim. The Republic of Slovakia, an independent state since 1993, has been the subject of much research and debate owing to its strong nationalistic orientation as well as to the organized and internationally well-documented resistance to state-building policies that discriminate against indigenous linguistic minorities, particularly the Hungarian minority (see Kontra, 1998, 1999; Langman, 1997b; Langman & Lanstyák 2000; László, 1998; Szigeti, 1995a, 1995b). Slovak political ideology, implicit in the Constitution, defines the Slovak nation as those individuals whose native language is Slovak. From the perspective of the Hungarian minority, who comprise around 10% of the population, this conception of the state leaves no room for minority national identity. A number of recent studies have focused on the Slovak language laws and other measures aimed at constructing a linguistically and nationally homogeneous state (Driessen, 1999; Kontra, 1995/1996, 1998; Langman, 2002; Pichler, 1994). Other studies examine the nature of minority identity among Hungarians in Slovakia (Langman, 1997a, 1997b). Langman and Lanstyák (2000) explore a set of myths that underlie a powerful discourse ideology that places Hungarian minority members in a conflictual relationship with the state through the view that Hungarians neither speak Slovak nor want to learn to speak it.

This chapter explores the practice of social identity with a particular focus on language use, within the context of a linguistic minority youth group. In other words, I explore the nature of socialization as learning that entails the development and practice of a social identity. In particular, I explore how the membership of a Hungarian dance group, which I call the Rock Crystal Dance Ensemble,[5] constructs a multifaceted Hungarian identity. I will argue that the identity practiced in the context of the Rock Crystal Dance Ensemble is one that is both reflective of and resistant to the dominant language ideologies of the Slovak state, seen through the contestation of the conception of the Slovak state as monolingual. In what follows, I will first locate the Rock Crystal dance group within the broader social setting of late twentieth century Slovakia. Thereafter, I will detail how Rock Crystal members practice their identity, in particular through an examination of how core members reflect on their identity practice juxtaposed against that of other communities of practice, as well as the perceived normative behavior within the society at large.

Locating the Rock Crystal Dance Group

The sizable Hungarian minority population in Slovakia derives from the historical shifts in territorial control in Central Europe. This history is central to situating the Rock Crystal Dance Ensemble as a CofP for Hungarian minority identity. Hungarians form the largest minority group in the Republic of Slovakia. According to the 1991 census, the population of Slovakia was 5.27 million, 85.7% of whom claimed Slovak nationality. Of the remaining 14.3%, 10.8% claimed Hungarian nationality. The Hungarian population is densely concentrated in the southern part of Slovakia, along the border with Hungary.

The last few centuries have seen many shifts in the relationship between Hungarians and Slovaks as they have been joint members of various political regimes. During the period of the Austro-Hungarian monarchy (1867–1918), Hungarians had political control over the territories that today form the Republic of Slovakia. With the formation of Czechoslovakia following World War I, the Hungarian population became a national minority group. Since that time, the Hungarian population has had minority status, and has experienced a wide range of policies directed at national minorities, ranging from repression and population exchange to benevolent neglect. Gyurcsik and Satterwhite (1996: 511) suggest that one consistent theme of (Czecho)Slovak state policy since World War II has been "the creation of the 'pure nation-state.'" Shifts in policies have been accompanied by greater and lesser degrees of support for minority institutions, notably schools and cultural organizations, together with a general climate of discrimination across all sectors of society.[6] A consequence of this has been assimilation of Hungarians on the one hand and the development of a strong and separate Hungarian minority identity on the other.

Constructing a Minority Identity: Growing Rock Crystals

The Rock Crystal community of practice

The community of practice that I examine comprises members and supporters of the Rock Crystal Dance Ensemble, a Hungarian dance ensemble located in Golden, which is a regional center of education and commerce with a larger catchment area population of 86,000 (Golden itself has 18,000). Golden lies in Eastern Slovakia on the "language border" between Hungarian- and Slovak-speaking populations, with all the villages to the south and east having a Hungarian majority, while those to the north and west have a Slovak majority. Golden, a former wealthy mining town, was originally established by German miners. Virtually all remnants of the German population have disappeared since the end of World War II.

According to official statistics, about 30% of the population of Golden claim Hungarian nationality. The surrounding villages, which are home to the majority of Rock Crystal members, range from 65–95% Hungarian, with populations ranging from 650–2,400. Golden is further characterized by a large Romany (Gypsy) population.

In spite of the large minority population, the visitor to Golden observes virtually no evidence of a Hungarian presence. There are no street signs or signs on shops in Hungarian (the last disappeared in 1996).[7] Spoken Hungarian is rarely heard on the street, much less in the post office and official administrative offices. Hungarian may be heard occasionally in shops, particularly if the shopkeepers are familiar with and know that all present speak Hungarian. In sharp contrast is the rich and full impression of Hungarian that one gets upon entering the courtyard just off the main square that houses the local Hungarian cultural organization. In addition to office space, the courtyard has, over the last six years, housed a Hungarian bookstore, a bar, and a hall with a small stage that serves as rehearsal space for Rock Crystal and also as a space for Hungarian religious and social events. Here signs in Hungarian tell of meetings, posters of Hungarian cultural events decorate the walls, and Hungarian singing can be heard if the dance group is practicing.

Rock Crystal was established in 1981 through the support of a local Hungarian teacher and cultural leaders as well as through the financial support of the state-supported Hungarian minority cultural organization.[8] The founder, an elderly Hungarian teacher, began a children's group, designed to provide culturally enriching activities for young Hungarian children through the performance of choreographed dances. As the first cohort of children became adolescents, a youth group developed separately from the children's group, but continued with choreographed dances.

In 1993, when I first had contact with Rock Crystal, the current leaders of the group had just taken control of the adult group, which consisted of young people aged 14–23. The trend that led to the (re)creation of Rock Crystal under youth leadership, was fueled from abroad, specifically from Hungary, where the Dancehouse (*Táncház*) folk revival movement had begun in the early 1970s, partly as a resistance to communism. Members of the youth group were among the first generation of dancers to have opportunities to travel abroad (to Hungary) in the mid-to-late 1980s. They became enchanted with the Dancehouse movement and wrested control from the founder, who had not embraced this movement. The Dancehouse movement, which entailed the practice of dance in improvisational peasant style, subsequently spread throughout the Hungarian language area and, by the 1980s, had spread to emigré communities in Western Europe, the United States and

Canada, supplanting the choreographed version of national Hungarian dance promoted by the communist regime.

My own contact with the group stemmed from the Dancehouse movement as well as from the establishment of cultural organizations to support Hungarians outside Hungary, following democratization. In 1993, I accompanied a choreographer from Hungary on a number of weekend workshops. As a member of a dance group in Budapest, I was able to participate in rehearsals and act as assistant to the choreographer. Through this initial contact, I developed friendship and professional ties with various members of the group. These ties allowed me to maintain a regular pattern of visits to Golden over the course of four years, during which time I was engaged in participant observation. In addition, after my initial contact with the group I also carried out occasional videotaping of rehearsals and performances, as well as in-depth interviewing of group members and others in the community. Through these visits, I joined rehearsals, occasionally performed with the group, celebrated its fifteenth anniversary, and hosted the dancers in my home in Budapest when the group visited Hungary. In subsequent return visits in 1999 and 2001, I visited and also carried out follow-up interviews with Rock Crystal members. In this sense, I, as a Dutch American with high-intermediate proficiency in Hungarian, as well as a dancer in a well-known performing group, became an apprentice member of the Rock Crystal CofP, learning from group members as well as sharing with them my perspective on dance and the world.

From 1993 to the present the membership of Rock Crystal has ranged from 12–35 dancers in a fluctuating pattern that is seasonal as well as tied to particular performances and events. Ages of members in the year 2000 range from 18–30. A stable core of six members has been in the group throughout this time period. The practice of these six individuals is central to the operation of the group, and forms the focus of this chapter. In 1993, Tamás (aged 19) began to organize the administrative aspects of the group; his partner Zsuzsa (17) focused her attention on costuming and women's styling; András (18) was artistic director and dance instructor, while his partner Béa (15) was a determined learner of dance and song. Finally Mihály (19), a strong dancer and moral leader, came from a village where dance was still a regular event. His future partner Kati (14), a cousin of Béa's, was an apprentice in things Hungarian, since her parents had sent her to Slovak school. Her study in technical school towards a sewing degree made her an invaluable assistant to Zsuzsa.

The majority of dancers came to know about, and then join, Rock Crystal through school, friendship, or family ties with members. Mihály explains how his friends enticed him to join and then he "stuck:"

> Well they talked and talked "Come on," they said, they kept filling my head. I, well, I don't know ... well I was shy and I was scared of it, like what will it be like, I won't know how, of course that's in everyone. But well in the end I went and watched what they were up to, I tried it and then I said, "It's not so bad."

In a town the size and ethnic make-up of Golden, Mihály explains joining the group as an inevitability:

> Sooner or later, I think I would have joined because, here in Golden, there are no other possibilities ... . So well they enticed me ... . There was always a good feeling there, so it got me, plus well once you're there for like half a year, then you've already got friends, maybe girlfriends ... . Well and then well folk, folk dance is not something you can neglect, because well I think it's really good to do, I like to do it and it's entertaining.

Central dimensions of Rock Crystal practice

Communities of practice are defined in terms of three core dimensions that characterize the nature of the relationship between members: (1) mutual engagement, in (2) a joint negotiated enterprise, through (3) a shared repertoire of negotiable resources (Wenger, 1998: 76). Mutual engagement essentially involves regular interaction. Members of Rock Crystal meet at a minimum once a week for rehearsals, sometimes extending to three times a week. Rehearsals are augmented by weekend workshops, social events, and performing trips and tours lasting up to two weeks in the summer months. In addition, Rock Crystal is the primary social group for older members. Among the core members, there are now three couples, two with children ranging from a few months to five years of age. Mutual engagement extends beyond the world of dance and performance to that of advice on employment, child rearing, and various other activities defined by members as ways in which to live life according to traditional Hungarian values within a modern Slovak state.

The primary joint-negotiated enterprise (that is, the shared goal and the practice involved in achieving it) is the learning, preservation and presentation of Hungarian folk culture through the study and performance of dance, primarily to audiences in the Republic of Slovakia and northern Hungary. The group has also toured Western Europe and participated in countrywide dance competitions. To accomplish these goals, the group meets regularly for rehearsal and seeks funds to bring in outside teachers and choreographers, as well as opportunities to travel to rural sites to collect dance material. In addition they travel to organized dance camps and festivals to learn new things and socialize with members of a network of dance groups across southern Slovakia, Hungary and beyond. In spite of all these activities, the majority of time spent by the group in mutual engagement takes place in the rehearsal hall, and later in the evening at various venues including the local bar or restaurant or in the home of Tamás and Zsuzsa.

The third dimension of a community of practice is a shared repertoire of negotiable resources, such as specialized terminology and linguistic routines, as well as physical artefacts, instruments, costumes, recorded music, and audio equipment that all form part of the community's practice. These resources, which the group has accumulated over time, include a wide range of dances, songs, stories, costumes, choreographies, jokes, and tapes, each drawn from different sources. Each has also taken on a special meaning within the group.

Particular status can be given to the shared repertoire of terminology and linguistic routines that constitute definitions of practice as well as actual practice. Indeed, some of the attributes that Wenger (1998: 125–6) suggests characterize a CofP include both the rapid flow of information and propagation of information, and a shared discourse that reflects a certain perspective on the world. Discourse or language then plays a central role in practice in two different ways, characterized as "talk within" and "talk about" practice (Lave & Wenger, 1991: 109). "Talk within" involves discourse that facilitates the practice of a community, while "talk about" (e.g. the telling of stories of practice) allows for the creation of an identity – the shared discourse that reflects a certain perspective on the world.

Within the world of dance, a particular terminology characterizes dance steps. Mutual engagement is marked further through "talk within" practice in the making of on-the-spot plays on words that highlight on-going activity. For example, during one rehearsal in 1993, I recorded numerous plays on words, involving inversions of morphemes, which served to mark knowledge of the world of folk dance and the physical and cognitive demands on dancers engaged in choreography, as well as to refer to the actual events taking place at a given moment. In describing the manner in which he wants one set of steps to be executed, the choreographer reminds the dancers that it should flow *"mint a karika csapás"* ("like clockwork"). Subsequently when one dancer moves to her position clumsily, with wobbling ankles, "unlike" clockwork, the choreographer laughs and points out *"kibokamodott a ficája"* ("she ankled her sprain") which is a play on *kificamodott a bokája* ("she sprained her ankle"), meant to suggest that tripping and clumsiness is her natural condition. Later, the choreographer wants to improve on the quality of these steps, which should move "like clockwork," and not like an *"üldözéses vásár"* ("a flea race") – a play on words of *üldözés verseny* ("motorcross racing") and *zsibvásár* ("a flea market"), in other words a rushed and disorganized mess. Later he fine-tunes further, making gender-specific comments on the way the men and women moved. He refers to the women's manner of stepping by juxtaposing *kicsi csalfa leányka* ("little deceitful girl") with *csalafinta* ("crafty/artful") to underscore the fact that the steps should be subtle and not exaggerated. Here the reference he is making is to the "modern" girl's too-overt attempts to attract boys, in contrast to the traditional and more subtle ways of flirting. In contrast, when the men first fail and then succeed at moving with "manly authority" across the stage, he congratulates them with *"kanfasztikus,"* an inversion of *fantasztikus!* ("fantastic!") that results in the high-lighting the desired quality of manliness, through *kan* ("stud") and *fasz* ("penis"). An important element of "talk within" this community of practice is the intensity of activity coupled with a joking about that activity, all laden with several layers of cultural meaning for members of the group.

"Talk within" practice further focuses on the establishment of a group ethos around the negotiated enterprise of performing. During the same rehearsal, the choreographer reminds dancers of their role as members of a team and the importance of working as a group: *"Szeretném mindenkinek a lelkére kötni azt, hogy ha ... valami baja lesz, ne adj Isten, akkor valaki be tudjon állni rögtön a helyére. Tetszik érteni?"* ("I would like to impress on everyone's soul, that, should someone have a problem, Heaven forbid, then someone can immediately step into their place. Please, do you understand?") Later, when the choreographer notices attention to the task at hand is waning after several hours of rehearsal, he emphasizes the centrality of maintaining active involvement in the task: *"Azt szeretném kérni hogy aki tud az gyakorol. Aki nem tud az figyel ... ha nem csinál semmit akkor nyugodtan haza mehet"* ("I would like to ask that he who can, practice. He who can't [practice], pay attention ... if you're not doing anything, then you may just as well go home"). Note that these comments contrast with the discussions of steps and dance-related movements. These comments are serious as opposed to joking in tone. While they are directive in nature, they are also characterized by a high degree of indirection, seen through the use of the conditional "I would like to ask" and the formal form of the verb *"tetszik érteni"*(please understand, inf.). They illustrate how the joint enterprise can not only lead to a discussion of "rules for dance" but can also be extended to "rules for life."

The activities of the evening of July 12, 1999 illustrate both the continuity and the change in this CofP. That night, when I returned to the group, the Friday evening rehearsal schedule was reminiscent of those I participated in five years earlier. The evening lasted from 4:00 pm to 6 am. The group began in the rehearsal hall, where an exchange of pictures and stories took the place of rehearsal, as most of the group had just returned from a tour to Finland: Béa, a new mother, had been unable to go. The storytelling was thus for her benefit and mine, as well as for the group members, who rejoiced in the joint retelling of the various events. The storytelling was complemented with the celebration of a birthday for Mihály. This celebration entailed the drinking of much homemade wine, brought in 1.5 liter soda bottles from various homes, the ritual of each woman dancing with Mihály, after the group had formed a circle around him and sung the *széki Zsuzsanna napi köszöntő* (Susanna Day Salutation). This traditional song from Szék/Sic, Romania[9] ties together Hungarians involved in folk activities across a wide range of countries. The text contains a traditional set of wishes for prosperity:

> Széki Zsuzsanna napi köszöntő
> *Sok születés napokat vígan megélhess,*
> *Napjaidat számlálni ne légyen terhes,*
> *Az ég harmatja szívedet újítsa,*
> *Áldások árja házad elborítsa!*
>
> Susanna Day Salutation
> May you joyfully live through many birthdays,
> May the counting of your days not be heavy,
> May the dew renew your heart,
> May a flood of blessings envelop your home!

The evening progressed to dinner at the one restaurant in town where the group feels they can speak Hungarian comfortably, although all ordering and exchanges with the waitress take place in Slovak. Here talk centers on upcoming dance possibilities, and job opportunities for the men, two of whom have recently started their own workshops – one in metalwork, the other in woodwork. Together they are approaching villages throughout the region, looking for work casting and carving traditional furniture as well as town signs. The group then moved on to a potential spot for disco dancing, a journey of approximately half a mile that took one and a half hours to complete. At each of two stops, a long discussion ensued as to whether this was the place they all wanted to go. These stops also served as opportunities to tell jokes, to continue drinking wine, and to comment on differences in tastes in music and evening activities between the group members. On the way, Marton, a former member who now lives in the capital Pozsony/Bratislava and dances in the best-known semi-professional Hungarian dance group finds the group. Home for the weekend to visit his parents, he had been following the likely route of the group until he caught up with us around 11:00 pm. The group ended up at the disco, where half the group ordered one drink, in order to hold a table, while the rest danced together as a group. Here, too, other friends, both Slovak and Hungarian, were greeted and a number of the men drifted to the bar. Finally around 2:00 am, the group of ten moved to Tamás and Zsuzsa's house, a quarter mile walk. Here Zsuzsa prepared food, and a serious discussion over family values and family structures ensued. This talk centered on the three couples present and the life decisions they were currently struggling over: one married couple over whether to have a second child, one unmarried couple with an infant over when to marry, and a third not-yet-married couple over when to marry. Slowly one after the other fell asleep on the couch and then was reawakened, by a question, an offer of wine or food, or loud laughter. At 6:00 am, as it began to get light, everyone prepared to leave either to walk home or to catch the first bus to their village.

This cursory recounting of events suggests the depth of attachment of members of the group and thus the extent to which they operate as a primary community of practice. In this recounting, additional attributes that characterize a CofP are notable. First is the "[a]bsence of introductory preambles, as if conversations and interactions were merely the continuation of an ongoing process" (Wenger, 1998: 125). Reactions to my presence at the rehearsal after a two-year absence, prefaced only by a phone call from a dance camp 20 miles away asking if someone would pick me up, were extremely casual. I was immediately incorporated into the evening's activities as if my absence had been one or two weeks rather than two years.

Just as during rehearsals when they were focusing on dance problems to be solved, here too we see the "very quick setup of a problem to be discussed" (Wenger, 1998: 125), first employment, then marriage. This talk further illustrates the extent to which members know "what others know, what they can do, and how they can contribute to an enterprise"(Wenger, 1998: 125). In the discussion of jobs, the conversation turned immediately to strategies for convincing mayors to make funds available, and to negotiating rides with a clear understanding of who had money, who had access to gasoline, and who had access to a car.

An additional central attribute of a CofP is the fact of "[s]ustained mutual relationships – harmonious or conflictual" (Wenger, 1998: 125). The discussion about
life choices late on Friday night was far from congenial, with a number of comments
along the lines of "mind your own business" or "you're one to talk, look at your relationship with x." Yet, at no time during the evening or in the subsequent days were
these conflicts considered grounds for ending a friendship; rather they were considered part of the business of the group and therefore welcome alternate viewpoints.

Rock Crystal national identity practices

Just as the community shares a discourse that reflects their perspective on dance,
this perspective is extended to the world as well. Through this shared discourse,
primarily "talk about" practice, we see the unfolding of a particular social identity
that outlines "the salient identities from the points of view of members themselves"
(Lave, 1991: 81). For Rock Crystal members, salient identities relate to a Hungarian
national identity. This identity is characterized as being a "respectable" Hungarian
in Slovakia in the face of a powerful ideological discourse that would negate such an
identity.[10] To accomplish this identity, members of the Rock Crystal "talk about"
who they are, and "talk within" by practicing who they are. Such talk involves both
positive and negative identity practices.[11] Positive identity practices are "those in
which the individuals engage in order to actively construct a chosen identity"
(Bucholtz, 1999b: 211). They define what speakers are, thus emphasizing intragroup
aspects of social identity. Negative identity practices are "those that individuals
employ to distance themselves from a rejected identity" (Bucholtz, 1999b: 211).
These practices define what users are *not*, thus emphasizing identity as an inter-
group phenomenon and comparing their group to relevant outgroups.

Rock Crystal members practice an identity that ties a distant past, in the form of a
traditional Hungarian identity, to a future that incorporates bilingualism. This
multifaceted identity that Rock Crystal members struggle to define and practice
stands in contrast to an identity that is monolithically anti-Slovak, as reflected in
memories of a more recent past, characterized by discrimination against Hungarians and forcefully brought home through their parents' stories of the post World
War II period, as well as changes in laws in the post-democratization period. Mihály
clearly states the central aspects of identity for Rock Crystal members:

> I'm a Slovak citizen, that's a fact. But I feel completely and totally Hungarian. I
> live here, but well, that means something too that a person lives in Slovakia,
> because, it's totally different being a Hungarian in Hungary versus somewhere
> else... . But the important thing is that one is Hungarian.

Mihály clearly highlights the central component of his identity as Hungarian,
while at the same time further defining himself through his Slovak citizenship and
residence, thus contrasting himself with Hungarians in Hungary. This distinction
allows him to highlight central elements of his identity, focused on the practice of
traditional culture, especially in a climate of adversity, namely as a minority

Hungarian in a state that discriminates against him. Because of the need to struggle to maintain their identity, Rock Crystal members express having a richer and truer sense of being Hungarian than Hungarians in Hungary have. Tamás explains, "Our perception of our identity is uh, a little deeper. But that's not true for everyone, just for that layer, for example, a particular layer, who practices it." Here Tamás is in essence defining his identity in terms of a community of practice – a group of individuals who build an identity by practicing it.

In discussing Rock Crystal's experiences when performing in Hungary, Mihály reflects further on his Hungarian minority identity using the common term of *külföldi magyar* "foreign Hungarian" to refer to those Hungarians who live outside the borders of modern-day Hungary but are still recognizably Hungarian in their language and behavior:

> I'm a little bit proud, a little, well and the people make you feel that, mainly in the villages where we go to perform. Fairly often, there well it's a good feeling that the people well they respect us a bit because we are "foreign Hungarians." And well you feel, then you really feel proud of the fact that you are a foreign Hungarian.

It is being a "foreign Hungarian" who practices traditional culture that makes Mihály proud. For Tamás, this minority Hungarian identity can be encapsulated in an identity that is local or regional in nature:[12]

> I'm the type of person that, let's say, this Golden area, well, it would be hard to leave it … . To a certain extent I am very happy that I live on this side of the border … . Ok there's Hungary or whatever, but still this is my home. Lots of people these days say Hungary is my mother country … I don't know, maybe it was once a "mother country"; and I don't say that Slovakia is my home, but rather the Golden region. What does it matter to me [what they do in Bratislava or Brno] … because then I could say that Europe is my home or I can expand it as far as I want. So neither Hungary nor Slovakia is my home… . I know this area like the palm of my hand, you know. For me it is this Golden area … .

Both Tamás and Mihály are happy to live on "this side of the border." Both also revel in their experiences visiting Hungary. Mihály feels at home there, because "Well it's just simply that you cross the border and then everyone speaks Hungarian and it's just, oh I don't know, pleasant. Homey." Here Mihály touches on the central component of Hungarian identity for this CofP, namely that to be Hungarian is to speak Hungarian. This component is so central that it is not always mentioned explicitly – it is part of breathing.

Kati, however, given her somewhat different experience at home, where her parents decided to send her to Slovak school, makes the centrality of Hungarian language explicit. For her, the importance of Rock Crystal is as a site for speaking and therefore being Hungarian. Rock Crystal is the only such group she knows of in the area, and is especially important for Hungarians, because :

It is different here for the Slovaks than for the Hungarians, for a Hungarian person, I think it's very good that there is such a place where you can go, because, well it's true that we are in Slovakia and so we must speak Slovak, that's what they always insist on, anyway that there is such a group where you can go out to and you can speak Hungarian there.

She further explains the importance of Rock Crystal as a safe haven, one of the few places she can speak Hungarian without fear of reprisal:

Because, you know for such a person, if her mother tongue is Hungarian then she'd like to speak it with her parents and if she's on the road with her girlfriend have nobody yell at them [for speaking Hungarian].

In further outlining their identity, Rock Crystal members outline similarities with Slovaks, a practice that is rarely heard among older Hungarians. In this way, Mihály points to similarities with like-minded Slovaks:

So well, this cultural preservation mentality is similar, in the Slovak–Hungarian environment, there's a place for both of them, well, like I see that the difference between the Slovaks and Hungarians is blurring ... . So well, here with us, we don't judge a person according to whether he speaks Slovak or Hungarian ... It's like the people live in one, one environment so their mentality is basically the same, they do the same things, they live the same way ... . So from that point of view, the way of thinking, there's no big difference ... . True, we preserve our traditions, we preserve our own [traditions], and our identity too, in that respect let's say the whole thing's a bit different. So we express a little something extra with this [cultural preservation].

Mihály highlights the similarities in behavior among rural Hungarians and Slovaks, in particular those who still focus on preserving traditions. He also, however, clearly shows where the boundary is between Rock Crystal members and like-minded Slovaks, in the "little something extra" they express through their practice.

Negative identity practices focus on one group in particular, a group that does not practice what Rock Crystal members practice in preservation of language first and traditions second, and thus endangers their world by shrinking it. Mihály explains his concern, shared by all the others in the group, about the world around him becoming more and more "Slovakicized," meaning to them primarily the loss of knowledge of Hungarian, and, by extension, the associated folk cultural traditions that rest on language. Today, it is "natural" only to Rock Crystal members to enroll their children in Hungarian language schools. In contrast, years ago it was natural for all Hungarians to place their children in Hungarian schools.[13] Rock Crystal members distinguish themselves through negative identity practices, from the group they refer to as *Félmagyar* "half Hungarians," those who are in the process of assimilating to the Slovak majority. Such half-Hungarians no longer admit to speaking Hungarian, send their children to Slovak schools, and actively dissociate themselves from Hungarian identity. In a joint conversation, Tamás and Sándor explain *Félmagyar* in the following way:

Sándor:	He will be neither Hungarian nor Slovak.
Tamás:	And he considers himself Slovak, but in contrast the others consider him Hungarian, the community, and that's why he won't know where to be.
Sándor:	And he puts his heart and soul into somehow drawing himself to the Slovaks.
Tamás:	Because he wants to be Slovak at all costs.
Sándor:	And those guys are more Slovak than the Slovaks.
Tamás:	Those *Félmagyar* (half-Hungarians) are the worst because they try to convince the others that they are Slovak by doing something against the Hungarians.

Two key elements stand out here. First, the *Félmagyar* has no community, doesn't know where to be. This leads to such a strong yearning to belong that he carries out negative practices against the group he has rejected, while not realizing that he will never be accepted by the group that he wishes to join.

Through these positive and negative identity practices, the Rock Crystal CofP members distinguish themselves from Hungarians in Hungary, who take their identity for granted, and from *Félmagyar,* other minority Hungarians in Slovakia, who have rejected their Hungarian identity. They also distinguish themselves from older Hungarians in Slovakia, with whom they share a deeper experience of Hungarian identity through cultural practices, but who couple that with a strong anti-Slovak stance. They, as opposed to an older generation active in the Hungarian community, advocate bilingualism as well as the maintenance of schools in which Hungarian is the language of instruction. They further actively reject attempts on the part of the Hungarian cultural organization in Golden to "co-opt" their performances as representative of the strong and pure Hungarian culture that is being oppressed. In responding to my question about the relationship between the Hungarian traditional dance movement and politics, Mihály sighs:

> Well, I don't think there's much connection, only, if someone for instance wants to use, takes advantage, like uses it, then yes, same goes for [using] culture to achieve their own political goals, but like I think just a connection, well you just can't mix politics with culture, just like that. Well, like you shouldn't mix them!

Rather, Rock Crystal members advocate cultural sharing and an exploration of similarities with like-minded Slovak groups, practicing their view that Slovaks and Hungarians are more alike than different. Hence, from 1995–1997 they worked to organize a joint dance house with the Slovak traditional dance group in the area. In their everyday practice, they also advocate and practice bilingualism that rests on situational and intersentential switching. When Zsuzsa goes shopping, she always makes a point of speaking Hungarian in every shopping encounter, when there are Hungarians present. If there are also Slovaks present, she greets everyone first in

Slovak, and then shifts to Hungarian. She addresses the salespeople in Hungarian, even those who otherwise never speak Hungarian "to let them know that one can speak both Hungarian and Slovak, that keeping their Hungarian is nothing to be ashamed of." On leaving a store, she always closes with both a Hungarian and a Slovak farewell. While this seems like a small thing, in the context of Slovakia, such practices reflect a desire to change the status quo, to create a new Hungarian identity, that may spread beyond the CofP to incorporate a larger percentage of the population in Slovakia.

Moving outside the community-of-practice: Confronting dominant ideologies

Members of Rock Crystal practice and perform an identity that is at one and the same time, strong in cultural and linguistic orientation to a traditional Hungarian identity, and a local identity supportive of a bilingual and bicultural identity that is non-oppositional to Slovaks. Through these identity practices, we also see the link of this CofP to the larger social formation as a whole. While much of the practice of Hungarian identity for members of this CofP takes place within the CofP, the performance of that identity, linked to the speaking of Hungarian in Slovakia, is a political act in the larger social formation. Hence, while members of Rock Crystal express their identity as "non-political," their practice is by definition political when seen in the context of the powerful ideological discourse within Slovakia.

First Rock Crystal members practice an identity that to some may appear contradictory to older Hungarians with whom they share a large CofP, in that they advocate at one and the same time, close adherence to traditional values and practices, and the acquisition of Slovak and the development of ties with like-minded Slovak youth. This apparent contradiction with "established" views of Hungarian identity as conflictual with Slovak identity, points to the richness of the CofP as a unit of analysis, as it allows for an examination of practice from the perspectives of the members themselves. As time goes on, these young Rock Crystal members are also taking on more central roles within the larger social categories, such as the Hungarian community in Golden, to which they belong. Meyerhoff (2002: 533) outlines that the "membership and boundaries of a CofP, including whether an individual is a core or peripheral member, are defined on the basis of criteria that are subjectively salient to the members themselves and membership is reciprocally recognized." With continuity and change within this small CofP and with respect to the relationships of its members with other CofPs we see how social change may begin to take place. The CofP indeed, "explicitly focuses on (1) individuals' social mobility and (2) the negotiated nature of social identities, thereby elucidating ties between abstract social categories and the social groups that people are members of on an everyday basis (Eckert, 2000: 40–1)" (Meyerhoff 2002: 533).

In this way, these youthful members of a dance group take on a different meaning within the larger society. Bucholtz reminds us that:

... one of the great strengths of the community-of-practice model ... is that 'marginal' members – novices, learners and so forth – move to the center of analysis. In this dynamic framework, *practice* takes on a double meaning, suggesting both habitual social action and rehearsal for later social action – that is, for performance." (Bucholtz, 1999a: 8)

Thus Rock Crystal members, rather than being perceived as marginal to both the Hungarian community and (all the more so) to the larger Slovak society, can be seen as practicing an alternate identity while at the same time influencing the definitions of what it means to be Hungarian in Slovakia.

Indeed, Lave (1991: 77) discusses the relationship of CofP to the "broader situatedness of such communities in a social formation as a whole" with respect to two principles. The first is the prevalence of negatively-valued identities within the society as a whole, of which one example in the present context is Hungarian identity. The second is the "ad hoc interstitial nature of communities of practice in which identities are formed, and sustained knowledgeabilities made possible" (Lave: 1991: 77). We see here in the Rock Crystal an example of just such a community of practice that circumvents the expected and has not only created a new identity for a small group of dancers, but also, through their interactions with other CofPs, may be influencing society as a whole.

While the Rock Crystal Dance Ensemble is but one group of no more than about twenty members, they are tied not only to larger social groupings in Golden, but also to a network of Hungarian dance groups across Slovakia. In these groups, similar practices tying a traditional culture to a modern multicultural world are evident. One aspect of this trend is apparent in the choosing of repertoires that include Slovak dances (and also Romanian dances) to celebrate the links between the traditions of peoples who have lived in close proximity for hundreds of years and have therefore shared cultural elements. This extension of the Dancehouse movement is present in groups throughout the Hungarian language region, and is tied to the types of identity practices outlined for the Rock Crystal group.

Shifting Identity Performances, Shifting Ideologies?

The instruments of social change are generally considered to be elite individuals who have differential access to the powerful discourse, and not individuals engaged in the daily practice and performance of particular identities. Can individuals engaged in the daily practice and performance of identity also bring about social change? Or are they rather sources from which the political elite draw examples that form part of their discourse in the practice of minority identity that centers around critical political issues? This is the next set of questions to address in exploring the mechanisms of social change. Meyerhoff (2002: 531) notes that "[t]he kind of role that [individuals] play in a CofP will partly reflect their own personal history and goals, and also the goals of the group that is jointly engaged in those practices." The same can in theory be extended to an examination of the inter-locking CofPs that make up a particular society.

Through a CofP analysis of performance of a particular ethnic/national identity, we can link this discussion to explorations of the mobilization of political groups. Within East and Central Europe, such mobilization is generally a form of ethnic mobilization and is thus tied to issues of nationalism. The question for political scientists is: why do the political stances and preferences of ethnic minority groups change over time? The answer may lie in the manner in which the CofP changes through the concept of legitimate peripheral participation, where old-timers as well as newcomers are in some sense peripheral to "the future of the changing community" (Lave & Wenger, 1991: 117). Hence newcomers with a different perspective on history and a different perspective on the future, in contestation with old-timers, practice and perform a new identity based on language, one that may allow for a multi-national state identity.

Notes

1. For Erikson (1963, 1968), adolescence marks the development of identity, and hence the identity crisis marks the coalescence of a new identity; the identity crisis entails trying on various identities, which suggests that adolescents shift their affiliation from group to group, sampling the prototypical identity each group offers (Erikson, 1968). Following such sampling, in late adolescence individuals seek an occupational niche to solidify their identity. I interpret that occupational niche here in terms of a central CofP (community of practice). Erikson's conception of the psychological development has more in common with a CofP approach, as he saw internal development as directly tied to societal processes. Hence, he sees the adolescent mind as "an ideological mind – and, indeed, it is the ideological outlook of a society that speaks most clearly to the adolescent who is eager to be affirmed by his peers, and is ready to be confirmed by rituals, creeds, and programs which at the same time define what is evil, uncanny and inimical" (Erikson,1963: 263).
2. See Eckert (2000) for an extended discussion of these issues.
3. A central question in socialization is the nature of the individual and the society to which he is socializing. As outlined in Schieffelin and Ochs (1986b), the individual in various theories of socialization has been conceived of as operating along an agentive, active-to-passive behavioral continuum. The role of individuals as agents of their own socialization can be traced to Mead's (1934) symbolic interactionism, and Schutz's (1967) and Berger and Luckmann's (1966) phenomenology. (See Ochs 1986 and Weigert *et al.*, 1986.)
4. In the remainder of this paper I will use the term "national group" to correspond with the practice in East Central Europe. In that setting, legal documents, social science researchers, and individuals in their everyday discourse, all make a distinction between national minorities and ethnic minorities. That distinction lies in the fact that national minorities "have" a referent "homeland" in which they are a majority; for example Hungarians form a national minority group in Slovakia, Romania, Ukraine, Yugoslavia, etc. In contrast, ethnic groups do not have such a referent homeland, as for example Gypsies throughout East Central Europe. Note, that this distinction also carries with it strong social hierarchy, as groups with no reference homeland are stateless and, by extension, culture-less.
5. This name and all other names of places, individuals, and groups are pseudonyms.
6. For a detailed discussion of the nature of institutional support see László (1998). See also Langman (2002) for an outline of policies directed at Hungarian mother tongue schools.

7. Note that some changes subsequent to the elections in 1998 have led to a loosening of laws, and the reappearance of a few signs.
8. The CSEMADOK (Czechoslovak Hungarian Cultural Organization), an organization of the former Communist government of Czechoslovakia, continued operations in Slovakia for a short time before being subsumed into a national organization supporting cultural arts. At that time, virtually all funding for Hungarian groups ceased. Other avenues for financial support are now occasionally available (especially from Hungary) for cultural activities.
9. I am following the practice of Hungarian scholars who list the Hungarian name, followed by the official name of the town. In this case *Szék* is Hungarian and *Sic* Romanian.
10. While the practice of identity within this group covers a complete range of issues related to gender, age, and national identity, as many of the examples suggest, here I focus on a national identity, as that identity is central to the conscious practice of all members.
11. In looking at both positive and negative identity practices, CofP is distinguished from Tajfel's social identity theory, which holds that "individuals' social behavior is a joint function of (a) their affiliation to a particular group identity that is salient at that moment in the interaction, and (b) their interpretation of the relationship of one's ingroup to salient outgroups" (Holmes & Meyerhoff, 1999: 177). While social identity theory holds that the primary process of establishing a social identity is through comparison with other social groups and boundaries established to distinguish groups (e.g. Barth, 1969), CofP does not see all identity behavior as directly related to outgroups. While such comparisons are important, much identity activity is internal to the group.
12. I have not discussed regional variants of Hungarian here. This is because my informants rarely if ever discuss their own situation in terms that require the inclusion of a distinction between Standard Hungarian and a regional variety – this in spite of the fact that, in dialectological terms, the region in which Rock Crystal is located is defined in terms of a strongly delineated and often stigmatized variant of Hungarian. Speculation on the lack of explicit linking between a regional identity and a regional variant fall beyond the scope of this paper, as I am writing from the perspective of the speakers themselves. In that sense, I am providing what Schiffrin (1997) refers to as a sociolinguistic self-portrait.
13. See Langman (1997b) for additional discussion of the relationship between language, identity, and schooling.

Chapter 12

Multiliteracies in Springvale: Negotiating Language, Culture and Identity in Suburban Melbourne

HEATHER LOTHERINGTON

This chapter focuses on a group of young Australians of South-East Asian background, who are studying the languages of their cultural heritage in Rosemount High School (a pseudonym), a state high school in Victoria. Rosemount High is located in an outer suburb of Melbourne, framed by factories and a bustling community that is living evidence of Australia's post-1970s immigration policy. Springvale, the sociocultural context of these students' lives, is just fifteen minutes away from a rather different picture of Australian suburbia, characterized by tree-lined streets, prohibitively expensive private schools with long waiting lists, and faces whose cultural roots reflect a different vintage in Australia's history of immigration. The understanding of what being an Australian means here is Anglo-Celtic and white – an understanding that grew out of Australia's pre-1970s racist immigration policy which, from the 1890s until the 1960s, effectively created an exclusionist notion of Australian citizenship (Cole, 2000: 31).

This chapter explores the world of Grade 9 and 10 students at Rosemount High School through their everyday language and literacy practices in three languages: Khmer, Vietnamese, and English. The discussion draws on a multifaceted study of the language and literacy practices of adolescent Cambodian-Australians and Vietnamese-Australians living in Springvale.[1] The data drawn on in this chapter include:

- a questionnaire survey of students' sociocultural backgrounds and their language and literacy practices and attitudes ($n = 55$);

- a diary of students' literacy activities over the period of one week ($n = 18$);
- a questionnaire survey of parents' and guardians' socioeconomic back-grounds and their language and literacy practices and attitudes ($n = 24$);
- observations of the language classes in which students participated, including Khmer, Vietnamese, English and English as a second language ($n = 6$);
- interviews with language teachers ($n = 5$);
- interviews with local business people in the community on their uses of and attitudes towards languages, both oral and literate, in daily business life ($n = 9$);
- interviews at factories in the community on their requirements for literacy and their tolerances and expectations of languages used on the factory floor ($n = 18$);
- a photograph study of the main business area;
- informal conversations with students at a local community center.

This chapter frames young peoples' language and literacy practices within the community of their transplanted families and the school, locating conflicting social, cultural, political, and economic pressures that mediate their learning opportunities, cultural obligations, and social networks in a country striving towards multiculturalism. We consider their precarious negotiation of an Australian identity where, given the shape of twentieth-century Australian immigration, only tentative and limited role models exist.

Australian Language Policy: LOTEs in Education

The final quarter of the twentieth century was, for Australia, a political about-face, irrevocably altering the demographics of the country and, in so doing, challenging political and cultural beliefs about what it means to be an Australian. Prior to the 1970s, in the era of the "White Australia Policy," second languages taught in school were seen as "foreign languages," in keeping with Australia's highly discriminatory Anglo-centric cultural orientation. With radical changes to the immigration policy, this label was seen as inadequate; LOTE, the acronym for Languages other than English, came into use in the mid-70s (Kipp *et al.*, 1995: xiii). Later, the designation "community languages" referring to LOTEs and aboriginal languages came into use (Clyne, 1991: 3), identifying post-colonial languages together with pre-colonial languages at home in Australia.

Australia at the turn of the century prides itself on being a multicultural country. The national language policy strongly encourages multilingualism. Each state has its own languages-in-education policy, providing for study of ESL and a range of LOTEs in school. Community language maintenance and learning enjoy strong political support.

In the state of Victoria, LOTE study is available in more than 50 languages (Department of Education, 1997). Eight key languages are prioritized: Chinese, French, German, Greek, Indonesian, Italian, Japanese, and Vietnamese (Clyne, 1997: 104). At the time of this study, ten community languages were taught as credit subjects at Rosemount High: Arabic, Chinese, Khmer, French, German, Greek,

Italian, Japanese, Spanish, and Vietnamese. Our participants were studying their respective languages of cultural origins in a politically and pedagogically supportive context, which, in theory, enfranchises literate LOTE learning and teaching within a system that typically establishes social and political norms for literacy achievement.

Negotiating Multiple Literacies

Rosemount students, studying Khmer or Vietnamese in LOTE programs, are bilingual and biliterate in the languages of their families and the language of social, political, and economic power in Australia: English. Bilingualism, however, is a vague descriptor. A fluent and capable bilingual is not necessarily biliterate, although in our highly literate world, concomitant literacy proficiencies are implicit in notions of language proficiency. Moreover, varied levels of language proficiencies in a person's linguistic repertoire may or may not earn him or her the designation of bilingual, depending on social, educational, and political norms. Although the majority of the participants in our study were dominant in the language of their Asian cultural roots (several were multilingual), all could function and were being educated in both languages.

Multiliteracies

Discussions of literacy engage highly-argued conceptual terrain. Gee (1996: 22), pointing out the inherent political dimensions of literacy, describes it as "a socially contested term." Multiple understandings of literacy bring with them consequent variable social evaluations of literacy success. Achieving socially-sanctioned literacy has been touted as everything from oppressive to empowering. To be found lacking in society's demands for literacy functioning is to be socially aberrant, and those labeled as "illiterates" are characterized in terms of disability, disease, criminal victimization, and imprisonment (Horsman, 1994; Street, 1994b). Despite the breadth of possible understanding of the concept of literacy, social demands for literacy tend to be narrowly constructed and expressed in terms of language proficiencies in specific, powerful languages.

Literacy is clearly too complex and too socially pervasive to be satisfactorily described as the ability to read and write. Written language imbues everyday life. To function in society, we critically mediate an encoded world. However, the exponentially increasing communication technologies we have at our fingertips increasingly complicate what used to be distinguishable lines drawn between written and spoken language. We "talk" in chat rooms that require literate access, input information on telephones using keypad knowledge, and "phone" interlocutors using keyboards and modems (Lotherington, 2001a).

As our world becomes increasingly connected, our needs for literacy diversify. Negotiating multiple discourses is now a crucial part of literacy. Given the increasingly multicultural nature of urban spaces, and global communication possibilities, literacy needs to be correspondingly dynamic. Street (1994a: 95) speaks of "... an 'ideological' model of literacy, that recognizes a multiplicity of literacies... . " The New London Group offers the term: multiliteracies, and in explanation: "... we attempt to broaden this understanding of literacy and literacy teaching and learning to include negotiating a multiplicity of discourses" (The New London Group, 1996: 60).

Preferred literacies

Not all literacies are of equal value. A preferred notion of literacy is created through the historically inextricable relationship between schooling and literacy acquisition. School notions of literacy tend to be socially and linguistically hegemonic. Furthermore, given that notions of grammar are grounded in texts (Street, 1984), the preferred languages of school literacies also have preferred standards.

The young people in our study engage in multiple literacies in two languages. The evaluation of such students, however, is measured in narrower terms, fixed on cognitive attainment and social fluency paradigms in the majority language: English. The young people we studied were assumed to be heavily at risk of not achieving "adequate" literacy skills, "adequate" meaning socially and culturally sanctioned, functionally oriented, academically-based literacy skills in English – although, technically, these students have a wider not a smaller range of literacies than monolingual Australians.

Australian literacies

The Australian *Survey of Aspects of Literacy*, undertaken in 1996, focused on "'functional literacy and numeracy' – those skills necessary to understand and use information from material which is printed in English and found in everyday life" (Australian Bureau of Statistics, 1997: viii). Tests were given for prose literacy, document literacy, and quantitative literacy, and results were reported in a 5-level rubric treating literacy as a continuum rather than as a threshold to be accessed (Australian Bureau of Statistics, 1997).

The results of the *Survey of Aspects of Literacy* identify several factors characterizing Australians "at risk" of inadequate literacy skills. Factors selected for correlation were, in the order reported (Australian Bureau of Statistics, 1997: 4–8): (1) whether English was the first language spoken, (2) educational attainment, (3) age, (4) labor force status, (5) income, (6) indigenous peoples.

The study's definition of literacy as entailing English, together with the reported strong correlations between English as the first language spoken and the levels of educational attainment in a system that runs predominantly in English, indicates that literacy in other languages was considered to be of a lesser value. Indeed, one might question whether literacies grounded in other codes and cultures were thought to legitimately contribute to a profile of Australian literacies at all, indicating a political mismatch between concepts of national literacy and of national cultural identity. Should not a multicultural nation recognize multicultural literacies?

Community Responses to Multilingualism

Springvale

The community in which Rosemount High School is located has traditionally been a major reception center for migrants to Victoria, including, particularly, the Indochinese refugees who form the focus of this chapter. According to the 1991 census, approximately half of the population of Springvale had arrived since 1980 (Markus, 1993: 43). Evidence of Springvale's settlement history is seen in the dramatically multicultural character of the present-day area. Springvale is the face of the late twentieth century in Australian political history: a vital, predominantly blue-collar community, home to a disproportionately high percentage of visible minorities.

A short drive from Rosemount High School, at a major crossroads where the streets bear names celebrating British royalty, is the heart of a thriving commercial community in which businesses are publicized in four languages: Chinese, English, Khmer, and Vietnamese (Lotherington *et al.*, 1998). Around the corner, there are still one or two businesses bearing Greek signs, attesting to Springvale's colorful history as a beacon for newcomers to Australia. Surrounded by factories producing everything from bread to cement, Springvale was a place where migrants could find work.

The Indochinese in Springvale

The latest and most visible wave of newcomers to Springfield is Indochinese. At the time of the 1996 Australian census, the Cambodian community in Australia numbered 19,334 speakers; the Vietnamese community numbered 146,265 speakers, making Vietnamese the fifth largest community language in Australia, and the third largest in the state of Victoria (Clyne & Kipp, 1997: 8–9). Springvale has one of the highest concentrations of both Vietnamese and Cambodian speakers in Australia. Vietnamese-speakers comprise the largest ethnic group in the area (Markus, 1993: 43).

Both the Vietnamese-speaking and Khmer-speaking populations of Springvale represent essentially post-1975 migration. Of the Indochinese youth we studied, 92% were first-generation migrants to Australia. They had settled in Australia during their own short lifetimes. Two thirds of both groups were born in their country of origin (Cambodia or Vietnam) with another 21% (Vietnamese) and 24% (Cambodians) born in other Asian countries, particularly Thailand, signaling that these students entered life in a refugee camp. Only a few participants had been born in Australia.

The Vietnamese-speakers in our study had been in Australia between 1 and 12 years, with a mean Australian residency of 4.43 years. The Cambodian-Australians were slightly more established, having spent from 1 to 14 years in the country, with a mean Australian residency of 5.45 years. In other words, the overwhelming majority of participants had moved into Springvale – their introduction to Australia – during the 1990s.

Multiliteracies in the Business Community

We investigated the language dynamics underlying this manifestly multilingual community in two ways. We explored the uses of the languages displayed in signs in the business community, and we investigated the language and literacy policies and expectations in the local factories where participants' parents might be either working or trying to find employment. A multilingual research team, which included both insiders and outsiders to the language communities being studied, made a number of field trips, eating in the local restaurants, and shopping in the stores, to observe and test out language and literacy practices against the languages used in commercial signs.

Spolsky and Cooper (1991) develop a theory of language choice based on a study of signs in Jerusalem. They posit three rules explaining language choice in signs:

(1) skill: the language/s used are known by the owner (and sign writer);
(2) presumed reader: the language/s used are known by the intended readers;
(3) symbolic value: the language/s used are ones with which the owner wishes to be identified (Spolsky & Cooper, 1991: 81–84).

Within the context of the marketplace, motivation for signing is assumed to be largely economic. However, given the complex multilingual signing on commercial businesses in Springvale, located on streets with British names written in English, a sense of sociocultural belonging is also manifest.

In this commercial area, despite the incessant pressure for English in order to maintain economic viability in an English-speaking country, written English did not figure as prominently as Chinese and Vietnamese in signs and other written material. Interestingly, the ceremonial Khmer script used in commercial signing was discovered to be the work of a single sign painter who had been extensively employed in creating the signs we were seeing on virtually all local businesses. Advertisements for Vietnamese and Cambodian movies as well as notices for cultural events were widely posted in both Vietnamese and Khmer. In one restaurant, the menu was written only in Vietnamese and Chinese, with icons indicating beef and chicken for those not able to read either language. Shopping for food and household products, we found items labeled in Indonesian, Korean, and Japanese in addition to the languages of the area. Indeed, the sole English-labeled product on one large display was toilet paper.

Nonetheless, despite multilingual exteriors, we formed a rather different picture of language values once we began to talk with people who run businesses in the area. The widely used Khmer signing, when put to the test, was found to have been used for presumed readers. Few employees could actually speak Khmer, although offers were quickly made to find someone who could. The script was used as a welcome mat for Cambodian customers. Most shops were actually owned by ethnic Vietnamese and Chinese, who did not read or write Khmer. The choice of languages used in signs thus had symbolic value extending beyond the language proficiencies of the owners. In this community the spirit of multilingualism is honored, but English will still buy you whatever you want.

Factory language and literacy practices and policies

Many of the parents of the young people we interviewed held local blue-collar factory jobs despite their professional or vocational backgrounds. As Markus and Sims explain (1993), post-70s Indochinese refugees did not have the luxury of choice in jobs that earlier migrants to Springvale did. Given the importance of the local factories to the stability of everyday life, we decided to investigate the language and literacy policies of a sample of local factories.

We interviewed supervisory or managerial staff in eighteen local factories, including large and small factories in heavy as well as light industry, and ranging in size from those employing fewer than 10 workers to those employing 500. Profiles of workers varied greatly in gender and cultural background from factory to factory, depending in part on the nature of the product manufactured. Some factories employed 90% or more male employees; others, such as clothing manufacturers, had 80% or more female employees, and only 28% of factories hired equal numbers of men and women. The cultural profile of factory workers was similarly varied, especially in smaller family-owned companies, ranging from factories hiring mostly "Australian" workers (i.e. Anglo-Celtic native English speakers), to those with extremely multicultural workforces, to those with mostly Asian or mostly continental European workers (Lotherington & Norng, 1999).

The language and literacy policies of the factories also varied widely. English only, or mostly English, was required in seven factories. English plus LOTE on occasion was required in four; and English plus one or more languages (including Chinese, French, Khmer, Greek, Italian, Spanish, and Vietnamese) was required in seven factories.

English literacy was not stated as a prerequisite to employment in one-third of the factories surveyed. Nor was either English or literacy in any language a requirement for getting a job in four of the factories, where it was stated that what was important was for workers to be able to do the job effectively. Literacy in English was, however, required in half the factories surveyed (Lotherington & Norng, 1999). Interestingly, despite wide tolerance for the use of LOTES in factories, it was noted that in every case the language of the foreman's instructions was English.

The factory survey indicated that, whereas English was used interculturally in one-third of all factories surveyed, in the majority of local workplaces cultural maintenance was not linguistically jeopardized. However, English language and literacy proficiencies clearly privileged workers economically by creating a wider choice of jobs.

Not surprisingly, workplace literacies in Springvale's blue-collar industries and in the commercial center were shown to be essentially economically driven, resulting in covert as well as overt demands for English, despite surface uses of and tolerances for multilingualism.

Studying at Rosemount High School

Parents' aspirations for their children's cultural literacy

Parents of the teenagers in our study worked at largely blue-collar jobs, including factory work, sewing, truck driving, picking fruit, and also in work in which they had more autonomy, particularly, the restaurant business. On the job, they reported using four languages. In order of descending frequency, these languages were Vietnamese, Khmer, English, and Chinese.

There was staggeringly high unemployment in the group of parents studied: 34.5% were not working. This figure jumps to 45% if those who returned to school for further education are included. Information collected on parents' past work history indicated serious downward mobility. It is little wonder parents pressured their children to be successful in their Australian education.

Parents wanted their children to maintain their Asian language and culture. Their support for their children's study of Khmer or Vietnamese at school was primarily for cultural maintenance, but included a basket of instrumental purposes which, interestingly, involved career prospects. This is salient, given that working parents spoke three Asian languages apart from English in their jobs, and that Springvale boasts a booming business area that is quadralingually sign-posted. The inference is that parents considered Australian multiculturalism to be economically resonant within the heart of their community. Other reasons given included communication with relatives, travel, and use as the default language of communication.

Valuing multilingualism and multiliteracies

Given the multicultural character of the community, local schools must cope with very large numbers of ESL students who live within their catchment areas. Rosemount High School takes pride in its extensive language programs. English as a second language (ESL) and ten community languages, including Khmer and Vietnamese, are taught at the school. Shortly after the completion of this study, the school began to offer bilingual education in Vietnamese and Chinese.[2] This is a learning environment in which multilingualism and multiculturalism are valued.

Vietnamese, designated by the Victorian state government as one of eight languages prioritized for LOTE teaching, was introduced as a subject in 1989. The teaching of Khmer was introduced the following year in response to the expressed needs of the students, parents, and school community.[3]

Teachers of Vietnamese and Khmer at Rosemount High School are well-qualified native speakers who are able to incorporate cultural activities into their classes. The teaching of Vietnamese and Khmer is seen not only as instilling cultural pride, and augmenting and maintaining proficiencies in the ancestral language, but it is also viewed as helping these bilingual and bicultural youngsters to improve their school grades by drawing on their life experiences, whether real or assumed.

Languages and literacies in class

We interviewed teachers of Khmer, Vietnamese, ESL, and English[4] in order to understand their philosophies of teaching, and we attended classes in all languages to observe lessons, implicit as well as explicit, in linguistic and cultural literacies. Teachers' epistemologies of literacy as manifested in classroom practice varied significantly from language to language, and from teacher to teacher. One reason for this was linguistic: the languages and the literary traditions they were teaching varied greatly phylogenetically. Khmer uses a complex syllabic alphabet derived from Sanskrit to represent 33 consonants, 13 independent vowels, and 24 dependent vowels (Coulmas, 1996: 268; Hornberger, 1996: 77; To, 1998: 130). Literacy acquisition in Khmer thus requires instruction in basic alphabetic conventions and numeracy activities as well as in the expected literary, social, and cultural discourses. Contemporary Vietnamese uses an adapted Roman alphabetic script to represent 18 single consonants, 8 double consonants, 11 vowels, and 6 diacritics to differentiate phonemic tones. Vietnamese, unlike Khmer, is a tonal language (Coulmas, 1996: 543; To, 1998: 130–131; Tuc, 1997: 132–133). Furthermore, Vietnamese orthography has a complex history that saw Chinese ideograms and their indigenized Vietnamese variant, Chu Nom, co-used for socially distinguished literacies, similar to the socially delineated, interactive scripts of contemporary Japanese (Lo Bianco, 2000).

Variable access to texts in LOTE and ESL/English classes created different possibilities in language teaching methodologies. In LOTE classes, political preoccupations with the origins of literacy materials meant that teachers had to work very hard at finding and editing suitable reading materials for their students to ensure that there was no promotion of political ideologies incompatible with views held by parents in the community. Notably, there was remarkably little interface with community literacy practices. One exception to this was a multimedia poster project completed in a Vietnamese class publicizing a school camping expedition.

English classes tended towards a genre approach in both reading and writing. This focus on language as a process was less available to LOTE teachers owing to limited text access. For learners of Khmer, product was, in any case, a serious concern, given script convention differences that had to be mastered. On balance, LOTE classes were more teacher-centered than English and ESL classes, reflecting both resources and cultural notions of education.

The essence of literacy education in the three languages is historically rooted in diverse cultural perspectives. To (1998) notes the importance of role models in Vietnamese learning. Literacy is highly valued; the teacher is expected to provide models for students to emulate. In Cambodian culture, the Buddhist temple serves as a cultural anchor; religious practice and the teaching of cultural literacy are both celebrated (Hornberger, 1996). These are not models of contemporary Western education, and certainly not templates for communicative ESL methodology. English is a language that has come to literary prominence only over the past few hundred years, and is typically taught for functional, often intercultural, communication purposes rather than for its literary and cultural history.

Analysis of classroom literacy practices in LOTE, ESL, and English classes also underscored the prominence of school literacies within the school community. Whereas school literacies permeated home and community literacies, e.g. in the treatment of homework as a social activity as well as a family obligation (to help younger siblings), very little incorporation of the rich multilingual literacy practices occurring within the community was evident in the classroom. School literacies were similarly seen to be invading home and community domains in a non-reciprocal manner in a study conducted by Bhatt *et al.* (1995), who investigated multilingual literacy practices in England. School-based literacy practices in language classes were treated as ends in themselves rather than as means to other ends, which we found more typical of community literacies.

Languages, literacies and cultural identity

Teachers' comments about the cultural identities of students revealed curiously conflicting stereotypes: LOTE teachers saw their students as Australians, while English as well as ESL teachers saw the same students as Asians. How could the same students be perceived so differently?

A worry that I felt over this dichotomous labeling was that young people were being assessed in terms of deficit, in terms of what they weren't rather than what they were, i.e. not sufficiently Australian or Vietnamese or Cambodian. Discrepant notions of students' identities also signaled a need for closer dialog between teachers about the linguistic proficiencies of their students across languages. Their comments may also indicate that teachers, particularly English language teachers who do not necessarily have access to Indochinese cultural life, need to learn more about the students they teach, and the lives they lead outside of school hours.

When asked whether they felt more Australian or more Cambodian or more Vietnamese, participants had difficulty answering, but indicated that they considered themselves to be a fusion, determined to some extent by linguistic practices. Placement of their self-concept on a sliding scale of Asian to Australian found them leaning markedly towards an Asian identity. Results showed that the Vietnamese speakers felt marginally more Australian (33%) than the Khmer speakers (29%). Such a profile, however, begs the question: can young people of Australian cultural backgrounds create an acceptable Australian identity in a nation where "Australian" is still understood as white and Anglo?

Communication with friends and family

The families we studied had variable proficiencies in a number of languages, including Khmer, Vietnamese, English, French, and Chinese. Most young people (62% of Khmer speakers and 59% of Vietnamese speakers) considered their home language to be their strongest language. Nonetheless, 27% of all young people participating felt that English was their strongest language.

In general, Cambodian families preferred to maintain Khmer as the language of the household. Although Vietnamese speakers certainly maintained their language in the home as well, they were more likely to code-mix. Some 85% of all Cambodian-Australian adolescents engaged in brokering on behalf of family members in situations where translation help was needed, such as in filling out forms for social services or in accessing medical help or consulting a teacher. This figure was lower in the Vietnamese-speaking population, where 67% were engaged in brokering for family members.

Profiles of who spoke which language to whom in the family revealed a familiar pattern of impending language shift. Whereas Khmer or Vietnamese was used exclusively with the mother and father of the family in 75% of cases, 60% of the participants also used English with older siblings, and 75% incorporated English with younger siblings. The fact that participants prefer to use their community language primarily with elders (usually for reasons of respect or because it was their language of highest proficiency), and incorporate more English with friends and younger siblings, echoes the findings about attitudes and language-use patterns amongst community language speakers that have been reported in other Australian studies (Fernandez *et al.*, 1997).

Community involvement

Community activity among our group of Asian-Australian adolescents was unexpectedly low. Only 13% were involved in any work outside the home, and this consisted mostly of helping out with the family business. Only a very slim 10% were involved in extracurricular activities, these being mostly sports activities. Participants were active in cultural and religious activities, centering largely around their Buddhist temples and churches, and they actively helped out in the home, often being charged with responsibilities for taking care of younger siblings, while parents did shift work in local factories. The picture produced from these findings is one of a community within a community: Asian youth engaged in culturally sheltered lives searching for a way into an Australian identity.

This observation prompts a concern expressed by a teacher, who feared that teenagers of South-East Asian origins were not getting sufficient exposure to English through "Australian" life. It also echoes reported pleas made by parents to the Vietnamese teachers to safeguard their children against an emerging Asian youth role model, that of druglord. Indeed, during the tenure of this research project, a tragic death from a heroin overdose occurred in this neighborhood: a Cambodian-Australian boy of only 13, whose parents were, understandably, beside themselves trying to understand how this terrible fate had befallen their son. Investigative reports described a home in which rooms were culturally divided – the Cambodian artefacts of the family rooms contrasting with the pop youth culture of the boy's bedroom. The space between Asian-ness and Australian-ness, especially as foregrounded against the recent, unsettled history of non-white migration into the country, creates a critical identity battleground for these young people.

Community literacy activities

Using as a framework the seven uses of community literacy proposed by Heath (1986: 21), which includes instrumental, social interactional, news related, memory supportive, oral substitutes, record keeping, and confirmation, we analyzed students' journals of literacy events. Four of Heath's uses of community literacy are relevant to the lives of the teenagers studied here:

(1)   instrumental: information about practical problems of everyday life (e.g. price tags, street signs);
(2)   social interactional: information pertinent to social relationships (e.g. letters, recipes);
(3)   news related: information provided about third parties, distant events (e.g. news items)
(4)   memory supportive : memory aid (e.g. phone messages) (Heath, 1986: 21).

These we classified according to domain of use, to reveal a picture of the kinds of literacy practices students were engaged in and with whom (see Table 12.1). Domains included community (friends/social), home (family and self-engagement), and school. It is important to note that these domains were found to be permeable and interdependent. For example, reading a novel could be either homework or a leisure activity, and as such could be either or both school and self-engagement. Furthermore, a story assigned in English class may inspire further reading of the same author or genre of text. Equivalently, information gleaned through vernacular media may be incorporated legitimately in schoolwork.

As can be seen in Table 12.1, school-based literacy activities, which include home-work, TV/news, and books, figure prominently in all domains of young people's lives. Homework, for example, is an activity communally engaged in with siblings and with friends, as well as being an individual activity. Comments from teachers signaled the parental pressure typically put on students to study hard and do well in school. Participants' incorporation of homework into the social fabric of their home and social life attests to this.

The literacy events engaged in by the participants were generally consistent with their age group. However there were two interesting cultural exceptions: the common use of karaoke with friends, and the need to provide assistance for their families where an interface between the Asian worlds of the household and the larger Anglo-centric, social fabric of Australia was needed.

The range of literacy activities that students engaged in and the languages they

Table 12.1 Participants' uses of literacy and domains of use

Domains	Community	Home	School
Community literacy	friends/social	family	self-engagement
Instrumental	homework with friends	siblings' homework	own homework
	shopping	shopping/errands	library research
		brokering/translating	specific reading
			specific writing
			computer-related media news
Social interactional	story-telling	writing letters	novels
	joking	cooking	computer
	singing/ karaoke	reading to siblings	electronic games
	card games	card games	movies
	sports		
News-related	chatting	writing letters	media news
Memory-supported		telephone messages	

used were patterned in many ways. Figure 12.1 tracks the most commonly reported literacy activities, and the languages young people used engaging in them.

Not surprisingly, homework was reported to be a dominant activity. School-work was conducted in both languages, reflecting students' bilingual study, but there was clearly a preference for English. Reading of books and stories, too, was biased towards English. One possible reading of this language bias is that most of the reading done by the participants is actually determined by school demands, and most of their subjects are studied in English. Another possibility is that market availability affects access to recreational texts written in Khmer and Vietnamese. Khmer books were burned under Pol Pot in Cambodia (Hornberger, 1996). Present day sources of Vietnamese and Cambodian written materials include France and California. Both require cultural as well as linguistic adaptations for teachers in Australia.

Both English and Khmer/Vietnamese were used in social activities with friends, although interestingly the Vietnamese speakers tended to use less of their home language with friends than did the Khmer speakers. English was, in fact, the domi-nant language used between friends for the Vietnamese-speakers; it was equally used with Khmer for the Cambodian-Australians.

Language choices with family also included both languages, with the inclusion of English tending to vary according to the age of the family member, and greater use of Khmer and Vietnamese occurring with older family members. Recreational

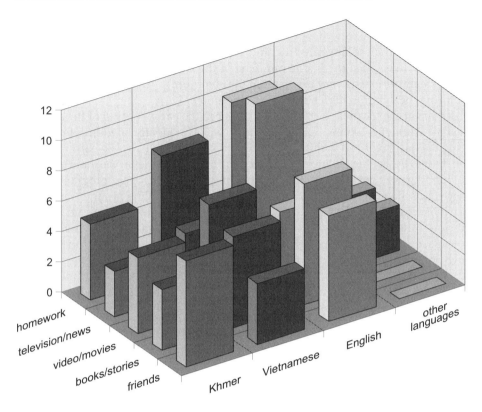

Figure 12.1 Most commonly reported literacy activities and languages used

activities were linguistically split with videos, CD music, and karaoke being enjoyed predominantly in Asian languages (including Chinese languages as well as their home language), but computer games were played predominantly in English, probably reflecting market availability. Mass media consumption tended to be more English-oriented, with television viewing involving more English than community language; radio involved mostly English, and newspapers, exclusively English. Our familiarity with the languages of electronic media (Lotherington & Ebert, 1997) suggests that these preferences are reflections of availability more than of agency.

Volunteer tutoring at a community center

Despite having local research assistants in our team who were native speakers of Vietnamese and Khmer, and also first-generation Australians who had followed difficult life paths similar to those of our participants and emerged as academically successful,[5] we had problems getting close to the families we were studying. I had expected to be kept at a distance as a white, native English-speaking researcher, although I had hoped that my own status as a migrant to Australia would strike a cord. However, the young people and their families were fearful, and sometimes resistant. Nonetheless I wanted to find a way to get a sense of young Asian-Australians' lives from the inside out. One of the Cambodian-Australians on our research team, who was very involved in the community, suggested that I join him in tutoring local high school students as a volunteer.

I arrived at the location, a community center in the early evening of the assigned weekday. Although I knew Springvale quite well, frequently spending time there during the day, I realized that it was a different place at night. It was hard to find an open door to the center; eventually I located the buzzer to be let in the main entrance. The building was covered in signs advertising needle-exchange programs, pregnancy counseling, STD and AIDS testing. A few people milling around outside the place looked at me oddly. I inquired as to the volunteer tutoring program and was sent down the hall. I found it easily. The three or four small rooms assigned to tutoring were full to the brim with Indochinese teenagers, who spilled into the halls, doing homework on the floor, tables, chairs, window ledges, wherever. Piles of coats were lumped here and there. In each of the rooms was at least one person leading discussions, or making explanations on the board. All were young, Indochinese people in their twenties. My research assistant spotted me right away, and set to work finding students who I could help. After sadly turning away one young person who wanted help with senior chemistry, I was introduced to another who needed assistance with an English composition. We set to work one-to-one in a comfortable corner on the floor, proofing and correcting a text written from the perspective of any teenaged girl concerned with clothes, boys, parental approval, and whether that special someone would ask her to the dance.

As the allotted time for the tutoring space came to a close, I was introduced to the other volunteer tutors. They were university students working towards their degrees at various universities in Melbourne. Their zeal was highly energizing. They were survivors; they had lived through the same academic and settlement difficulties as the young students they tutored for hours every week absolutely gratis. They had found a way through the academic maze, despite their traumatic refugee pasts, the constant cultural and linguistic mediation, the lack of academic support, the economic hardship, the palpable racism. They had learned to use English well, and had competed favorably to gain entrance to tertiary education in Melbourne. Many of them were studying to be teachers; all were cultural and linguistic mediators of learning to high school students in Springvale in the same rooms where during the day, needles for hard drug users were exchanged, and those suffering from AIDS or other STDs were counseled. I was deeply impressed with their altruism. Though their mission was to help students succeed in school, they were presenting powerful, positive role models to these local high school students who had no social space to fill, no archival identity to look to. As I left the building to drive west into town and into progressively whiter, more identifiably "Australian" Melbourne, I got more strange looks. I realized that mine was the only white face in the entire place.

Negotiating Sociocultural Identity

Tensions in language choice, practices, and values

What are the tensions mediating young people's language and literacy learning, opportunities, requirements, aspirations, and practices? A number of specific tensions create problems for their lives in and out of school. These center around two predominant concerns: first, negotiating a sociocultural identity as first-generation Asian-Australians within a country that has only welcomed non-white migrants for one generation; and second, successfully acquiring an Australian education.

Comments made both by and about participants show how they are caught in an identity conflict. Family tensions in children's socialization counterpose the desires of parents for their children to maintain their cultural identity through study of the home language at school, and the economically-driven pressures they impress on their children to succeed at school, where they are academically judged in English.

Parents are struggling to relocate themselves and their families within the Australian context: they have had a low success rate in finding employment, and what they have found has been downwardly mobile. They want their children to have better economic opportunities, and at the same time, they are highly fearful of the emerging druglord role model for young Asian-Australians that is, in itself, a manifestation of this battleground for a socially and economically acceptable identity. Young people are negotiating the border between them and us in a racially charged environment. People of all ethnic backgrounds are still trying to learn what multiculturalism means in a country that just a generation ago militantly promoted an image of Australians as white, and continues to include this stereotype in high profile, present-day party politics. Where are the social and economic rewards for an Asian becoming Australian?

Although Springvale offers strong community support for the use of local Asian languages, there are threats to community language use through sheer economic force. Customers may be served in the language they want but, with the spread of multiculturalism, this will increasingly be English, used as an intercultural language. There is also evidence in the factories: in many cases workers were hired if they could do the job despite their language and literacy proficiencies. However, their supervisors were most likely to be speaking English.

Changing patterns of language use were in evidence with younger generations of Vietnamese-speakers and Khmer-speakers in negotiating their various roles as student, friend, sibling, and child. The Cambodian families were less likely than the Vietnamese to code-mix in the home, and more likely to require assistance brokering on behalf of family members in situations where translation help was needed. It is not possible to discern whether this tendency for stronger maintenance reflects the greater learning required to become literate in Khmer due to script divergence, or simply reflects different cultural values. Also, the Cambodian population in Springvale, though a very strong regional presence, is much smaller than that of the Vietnamese.

Acquiring an Australian education

It was clear that school literacies had interpenetrated home and social life, but there was very little evidence of the reverse. There were apparent discontinuities in kinds of literacy practises between home and community, where literacies were incorporated into life as means to an end (whether social, cultural or economic) and school literacies, which were treated as ends in themselves – perpetual tests of sufficient Australianness. Bhatt *et al.* (1995), studying multilingual literacy practises in the home, school, and community in England, similarly found that individuals had their own purposes for literacies in the home that literacy both facilitated and was incidental to, whereas literacy activities in school focused primarily on literacy learning.

School structures also tend to dichotomize identity by separating literacy activities into different language subjects. Khmer, Vietnamese, and English were taught by different teachers, who had different impressions of their students. Although the teaching of all languages was unquestionably competent, teachers were posed on different ends of an ESL–LOTE continuum, on which were balanced different social and academic expectations. Teaching together within a system that offered boutique literacies in Vietnamese and Khmer versus academically rewarding literacies in English, obfuscated teachers' common ground of language and literacy education.

Despite the positive national policy on maintaining community languages, social messages as to the linguistic value of Vietnamese and Khmer are mixed. Current concerns about Australian literacy levels clearly indicate that literacy is constructed as English literacy, despite Australia's widely publicized policy of multiculturalism. Literacy in English is clearly a priority of the school, boards of study, and the nation, as seen in the *Survey of Australian Literacies* (Australian Bureau of Statistics, 1997). Academic excellence is construed as a function of English literacy.

We need to ask serious questions about the gaps between political positions. Where is multiculturalism in literacy? Can schools accommodate and facilitate a concept of multiple literacies? Who are "Australians" in this post-modern age of multiple cultures, literacies, and identities? How big is the Australian cultural space for linguistic minorities?

Conclusion: Negotiating Identity in Multicultural Australia

Australia's multicultural policy does not pervade public social conscience in terms of literacy practices. Australian education is politically well-intentioned, but is not yet creating the social space for constructing a multimembership Australian identity. There is a need to rethink how to conceptualize, validate, teach, and assess literacy proficiencies in a multicultural society. There is also a need for closer collaboration on all fronts in the lives of these young people (among their teachers, between the school and the home, the school and the community, and the home and the community) to help them build an Australian life within a dynamic and potentially inclusive multiculturalism.

Notes

1. I acknowledge with gratitude Language Australia who funded the study: *Biliteracy at Home and School* that I conducted with the assistance of the following research assistants in the Language and Society Centre, Department of Linguistics, Monash University: Simone Ebert, Tetsuta Watanabe, Sorn Norng, Tuc Ho-Dac, and Sopea Sao.
2. For information on this project, see Lotherington (2001b).
3. This information is from school brochures. However, in order to protect the anonymity of the school, I cannot include these publications in the references.
4. English as a second language (ESL) and English classes were parallel streams into which students were placed depending on their assessed proficiencies in English.
5. Dr Tuc Ho-Dac had recently been awarded his PhD. Sorn Norng and Sopea Sao were students nearing graduation from Monash University.

Chapter 13

Terms of Desire: Are There Lesbians in Egypt?[1]

DIDI KHAYATT

I was born and grew up in Egypt more than half a century ago. All my life I suspected that my mother's dreams for my marriage and parenthood would never quite materialize because my desires did not seem to coincide with her fantasies. I finally became sexually involved with a woman at nineteen, in my third year of university in Egypt, knowing in my heart that I now was a "lesbian," although this was an identity that was only in my mind, and ambiguously so. By that time, I already had the words for what I was becoming. At the time I told no one but my middle sister about my suspicions regarding my possible predilection, not because I did not have the correct terminology, but because even then I realized that being involved with a woman was even more reprehensible than being involved sexually with a man when custom demanded that I remain a virgin until marriage. The interesting part of this story is not that, even then, in the early sixties, I had words to represent my unfolding identity, but that those words could be spoken in only two of the three languages that I spoke: English or French, but not in Arabic. Since my native language is Arabic, and since this is not my language of education, it never occurred to me at the time, nor for many years later, that if I had not been educated in a European language, I may never have been able to articulate my sexuality in terms of an identity, rather than as a set of practices with no name.

Although Arabic does have words that are in some sense equivalent to "homosexuality," "gay," and "lesbian," most of these do not occur in Egyptian colloquial language. The exception is *"khawal,"* a term comparable to the English "faggot" (in terms of the derogatory intention of the speech act, but not as an identity). I spent six years explicitly looking for "lesbians" in Egypt. Although I found women who were homoerotically involved with other women, it became clear to me that they were not "lesbians," an identity whose history is located in nineteenth century Europe, and whose current significations are associated generally with *being* particular sexual orientations rather than *practising* specific acts. My question became: if sexual categories can be called into question when we attempt to apply these to trans-national locations, what other subject locations are troubled, shift, or even do not make sense, when the cultural context is different from the one in which we are working and naming social behavior?

This chapter is based on the work I have been doing in Egypt for the past six years. I began the research because of a statement I read in Schmitt and Sofer (1992: 5) that the Arabic language contains no equivalent words for either "homosexuality" or "heterosexuality." Although I now question the assertions made by Schmitt and Sofer, they nevertheless led me to interrogate how women whose language and culture is Arabic, who do not have access to semantic categories that would describe their experiences in their informal speech systems, and who have not been in contact with "Western"[2] sexual terms, make sense of their sexual relations with other women. Furthermore, in terms of doing research, how can one find lesbians in Egypt when the local language contains no current colloquial referent for such terms as "lesbian" or "heterosexual"? What are the implications of universalizing the term "lesbian" for women in Egypt involved in same-sex relationships but whose sexual orientation developed outside the context that originally gave meaning to the term? Sexual identities are not universal, even if sexual practices are generally similar around the world. As Anna Livia and Kira Hall argue: "Clearly, one cannot study gay, lesbian, bisexual, or transsexual discourse cross-culturally, or transhistorically if the terms are defined in such a narrowly culture-specific way as to be ungeneralizable" (Livia & Hall, 1997: 11). The meaning people give to the practices depends upon their cultural contexts as these intersect with social class, religion, and gender, and so on. For instance, one of my interviewees, a social scientist in Egypt who was completing major research on women's health, maintained that there are no lesbians in that country. In her words:

> I said in a rural village you would not find a lesbian if you want to define lesbianism the way it is defined in the West. The term does not exist. The relationship between a female and a female does not exist in our culture. For us to ask the question – not that people did not respond, but how do we ask about something that has no description or terminology to describe it? How do we describe it? Do we use practices or definitions that come from the West? It could not be. So what we tried to do is just describe: "they do this, they do that," to make ourselves understood. There wasn't resentment to the question, but there was a sort of "what are you talking about" confusion. So I did not feel that homosexuality existed – but with men, most [of the women interviewed] recognized the practice.[3]

In a related way, when I read a detailed footnote in Franz Fanon's *Black Skin, White Masks* (Fanon, 1967:180) that insisted that there was no homosexuality in the Antilles, I had to agree with his contention. I concur that the practices that existed in the Antilles at the time Fanon was making his assertion could not appropriately be described by using a referent (homosexuality) that had a history in white Europe in the nineteenth century. As Kramsch (1998: 9) would have it, "Knowledge itself is colored by the social and historical context in which it is acquired and disseminated."

The object of my study was not to find "lesbians" in Egypt, but to disrupt the unproblematic transposition of sexual categories by many Euro-North-American scholars. There have been several volumes that recount looking for gays and lesbians, bisexuals, trans-gendered, and trans-sexual people in various nations around the globe (see Herdt, 1997; Penelope & Valentine, 1990), some of which recognize differences in conceptualizations of such terms. The tendency, however, is to seek individuals who exhibit sexual desires that parallel "Western" sexual identities. When, however, particular societies do not yield terms or behaviors that correspond to sexual categories assumed by the authors, the society in question is presumed to be lacking in sophistication. By that I mean that, when conceptualiza-tions of gender/sexuality categories occur in various areas of the world, they are measured hierarchically against a Euro-North-American understanding of sexual identities, and are often found wanting. Practices that can conceivably be compared to "lesbian/gay/homosexual" categories are perceived as a primitive instantiation of the Euro-North-American model, and one that will eventually develop into iden-tity categories familiar in this part of the world. It is this very tendency that led me to research how gender/sexuality practices are articulated, understood, and played out in Egypt.[4]

The research I undertook included interviewing people of different social classes. As a previously-colonized nation, Egypt's upper classes are educated in either English or French (or other European language) schools and, as such, often read and think in the languages of the colonizers. The majority of Egypt's population is not functionally literate in classical Arabic, the language of writing, and is therefore unlikely to have read the rich erotic (including homoerotic) literature. For those who (like myself) attended European schools, however, intellectual and scholarly bodies of knowledge existed in various libraries and were/are available to the few who read in those languages. As a teenager, I had access to my mother's extensive French library. She was interested in poetry, history, and philosophy, and often read to us children pieces she found interesting, just as mothers in North America read stories to their children at bedtime. As quite a young girl, I remember my mother's voice reading a French poem she loved called *Les fleurs du mal* by Beaudelaire or poetry by the Ancient Greek poet, Sappho. I remember at one point in her reading registering an image of a woman sleeping on another woman's nipple and having the imprint of her lover's nipple on her cheek when she awoke. I remember asking and being told about women loving women, about the word "lesbian," and about "homosexual" men whose love for each other was often ambiguously mentioned in much of the literature that my mother owned. Much of what she read to us made no impression because the language of the poetry was difficult to understand for the child I was; but some of it did cohere because of my budding curiosity in sexual matters. Later in my young life, it was easy to go back to these poems, to read André Gide, Sartre, Camus, and others who mention some form of homoeroticism, by then knowing the words, guessing at the illicitness of my task, and yet craving a reflection of my troubled and troubling feelings.

My own history allowed me to recognize that to talk to women whose only language is Arabic would be different than speaking with women from my own class. My task as a researcher was to find women, regardless of their sexual practices, who would be willing to speak to me on the subject of same-sex eroticism. Because of religious and cultural taboos, this was close to an impossible task. In the end, however, I did find several individuals who agreed to be interviewed. I was also able to speak to several people who, either because of their sexuality or because of their profession, could talk about the prevailing notions of same-sex practices in Egypt.

It is very difficult to write about social classes in Egypt especially since the 1952 Revolution dismantled what was then recognized as the "upper" classes: families that were landed gentry and/or that were politically connected to the monarchy. Although the "old" families did not completely disappear, many lost much of their power. The social hierarchy that replaced the old system is for the most part made up of an entrepreneurial class whose money was made in the last forty years or so. It is therefore perhaps more appropriate to look at other ways of distinguishing among the diversity of classes that currently make up Egyptian society. Despite Egypt's long colonial history, what is today considered as mainstream culture can be recognized as a conglomeration of values and attitudes that are, for the most part, Islamic, but are adapted to a local culture that was already imbued by Ancient Egyptian, Greek, Roman, Christian (read Coptic), Arab, Ottoman, English, and French influences. It is therefore more appropriate to describe the cultural mainstream of Egypt as geographically variable, socially diverse, and culturally fluid. In other words, depending where you are in Egypt, the variety of responses on any given issue will depend on such variables as education, religion, gender, and location.

Baladi Values

A concept that would subsume yet nuance social class is *baladi*. It is a term that captures the distinct flavor of mainstream Egyptian society. Evelyn Early describes the term like this:

> Historically, "baladi" indicated the locals, the Egyptians, as versus the Turks, the Mameluks, the French, or the British. To be *"ibna' al-balad"* sons of the country, was to defend Egypt against French and British occupiers. *Balad*, a noun, means community – whether country, city, town, or village; in colloquial Egyptian it can mean "downtown" or village. *Baladi* the adjective form, means local or indigenous. (Early, 1993: 54)

Baladi is often contrasted to *afrangui*, a term that denotes "foreign," but which has come to mean simply that which is not considered *baladi*. What is interesting about these two concepts is that the terms are self-descriptive and both concepts permeate, to a certain extent, all social "classes." People who would consider themselves *baladi* are more likely to be poor, although the term could be used disparagingly to mean "not sophisticated, or not tasteful" when referring to new money. Where some *baladi* people aspire to *afrangui* ways, most of what is considered *afrangui* is imbued by *baladi*. The terms become more specific when describing particular values or specific ways of understanding the world. Therefore, although born and raised in Egypt until I was twenty-three, my English education, and later, my emigration to Canada, separated me from many current *baladi* ways of thinking. When, however, I decided to do this research, it was the *baladi* perspective that I was after. I expressly sought out women who did not speak any language other than Arabic, and who were more likely to be illiterate. My choice of respondents reflected what I perceived to be a large majority of Egyptian women. Because they are unlikely to have access to *afrangui* terms, interviewing *baladi* women would allow me to understand how same-sex practices are articulated or conceived if there is no word to describe these actions.

I went to Egypt on many occasions with the intention of speaking with women who, I thought, would not have been tainted by foreign television through satellite, and therefore would have no words to refer to women who had sex with other women. Whenever I planned a trip to Egypt, my intentions were very clear: I would go to a village or to urban *baladi* areas, I would speak with women, and would ask those questions that would lead me to understand how they thought about sexuality. When I got to Egypt, however, the impossibility of my task was manifestly evident to me: there was absolutely no way to speak to village women about such topics. I could not even speak to servers in my mother's house who were *baladi*. The reasons for what I thought was an inexplicable turnaround are numerous. First, a distinct social class difference, both in education and in financial means, made such conversations impossible. Second, sexuality is not a topic one can discuss as an issue, even among women who were members of a speech community. It may come up in a conversation, but only in intimate contexts, and I had no relationships with anyone outside of my class that included such intimacy. Third, as an "unmarried" woman, despite my age, I could not bring up a topic such as sexuality as easily as one who is married. Fourth, what seemed like a simple task of finding a language for discourse with Egyptian women informers about sexuality, turned out on closer examination to be a daunting task, since sexuality is an unmentionable subject.[5] Finally, I was attempting to interview *baladi* women in an era of resurgent traditional Islamic values where discussions about sexuality are taboo, and where issues about women's sexuality are covert, indeed, secret and shameful. On some level, I knew all of the above. The problem arose between, on the one hand, being in Canada when planning my research and, on the other, the reality of Egyptian culture. My role and location in Egyptian society escaped me when I was "away" living in a land where neither family nor name gave me the privileges I derived from my social class in Egypt. In the end, I succeeded in interviewing about thirteen people, only two of whom can be considered *baladi*.

Regardless of social class, when I broached the subject of names for women who are sexually involved with other women, I got blank stares. Except for the one man I interviewed, those interviewees with *afrangui* education could not think of an equivalent term for "lesbian." An intellectual whose ability to read in four languages (three of which are European) allowed him a fundamental understanding of the Arabic language and its literature, he confirmed that in classical Arabic a term did indeed exist that referred to women who are sexually involved with other women. The word is *mussahaqah*. Another scholar, As'ad AbuKhalil (1993: 32), confirms that "lesbian sex is described in Arabic as *sihaq* or *musahaqah*." It should be understood that a term such as *mussahaqah*[6] is not available to most Egyptians. But then, none of the people I interviewed, across class and education, denied that the practices existed. The problem was that whatever happened between women sexually was not made an issue, and was certainly not talked about publicly.

Two of the interviewees ventured to speculate why sexual practices between women are invisible, not significant enough to be discussed. These two women, who are social scientists in Cairo, believed that part of the reason may be that women in Arab cultures in general, and specifically in Egypt, have no trouble touching each other. One informant said:

> If you go to places like el Wali, [a *baladi* section of Cairo,] the woman has no problem touching another woman. Women touch each other, bathe each other, embrace each other, rub each other's backs. There is no idea that a woman would be ashamed of her body or be shy about her body in front of another woman, whereas it is not the same in front of a man. How much in this case there might be sexual feelings involved, this is something very hard to know, very hard to investigate.

The other woman concurred: "[women] touch each other and hug each other, [but] how much of this is sexually satisfying, one has to study it." She adds a little later that she thinks that women, in their generalized touching: "may acquire a certain emotional and sexual satisfaction to some extent, but I did not find [in my research] an Egyptian girl who would not marry because she is a lesbian and would rather have a relationship with another woman. Not even in the city. "

Other interviewees, while not contradicting the above contentions, nevertheless recognize the existence and the practice of woman-to-woman relations. One of the interviewees, an upper class woman, told me that, when she was a girl of twelve or fourteen, a "peasant" woman from one of the villages on her family's land came to Cairo to learn to be a servant. As is typical of female employees who go to Cairo on their own, she lived with the family. My interviewee explained that this young "peasant" woman was in her early twenties and that they became close. It was the young peasant woman who seduced the younger girl. Although the former eventually returned to her village to marry, the latter continued to seek women as sexual partners.

From interviews with two different *baladi* women, it became evident that, while they may not have the term for it, they certainly were aware of the practices. When I pushed one of them to tell me what she meant when she was talking about a woman being *bita'et settat* (an expression in colloquial Arabic that can be loosely translated as "those who like women," or "those who belong to women"), she explained[7] that "those kinds of women are found in Saudi Arabian princess (*amirat*) classes and that these women preyed on innocent Egyptian women." I asked if there were any Egyptian women who practiced the same "perversions," and she replied that there must be, but that she never heard of it in her neighborhood. The other woman assured me that, although she had heard of such practices because she had traveled abroad, she claimed: "I have never met anyone here in Egypt. Not one." She went on to nuance her assertion by quoting a saying in Arabic that declares that, for every rule in the world, a similar one must exist locally. But, she assured me, such "perversions" can only be considered a social disease. Later in the interview, the same woman admitted that:

> There are women whose sex is *multahib* [inflamed], the worse kind of sex is woman with woman. I shall tell you why. Because their [women's] nature is flat, so that the worse sex is in them. Horrible. When you find a man – with a man you can find a reason, but women with women, it is the worse. It brings shivers. Why? Because it is one of the types of sexual perversions, but it is the five-star perversion.

The contradictory claims evident in this particular respondent's interview are, I found, indicative of the general reluctance to speak about such issues as sexual intimacies of women with other women. Several authors support this notion. For instance, Stephen O. Murray (1997: 97), even as his chapter refers to "women–women love in Islamic societies," assures the reader that it "remains thoroughly submerged." AbuKhalil (1997: 102), another scholar, maintains that: "Contemporary Islamic attitudes recognized the sexual desires of men while women's sexuality is ignored, assumed to be nonexistent at least among Muslim women .... It is left for the Arab erotic literature to compile poems by lesbian women." The two *baladi* women I interviewed assured me that one of the reasons that women may not be involved sexually with other women is primarily due to the predominance of the practice of cliterodectomy. One of the women said that: "a girl should not have animal desires where she might substitute a woman if she does not find a man." While there might be an argument that cliterodectomy is a factor in discouraging women from getting involved sexually with other women, a number of scholars (Berkey, 1996; Guenena & Wassef, 1999; Kennedy, 1970; Khattab interview, 1995[3]; Wassef, n.d.; Wassef & Mansour, 1999; Zénié-Ziegler, 1988, to name a few) have shown that the practice does little to extinguish desire, although it does affect orgasm. There is also irrefutable evidence, from the women I interviewed, from the literature (see, for instance, Dunn, 1990; Murray & Roscoe, 1997: 97–104), and from my own experience, that women in Egypt are involved sexually with other women.

How is it that the majority of people, educated or not, are unaware of the existence of terms that describe such involvements? How can we explain the invisibility of same-gender sexual practices among women? How is it that men's involvements are recognized, while women's are invisible?

Traditional Views of Sexuality

The above questions may be partially understood by referring to Arab history and literature, and by consulting the Qur'an. Religious law, the Shari'ah, governs most Arab countries, and where this is an exception, for instance in Egypt, religious law is practiced side by side with secular law, each consulted appropriately according to the type of issue at stake. The Qur'an is clear in its acceptance of sexuality as being a natural part of the human condition, and this premise is often reflected in Arab literature. According to Bouhdiba (1985: 155): "Indeed eroticism is so inextricably bound up with the cultural life of the Arabo-Muslim societies that annotations, passages, even whole chapters are found interpolated in any work of literature, law, history, etc. Eroticism is not exclusive." Bouhdiba insists that the Qur'an "does not itself lay down prohibitions; it merely regulates sexual practices," because, he claims, "the sexual function is a sacred function" (Bouhdiba, 1985: 155). Furthermore, he states, "[i]n Islam temptation does not have the same meaning and significance as it has in Christian theology. It does not derive from human culpability, since Islam has no conception of original sin"(Bouhdiba, 1985: 59). Implied in that last sentence is the understanding that Islam does not recognize the concept of sin as it is defined in Christianity. It does, however, have a system of sanctions that regulate the everyday lives of the faithful, while acknowledging human weaknesses in the face of temptation. Therefore instead of the concept of *sin*, there exists the *prohibited*. Yusuf Al-Qardawi, in explaining the lawful and the prohibited, says:

> The Islamic Shari'ah removes from human beings harmful, burdensome customs and superstitions, aiming to simplify and ease the business of day-to-day living. Its principles are designed to protect man from evil and to benefit him in all aspects of his life. (Yusuf Al-Qardawi, 1960: 6)

For instance, where wine and sex between members of the same sex are prohibited on Earth, both are mentioned in the Qur'an in the description of what is available to the faithful in paradise.[8] What looks at first to be a contradiction makes sense within the context of a system of prohibition rather than sin. The distinction is between sin as a transgression against God as opposed to the breaking of a rule of God, a small difference, but a significant one. God's rules are in place to preserve society. This means that an act such as drinking alcohol or becoming sexually involved with a member of one's sex is not in itself abhorrent but becomes loathsome because it causes social devastation.

Same-sex relations in Islam

Same-sex references in the Qur'an exist ambiguously because most allude to a version of the Biblical character of Lot and are articulated in vague terms, using words such as "abomination" and "depravity." Conversely, there is no doubt that such references are condemned in the *Ahadith*. Analyzing the texts of Al-Ghazi, an eleventh century Muslim theologian and learned man, Madelain Farah (1984: 38) says:

The hadith mentioned repeatedly that sodomy and homosexuality, including lesbianism, were forbidden by the Prophet. That is, he forbade sexual intercourse between man and man, and intimate relations between woman and woman. There was no exposition on this point, other than that found in an injunction relayed with slight variations from the hadith forbidding intercourse between two undressed male or female partners; neither should one male or female come upon a partner of the same sex in "one garment." The limitations regarding the latter are difficult to ascertain, unless impersonation of the other sex is what is implied. (Farah, 1984: 38)

Al-Ghazi's only reference to same-gender sexual relations is, according to Farah (1984: 38–39), "that it is shameful for a man to look at the face of the beardless boy when it may result in evil" (which, in itself is an acknowledgment that such a temptation is possible or even probable). Indeed, explains that the Arab system of extreme segregation of men and women led each to turn to his/her gender for sexual relief. He states:

Thus homosexual relations were relatively encouraged by the Arabo-Muslim societies, to the detriment of intersexual relations. In the end, segregation exalted promiscuity. It is difficult for those who have not experienced it to imagine what life under strict separation of the sexes is like. But it is understandable that homosexuality, so violently condemned by Islam, could be so widely practiced among both men and women ... The fact that homosexuality was always being condemned proves only one thing: neither the religious nor the social conscience could put an end to practices that were disapproved by Islamic ethics, but to which in the last resort society closed its eyes. (Bouhdiba, 1985: 200)

He adds that pederasty and lesbianism, precisely because they resulted from the sexual division, were perceived as second best. His whole chapter on what he calls "certain practices" describes in detail how the culture lent itself to the eroticizing of men in that even concepts of beauty for women tended to lean toward a look that resembled a young boy.

Same-sex relations among women

Mention of women's sexual interest in other women comes from several historical sources. Mervat Hatem (1986) writes about a specific era of Egyptian history, the eighteenth century period of the Mamluks, a Turko-Circassian military caste who originally came to Egypt as slaves. She describes the concubines in the Mamluk *harems*, showing how homosocial relations provided women with a sense of strength and support and allowed them limited autonomous political power:

In this segregated social setting, women – not men – became the major sources of emotional and social support. Both lesbian and homosexual relations, in fact, were sexual responses to the social segregation of the sexes. As women and men looked for emotional support from members of the same sex, homosexuality emerged as a challenge both to Muslim values (which condemned it in very strong terms) and the heterosexual ideal that the segregated patriarchal system upheld. (Hatem, 1986: 259)

Leila Ahmed (1992: 121), writing about women and Islam, mentions that no written records by women were left that mention women's relationships. European visitors to the Middle East of the eighteenth century, however, describe the lives of the upper class women of Turkey and Syria. These "Western" chroniclers observed and recorded intimate relations between women friends as well as between women and their female slaves.

The consensus among the scholars I examined is that same-sex practices were prevalent historically, especially during those periods that demanded strict segregation of the sexes. Incidences of such practices appear in literature, historical accounts, and poetry, as well as by "Western" visitors to the area. Musallam (1983: 108) ventures some conjectures regarding women: "There were, in medieval Arabic, stories that attempted to explain homosexuality as resulting from the fear of pregnancy, and the same fear was an excuse given by women for hesitating to see their lovers."

If both the history and the literature of the Arabs are replete with references regarding intimate relations between women, how is it that Hind Khattab did not hear one incident in her exhaustive study? How is it that these practices are, for all intents and purposes, invisible? And finally, how is it that no one knows of a single current term that denotes those practices that seem to be so prevalent throughout history, so present in the culture?

Same-Sex Relationships Among Educated Women

One night in Cairo in 1998, I was invited to go to a very small party given by a woman I knew slightly. I wondered at the invitation precisely because we were barely acquainted. I decided to attend simply out of curiosity. There were eight women in total at that extremely rich and elaborate apartment in an exclusive part of Cairo. Almost all of the women present were stunningly beautiful, all very obviously rich, well traveled, and educated. They all seemed to be friends with each other. I knew none of the women except for the hostess, although their names were familiar to me. The evening focused on a new video that mentions "perversions" and was made in Lebanon for the purposes of teaching school children. The video was in an Arabic dialect that I found hard to understand, although I could discern that nothing complementary about that "condition" was being expressed. No terms that specifically described sexual categories were used on-screen, but the message about the "perversions" in question was very clear and elicited much laughter amongst the women. Since the video itself was of little interest to me, I watched the women viewing it instead. There was a profound silence for most of the video, as all eyes focused on the screen.

When the video was over, the discussion began, most of it in colloquial Arabic. What was unique about the evening was not necessarily the topic under discussion so much as the incredible undertow of sexual tension among the women. All were married and some had children. I suspect (but have no way of knowing) that I was invited because one of the women knew my work. Although I am not "out" in Egypt except to my immediate family, any one of these women could have come across my published work in her travel. When I asked my sister later about the evening, she confirmed my suspicions: all those women present, it was rumored, were involved sexually with other women or with each other. None of the women had "come out" in conversation, none had mentioned a sexual involvement with another woman, yet the "signs" were there: women who looked at each other and at me in a prolonged way, touching that indicated intimacy, languid postures, tacit references, veiled hints, all spoke clearly to me of an atmosphere that I recognized from my life before I left for Canada. What was happening that evening was concealment that I appreciated and that I could read plainly because I had participated in similar subterfuge more than thirty years ago. It was a concealment that proceeded from an understanding of sexual categories, of the term "lesbian," of the sanctions that accompany it: a recognition of what is forbidden couched in what is considered appropriate behavior for women of that social class.

The concealment to which I am referring is not the same as what I described with the *baladi* women: the reticence to speak about women's sexuality publicly. An analogy may explain my point: when two children are playing sexual games, they know they are doing something "wrong," and will therefore conceal their activities. They know that anything involving the general area of the genitals is wicked, dirty, bad, because they have been told often enough "not to touch." When, however, an adult is involved sexually with another adult of the same sex and both can name what they are doing as forbidden or taboo, the concealment is played out in a specific way that masks the condemned behavior. I am by no means suggesting by this analogy that *baladi* women are like children. What I am saying is that there is a different level of awareness of wrong-doing when there is a term to describe what exactly is forbidden and consequently, the concealment is different. On the one hand, if a *baladi* woman touches another woman and is aroused, she will know that what she is doing is wrong because it concerns sex (even if it is one-sided) although there may be no word to describe what she is feeling. She may or may not stop touching the other woman, she may think of herself as a freak, she may even feel that she never wants to stop what she is doing, but throughout, she will not know the full implications of belonging to a religiously (and socially) outlawed category such as "lesbian." What is qualitatively different about the women at the party (most, if not all, of whom had access to "Western" terms) is that they knew that their desires were prohibited and had therefore developed an intricate set of "signs" to express their attractions. Having a word to describe their desires allowed those women to recognize that they all belonged to the "same group." Having a word for their actions permitted them access to one another and to literature (should they so choose) to confirm, arouse, or to reject what they were feeling.

Same-Sex Relationships as a Problem of Representation

Thus far, I have refrained from explicit discussion of the sociolinguistic dimensions of the problem I have delineated. I was trained as a sociologist, and have only recently developed an interest in same-sex relationships as a problem of linguistic representation. In truth, until Sandra and Robert invited my participation in this volume, I consciously avoided engaging this dimension. For years colleagues had called to my attention the well-known theories of linguists Edward Sapir (1949) and Benjamin Lee Whorf (1956) concerning the pre-eminent role of language in providing semantic categories for the representation and, hence, construction of experienced reality. I resisted these theories because, as I have described here in some detail, I attribute the pervasive reticence within Egyptian society to acknowledge same-sex relations to Islam's condemnation of homosexuality as a perversion of societal mores. I regard linguistic patterning as a secondary effect of this prohibition, certainly not as a causal influence on cognition.

However, after coming into contact with recent sociolinguistic work on "rethinking linguistic relativity" (Gumperz & Levinson, 1996; Lucy, 1992; Schultz, 1990), I have developed an interest in how the relationship between language diversity and thought impacts on our understanding of same-sexuality in cross-cultural perspective. Schultz' elucidation of Whorfian theory from a Bakhtinian perspective is illuminating in this regard. Schultz (1990: 42) called attention to Bakhtin's success in "opening up [of] a theoretical space" for examining the tensions in Whorf's work by explicitly separating theories about language-in-the-abstract (theories of grammar) from theories about language-in-the-concrete (theories of discourse). Bakhtin (1984: 69) signals a polyphonic approach that, he argued, "has nothing in common with relativism (or with dogmatism)" but is concerned, rather, with "a plurality of consciousnesses" (Bakhtin, 1984: 81). Indeed, Bakhtin takes delight in heteroglossia, or the existence of "many-voicedness" within a single national language, and finds this to be the normal state of affairs in speech communities. (This is not to deny that the speech community may also be multilingual; but this dimension is not where Bakhtin places his emphasis.) For Bakhtin, who had to elude the censors of Stalinist Russia both to stay alive and to communicate on dangerous topics, this state, where the resources of language can be manipulated to create a diversity of content, was a lifeline. In emphasizing that there are "varied resources that exist *within* any particular language ... for saying the same thing in different ways, or different things in the same way" (Schultz, 1990: 25), he found a way to give hope to those who live under restrictive linguistic circumstances by pointing to areas where freedom can be claimed.

Thus, from a language-socialization perspective, the compelling problem lies not, in the words of Roman Jakobson (1959: 142), "in what may or may not be expressed but in what must or must not be conveyed by the speakers." In Egyptian society, educated women have found their way to a discourse – and a discourse community – where they can manipulate the referential capacity of language and metaphor in pursuit of their authentic voices (cf. Lakoff & Johnson, 1980). They have done this by participating in a social network that yields different meaning systems for the same set of practices that must remain unspoken for their *baladi* sisters, and by engaging in discrete but persistent contextualization processes that instantiate these practices as societal realities (Gumperz, 1996a). Indeed, the study of same sex relations in Egyptian society yields an excellent case study of the state that Bakhtin refers to as *heteroglossia*, or multi-voicedness, in that, as we have seen, "we can have speakers of the same language fractionated by interpretive subsystems associated with distinct social networks" (Gumperz, 1996b: 361).

Finally, examining same-sex relations through a language-socialization lens has created in me a heightened awareness of how "linguistic usage can transform one kind of relationship into another" (Schultz, 1990: 120). In my wildest fantasies, having a name for the practice, may (as indeed happened in North America, although it seems highly unlikely in Egypt), lead to political mobilization for human rights.

Notes

1. To Sandra Schecter, my most heartfelt thanks for the support, for tightening sections of the chapter, but mostly, for being such a great colleague. This paper was made possible through two consecutive grants by the Social Sciences and Humanities Research Council. I want to thank especially Kate Eichhorn whose exquisite ability to find material in unlikely places is unparalleled. I would also like to express my deep gratitude to Celia Haig-Brown who patiently reads and always improves my work. I would also like to thank Nadia Wassef for her ideas regarding sexuality in Egypt. I dedicate this paper to the memory of my dear friend Marian McMahon.
2. I am using the term "Western" in quotation marks to denote a general cultural area that, in this specific case, is English-speaking and that is mainstream and dominant in North America. It is by no means an exact term, nor is it used to indicate a monolithic understanding of Western capitalist nations. Finally, the term " Western" is not intended as a binary opposite of "Eastern."
3. Interview with Dr Hind Khattab in Cairo in her office at Delta Consulting on March 9, 1995. Dr Khattab had just completed extensive research funded by the Ford Foundation on the reproductive health of women in Egypt.
4. This is not to say that, because of the influence of American and Western European satellite television, films, and books, that the concepts of sexual identities will not seep or have not already trickled into Egyptian awareness. Nor does it mean that there does not exist some understanding of the term by some people in the society, even if it causes a perplexed reaction because most Egyptians would find very difficult to understand the need to define oneself by a particular sexual practice, one that is perceived as perverted.
5. It is not entirely true to say that women in Egypt do not talk in public about sexuality, as Nadia Wassef, in a private conversation (January 2001) maintained. Wassef draws upon the work of Lila Abu-Loghod (2001: 198–207) to demonstrate that there are competing notions of sexuality where, on the one hand, the topic is taboo but, on the other, within the context of institutions such as marriage, divorce, and pregnancy, women's sexuality becomes both public and culturally condoned. The tension between these two positions depends on context and, for an unmarried woman like myself, there is no entry point into a conversation about sexuality unless I could spend enough time with some of these women to become accepted by them and eventually taken under their wing so that they would encourage me to marry.
6. Stephen O. Murray (1997: 103), in an endnote to his chapter entitled "Woman-Woman love in Islamic Societies," gives several terms that refer to woman-to-woman relations,

"including *sahq, sihaq*, and *musahaquah*." Murray goes on to explain that the common root to the terms above and, he adds, to the nominalization of a person: *suhhaqu*, means grinding. The spelling is transliterated and depends on the scholar. I chose the spelling with which I was most comfortable.

7. It should be noted that in almost all cases, but especially when speaking with *baladi* women, the language of the interview was Arabic. I translated as I transcribed each interview. Even when interviewing English-speaking informants, as is prevalent in Egypt, the language varied from English to French to Arabic depending on the sentence and on the speaker's whim.

8. For wine, see Sura XLVII: 15; and for the availability of youths, see Sura LXXVI: 19.

Part 4

Language Socialization in the Workplace

Part 4

Language Socialization in the Workplace

Chapter 14

Language Dynamics in the Bi- and Multilingual Workplace

CHRISTOPHER MCALL

Most people spend most of their adult lives at work. Access to paid work is the key to financial independence, social status and recognition, and, for the privileged few perhaps, personal satisfaction and fulfilment in terms of the realization of career goals. It is also, for many people, the principal place in which they come into contact with others on a daily basis – outside the family and the immediate neighborhood. Language is central to the workplace in two ways. First, work, as a set of tasks individually performed and collectively integrated, requires different kinds and levels of communication. Second, in so far as the workplace is one of the principal sites in which people establish their social connections with others, language plays a central role as a social connector, binding together individuals, groups, and larger networks. These two ways in which language operates in the workplace can be thought of as the more professional (or work-related), and the more socially oriented. In reality, all workplace communication has a work-related aspect to it, and all communication of any kind is socially oriented. However, it would seem to make sense to distinguish between the types of workplace communication and language use that are primarily work-oriented (in terms of their goals) and other types that are more purely social.

Given that access to paid work is essential for most people (in terms of financial security, social status, and satisfaction with life), and given that language is omnipresent in the workplace in both a work- and socially-oriented sense, the use of different languages at work in bilingual and multilingual societies can be a means for ensuring the privileged access of certain language groups to better-paid jobs (or to work itself) and the exclusion of other groups. In order to understand the way in which language difference can come to play such a role, however, we need to take two preliminary steps. The first step is to get a better understanding of what it means to talk about language *as such* in the workplace – that is, language in the sense of oral and written communication. What is the relationship between different kinds of language use and different kinds of work processes? We then have to think about the relationship between different social groups in which language difference plays a central role, and the importance or otherwise of the control of access to work in that relationship. In sociological form, this means thinking both about the relationship between specific language groups in particular historical contexts, and about the general features of those relationships that can be extrapolated from such examples. In what follows, I shall first look at language at work, and then at the broader relationships between specific language groups in which work is a central issue. Examples from Montreal case studies will be brought to bear to illustrate different aspects of language use in bilingual and multilingual workplaces.[1]

Language at Work

The use of languages in the workplace, or the relationship between different language groups at work, requires us to think about the work-related use of language itself. In some work settings, communication is at the center of the work process; in others, noise levels, or the nature of the work, may preclude any communication. For example, while written and oral communication are at the heart of the work-related activities of such categories as teachers, doctors, social workers, receptionists, bank clerks, managers, supervisors, and waitresses, for other categories (such as assembly line workers, machinists, and office cleaners) the use of language may be more or less marginal or absent. Different types of work can thus be classified on a scale based on the relative presence or absence of language, both in the work-related sense of language use and in its more social orientation. Teachers, for example, would presumably rate highly on both counts, while machinists in an aero-engine plant might spend much of their workday not being able to hear or talk to anyone, as their grinding machines cut out cog wheels and gear shafts.

The relative presence or absence of language can also be taken as being indicative of the degree of isolation of different categories of worker. That isolation can be understood either in a physical sense (for example, night cleaners in downtown, high-rise, office buildings working on their own for hours on end), or in relation to noise levels that prevent or limit contact. Isolation can also be imposed by management in an attempt to prevent people from "chatting" to each other, thereby reducing productivity and wasting company time.[2] At the other end of the scale, high oral language use during work time presumes contact, and may mean a greater degree of insertion in work-related social networks, or involvement in a succession of one-to-one encounters in the case of service providers. Writing and reading also imply involvement in communication networks, although the nature of that involvement can vary from the more or less immediate sending and receiving of messages, to the reading of company directives, machining instructions, or any of a variety of documents in which the connection between sender and receiver is more distant and diffuse.

If language use at work can be seen in terms of isolation from, or insertion in, work-related social networks, it can also be seen in terms of its centrality or marginality to the work process itself. High language use, in the work-related sense, implies that people are *using* language to produce units of meaning, whether in the form of opinions, or diagnoses, or lectures, or operating instructions, or other bits and pieces of information that may or may not be useful to the people for whom they are destined. Language in such cases is the raw material that is worked up into a finished product or text. One could say that it is at the center of its own production process, and that high-level language users transform language into text in the way that others might transform lumps of steel into cog wheels, or assemble aero-engines from their three thousand or so component parts.

There is thus a distinction to be made between work where language is itself the principal raw material that is subject to transformation (in the production of texts, for example), and work where some other raw material is being transformed. Language may be used in the second case among those who are involved in the transformation process, but it is not itself the main object of transformation, and may disappear altogether where there is no communication involved. At best it plays an ancillary or supportive role in the transformation of some other raw material. This suggests that we could make a distinction between, for example, metal workers or wood workers, on the one hand, and "language workers" on the other, the latter being defined as those whose work process revolves around the transformation of language as raw material.

This distinction takes on particular importance in workplaces where the production of language texts precedes and allows for the transformation of others kinds of material, where, in other words, the text is a "pattern for action" for other kinds of work at other stages in the production process. In an aero-engine plant, for example, the engineer produces language texts (based on different kinds of language, including written instructions, graphics, and mathematics) that are in effect the symbolic representation of the engine parts that are to be produced.[3] These written and drawn texts are then transmitted to the machinists, who enter the required dimensions and tolerances into the machines and transform the metal as raw material into the appropriate engine part. The transformation of language as raw material into a language text thus serves in this case as a pattern or guide for the subsequent transformation of another kind of raw material. What we see here is the transition from the engine part (and eventually the engine itself) as "conceived" and symbolically represented on paper (or on screen) by the engineer, to the engine part as cut out of the metal by the machinist. The engine part thus "comes into existence" on the basis of the preceding language text.

The story of the relationship between "language work" and other kinds of work does not end here, however. The language text is not just the symbolic precursor of the "real" thing. Apart from its subsequent ancillary role in allowing the production process to take place, language continues to play a part in tracing the events that make up the production process itself. To come back to the example of the aero-engine, every aspect of the production process has to be recorded in the form of process sheets or inspection reports such that the purchaser of the engine knows what happened at every stage in the process.[4] The aero-engine emerges from the other end of the plant not only in a real, concrete form – as a three dimensional, existing and functioning object – but is also accompanied by several thousand pages of graphics, numbers, and written text that tell the story of its own production. Most of its thousands of component parts are no longer visible, being buried at the heart of the machine, and can be accessed only through the accompanying symbolic representation and explanatory text. The engine thus continues to exist in both its material and its symbolic forms.

While some kinds of work process are thus centered round the transformation of language into language texts, and others are centered round the transformation of other kinds of raw material (with language playing an ancillary role), the division of labor within the production process frequently means that the one follows on from the other, with those who plan and conceive products sending them "downstream" to production workers in the form of language texts. What this suggests is that there are often two phases in the production process, a "language-centered" phase and a "language-marginal" phase.

The relative presence or absence of language in a particular kind of work process does not tell us anything about the complexity of the language that is being used. Receptionists, telephone operators, salespersons, and various other categories can be talking all day but may be restricted to a succession of short-term conversational exchanges based on a standard set of questions and answers and a limited range of vocabulary. Laboratory research work, on the other hand, may include long periods of low language contact but nonetheless require the mastery of complex technical language codes when such contacts do arise. The criterion of complexity of language – in terms of the mastery of complex technical codes or simply the breadth of vocabulary used – needs to be brought into play when evaluating the language content of different kinds of work. Maximum language content would mean a language-centered work process with a high degree of complexity.

One further point needs to be made concerning language use at work before we can look at what happens in bilingual and multilingual workplaces. Most workplaces are hierarchically organized and imply bi-directional information flows. Upper levels of management must know what is happening in the different areas of the production process (based on an upward flow of information) and be able to transmit their directives downwards. Language is at the heart of management as a process and is directly linked to the exercise of power and control over production and the workforce.[5]

Language thus enters into work in a variety of different ways, both at the heart of the work process itself and in the overall control of work and production goals. All of this is of paramount importance when we try to understand how different language groups attempt to take control of, or are relegated to, particular kinds of work. Such an understanding requires us to set the workplace in the broader social context of the relationship between specific language groups. A series of Montreal case studies will serve to illustrate some of the issues involved in bilingual and multilingual workplaces.

Language and Territory

From a sociological perspective, Fishman (1972) identifies two sociolinguistic models for what he describes as societal bilingualism, the Urban French Canadian Nationalist model and the Urban American Migrant model. The first model refers to a situation where a historically subordinate group gradually comes to occupy territory that had previously been occupied by a dominant group; the second refers to one where the language of an immigrant community is gradually restricted in use to the private domain.

In contemporary Quebec society, we seem to be confronted by the combined effects of these two models at the same time. French Canadians, who constitute the overwhelming numerical majority (83%) of the population of the province, have dramatically improved their socio-economic status with respect to the English-speaking non-immigrant population over the last thirty or forty years. The major economic inequalities that existed between the two groups in the 1960s had more or less disappeared (at least in terms of mean annual income) by the mid-1980s (Vaillancourt, 1991). This disappearance is directly associated with access to various categories of employment in the private sector that had hitherto been largely confined to Anglophones, as well as with the increase in public sector employment from the 1960s onwards – public sector jobs being disproportionately occupied by Francophones up to the present day (Conseil des relations interculturelles, 1999).

It is an open question as to whether the famous (or infamous, depending on one's point of view) language legislation, by which Quebec governments have sought to make French the language of the workplace since the end of the 1970s, has had much of an effect. Over the same time period, increasingly highly trained Francophones have moved into many areas of work in which they were previously under-represented, bringing their language characteristics with them, while the proportion of maternal-language Anglophones in the population has gradually declined to around 10%. The increasing presence of French in the workplace is probably due as much to these socio-demographic changes as it is to the impact of the law itself (which was of course itself carried by socio-demographic pressures). Whatever the relative importance of a critical mass of Francophones in a given sector of the labor market on the one hand, and the existence of the language legislation on the other, the occupation and control of territory within the labor market has been a key issue in the relations between the two principal language groups.

It is with respect to this relationship that the arrival of immigrants of various origins and at different periods has had an impact. At the end of the nineteenth and the early part of the twentieth centuries, incoming Francophone migrants from the Quebec countryside find themselves in direct competition not only with skilled, immigrant British workers, but also with Irish and Italian immigrants. In the period following World War II, and with the rapid transformation and mechanization of agriculture, the bulk of the French-Canadian population moved from the country-side to the towns and, especially in the Montreal metropolitan area, found them-selves living alongside and competing with more recent immigrant populations from Southern European countries such as Portugal, Italy, and Greece. Many of the latter immigrants found work in the construction, cleaning, catering, and garment industries, often in areas where English was the dominant language.

This ethnically (or ethnolinguistically) structured labor market came to be all the more complex with the increasing arrival of immigrants and refugees of other than European origin (referred to in Canadian employment equity law as "visible minor-ities") from the 1970s onwards, following the changes in Canadian immigration law. With the recessions of the 1980s and 1990s, the issue became not just that of access to better-paying jobs, but access to work itself. At the same time, the children of immigrants have been required to attend French language schools since the beginning of the 1980s, and this has in turn increased the number of young adults arriving on the labor market with competence in French, particularly from the mid-1990s onwards. This, paradoxically, can increase competition in those areas of the labor market where French has acquired dominance. This has notably been the case in the public sector, where the non-immigrant Francophone majority has been faced with the need to give access to jobs to an increasingly diverse population (in terms of national origin), even though its own socio-economic progress in the past has been largely due to the setting up of such protected territories (Guindon, 1978).

These changing relationships between language groups and populations of different national origins revolve largely around the control of the labor market and the occupation of particular niches or territories within that market. Language has been, and still is, central to the occupation and control of such territories. It serves as an instrument of communication among those who belong to the group in question and, equally importantly, serves as an instrument of non-communication with those who do not. It can also be a key element in the construction of identity based on the idea of belonging to a historical language community. It is here that we come up against the interface between language as a defining characteristic of different groups in their relationship with one another, and the use of language as a central feature in the work process itself.

Language Frontiers and the Work Process

The study of the Montreal labor market over the period since World War II shows how language can be a central factor in the occupation and control of territory. Specific categories of employment – such as management, engineering or work in the public sector bureaucracy – can be seen as being largely dominated by given language groups both across the market and within individual companies. The classic case, in the immediate pre-war period, is described by Hughes (1943). In the small industrial town (outside the Montreal area) studied by Hughes, a French-speaking workforce in the textile industry finds itself facing English-speaking owners and managers. Communication between the two groups is made possible by the presence of bilingual supervisors who act as go-betweens across what amounts to a language frontier running through the workplace.

The Montreal labor market is still marked by such frontiers, even if Francophones are no longer contained within subordinate employment categories. The increasing presence of Francophones in various categories of employment does not necessarily mean that they work in French. Between 1971 and 1991, for example, the proportion of Francophones among company administrators in Montreal's private sector had increased from 41% to 69%, among professionals, it had increased from 45% to 67%, and among technicians, from 53% to 69% (Comité interministériel, 1996: 65). Francophones were, therefore, no longer under represented in these categories, since they made up 69% of the population of the region of Montreal in 1991. However, little more than half (56%) of the Francophones working in Montreal's private sector at the end of the 1980s were working in French (Béland, 1991). Although some commentators suggest that the continuing presence of English may simply be the result of the integration of many sectors of the Montreal economy into international markets where English is the dominant language, there may be other explanations closer to hand in the internal dynamics of the bilingual and multilingual workplace.

One such explanation could be proposed on the basis of an analysis by Tremblay (1993) of the language use of lower-level Francophone white-collar workers in a Montreal pharmaceutical company. Tremblay used the method of the reconstructed workday, whereby language use over the preceding eight hours is reconstituted retrospectively in interview at the end of the workday (McAll *et al.*, 1994). She found that interviewees tended to use French only while chatting to each other informally about issues that were not work-related, and when communicating with employees who worked in the factory alongside the administration building – referred to by one of them as the "people from down below" (*les gens d'en bas*). Otherwise, they tended to work in English, and even felt some embarrassment about using French.

Tremblay's analysis suggests a clear territorial division between the administration building, in which most work-related communication takes place in English, and the factory, where most communication is in French. The maintenance of the language frontier in this case can be related to the predominance of English speakers at the upper levels of management, and to the requirement that information flows within the administrative hierarchy have to be in a language that upper-level management can understand (following what I have described as the "rule of bureaucratic transparency" or ease of access to information from below; see McAll, 1993b). It may also be related, however, to the overall opposition or distinction between management and labor, in which it is not necessarily in the interests of management for there to be easy access on the part of the workers on the factory floor (or their representatives) to the "secrets" of management, whether in terms of budgeting, long-term planning or day-to-day administration. The maintenance of language difference, while not necessarily being intentional policy, can have the effect of maintaining distance and a certain opacity concerning company operations.

One further factor relating to internal dynamics in this case concerns the way in which the white collar workers we interviewed see the development of their own professional competence and career advancement as being somehow associated with working in English, particularly in that working in French (in the context of this company) is associated with production and blue-collar work. Low-grade white-collar workers themselves may, therefore, have an interest in the maintenance of the language frontier for reasons of what Bourdieu would describe as "distinction" (Bourdieu, 1979, 1982a).

If it is true that the maintenance of the language frontier is not just the reflection of broader inequalities or differential access to the labor market on the part of distinct language groups, but may flow in part from internal workplace dynamics, then the bilingual workplace may be telling us something about those dynamics that would emerge less clearly in a monolingual situation. It has to be remembered that administrative work is highly language-intensive, or language-centered, while production work tends to be "language-marginal," to use the concepts suggested earlier. If English is the dominant language in the pharmaceutical company, that dominance is associated with the presence of English in precisely those areas of activity where language is central, areas revolving around "language work."

However, we should avoid falling into the trap of seeing language as a thing in itself, capable of domination. To speak of a language being "dominant" in one or other area of activity really means that a dominant language group exercises control over that area to the exclusion of another group, and that language plays a key role in that process. It also means that employees working in that area, whatever their maternal language might be, work in the language of the dominant group, and effectively become part of that group in terms of internal company dynamics.

A comparable example is to be found in the aerospace industry. In the case of two Montreal companies (including the world's third-ranking producer of civil aircraft, and an aero-engine plant), as far as the presence of Francophones is concerned, major changes have taken place over the last 15–20 years at all levels of activity.[6] Francophones have not only come to be predominant at the level of production and among technicians, but are now represented at all levels of management. Interviewees from both companies suggested to us that French was increasingly present not only on the shop floor but also as the language of administration (McAll *et al.*, 1998). Of the various explanations offered above to explain the maintenance of the language frontier in the pharmaceutical company, the maternal language of upper management emerges as key. In both aerospace companies the existence of a critical mass of French-speaking managers and executives seems to be shifting the balance towards the use of French (or at least administrative bilingualism) as the internal language (or languages) of administration, in spite of the strong presence of English as the international language of commerce, science, and technology.

One area of activity within these companies that seems to remain rigorously English-speaking, however, is that of engineering. Here again, the critical-mass explanation comes into play, in that it is only in recent years that Quebec's French-speaking universities have been turning out engineers in aerospace with the training necessary to compete against candidates from other parts of the world. Our interviews with Francophone engineers suggest that there is now increasing recruitment of French speakers, but that nonetheless English speakers remain numerically dominant, and the engineering component in the Montreal aerospace industry continues to operate mainly through English.

Again, the language distinction between the territories of engineering and production highlights a feature of internal dynamics that would be less visible in a monolingual environment. An aircraft, or an aero-engine, exists first as an idea before it is symbolically represented on paper or on screen in words, numbers, and graphical form. Engineers thus operate in a realm of conceptions, ideas, and symbolic representations – in other words, in the realm of language. As suggested above, it is their "language texts" that are to determine what it is that production workers make. These texts circulate through the various work spaces and provide the guidelines for the transformation of other raw materials. Engineers may be working within product guidelines laid down by upper management, but they nonetheless exercise power in terms of conception, design, implementation, and testing. Any changes that are to be made, or mistakes corrected, can be done only on the express authority of an engineer.

The predominant use of English in engineering thus coincides with a significant frontier in the use of language itself, where language-centered work precedes and has a determinant effect on the language-marginal work that is to follow. English thus enters into the production process in the form of operating instructions, process sheets, and technical terms referring to parts and process, which are then interpreted by mainly Francophone workers, working (orally) through French. English-speaking engineers come down to the shop floor every now and again to supervise testing or authorize changes or simply to make sure that things are being done as they should be, bringing English with them into the production environment.

The critical-mass argument (that there is an insufficient number of Francophone engineers to support the use of French) may explain why it is that English continues to predominate in engineering. The differential use of English and French in this case, however, also coincides with a key frontier in terms of the use of language itself between those who conceive and those who execute, or between what some might have described as "intellectual" and "manual" labor, if those terms can be considered to have any clear meaning, since all manual work involves intellectual input. Interestingly, the use of language itself (in terms of intensity, quantity, and complexity) is a defining characteristic of this frontier, and the dominant language prevails (or the dominant language group exercises its domination within the production process) precisely in that area where language use is maximized. This form of language dominance would be less visible, but nonetheless present, in a monolingual environment.

As in the case of management, the critical-mass argument may be the principal explanation for the maintenance of one language rather than another in engineering, but it is not the only one. Internal dynamics, and notably the role of language itself in the production process, suggest other complementary explanations. Leaving aside the increasing presence of French in administration in one or two of the companies studied, the differential presence of English and French in conception and production could be taken to suggest that, where work in aerospace is language-centered, it tends to be in English. Where work is language-marginal (that is, centered around the transformation of other raw materials), it tends to be in French. This situation will probably maintain itself, supported in part by internal dynamics, up to the point at which the presence of a critical mass of Francophones in language-centered work will shift the balance towards the use of French.

The question arises as to the moment when that shift is likely to take place. Our research suggests that there are two principal factors that bear on the use of one or other language among engineers in the central part of their work process, that is, in the day-to-day resolution of engineering problems. The first, and most important, is the language competence of the colleagues they are working with. Most of the employers studied seem to encourage creative teamwork in the resolution of problems, and design office space to make such teamwork possible. As far as language is concerned, everything depends on who is in the team on any given day. With the increasing presence of French-speaking engineers, it is possible for a given team to be composed of a majority of French speakers, or even, as happened in one of our reconstructed engineers' workdays, of *only* French speakers. In the latter case, the team worked in French for part of the day on a high-level technical problem. Where one or two English speakers are present, however, the language used tends to be English, because of their insufficient competence in French. On the basis of this example, one could suggest that, even in language-centered work, where one language is dominant, speakers will switch to the other language if the balance of language competence in a given group shifts in the direction of the second language, and everyone in the group is capable of functioning in that language. There is nothing therefore "given" or permanent about language dominance, if the territory in question is gradually being opened up to members of the second language group.

The other key factor is the impact of the language of management on engineers. In one case, the company had recently hired a monolingual English speaker as team manager, even though the team members themselves were all Francophones. More generally, the language of management imposes itself on everything that is consigned to writing, whether for administrative purposes or for production. Here again, one can imagine that an increasing critical mass of Francophones among upper management could eventually allow a shift to the use of French in the day-to-day internal operations of the company, where the presence of Francophones in the workforce allows it to happen.

On the Margin: The Language of the Shop Floor

The work-related language of Francophone production workers in the Montreal aerospace industry may be French, but it is a French that is shot through with English terminology. Not only is the use of language marginal to the production process, but the presence of French itself is subject to an additional form of marginalization by offering often little more than syntactical support to English words that are the principal carriers of meaning.

Examples of such English words embodied in French texts and taken from the transcriptions of the interviews, include: words associated with the process itself (set-up, rework, insert, check diameter), machine tools (chucks, jaws, blocks, bits, drills, face plates, dust collectors, buffers, cutting wheels), product parts (long shafts, bull gears, bearings, small ducts, liners, housing, gaskets, flanges, hoses, brackets, gas generators), internal administrative documents (manufacturing operation sheet, quality assurance inspection report, carry over sheet, request for services), phrases to be written on such documents (accepted as is, checked and found acceptable, waviness accepted), descriptive personnel titles (line manager, dispatcher, set-up man, lead man, foreman, park-controller), shop departments (machine repair, shipping, miscellaneous and blades, cleaning, gear lab), and even the sundry bits and pieces used in and around the work station (pad, bins, rack, truck, chain block, nuts, bolts).

It would thus be somewhat inaccurate to suggest that the language that is used in and around production on the shop floor is French in the full sense, given that English remains present in the key terminology, much as it remains present at the heart of the entire manufacturing process. The received explanation is that the aerospace industry is both high-tech and internationally integrated, and that therefore it is only to be expected that English terminology will be found at all levels of operation. In fact, the situation seems to be more complicated. As can be seen from the terms above, most of them have little to do with science, high technology, or the international market place, and a lot to do with day-to-day procedures, the naming of departments, machine tools, and job descriptions. What these terms are really telling us about is the history of the relationship between the two language groups in this particular work setting.

Historically, and within living memory, production work in the Montreal aerospace industry was dominated by an English-speaking workforce. Over the last 15–20 years, shop floor production workers seem to have become predominantly Francophone. There has thus been a process of what one could describe as succession/replacement, whereby the occupation and control of a given territory or niche has passed from one language group to another. This process has been a gradual one, which means that French-speaking production workers were, for a long time, a numerical minority with respect to their English-speaking counterparts, much as French-speaking engineers are today. They had therefore to adjust to an environment where everything took place in English – management, engineering, and production work. This led, presumably, to the emergence of a workplace dialect of French, referred to by the workers themselves as *"jargon,"* which is a mixture of English and French.

What would seem to be the vestiges of the period when English speakers were numerically dominant in production are now part of the "language of the shop" to such an extent that young Francophone technicians and machinists have to divest themselves of the French terms they learned at technical college in order to become linguistically and socially integrated into the workforce. It is not just a question of the inability of older workers to understand the French terms (since the English terms include such run-of-the-mill words as "cleaning," which could easily be translated, although older workers would have difficulty in understanding some of the more technical terms in French), but more an example of an established workplace dialect into which newcomers are socialized. The workplace dialect may therefore, among other things, serve to distinguish (in Bourdieu's sense of the word "distinction") the old hands from the new arrivals.

The continuing use of Anglo-French jargon in the workplace would thus have its roots both in past relationships among French-speaking and English-speaking workers (the former gradually replacing the latter) and in present relationships between the established French-speaking workplace language community and the new Francophone arrivals, fresh from college. Again, the emergence and continuity of the workplace dialect seems to tell us more about internal social dynamics in the past and in the present than about the global market place or the international language of science and technology. We could go further and see in the survival of many of these English terms the relics of the establishment of Montreal's industrial base at the end of the nineteenth century, and the handing on of English terminology from the first generations of British working class immigrants to their French Canadian successors.[7]

Attempts to replace the technical English terms by French ones have so far largely failed, partly for the reasons already given, but also, according to the workers themselves, because the equivalent French terms have been coined by academics who may be specialists in technical terms, but seem to be light years removed from the language of the shop floor. Thus "flap" is supposed to be replaced by the French term *"volet hypersustantateur"* and "plug gauge" by *"tampon a coulis."* Such terms have no echo or grounding in the workers' own everyday language, while the workers themselves invent words such as *"flute"* (in French) to describe an engine part that looks like a flute, a usage that terminological purists would find unacceptable as the officially-recognized term.

These examples show how the use of language in the bilingual workplace not only reveals something about the use of language itself in management, conception, and production that might be less visible in a monolingual work setting. It also tells us about the history of relations between language groups in their attempts to occupy and control different sectors of the labor market and different territories or niches within the workplace. Hitherto we have looked only at language and work in the context of bilingualism. But what happens in the multilingual workplace?

The Multilingual Workplace

The emergence of a workplace dialect based on French, but laced with numerous English terms, flows from the fact that language may be marginal to the central work process (or to the transformation of other raw materials). But it is nonetheless essential to that same process, whence the need to develop a basic vocabulary that allowed for communication between Anglophones and Francophones. However, in our research we have also studied workplaces where language scarcely enters into the work process.

One such example is Montgomery's study of the use of language as such, and of different languages, in the Montreal garment industry (Montgomery, 1993). Immigrant workers are heavily concentrated in this sector of the Montreal labor market. In a recent project on a sample of asylum seekers, we calculated that 31% of the time spent at work since their arrival in Canada at the end of the 1980s was in this one sector (McAll, 1996). According to Montgomery's study, the use of language as such varies according to the type of occupation. Whereas some of the occupations studied (e.g. cutting out) do allow for some largely socially oriented language use during work time, others, such as the operating of sewing machines, tend to allow for little or no language use.

The principal reason for the lack of language content is that the work performed does not require more than a minimum level of communication, and may actually inhibit it altogether. Noise levels make communication difficult with anyone other than one's immediate neighbor, and supervisors may intervene to cut short any conversations that distract from the work in hand. For example, during one of the reconstructed workdays, an interviewee was told by a supervisor to "keep it for the break" after she had said something to one of the women working alongside her. According to one of the women interviewed, the women themselves also have a vested interest in talking as little as possible, given that they work on piece rates and are constantly seeking to maximize their output. "[The supervisors] don't need rules [concerning language use] because nobody wants to lose their time" (Montgomery, 1993: 41). When sewing machine operators do communicate while working, it tends to be in bits and pieces, snatches of conversation, a word or two to a supervisor or colleague. They have to keep an eye on the work being done, however, which means that they cannot look at the people they are talking to without stopping work altogether, another factor that makes verbal communication difficult. The pressers and cutters-out have more of an opportunity to "chat," but the former tend to work back-to-back, which makes conversation difficult. The fact that pressers also work on piece rates tends to reduce time spent on unnecessary talk. For all these categories, the only time of day when language really comes into its own (but only in the socially-oriented sense) is during coffee and lunch breaks, when workers either split up into their own language groups, or manage some form of overarching conversation in French or English (in so far as they are able).

In these work environments where language (in the work-oriented or professional sense) can be more or less absent from the work process, the concentration of immigrant workers from many different backgrounds also means a multiplicity of languages. The bits and pieces of language used around the work process thus tend to be in different languages, sometimes used together in the same phrase. The women interviewed by Montgomery, for example, had spent their day exchanging occasional words and phrases in mixtures of English, Italian, French, Spanish, and Creole depending on who was talking (or shouting) to whom.

Such a range of language competence within the same workplace is made possible by the fact that there is little need for communication. At the same time, language difference can emerge as a definer of frontiers in such work settings in the same way that the use of English and French marks territories and frontiers in the aerospace industry. Teal's (1985) record of nine months' participant observation as an employee in a Montreal underwear factory, for example, shows how the workforce is divided by ethnicity and language, with specific ethnolinguistic groups keeping the best work (in this case, white underwear, which is easier to work on) for themselves, and using language as the basis for setting up an exclusionary network. Language can thus be minimally present in the work process, but none-theless play an important role in the control of the various areas of production. What languages are actually used varies from one workplace to another.

On the basis of Montgomery's case study we could suggest a third type of language use at work to set alongside the "language-centered" and "language marginal" examples already cited. In this case, we could refer to the work as "language minimal," meaning that the work process has little or no necessary language content. This type of work, by its very nature, allows for the presence of several languages at once, since it does not require people working alongside each other to be able to communicate. In some cases, it may even be an advantage for employers that employees are unable to communicate with each other, if that means the inability to share grievances or plan collective action to improve conditions. Whether or not employers see such an interest in a multilingual workforce, however, internal dynamics and the work process itself do not require a common language in the different workplace territories concerned, other than in a minimal sense.

The multilingual workplace thus again brings out certain characteristics of language use at work (and in society) that would be less evident in a monolingual setting. Teal's study suggests that there are some parallels to be drawn between bilingual and multilingual workplaces. In both cases, there can be a dominant language group that exercises control over the language-centered aspects of work. In the case of the pharmaceutical company studied by Tremblay (1993), and in our studies on the aerospace industry, that dominance has been exercised historically through English. In the case of Teal's participant observation in a Montreal clothing factory, dominance was exercised through Italian. In the first two cases, however, production work requires a degree of horizontal communication – albeit marginal to the central work process – and French fills that role. In the clothing factory, however, no such horizontal communication is required other than in a minimal sense, and various languages are spoken or not spoken, as the case may be.

Discussion: Language and Differentiated Employment

The differential use of language as such in relation to the work process in various sectors of the labor market, and within specific work settings, facilitates what Max Weber would describe as monopolistic closure on the basis of the use of different languages. Given that in the workplace power is exercised precisely in those areas where language use is most intense, or where the work is most "language-centered," to use the term suggested here, employment in those areas requires a high degree of language competence. Where the group exercising power in the workplace has a different language from those over whom power is being exercised (within a broader social context where the two groups are opposed to each other), the incompetence of the subordinate group in the dominant group's language prevents its members from being effective in the language-centered work on the other side of the boundary. Language difference thus becomes a key instrument in the maintenance of relations of inequality between the two groups.

The same holds for "other language" immigrant groups attempting to gain access to even language-marginal work. Renaud (1992), on the basis of quantitative research on the access of immigrants to the Montreal labor market, suggests that language competence has little or no effect on accelerating access to entry-level jobs. This probably means that competence in English or French is not necessary in the kinds of jobs to which most immigrants are given access, since those jobs have low language content, or are "language-minimal." We could look at this problem another way, however, and suggest that low levels of competence in English or French preclude immigrants from gaining access to jobs that are either language-centered or language-marginal, since both kinds of jobs require the ability to communicate. Thus, language competence, in a linguistically divided labor market, comes to be a convenient tool for discriminating against other language groups in an apparently 'legitimate' way, since no one can deny the importance of language in order to function in areas of the labor market where language is necessary to the work process.

It is notoriously difficult for first-generation immigrants to acquire sufficient expertise in a second language to escape from traditional immigrant work ghettos. Less noticed is that the frontier between many of these ghettos and the more attractive (and lucrative) sectors of the labor market is also often one between types of employment that are differentiated according to language content or language use. The issue for such immigrants, and for their children, is therefore not just access to such coveted sectors of the labor market, but also access to language competence. Non-immigrant populations (or dominant language groups) do not necessarily have an interest in providing that access, since by doing so, they increase labor market competition and decrease their own chances of gaining or maintaining access to jobs.

Notes

1. Research on language use was conducted in several workplaces in Quebec in the 1990s by the *Équipe de recherche en sociologie du langage* of the Department of Sociology at the University of Montreal. Workplaces included the garment industry, a pharmaceutical company, a public research facility, a variety of companies involved in aerospace, and health and social services (McAll, 1992; McAll, 1993a; McAll, 1997;McAll *et al.*, 1997; McAll *et al.*, 1998; McAll *et al.*, 2001).
2. Such practices on the part of management – with respect to certain categories of worker – emerge clearly in Montgomery's study of language-use in the Montreal garment industry (Montgomery, 1993).
3. As part of a research project on language use in the Montreal aerospace industry, the workdays of 20 engineers were reconstructed in interviews at the end of the day (McAll *et al.*, 1998). For a discussion of the methodology used, see McAll *et al.* (1994).
4. The Montreal aerospace language-use project included the reconstructed workdays of 30 production workers, supervisors, and technicians (McAll *et al.*, 1998).
5. See Tremblay's (1993) study of language-use among low-level white-collar workers in a Montreal pharmaceutical company.
6. For an overview of the Montreal aerospace sector and details on the Montreal aerospace language-use project (funded by the Social Sciences and Humanities Research Council of Canada) see McAll *et al.* (1998) (available at www.ceetum.umontreal.ca).
7. This period in Montreal's industrial history is well described by Reynolds (1935).

Chapter 15

Back to School: Learning Practices in a Job Retraining Community

JILL SINCLAIR BELL

Increasingly, research into language socialization is coming to recognize that the process is a lifelong one (Li, 2000: 62). As the world around us changes, the roles and practices available to us, and the language through which we both understand and shape the world, change too. In the twenty-first century, with increased global mobility and technologically driven communication, the phrase "life long learning" has become a cliché as people acknowledge the inadequacy of their early education in trying to adapt to new contexts. Increasingly, adults are returning to formal learning situations in response to a changing employment scene and the demands of the new marketplace. In North America and elsewhere, employers are being influenced by the tenets of "fast capitalism" or the new demand-driven workplace to require higher levels of linguistic and literate performance (Bailey, 1997; Lankshear & Gee, 1997; Sticht, 1997). As Lankshear and Gee (1997: 89) point out, workers who are unable to respond effectively to these increased demands are being seen at best as peripheral and often as defective. Unemployed workers are, therefore, increasingly being asked to develop new skills to help them adapt to the new workplace. As they struggle with the loss of income and status that accompanies their job loss, the retraining process forces them into new contexts where they must learn to use language in new ways if they are to participate fully.

The challenge for unemployed workers in formal retraining programs is not merely their understanding of language, however, but also their understanding of self. Such learners have been socialized into one identity, that of workers, and are now forced to grapple with a different identity, that of student. In this chapter, I explore the learning experiences of a group of unemployed adults from a wide variety of language backgrounds who return to school to be retrained as refrigeration mechanics. Their experiences demonstrate that learning at any age, by definition, involves socialization into particular community practices, some of which may involve difficult choices relating to personal identity.

In discussing this research, I draw on the work of anthropologists Jean Lave and Etienne Wenger, whose research on situated learning has helped frame my understanding of the learning situation described. In their book, *Situated Learning: Legitimate Peripheral Participation*, Lave and Wenger (1991) suggest that all learning should be understood as a process of participation in communities of practice. Whether the learners are children in school, adults in job-training programs, or alcoholics joining AA, their learning involves coming to understand and participate in the practices of the new community. Rather than seeing learning as the acquisition of particular discrete pieces of knowledge, they see it as a growing ability to participate in the practices of a particular community. This learning comes about not merely by observation of others' participation, but as a direct result of participation, which requires performance opportunities. Initially, as newcomers to the community, learners will participate or perform only in peripheral ways, with limited responsibility for the outcome of the practice. As they engage in the process of performing with established community members, or "old-timers," their participation gradually increases in responsibility and complexity. As they become increasingly proficient, they come to identify with the community and move towards old-timer status themselves. We might perhaps think of medical students as legitimate peripheral participants in the medical community. They are legitimate in the sense that they have an unquestioned right to be present and participate, but they are peripheral in that they have not yet learned how to perform fully. As they learn through participation in the activities of the community of health professionals, they come to perform with increasing confidence, skill and responsibility the practices that define the community and in doing so move toward a less peripheral status. Importantly, they also have an impact on the community of practice itself, which is not a fixed structure but is constantly in flux. Communities always seek to reproduce themselves, but this reproductive process always involves change. The medical community of today differs in significant ways from that of a few decades ago as a result of the participation in community practices of successive newcomers. In this sense, the community learns along with the newcomer.

Not all learners make the move toward full participant status, and newcomer participants may disengage from the community, or drop out, before attaining mastery over core skills. Language and access often play key and inter-related roles here. As Lave and Wenger (1991: 105) point out, "learning to become a legitimate participant in a community involves learning how to talk (and be silent) in the manner of full participants." Developing appropriate language skills is thus a critical part of successful participation. This process involves much more than knowing appropriate grammatical forms, or even knowing how to verbalize specific community-related knowledge. Learners must be able to perform the practices appropriately, which requires them to have access to performance opportunities. "To become a full member of a community of practice requires access to a wide range of ongoing activity, old-timers and other members of the community; and to information, resources and opportunities for participation" (Lave & Wenger, 1991: 101).

In her work on the socialization of young immigrant children in kindergarten classrooms, Toohey (2000) found that one of the most significant features of access in the classroom situation concerned access to the classroom language. Those community participants who failed to understand and work within accepted community practices were excluded from community resources, both material and linguistic, so that the opportunities to develop competence were restricted. Toohey also found that the question of access was linked to issues of identity, arguing that:

> Learners' identities as well as their learning [are] constructed in the practices of the communities in which they are situated ... a classroom being a kind of community, one can examine its practices not only in terms of how they identify learners, and how the learners take up and are assigned identities, but also in terms of how differential access to the classroom language arises. (Toohey, 2000: 16).

Job Retraining: A Reluctant Community of Practice?

We will see that language and access issues played a critical role in determining the degree to which adult learners were able to participate successfully in the community of practice represented in the retraining program. Schecter and Bayley (1997: 514) have pointed out that "an integrated view of the role of language in identity construction acknowledges the relevance of ideological and power relations," and there is no doubt that differential access to classroom language is one of the sources of power variance. For adults in retraining programs, the community in which they are learning sits within a complex web of power relations that reflect the learners' roles as both worker and student. Issues of power and identity also affected the degree to which the learners aspired to full legitimate participation. As mature adults, previously well socialized into relatively prestigious identities as workers, these learners were now being asked to identify themselves within a community made up primarily of young students. Both the learners and their instructors demonstrated some ambivalence regarding the desirability of making this change.

In the example of medical students, we can broadly assume that the students have joined their community of practice by choice, and that the identity of full participant is one they seek out. For the unemployed workers in this study, however, while the community of practice they would like to join is that of employed refrigeration mechanics, the college program that they are invited to join instead is a community that involves very different practices, much more like school than the workplace. The learners therefore face a dilemma. To gain access to the desired community of practice, they have to learn first to perform within a community where many of the practices are unappealing. In addition, since every time we use language, or engage in language practices, we are demonstrating our assumptions about our identity and the community to which we see ourselves belonging (Gee, 1990), for these adult learners, successful completion of the job-training program may necessitate engaging in practices and taking on identities that are not desired. Many find this condition sufficiently stressful to prefer to disengage from the community prior to completion.

Research in a College-based Job Retraining Program

Background

The material discussed here is drawn from a study of the language and identity challenges faced by a group of unemployed workers enrolled in a job re-training program held at a community college in a large Canadian city. The work was done as part of a large-scale research project[1] that included surveys of trainees in a number of different Canadian community colleges, interviews with trainees and instructors in a range of programs in two colleges, and detailed ethnographic observation of one particular focal class, a 36-week pre-apprenticeship program in refrigeration mechanics. Most of the material discussed is drawn from the ethnographic study, together with interview data from students in the focal class, students in the subsequent cohort of the same program, and program instructors.

The 28 men and one woman in the focal class under study came from a wide range of backgrounds. Most of the workers had attended English-language schools in Canada or abroad, and only three men initially identified themselves as non-native speakers of English. However, many of the others came from homes in which other languages were used, including Tagalog, German, Maltese, Greek, Italian, Spanish, French, Cree, Polish, and Bahasa. Often these learners reported that they spoke very little English on first attending school. A number of participants in the program came from the Caribbean and Guyana, and spoke non-standard English dialects. Ages in the group ranged from 18–45, though most of the workers were in their twenties and thirties. A few of the younger members of the group had been unemployed since leaving high school, but the majority had work experience, often in more than one field. All 29 workers were now unemployed and were taking this course in the hope of gaining skills that would lead to more permanent employ-ment. In particular, they hoped to find employers who would accept them into a formal five-year apprenticeship agreement that would lead to a full trades-person's qualification. Some had been referred to this pre-apprenticeship course by their unemployment, welfare, or workers' compensation counselors. Others had found the course on their own, and were paying their own college fees.

Although one member of the group had a university degree from Poland, most of the learners had had less success in the formal educational system, and had dropped out of high school prior to graduation. Many of those whose home language was not English reported that they had ongoing difficulties in school with language and literacy (see Bell, 2000 for a full discussion of this issue). As is discussed later, the program demanded high levels of language and literacy skills, a feature that had a significant impact on learners' performance opportunities.

The college community

The multi-campus community college in which this program took place offered a range of trade and professional training programs. The college was gradually shifting away from its previous base in trades training towards a focus on more academic programs in areas such as engineering technology or architectural design that were offered on the same campus as the program under study. Students in the academic programs were different in many ways from those in the job-training programs. Approximately half of the students in the academic programs were female, in contrast to the heavily male population in the trades area. Typically, the other students were younger, having been admitted directly from local area high schools. Higher admission requirements for the academic programs ensured that most were better educated, with more successful school experiences behind them. A number of signals such as their fashionable clothing suggested that they had access to more disposable income than did the unemployed workers, and many came from middle class homes and were still being supported by their families. These students appeared to exhibit a comfort level in the college environment that was reflected in their willingness to spend extra time there outside of class. They could be seen routinely hanging out in large, often rowdy, groups in the cafeteria and student lounges, or outside on the steps where people went to smoke.

The workers in the job training programs did not appear to mingle with students from academic programs. The large workshops for trades training were all located in the basement of the building, and the workers were assigned lockers on the same floor. Although lectures were scheduled in various above-ground classrooms, the workers rarely made use of the upholstered chairs in the lounge space on these upper floors, tending to return promptly to the hard benches of the basement corridors after class. They did not hang around the college once class was over, and could be found in the cafeteria only in the break between classes or when a class was unexpectedly canceled.

The instructors in the trades program seemed to feel a similar comfort level in the basement. I never saw any of them make use of the attractive and spacious staff lounge located upstairs. Instead they worked and relaxed in the windowless bare basement room assigned as the program office. Like the learners, they appeared to feel somewhat defensive in relation to their supposed peers in the more academic programs. They had been hired on the basis of their experience in the trades, and had few academic qualifications, and no pedagogical training.

In interviews, a number of the instructors commented that they experienced some tension between their role as teachers and their role as trades people. When first interviewed, one instructor, Jeff, told me that he was very proud to tell people he was a teacher and that he thought he had done well. Later, when he got to know me better, he confessed that when he met people outside of the college environment, he always described himself as being "in refrigeration mechanics." He wasn't quite sure why he did this. He felt a bit of a fraud claiming to be a teacher, and there was also something about the identity that didn't really appeal to him. It didn't seem productive enough, and it wasn't very masculine. A number of other instructors indicated similar concerns, along with some scorn for colleagues who appeared to take themselves too seriously. At the time of the study, the title of "Professor" had recently been awarded to the college instructional staff, replacing the previous title of "Instructor." Offering me his business card with some embarrassment, another trades instructor, Sean, commented, "It's ridiculous, isn't it, calling us professors? Mind you, the ones in the academic programs, they like it. Kidding themselves, they are. We're instructors."

As trades instructors, the teachers in the program were answerable to many masters, which seemed to aggravate their confusion over their role. Stakeholders with the power to shape their daily work included the students themselves, the college authorities, the trade unions that set licensing examinations, and potential employers who expected them to keep up with changes in the field. At the time of this study, the college authorities posed a particular challenge. Provincial cutbacks to education funding had led to a number of layoffs among the instructional staff. Fewer applications were being received for apprenticeship programs, leading to the threat of further layoffs if student registrations could not be increased. The pre-apprenticeship program was seen as a way to attract students and maintain staff numbers, so instructors had a personal stake in the success of the program. Simultaneously, however, the authorities were stressing the need to maintain academic standards, and to avoid "dumbing down" the curriculum. Assessment was therefore based on standards developed to assess the progress of those in true apprenticeship programs, whose classroom studies would be supported by many months of hands-on training. Significant numbers of students failed courses and, though some dropped out, often they were encouraged to re-register to take the same courses again. Of the focal class of 29, 17 (58%) completed the program on schedule. A further 5 (17%) graduated after repeating certain parts of the program. Instructors disagreed as to the merits of encouraging students in difficulty to continue. While most instructors encouraged re-registering, Sean commented that he found the process a waste of time, because he had never had a "repeater" who didn't eventually end up being advised to cease training.

The chances of graduates actually getting an apprenticeship at the end of the program were acknowledged to be rather slight. The instructors rationalized this by saying that, even if the learners didn't get jobs as a result, all the skills they were learning would be useful "when they owned their own homes one day." Perhaps because of this ambivalence as to the purpose of the training and the competing pressures from stakeholders, there seemed to be considerable confusion among both instructors and learners as to whether they were in a school or in a workplace environment. Some of the expectations and practices of this community of practice were clearly congruent with a workplace. In the workshops, for instance, evaluation was based on the functionality of a finished product that could be attempted many times until success was achieved. Other practices, such as the testing of abstract knowledge in theory courses, seemed more congruent with a school setting. An exploration of the ways in which these unemployed workers engaged in legitimate peripheral participation in the college community highlights an interesting ambiguity that demonstrates the challenges to language socialization and identity issues faced by adults in such a context. In their book, *Language as Cultural Practice*, Schecter and Bayley (2002) explore the complexity of the relationship between language socialization and identity issues, pointing out the "dialectical tensions in play in the relationship among language attitudes, situational circumstances, and personal agency." Participation in the community of practice shapes the learners, but not all learners are affected in the same way, and the impact that the participants have on the ongoing community is not easily predictable. Learners bring with them entire narrative histories (Bell, 1997; Connelly & Clandinin, 1988, 1990) that include and shape language attitudes and personal agency. The ways in which these influence their reactions to community participation are complex.

The training program community

If we view the training program as a community of practice, we can understand the community by examining the practices in common use. Membership in communities such as college programs shifts over time, and practices are set up in ways that allow for the induction of new participants. However, the norms of interaction are largely determined by the old-timers, and newcomers are inducted by being allowed to participate, though often in attenuated ways, with old-timers. In the context of the specific job retraining program under discussion, only the instructors have real old-timer status, and the types of interaction they offer to the newcomers, and the degree to which they legitimate their entry, determine the degree of access to the program resources. The social world is, of course, reflexive (Vygotsky, 1978, 1986), in that it is not merely constituted of humans or even just a context for them, but is constitutive of them. In other words, the community we live in shapes us, just as we shape it. But, for newcomers who are unfamiliar with the practices of the community, interaction, while legitimate, is always peripheral, minimizing the newcomers' impact. The community makes available only certain roles – which may be more or less desirable, powerful, or equitable. Participants learn how to act within this community and they construct their identities according to choices offered to them by the old-timers, in this case, primarily the instructors.

With very few exceptions, the learners coming into these programs had supported themselves, often for many years, before beginning the training. They were adult taxpayers, with responsibilities and commitments, with marketable skills that allowed them to support themselves, and sometimes a family, too. Much of the time it seemed that these identities went unrecognized in the college setting. The instructors assumed a hierarchical role, in which they had the privileges of rank, and the needs of the students were not much considered. For example, classes were canceled with no advance notice or apology, which seemed indicative of the assumption that the students had nothing better to do with their time than to hang around the college. One student commented, "The teachers keep missing classes and we have to pay for it in the end. We have to reschedule. Well, we were here, you weren't, why do *we* have to reschedule?" Timetables were also routinely changed every six weeks. As the college maximized classroom use with an informal shift system, this meant that after six weeks of primarily afternoon and early evening classes, the program might shift to a pattern of early morning starts. This was especially problematic for those class members with young children and babysitting arrangements.

As I spent time in the program, it became clear that the instructors unconsciously assumed that their students shared a particular identity profile. For instance, the comment cited above about "when they get houses of their own" presupposed that the workers still lived either with their parents or in apartments. For instructors the prototypical student seemed to be a young version of themselves and the men who had been their fellow apprentices some twenty or thirty years earlier. The assigned identity was, therefore, a young, white, working-class male, accustomed to working with tools to mend cars and motorbikes. He was assumed to be single, free of major responsibilities, and to have dropped out of school prior to graduation. If English was not his first language, he nonetheless spoke it comfortably, though he might use Italian or Greek at home. In their role as old-timers, the instructors influenced the opportunities for learners to engage with other community members and to learn from that participation; and, inevitably, there was a tendency to make opportunities available in ways that supported the learning of those who fitted the assigned profile. There was no doubt that a number of the men in the focal class did appear to fit this image, but the population of the multicultural city in which the college is located has changed in the last thirty years, as has the employment situation. A significant amount of diversity could be seen and heard in the classroom; and interviews with students confirmed that variation existed on less easily assessed parameters as well. An example of a student who did not fit the pattern, and hence encountered limited performance opportunities, was Samantha, the female student. Samantha was an intelligent, young, single mother struggling with day-care problems out of school and with sexism on campus. Not surprisingly, she dropped out early in the program, leaving the focal class as an entirely male group.

Despite the evident maturity of many of the workers, instructors still saw themselves as being responsible for policing the students' behavior. They worried about leaving the room in case the learners made too much noise and disturbed another class. They discussed with me their problems regarding students who arrived late for class. One instructor went so far as to lock the door to keep out late arrivals. Another instructor worried that I would think he was a bad teacher, because he had allowed one young man to leave class for a few moments without asking permission. Sean, the electrical instructor, confessed to me that he preferred to teach in the older classrooms. He was uneasy when his lectures were scheduled in the newly renovated part of the college, in case his students damaged the rooms. It is hard not to see here a reflection of his own feeling that trades programs had a second-class status in the college, and that his students were not entitled to the best facilities.

When discussing discipline, the instructors often commented that students had to learn what life was like in the workplace. "They won't be able to turn up late once they have jobs," was a common comment – one that ignored the work history of the people involved. A surprising ambivalence was inherent in the way that most of the instructors constructed their jobs. Lip service was paid to the workplace reality, but most of the deep-seated assumptions that shaped practice seemed to come from school-based settings. The instructors had never taught in schools, and had been given no formal teacher education, so one might have expected the community practices to be reflective of the apprenticeship model of workplace training.

Polanyi (1962) describes the traditional educational mode of apprenticeship as one where the apprentice learns holistically by observation of tasks being completed in natural contexts and then by imitation and practice. He stresses the value of the unspoken and often unformulated knowledge that is acquired tacitly from such lengthy periods of observation and practice. The learner makes progress at his or her own pace, with performance continuing to be refined as craft develops. In contrast, much school learning focuses on explicit knowledge – on that part of knowledge that can be broken down analytically and presented in pieces to learners to be absorbed and tested in abstract ways. As I will explore later, when the instructors were supervising hands-on classes in the big workshops, they worked largely within an apprenticeship model that valued tacit knowledge. They set tasks and allowed the learners to discover how to fulfil them through a process of trial and error. In the theory classes, however, the instructors taught only explicit knowledge and demonstrated a rather rigid understanding of how classrooms operate, and what roles students might play.

Community practices in the classroom

To a man, the instructors endorsed the assumptions that they were the holders of knowledge and that their task was to somehow get that knowledge into the students' heads. They did not question the program framework that showed an artificial separation of theory and practice. They did not question the time tabling that assigned three-hour "lectures." On the contrary, for the most part they took these instructions at face value, and lectured for three hours, interspersed only with a few questions from the students. Students were never positioned as a source of knowledge, even though the class included students with previous work experience in the field, and one man had a degree in mechanical engineering. Following some direct questioning on my part about whether group or pair work was ever used, one instructor assigned a group activity as homework. Other than on this one occasion, I saw no group work or pair work assigned in the theory sessions. Despite the learners' experiences as member of worker teams, there was little formal encouragement for learners to support each other in approaching the learning task. Of course, students did try to help each other, but this was done furtively, in whispers. On one occasion when Samantha (the only woman in the class) was asked by another student what result she had got to a problem, she angrily refused to answer, as if she thought he was trying to cheat. It was never suggested that students should approach a problem as a group or attempt a task in pairs, so students had little opportunity to learn from one another, or to position themselves as being able to construct knowledge, or even discover it.

There was surprisingly little individual work assigned during class-time. Occasionally students were assigned a problem to calculate and, sometimes, in a review of homework questions, a student would be asked to come up to the front and explain his answer. For the vast majority of the time, however, the instructor talked, and the students listened. The most common, if not only, subject role available to students in these encounters was that of naive listener.

These long theory classes put an enormous strain on people's language abilities. Listening skills were clearly in demand, to make sense of this flood of mostly abstract spoken language, which included a highly specialized technical vocabulary. The learners also needed quite sophisticated literacy skills to listen to the lectures and simultaneously make notes that summarized the material and recorded it in their own words. Many of the students struggled, constantly attempting, and inevitably failing, in a word-by-word transcription. Others tended to merely copy the blackboard notes and to allow the rest of the material to go unrecorded. The more successful students seemed to understand that their task was to identify and record only significant material. Understanding how to do this, required not so much the ability to identify important concepts in refrigeration, as the ability to pick up communicative signals from the instructors. While these signals were sometimes very straightforward (such as "Now listen up guys, this is important"), at other times they were carried by a shift in intonation or body language, or by simple repetition of the material.

Again, there were significant differences among the instructors in the degree to which language accommodations were made. One instructor, Phil, assumed that students (from all language groups) had limited literacy competence and needed a "translation" of written language. He rarely used the text except for homework reviews, and he presented information in non-technical language wherever possible. When reading homework questions from the text book, he would often try to rephrase material, as in this example where he is addressing a native speaker: "Question 6, what is the function of the start relay? What is the function of the start relay? Brian, what do you think – what's the purpose of the start relay? What's it for?" Other instructors were less accommodating and tended to work more directly from the textbook for their basic presentation. At one point, when Phil was replaced by another instructor, the three recent non-native speaker immigrants came to me and asked if I could intervene, as their marks had fallen significantly.

Within the classroom community it was soon evident to the various learners which members of the group were being most successful at participating in community practices, and status was assigned accordingly. In part, this assessment reflected an awareness of test scores and homework grades as indicative of the ability to perform the required academic practices; but such successes tended to reflect the learners' abilities to engage in a range of underlying practices. One such practice was recognizing when and how it was permissible to ask for help. Phil was willing to take questions, but expected students to recognize what he considered to be appropriate times to ask. Juan, a student of Mexican descent, demonstrated some difficulty in this regard. The instructor would pause after explaining an item, offer some summary comments, pause again, and then begin on a new piece. Because it took Juan a little longer to process what he had heard or perhaps because he didn't recognize the pause as a cue for questions, he would not indicate a question during the pauses. Instead, he would raise his hand once Phil was launched into his next theme. Not wanting to break his explanation, Phil would ignore Juan's raised hand. Eventually, Juan would give up. Soon after, Phil would reach a suitable pause point, look around for the hand that he had noticed earlier, see no sign of it, and carry on.

Asking appropriate questions was not merely a matter of reading the teacher's signals, but of recognizing the implications for participation in the classroom community of practice. In general, questions were taken as a sign of weakness – the tougher the material, the fewer questions would be asked. Asking questions was seen as a sign of the learner's failure to understand, not the instructor's failure to teach adequately. The "prestige" students did not ask questions; they answered them. Even when the teacher's presentation was unclear, the strong students did not ask questions. They expected that the weaker students would ask and, as one student confessed to me, they found it quite helpful to hear the material explained again. However, there were "rules" regarding which questions were appropriate to ask, and who was allowed to ask them. Budi, an Indonesian man in his forties, routinely came to class late, after a timetable change gave him a conflict with some part-time work. As he had more related trades experience than most of the learners, his questions were always sensible and to the point. However, it incensed other class members that he would waste their class time to ask about material that he had missed.

Robert, a Jamaican student, found the program difficult. He asked numerous questions in class, often phrasing the questions in circuitous ways that were difficult to follow. One typical example concerned the nature of flash gas, " Er, yeah, you, you were talking about flash gas, er, I, er wondering what the difference was between flash gas and percentage of flash gas, what the response was?" The instructor appeared to make a wild guess at the likely question, and interpreted this to the class as "Robert's question is what causes a flash gas to make a better efficiency?" Despite the somewhat unclear and often lengthy questions, Robert attended regularly, worked hard, and asked out of a genuine need to understand. As such, his questions were remarkably well tolerated by most of the class, as legitimate uses of class time. He did, however, cast himself as "dumb" by this display. Dumb was an acceptable classroom identity for a legitimate peripheral participant, but was not one of the prestige identities available. James, a young man who had failed a number of courses, commented to me that he didn't want to look "like a dummy" in front of his peers, so he rarely asked questions. He said that he found the process difficult because "I find if I explain it [the question] my way, I'm going to make it sound like there's two or three answers involved when there's only one. So I got to think about how I'm going to ask the question."

Although asking questions was identified as low status, the community practices available in the lectures did not allow anyone other than the teacher to be cast as powerful. The roles available for learners in the theory class were limited, and none of them allowed for adults with wide work experience to contribute to the classroom exploration. Those who had earned status by demonstrating expertise in the shop and outside of class maintained it here by being silent. Typically, the students perceived by others as powerful would arrive promptly, sit with their peers in the middle rows, talk quietly before class or flip through their textbooks, answer correctly when spoken to, and volunteer nothing.

While all experiences lead to learning, not all learning is necessarily productive. A number of the younger men, especially those who were not long out of high school, chose to engage in community practices that ultimately worked against them. They measured their success purely in terms of test scores and, in contrast to their reticence about content issues, would plague the instructors with questions about the content and format of upcoming tests. When tests were returned, they invested much energy in checking the marks for each question and complained vociferously if they felt there had been any inequity in the marking. Their focus was entirely on passing the tests necessary to ensure graduation, rather than on understanding the material in ways that would allow them to use the knowledge in the workplace.

Community practices in the shop

The atmosphere was very different in the shop classes. These were held in large basement rooms, each of which was dedicated to a specific trades program and used only by the program members. Rooms were laid out in ways chosen by the trades instructors, so their control over their environment was absolute. Unlike the upstairs rooms where the instructors often seemed to feel under observation, here they had complete privacy to teach in their own way.

Basically, in shop classes, the learners were to develop the physical skills of handling equipment and tools. They were to learn how to cut and shape pipe, how to solder joins, and weld seams. Performance was typically tested by assessing the functionality of the finished product – whether or not a seal could withstand the appropriate amount of pressure, for example. Each project during the six-week block required the learners to construct a piping structure of increasing complexity. The particulars of the projects were never discussed in words. Instead, learners were given a hand-drawn diagram of the completed structure. Usually, the only written text would be the title of the project and some specification of sizes and measurements. Occasionally, a note such as "Must withstand pressures up to 200 psi." would be added. There were no instructions as to how to go about creating the structures, and no group demonstrations of the techniques involved. Essentially, then, the practice required a workplace-like pattern of independence in taking responsibility for producing work that satisfied the blueprint provided. Teamwork was considered acceptable in this context, and the workers shared resources such as tools. People worked at their own pace and largely assessed the standard of their own work, deciding whether or not a piece should be repeated, or whether it was ready to go forward for formal assessment.

Access to the instructor and to resources was critical in assigning community positions, and there was no doubt that access to these resources was not equally distributed. Tools were always in short supply because of funding restrictions. As all students were assigned the same tasks in the same order, and thus required particular tools at the same time, the competition could be quite intense. Those who were unsuccessful at gaining access had no option but to wait for tools to be available, letting limited shop access time tick away unused. Access to information was also critical. Workers had to know how to read the project diagrams distributed by the teacher. Much of the necessary information was missing from these hand-drawn sketches, and it required a knowledge of context to select appropriate materials, or decide the most appropriate technique to follow. While the instructors would often demonstrate some of the steps required, the help was offered on a one-to-one basis, rather than to the whole group. Almost invariably, such help was offered to the more advanced students, since they were the ones moving on to new projects first.

The teachers assumed that the students would seek help from one another, but participating in the practice of seeking clarification from others required an understanding of whom, when, and how it was appropriate to ask for help. Some learners, mostly men who fitted the teachers' expected identity profile, worked well within this system. The strongest students in the class chose tables near the front of the shop – this gave them easy access to the instructor, and also put them near the partitioned-off tool crib. They were first to start any new project, and benefitted from the instructor's demonstrations of technique, and the tips and shortcuts he offered up as he watched the men working. They did not wait until they needed a tool before going to the tool-crib, but looked ahead at their likely needs for the session and collected a set of tools prior to beginning work that they held in common in the group. Often they expedited the task by working together, perhaps with one holding the pipe while the other sawed, or by trading work, where each made two of a necessary component. They were comfortable asking each other for help, or offering unsolicited advice such as "Phil says that's easier if you heat the pipe first." If they needed help that the rest of the group couldn't provide, they approached the instructor directly.

Such tasks seemed less easy for other class members. Samantha, the only woman in the focal class, found shop classes difficult. She had no previous experience in using tools, and found that some tasks required a degree of physical strength that she lacked. In my role as participant-observer, I encountered similar problems using the tools, but was helped when one of the instructors showed me a number of tricks that compensated for my lack of physical strength. However, he never showed these to Samantha. When I asked about this, he told me that she never asked for help, and he didn't want to be seen "hanging around" her in case people thought he was "hitting on her." Samantha claimed that she did ask him for help, but never got any because he was too busy with the guys. She reported that if she asked the other men for help regarding technique, they took over the task and presented her with a finished product, which essentially denied her the right to learn. Consequently, she resisted asking for help, and got further and further behind.

Budi, the Indonesian mechanic, had no difficulties using the tools, but encountered challenges in finding the tools that he needed. Budi usually worked at one of the lower tables, mostly populated with those who were making poor progress. He often seemed to be short of tools, and would be looking for them long after the toolroom supplies had run out. In such cases, it was common for people to borrow a tool in use at a nearby table, but there were expected procedures for how this should be accomplished. These might include a query as to whether the tool was in immediate use, a request to borrow, or a pledge to return the tool promptly. Budi, however, would walk up to one of the other tables, pick up a tool one of the men had laid down for a moment, and walk off with it. This led to a number of arguments with the more vociferous class members, while others started hiding their tools when Budi came by.

In the shop, asking for help from peers involved quite complex protocols. Although everyone in the class identified the same few men as knowledgeable, only those in their immediate peer group would ask them for help. Those with less status asked each other, even though the advice they gained was often proved wrong. The instructors did not seem concerned about the limited access to instructional resources that many learners experienced. They commented that the process of trying, failing, and trying again was a good learning situation and claimed that all the knowledge ultimately filtered down through the members of the group, as they learned from one another. I asked one of the stronger students about whether he felt such information was well shared. He commented, "There's really no hidden information – you don't keep it to get ahead. If someone asks you, you tell them, but you really can't go out of your way, running around saying, 'you're not doing that right.'" This seemed an accurate assessment. This was not a community whose practices were marked by cut-throat competition, and information was not deliberately withheld. However, the practices of information sharing, like those of resource sharing, were complex and layered. In time, the necessary information would trickle down to the weakest students just as tools would ultimately become available, but participation in this community of practice was of limited duration. Those who were unduly delayed by lack of access to resources or knowledge, including language, were unlikely to complete the requisite number of projects within the allotted time frame, and were thus pushed toward failure.

Conclusions

The experiences of these unemployed workers demonstrate that: (1) language socialization can be a lifelong process; and (2) the modern workplace is now demanding greater language and literacy skills from workers than used to be considered necessary. Also, when job retraining is offered through educational institutions rather than in workplaces, the language and literacy demands are likely to be more complex, since the community practices are drawn from academic models rather than from apprenticeship ones.

Socialization into community practices that involve language use require more than simple language learning. Using language, or indeed failing to use language, in certain approved community practices has direct implications for one's ability to perform within a community, and the degree of acceptance one meets there. Roles within a community are shaped by the skill with which community practices are carried out. Only those allowed access to "information, resources and opportunities for participation" (Lave & Wenger, 1991: 101) can become full participants in the community. As the experiences of these workers demonstrate, not all educational practices lead to equality of access for students from varied linguistic and cultural backgrounds.

In the classroom sessions, successful participation requires high levels of language and literacy skills. The language in use is dense, technical, and abstract. Successful participation requires skillful performance in areas such as summarizing, note-taking, gisting dense text, and writing exams. Workers with successful school experiences behind them have developed related skills that support their ability to perform in this new educational environment. Samantha, for example, had dropped out of high school because she was pregnant, not because she had academic difficulties. While faced with some new language challenges, such as the trade-specific vocabulary, she nonetheless was in a strong position to perform well in these new classroom community practices. She knew how to work with the dense textbook, and had little difficulty with homework because she knew how to find necessary information. She could identify significant points from the teacher's presentation, and dismiss the supporting illustrations. Years of performance practice had developed her physical writing skills, so she was able to encode rapidly and keep pace with the flow of information. In addition, she had operated successfully within Canadian high school classrooms and understood the underlying performance requirements of the classroom. She knew how to read the teachers' intentions. She knew what behavior patterns were appropriate. She knew what to expect from test formats, and what they implied for grading schemes. She had a great wealth of practical classroom knowledge combined with a confidence in her own ability to be successful within this community. Not surprisingly, she did well within the academic part of the program.

By no means were all of the workers equally fortunate. Many had dropped out of school because they could not adequately perform the necessary high school academic practices. Now they were facing similar challenges with literacy skills that had grown weaker with years of disuse. Since there is little interaction in this classroom environment, performance opportunities are restricted for all participants. There is only one old-timer with whom the peripheral participants can interact. Many of the required practices involve interaction with written texts rather than with other individuals; and texts cannot mediate a learning process in different ways for different participants. Consequently, success in this environment is restricted to those who have already learned academic practices in other settings. Not surprisingly, many of the learners found the challenges overwhelming, and chose to disengage before they had learned how to perform core competencies.

For non-native and non-standard English speakers, the challenges were intensified. Even a learner like Tad, the Polish student with a degree in mechanical engineering, faced additional problems when working with dense abstract texts in a foreign language. For those without his educational background and ease in academic situations, successful performance of required academic practices was extremely difficult. Excluded by language barriers from attempting many tasks, they failed to gain performance opportunities, and were thus excluded from the participation necessary to developing competence. Juan failed to recognize suitable opportunities for asking questions, and was thus excluded both from acquiring the information he needed to allow him to comprehend the content being taught, and from the performance opportunity of asking questions in an academic setting. Without these opportunities for practice, he was unlikely to develop the skills he needed. Other workers, both native speakers of English and non-native speakers, demonstrated confusion over the purposes of activities such as note-taking. In their efforts to record every word, they excluded themselves both from the development of a useful set of crib notes necessary for homework, and from test success. Most striking, of course, is the instructor's failure to engage in drawing the attention of the learners to the necessary practices and to offer guided performance opportunities. The movement towards full participation in a community of practice requires interaction with old-timers, and the patterns demonstrated in the classroom setting minimize the opportunities for interaction, thus penalizing those for whom the patterns are least familiar – the non-native and non-standard English speakers (McCall, this volume).

The patterns were different in the shop setting, however, where learning was based entirely on the apprenticeship model, with greatly increased performance opportunities. While the instructor was still the only true old-timer, the previous work experiences of many of the learners allowed them to make rapid progress toward full participation in certain practices, thus allowing those still on the periphery to engage with and learn from a wider range of informants. In this noisy environment where lectures were impossible and written text was restricted to annotations on a diagram, the academic linguistic demands were minimized. Nonetheless, successful participation still required workers to be socialized into appropriate language practices, as Budi's difficulties with tools indicated. Samantha, for example, notwithstanding her success in the classroom, did poorly in the shop environment. Unwilling to tolerate the heavy flirting and sexist teasing, she chose to work alone where possible. This effectively excluded her from the opportunity to interact with and learn from other community members, and from access to tools and information. These exclusions led directly to her failure to complete the assigned projects in the required time frame, and her consequent withdrawal from the program.

In general, the non-native and native speakers of English did much better in the shop environment than they did in the classroom. If they failed to understand an instruction, they could see from the work being done at other tables what the assigned project should look like. With many more informants available, they could seek help repeatedly, practising their questioning performance skills as well as finding necessary information. If they made errors, the task could be repeated without major penalty. All these opportunities to engage with the practices of the community allowed them to build their competence in an atmosphere of relative comfort. Not surprisingly, they, like the native speakers, almost unanimously identified this part of the program as the most useful and relevant to their needs.

In indicating their preference for the shop environment, the learners were also reaffirming their identity as workers. The shop environment, and the shop model of education, was more congruent with the community of practice with which they had previously identified when they were employed workers and was closer to the community of refrigeration mechanics with which they soon hoped to be able to identify. Learners recognized the value of the practices in which they were being invited to participate, and they were prepared to invest the necessary time and resources to engage with these practices until they could perform them as full participants.

Some of the workers had made a similar commitment to working toward full participation in the classroom practices, but significant numbers found this to be a daunting undertaking. For those from non-native and native speaker language backgrounds, the combination of linguistic challenges together with limited performance opportunities, poorly explained expectations, low-status role options, and restricted access to old-timers meant that there were major barriers to successful performance. They were not only being asked to give up the identity of worker and take on the new identity of low-status student, they were also being asked to see themselves as unsuccessful within this unattractive position. Not surprisingly, many of them chose to disengage from this community of practice.

If, as current trends suggest, as adults many of us will face the need to retrain for new vocations, it is important for the educational system to find ways to make that training as successful as possible. All unemployed workers face identity challenges as they, often reluctantly, join new communities of practice. Educators in training programs need to become aware of the community practices into which they are attempting to induct the trainees, so that performance opportunities can be maximized along with access to resources, information, and other community members. Consideration also needs to be given to the kind of community that the job training represents, and its relationship to the learners' target community. For example, it may not be appropriate to require full participation in academic practices such as note-taking when these skills are not required in the target occupation. While apprenticeship models also have certain drawbacks, for the most part they do allow for more effective socialization and greater access to performance opportunities. The experiences of the learners in this program suggest that the needs of students from multilingual and multicultural backgrounds can be more easily addressed within such a model, and their identity challenges minimized.

Notes

1. The research on which this chapter was based was supported by the Social Sciences and Humanities Research Council of Canada.

Chapter 16

Bilingualism and Standardization in a Canadian Call Center: Challenges for a Linguistic Minority Community

SYLVIE ROY

This chapter explores how the linguistic varieties of a Francophone minority in the southern part of Ontario, Canada, are devalued as a result of standardization of communication in a service-oriented workplace, and how members of this minority community are adapting to these changes. By so doing, it also addresses the manner by which the marketplace in the new economy is redefining who is seen as "bilingual" as well as the consequences of this redefinition for social relations.

The setting for this study of workplace language socialization is a call center in a small community in rural Ontario province. Typical of such low-industry settings, residents depend on this workplace to ensure the economic survival of the Francophone community. However, in order to stay competitive in a global workplace, the call center management determined that they had to change the ways in which they did business. By introducing new hiring, training, and evaluating processes and procedures, they positioned the varieties of French normally spoken by Francophones in the community as not good enough to satisfy the new company standard – in other words as substandard. Francophones in the community frequently used French–English code-switching, as well as English terms and French colloquialisms. These vernacular usages were not seen by company management as sufficiently professional to ensure work as a bilingual in the call center; and the meaning of "bilingual" came to be redefined as speaking both languages well, in a standard way. Thus, in the name of "professionalism," an ideology of language purity replaced an earlier value placed by community members on the local vernacular.

New Ways to Do Business

The topic of the new enterprise culture in the "global" economy has been receiving considerable attention in professional journals and the media. This topic has been the focus of numerous articles in the Canadian magazine, *The Economist*, and in the financial sections of newspapers across North America. For example, an article published in the *National Post*, a Toronto-based newspaper, discussed how CEO's have an interest in being in the public eye in order to satisfy new ways of doing business and attracting investors (Howes, 2000). University researchers also have shown interest in the question of doing business in the global world. Castells (1996) and Gadrey (2000) have provided overviews of the new enterprise culture and its effects on business, people, and the economy. Gee *et al.* (1996) described the new era using the term "New Work Order." In their volume, they explained how the new economy is based on a capitalist ideology that seeks to adapt and change – even to the point of customizing the product – and that this orientation is considered the only way for large businesses to survive in a competitive market. The new workplace ideology also seeks to empower workers, and encourages them to take on new responsibilities in workplace decision making. This is accomplished by developing a shared culture between management and workers with a rhetoric that encourages "*empowerment*," "*vision*," and "*shared decisions*" while playing down talk of profit sharing. Thus, decentralization and flexibility comprise the motif that enables access to a competitive structure. We will see that the notion of flexibility as it pertains to the standardization of language is important in relation to this particular study, because it provides a rationale for standardizing the ways in which people talk. If they all have similar interaction patterns and use standardized forms in doing their jobs, employees would be able to work in different areas of the company – which is the link between flexibility and profitability.

Studies of language in the new economy

Studies on language ideology have demonstrated how some languages are valued and others are not, how some languages are considered "pure" and others not, and how some languages gain sociopolitical power over others (Blommaert, 1999; Joseph & Taylor, 1990; Kroskrity *et al.*, 1992). Lippi-Green (1997) studied language and ideologies in different areas such as education and the information industry, and documented how discrimination is created in these sectors because of people's attitudes toward languages. Many authors have examined language and the workplace (Daoust, 1987; Grin, 1996; Heller *et al.*, 1982; Henderson *et al.*, 1993; van Langevelde, 1999). Some have focused specifically on the choice of language in bilingual or multilingual workplaces (Goldstein, 1997b; McAll, this volume). Still other researchers have looked at the ways in which languages are used in the new global economy.

Sarangi and Roberts (1999) edited a book on professional workplaces (medical, mediation, and management settings) in order to integrate a different approach to workplace study that merges interaction order and institutional order. Their descriptions of talk, text, and interaction in the workplace allow us to better understand how workplaces are social institutions where "resources are produced and regulated, problems are solved, identities are played out and professional knowledge is constituted" (Sarangi & Roberts, 1999: 1). These authors also argue that workplaces are sites of social struggle where ways of talking, recording, and acting are produced and ordered over a period of time. This regulation of communicative resources controls access to the workplace and the opportunities available within it.

Cameron (2000a) studied communication in different service-oriented work places such as call centers and grocery stores. She examined how linguistic training takes place, and reviewed the documents used to provide such training. From her research in the UK and US she discovered that standardization involved the use of scripts which employees were required to memorize. The goals were to ensure greater efficiency and to create an image of professionalism by shortening the length of time in telephone interventions, thus saving time and money. Standardization also results in greater control over employees through codification and surveillance. Codification means that every single interaction between the employee and the customer is controlled from the moment a call begins through to final leave taking. As Gee *et al.* (1996) have pointed out, this increased control over employees represents a contradiction in relation to the new economy's stated goal of empowering employees. Cameron (2000a) sees some consequences resulting from this form of standardization in "The New Work Order." Among these, she notes a high level of stress and absenteeism at the employee level. She also notes a higher rate of personnel turnover, as workers tire of the repetitive nature of their jobs. Also, employees experience difficulty with having to follow a script when some calls require a more personal approach. We shall see that, for a Francophone minority in Canada, standardization also entailed a devaluation of the way in which they spoke and used their language inside their own community.

The new work order in the Canadian context

Anglophones and Francophones in Canada share a long history of struggles over access to linguistic, social, and political resources. After 1960, Quebec's political mobilization made possible the development of an ideology of language and state that placed increased value on bilingualism in the country (Heller, 1999). However, notwithstanding their access to employment as bilinguals at the federal level, Francophone minorities outside Quebec continued to struggle for rights and services in French. Before 1968, full education in French was not available to the French minority in Ontario, leaving generations of French speakers without access to education in their mother tongue (Heller, 1994; Welsh, 1988). The choices available to these Franco-Ontarians were: to leave school early to access the workplace, to attend English school where they would more than likely struggle and drop out, or to became English-dominant and lose their heritage language. In settings where linguistic minority members lived, bilingualism was a phenomenon that could be observed at the community level or in the home. Few people could work in French only; they had to know English in order to succeed.

More recently, with the emergence of new sectors of communication and technologies, bilingualism is now being valued in Ontario workplaces. However, in these settings being bilingual represents more than being able to speak two languages at home or in the community. It means being able to speak them in specific ways that can attract and retain clients.

Work in a Small Town in Southern Ontario

In the 1920s and 1940s, Francophones (from Quebec, northern Ontario, or New Brunswick) and other immigrants (e.g. Ukrainians, Poles, Italians) came in two waves to a small town in southern Ontario whose population was previously primarily English-speaking. They came looking for work opportunities and sought to establish themselves in this region's steel, textile, and power plants. Around 1940, 1,015 Francophones (there were about 3,000 in 1946)[1] organized and created Francophone organizations around the Church, consolidating a French neighborhood that came to be known as "Frenchtown." For years, Francophones worked in different industries and were part of community life. In 2000, Francophones still constitute 10–15% of the population of this little town.[2]

Between 1975 and 1990, the industrial economy linked with this community life, notably the textile and metallurgy industries, underwent a radical shift. The industries went under. This collapse of the economy left the Francophone population with various choices. Some moved away; some tried to make it on their own by starting a small business (such as a corner store, or a construction business); others turned to the Anglophone majority for opportunities. These conditions opened the door for some Francophones to assimilate to the English language and way of life, a phenomenon that represented a threat for the survival of the Francophone community.

At the end of the 1980s, after the economy had remained stagnant for ten years, the French language again became valuable in the new service-oriented sectors, a change that represented a vehicle for survival for the Francophone community. In order to access the global marketplace, the council of this industrial town initiated the installation of fibre optics to strengthen its communication infrastructure. Being well-positioned geographically and strategically, and with a bilingual (multilingual, even) population, the town was in a position to attract new businesses to the region. The publicity appeared to have a positive effect, as many call center businesses came to establish themselves in the region. These call centers expanded rapidly, and one became a large and important employer in the region. This call center was the setting for my study.

Research in a call center

The call center is a financial institution where telephone representatives provide services to customers who have credit cards from different companies such as retail outlets. The center represents both an inbound and an outbound workplace where customers call for information about their accounts and payments, and employees call customers in order to remind them of their overdue accounts. The call center also provides road assistance services in which customers phone a telephone representative in an emergency involving their vehicle, and the center arranges for the appropriate service, such as towing.

In this setting, I engaged in ethnographic and sociolinguistic research that entailed four months of observing and meeting with the staff on a daily basis in order to understand the ways in which a workplace tries to stay competitive in the global market and survives as a Canadian enterprise. I conducted interviews with people holding different positions in the workplace (vice-presidents, directors, managers, supervisors, coordinators, trainers, coaches, telephone representatives) as well as with people from outside who were directly connected to the call center. The latter group included members of the community college involved in preparing new candidates for work in the call center. My observations involved sitting with telephone representatives and listening to calls with them. I also observed training and hiring processes. In addition, I became familiar with different documents that were produced in the call center, and participated in conversations through the internal mail. As a member of a larger research team working for four years on a project entitled "Prise de parole,"[3] I learned about the history of the town and got to know its Francophone citizens. This ethnographic approach allowed me to begin to understand the realities of this Francophone minority caught up in the new "global world," where only those who can adapt survive.

In 1998, new rules were put in place in different sectors of the company. First, the task of hiring (which had previously been carried out by an external firm)was assumed by the company itself, whose management personnel introduced a policy of testing bilingual workers (in the past, Francophones who mentioned that they were French speaking were hired as bilinguals). Prospective employees had to achieve a grade of 80% to be considered bilingual. (I asked a Human Resources employee whether the company also tested monolingual English speakers for language ability, and she responded: "No! No we're not doing anything like that ... it's more their ability to be verbal and communicate.")

A second change involved a standardization policy that included the evaluation of the way employees spoke on the phone. When on the phone, telephone representatives now had to follow a script. Employees were required to include all steps and nuances in completing a telephone conversation from a standard opening – "Hello (the company's name). This is (the employee's name). How may I help you"? – to protocols for voice inflexion in handling difficult calls. Each employee was to be "coached" by his or her peers in order to learn and gain practice with the way in which calls were received and handled.

A third change was in the allocation of salaries. Telephone representatives now received extra money if they were designated as bilingual employees. In addition, employees received a bi-yearly bonus if they followed the script faithfully. Their performance on phone calls, as evaluated by coaches, counted for 20% of the overall performance as established by the company. It was, therefore, important for bilingual employees to follow the prescribed script; if they did not, they would lose their bonuses.

Thus two processes involving standardization occurred simultaneously: Employees had to demonstrate that they mastered standard French forms in order to be designated bilingual employees (and as such receive extra remuneration), and they had to follow the script in order to receive their bi-yearly bonus. These changes were not without consequences for the Francophone minority of this small southern Ontario town.

Access to the job market and/or survival of a community

From the late 1980s to 1998, being bilingual (and Francophone) in this small town signified being able at any time (immediately after school graduation or later on) to have access to a job in the call center. The idea of being able to find a job in the call center is still very strong in the community. Anglophones and Francophones alike believe that someone who speaks other languages (especially French) will find a job right away. This belief has been reinforced since the town invested in the industrial sector in order to boost the regional economy. The following interview excerpt is illustrative of the belief concerning the advantages of being bilingual in the new sectors of the economy.

Excerpt 1: Interview with a manager, 1998

Joseph: *Quelqu'un de qui est bilingue? i a pas un grand avantage à travailler dans les usines pour exemple mais pour exemple je pense que je suis peut-être un exemple que j'ai utilisé ma langue à mon bénéfice et non seulement le pratiquer mais d'avoir peut-être un avantage au lieu de d'être à côté de quelqu'un qui est unilingue que si on peut faire la même chose le fait que je peux parler la*

Sylvie: *les deux langues*

Joseph: *les deux langues officielles ça me donne un avantage*

(**Joseph:**   Somebody who is bilingual? doesn't have a great advantage to work in industries, for example, but for example I think that I am maybe one example that I used my language to my benefits and not only to practice it but to have maybe an advantage instead of being near somebody who is unilingual if we can do the same thing the fact that I can speak the

Sylvie: Both languages

Joseph: Both two official languages it gives me an advantage)

According to both Francophone and Anglophone respondents, being bilingual represents an advantage in accessing jobs in the workplace. Even people who are monolingual conclude that being bilingual is the key to accessing the call center. The following excerpt is part of an interview with a new employee being hired as a monolingual representative:

Excerpt 2: Interview with an employee, 1998

Whitney: Something like that here but (...) hm? Now he works in the [road assistance department] he worked in the [road assistance department] for a little while now and euh? He just talks about he would talk about calls he had or something you know it just be kind of funny and I just used to think it be kind of fun to do it you know? And so he told me that they were they were hiring for winter the winter staff the one year last year actually and so he said why did you put your name in and try but I mean I have to admit I didn't I really didn't think that I would get get hired because I only speak English and I know it's DEFINITELY euh? An advantage you know to be bilingual!

The preceding two examples show how important being bilingual is to getting access to the service-oriented sector of the workplace. In fact, most of the towns-people I spoke with for the purposes of this research believed that bilingualism was the key to accessing the job market. For the older members of the community, these new sectors represented more than bilingual jobs: they were regarded as the answer to their prayers regarding the survival of the Francophone community within an Anglo macro-context. In fact, the community elders saw call centers as the vehicles for the linguistic and cultural reproduction of *la francophonie* and, therefore, for the delivery of their people from the jaws of assimilation.

New rules, fewer opportunities

The new way of doing business in the call center also changed the way in which people assessed individual bilingualism. As mentioned, in the call center a new hiring process was put in place that assessed candidates to ascertain whether they could be considered bilingual in the context of the workplace. In the following excerpt, a Human Resources manager talks of how being bilingual – in the community sense of speaking French and English fluently – does not satisfy the company standard.

Excerpt 3: Interview with a manager, 1998

Marion: To get the bilingual calls? Through some recent contract hiring that was done we have hm? Assess, we assess people bilingual language skills verbal language skills and some people who have said they were bilingual have not met our STANDARDS.

As noted earlier, community members believe that the call center will foster the linguistic and social reproduction of the Francophone community by providing opportunities for individuals to practice their French in the workplace. However, we note a paradox here. The Francophone community and the town community in general believe that bilingualism helps individuals to gain access to the particular job market represented by the call center ("because it's a bilingual environment," in the words of one manager). Conversely, the call center is a positive factor in promoting the maintenance of the French language. On the other hand, the company's new hiring process separates those who are good enough to be bilingual from those who are not considered bilingual, even though these latter may be Francophone and also speak English fluently. Thus, to be hired as a bilingual, one has to practice "good" bilingualism that corresponds to the company's criteria. But what, precisely, are the criteria of the new standard? The new standard in the company stipulates that, in order to be considered professional and meet customers' needs, employees have to use proper business language. The following is an excerpt from an interview with a training manager.

Excerpt 4: Interview with a training manager, 1998

Doris:	hm?/4 sec Where we come up with standard? I don't know I can't really // (XXX) to proper English
Sylvie:	What what is proper English, proper French, for example for you?
Doris:	Using good grammar full sentences
Sylvie:	OK
Doris:	Euh? Appreciating the customer assuring that euh? There's a lot more about than just proper you know also? Hmm? Hearing or hmm? Ensuring that your tone is look for that the customer understand and eventually even some of the book we may get in to voice training! (...) voice inflexion yeah they use the right voice inflexion that's what it's all about ensuring that you use the right voice inflexion ensuring you use sentences ensuring you're not using SLANG?

For this manager, the "proper" way of speaking involves not using slang, but instead using standard grammatical forms and full sentences. The same respondent also refers to voice inflexion. Cameron (2000b) found that references to voice inflexion on the part of managers were often code phrases used to signal that female employees were expected to use a feminine approach in their phone conversations, characterized by a soft and empathetic voice quality. Further on in the interview, in his discussion of how the company has to ensure that its employees behave in a professional manner, the training manager embeds comments about the use of French by Francophones in the community.

Excerpt 5: Interview with the training manager, 1998

Doris:	(...)// French, although French is predominant in [the community] we have three schools where they teach French and a lot of people grow up in French families, there's a lot of slang and

anglicisms (X) the French language and: even compared to Quebec French [of the community] the French has always been different and compares to (X) in French different (X) and even actually compares to New Brunswick or when you get in to Quebec compare to Montréal to

Sylvie: Yeah

Doris: Chicoutimi yeah so hm? but try to stay in tune with all that!

Sylvie: OK

Doris: and, and ensuring that that we're meeting the professionalism customer expect from us.

The variety of French spoken by Francophones in this specific community seems not to satisfy the criteria of professionalism that management wants their employees to display in order for the company to stay competitive in the global economy. In this town Francophones mix English with French by engaging in code-switching. Thus, employers believed that they needed to raise their standards in order to serve clients better (and exercise more control over their employees). The following is an example of what a trainer thinks of the variety of French spoken in the community, a variety that he sees reproduced in the discourse of many call center employees .

Excerpt 6: Interview with a trainer, 1998

Sylvie: *Hmm? Toi ici à [la compagnie] quelle sorte de variétés tu penses que les gens parlent – en francais?*

Josiane: *(...) en différentes langues? oh ici?*

Sylvie: *la variété de francais de langue aussi parce que*

Josiane: *Hmm? Des niveaux de langue?*

Sylvie: *Euh? Niveau comme tu veux là? Variétés peut-être aussi, euh? Quelle sorte de francais qu'ils parlent?*

Josiane: *Hmm? Magané parfois.*
[rire]

Sylvie: *Magané qu'est-ce que tu veux dire par là?*

Josiane: *Ben souvent hmm? En parlant avec les gens ils ils mettent des mots anglais dans leurs phrases.*

Sylvie: *Oui.*

Josiane: *Pis parfois i i ne savent même que c'est que c'est un mot anglais?*

(**Sylvie**: Hmm? You here in (the company) which kind of variety you think people speak – in French?

Josiane: In different languages? Oh here ?

Sylvie: French variety language also because

Josiane: Hmm? Language levels?

Sylvie: Euh? Level like you want? Varieties maybe also euh? Which kind of French they speak?

Josiane:	Hmm? broken sometimes
	[laugh]
Sylvie:	broken what do you mean by that?
Josiane:	Well often hmm? When you talk to people they they put English words in their sentences
Sylvie:	Yes
Josiane:	(...) and sometimes they they don't even know that it's that it's an English word?

Indeed, Francophones in the community speak a variety of French that is criticized by many. The standardization of language in a specific workplace – as represented by the call center's revised hiring practices – reinforces the ideology of a norm that does not correspond to the way in which the French language is used by a majority of its speakers in the community. It also establishes as the definition of a bilingual someone who is able to speak two languages in a standard way (see Dabène, 1994, for a discussion of the "balanced bilingual").

The question arises: is a Francophone still considered "bilingual" if s/he doesn't speak French in this prescribed manner? Following is an example of a man born to a French family in this community. His father is well known by Francophones in the community and participates in many community organizations. For this employee, who no longer considers himself bilingual, being bilingual means being able to speak both languages well.

Excerpt 7: Interview with a supervisor, 1998

Marc:	So I do not consider myself so if they are the same way I am I don't consider (myself) fluently bilingual
Sylvie:	So bilingual than, it's somebody who answers fast or can use [the language] without thinking too much?
Marc:	Exactly. If they can use their French language the same as their English language? (X)
Sylvie:	OK
Marc:	If they can't, they need, they're like me, they need practice. It's not that they don't know it. They just need practice.

In the next excerpt, another example – this one provided by an Anglophone in the community and a Human Resources Officer responsible for the hiring – illustrates the view that being a good communicator entails being able to use both languages in a standard way.

Excerpt 8: Interview with a Human Resources officer

| **Kathy:** (...) | but you have to make sure that these people can communicate well even in both languages! Not just one not just in French or just in English! |

Thus, according to the new company criteria, the majority of Francophones in the community are not considered strong bilingual candidates because their variety of

French does not correspond to the professional image that the company wishes to project. From this, one can conclude that even if in the community the rhetoric about hiring bilingual Francophones remains strong, the true sentiments behind this rhetoric are revealed in the realities brought on by the new policy of standardization of language practices in the workplace.

Consequences of standardization for Francophones

What are the consequences of the devaluation of their spoken language variety for Francophones who wish to work in the call center? As concerns hiring, some Francophones are eliminated from the potential pool of employees who could be employed as bilinguals. Instead, they are hired as monolinguals (although they can be retested at a later time, presumably, if they practice their French).

Excerpt 9: Interview with a Human Resources officer

Kathy:	(...) we offer a lot of opportunity some a lot of people come to us because they want to have a job?
Sylvie:	OK
Kathy:	(...) to speak both languages because they don't want to lose it! They know that it's something very very valuable? So a lot of people would come to us like the girl we just hired yesterday. She said to me: "That's why I want to work here!" and she didn't, she did score 62% on her French level assessment, so we said to her: "We've got to hire you still but we're going to hire you as a unilingual rep? You're only getting the $10.50 an hour, $10 an hour BUT when you're ready to be retested, we will retest you. So talk to your person who you're sitting talk to your co-worker in French and she's been out of, she's been out of her parents' home for two years out of school for about three years she never used it."
Sylvie:	Yeah
Kathy:	So she said: "I don't want to lose it. I want to train to get it back and I want to use it all the time. So that's why I want to work here. I want to work in a environment that allows me to speak both languages."
Sylvie:	OK, but do people speak French in the workplace? Do they use it?
Kathy:	Besides the customer?
Sylvie:	Besides the customer.
Kathy:	Yes.

In this excerpt, the Human Resources officer makes several important points. If the new candidates do not satisfy the hiring criteria – they have to achieve 80% on the French test that measures oral skills – they can be hired as monolinguals. (However, they would not have access to the extra money they could receive as bilinguals.) The Human Resources officer also suggests that these individuals could be retested for bilingual positions after they practice their French. However, perfecting one's French is a process that is not evident in the call center. In fact, only a few Francophone employees actually used French in day-to-day interactions. Even "bilingual" employees who speak in French with customers rarely use French among themselves. In the broader community, French is spoken by the older members, and those who originally came from a unilingual region such as Quebec or northern Ontario.

And if they do practice French among themselves, what are the chances that potential candidates for bilingual positions will improve sufficiently to meet the company's expectations? The chances are slim. In fact, the trend is more in the other direction, with some employees already hired as bilinguals taken off the bilingual phone lines, as illustrated in the following excerpt.

Excerpt 10: Interview with a supervisor

Marc:	Just to give you an example, hmm? We have two reps that speak French however don't speak French in sense of euh? How can I put that? I mean if I have somebody from Quebec Montréal that were calling in and they speak (XX) and they're talking to a rep trying to speak French however can't pronounce the words you know what I mean it's an English person which took French course they not gone (XX)
Sylvie:	Yeah
Marc:	Me? I don't think that's right and I'll put them off that queue because I think for me it's insulting I know my dad gets insulting that's the same as somebody who English calling in they get upset (X) completely French rep trying to talk English to them because they don't understand them

If the company puts aside some bilingual candidates, either in the hiring process or once working on the telephone lines, employees have two options. These individuals may explore strategies to improve their competencies or communication skills in French, or they may refuse to be considered as bilingual. In the next excerpt, a supervisor is discussing the case of a telephone representative who chose not to work in the bilingual queue, because she believed that her French was not good enough.

Excerpt 11: Interview with a supervisor, 1998

Martin:	There's a need to have French people and why not compensate like the other day I had a representative in my department that I found out that she spoke French?
Sylvie:	Ah yeah? You didn't (X)
Martin:	(...) and she nobody knew about this and euh? I spoke to her and said why not get compensate for it? So and she said I don't know my French same thing as what I did I went to French

school and all that stuff and than she left high school and all that stuff and kind of lost it a little bit but I listen to her on the phone sat with her and I got her some testing? _on November 1st_

Sylvie: _ she was (X)_

Martin: Yeah. She passed. She just passed with an 86% euh? hmm?

Conversely, in the following excerpt, we see an employee who wishes to improve her French in order to both maintain the language and become more professional (that is, use fewer English forms in her spoken language). Regarding the need to improve her spoken French, she comments as follows.

Excerpt 12: Interview with an administrative assistant

Roselyne: *Mais c'est ça que je veux faire dans la nouvelle année prendre un cours en français juste pour m'améliorer?*

Sylvie: *Hmm, hmm.*

Jürgen: *Hmm.*

Roselyne: *Parce que je veux pas le perdre mais c'est juste je l'utilise pas souvent*

Jürgen: *Est-ce que tu as tu as peur de perdre le français?*

Roselyne: *Oui.*

Jürgen: *Pourquoi?*

Roselyne: *Parce que c'est une langue que j'aimerais garder mais je m'en sers pas souvent des fois je vais parler les deux langues ensemble pis je veux pas faire ça je veux être capable de parler en français penser au mot en français comme c'est quand que tu essaies de parler en français pis le mot ça tu peux pas penser au mot au mot en français t'as retourne en anglais je veux pas faire ca je veux être de capable de penser au mot en français aussi (...)*

(Roselyne: (...) but this is what I want to do in the New Year, take a French course just to improve myself?

Sylvie: Hmm, hmm.

Jürgen: Hmm.

Roselyne: (...) because I don't want to lose it but it's just I don't use it often

Jürgen: Are you afraid to lose the French?

Roselyne: Yes.

Jürgen: Why?

Roselyne: (...) because it's a language that I would like to keep but I don't use it often sometimes I will speak both languages together and I don't want to do that, I want to be able to speak French think of a word in French it's like when you try to speak French and the word you can't think of the word the word in French you put it back in English I don't want to do that I want to be able to think at the word in French also (...))

This example illustrates the language ideology in the call center. Even employees believe that they do not speak French well enough, because their spoken French is interspersed with English. They want to improve their French, that is, learn to speak a standard variety, by taking courses or by being coached and evaluated by their peers. In my research I met a few employees who refused at first to be evaluated by their peers, but accepted in the end because they wanted to receive their bonuses, and also because they believed that the process entailed in being hired as a bilingual employee would enable them to improve their French.

However, not all employees expressed agreement with the standardization policies and practices. Of course, because of the bonuses they had to follow the script when they spoke (in French or English) with customers. However, these employees are aware of the price they must pay for adhering to a scripted dialogue – the loss of natural communication in their native language. For the employee in the following excerpt, standardization practices cause employees to feel like machines. However, at the same time she believes that she does not have a choice in the matter because in the end she will be evaluated by her peers on how well she follows the company's script.

Excerpt 13: Interview with a telephone representative

Maryse:	*Hmm? Ben pour être honnête je pense que beaucoup de choses qui se passent avec le coaching hmm? Nous fait sentir comme i veulent qu'on soit des des des robots [rire] c'est hm? C'est difficile quand quand que t'es au téléphone t'es tu penses à ta liste de critères faut tu faut tu tu fais dans ta tête tsé pis l'appel on dirait que elle va pas aussi bien que tu penses tu finis une phrase pis j'ai tu penses ah j'ai oublié de dire ça ou? C'est parce que tu sais que qu'i vont _t'enregistrer_*
Sylvie:	*t'écouter_*
Maryse:	*i vont t'enregistrer pis? si tu le dis pas ça va pas être un mastering ca va être un* did not meet so you'll constantly thinking about tha*t ça ça te garde avec l'impression que tu es un peu des robots au téléphone*
(Maryse:	Hmm? Well, to be honest I think that a lot of things happening with the *coaching* hmm? Makes us feel like they want us to be like robots [laugh]. It's, hmm? It's difficult when when you are on the phone, you're, you think of your list of criteria you have you, you do in you head you know and the call one could say that it wasn't as good as you thought you are finishing your sentence and I have you think I have forgotten to say this or it's because that you know that they will _recorded_
Sylvie:	_listening_
Maryse:	They will recorded and (...)? if you don't tell them this it won't be a mastering it will be a did not meet so you'll constantly thinking about that it it leave you with the impression that you are a little bit like a robot on the phone.)

Finally, it bears mention that, while standardization is a strategy that the company uses to create a professional image and to survive in a competitive world, the use of a script on the part of employees does not always have the intended result. The use of standardized responses can undermine what customers are really seeking in their interactions with telephone representatives. Some customers will not master the linguistic standard and therefore will not understand what the representative is talking about. One given example related to road assistance – where a Francophone customer in distress was familiar with the English term for a particular part of the automobile but not the French term that the employee was obliged to use. Thus, bilingual telephone representatives have an additional onus: they must appear to follow the rules of standardization while at the same time being sufficiently flexible to understand and respond to the needs of customers.

The Global Workplace as the New Standard Setter

In this chapter, I have attempted to show how the varieties of French spoken in a Francophone community in southern Ontario are devalued as a result of a call center's standardization of language practices in the workplace of the new economy. I have also attempted to show how individual bilingualism comes to be re-defined by these workplace practices. Thus, bilingualism, in this re-visioned context, means being able to speak two languages –French and English – in separate and standard ways.

In order to stay competitive, the call center seeks to follow market trends. Thus, products and services are customized in order to maximize professionalism and efficiency. Inside the call center, standardization is synonymous with professionalism, an attribute considered necessary for success. Standardization is thought to be the key to effective communication with customers. Following a prescribed script shows that employees are professional, and care about the customer's needs by providing assistance in the same idealized way. Also, by standardizing the ways in which employees are trained and evaluated, the employer seeks to create a flexible workforce, one that is able to manage change. Thus, if a new product is marketed, employees will be ready to adapt, to quickly learn how to talk about it and promote it.

The above company protocols, however, do not detract from community members' awareness of the role of language standardization in rearranging the place of Francophones in the region's social structure. Before, Francophones were seen to have an advantage because they were bilingual, that is, they spoke French and English fluently. Now, for the most part their French is not considered good enough to satisfy the criteria of the new workplace; and the pool of 'bilingual' candidates is getting smaller and smaller. The call center now looks to hire people from elsewhere – from Quebec or northern Ontario – who possess the French language competencies required, provided that their English is also of a high caliber. However, in order to encourage potential employees to make the move, the company would have to offer permanent jobs and good salaries. The fact that it is not willing to do either makes it difficult to attract people to the town from other regions or provinces. Thus, both employers and employees are frustrated. Employers are unable to find bilingual employees who satisfy their criteria; and fluent French speakers discover that they do not possess the language skills required to access the global workforce as represented by the call center.

These findings raise critical questions about: (1) who defines what counts as appropriate language practices; and (2) how people can adapt themselves linguistically in order to be able to work and live in their chosen – in this case, their own – communities. Clearly, standardization of linguistic practices is not a new phenomenon. Milroy and Milroy (1985, 1999) noted that for years written languages have been codified and standardized so that everyone can write in the same way and, thus, communicate more effectively. However, oral language has been more resistant to standardization, since it has been viewed as a key social vehicle for cultural continuity and preservation of community values. This case study of standardization of oral communication in the workplace shows that, in the name of the global economy, those who hold power – who quite literally control the means of production – are now establishing and reinforcing the standards for spoken languages. In fact, the global workplace is challenging the position of the school as the social institution where language norms are reinforced. After all, in the community studied it is the call center that determines the definition of bilingualism and reinforces the ways in which people look at their language practices and competencies.

In southern Ontario, Francophone communities see the new economic order as an opportunity for maintaining their language and culture because of conditions that permit members to practice their French in the workplace. However, it seems that only those who already possess the standard language have real access to jobs as bilinguals. For the others – the majority – the process leading to qualification for these jobs is lengthy and arduous, involving the investment of time and financial resources in courses that will help them to improve their maternal language competencies.

What consequences will these changes have for the ethnolinguistic vitality of the Francophone community? To be sure there will be some positive impact. It is reported that many adolescents at the high school level now recognize the potential benefits of their French studies in terms of access to the job market, and are motivated to practice their native language. Those who already master the language sufficiently well to enter the workplace will improve their French through the practice they gain by speaking to customers. But for many others, the choices are limited. To work at the call center, they will have either to improve their performance in their maternal language to conform to company protocols, or become part of the majority of English speakers working in the call center, and therefore risk losing their French. And there are those who may elect to forfeit a role in the new economy, and instead aggressively practice and maintain their native vernacular in their community context. Thus, in the long term the community will lose some members, but it will acquire others. I look forward to further inquiry on the processes of linguistic change brought about by service-oriented workplaces that will shed light on the extent and manner in which those implicated in this re-visioned global market adapt to these new rules or else choose to resist them.

Notes

1. The statistics come from Historical and Architectural *Reflections of the Founding Peoples of [the city]. Ontario,* a document published in 1992 by the Local Architectural Conservation Advisory Committee of [the city].
2. The Statistical Profile of Canadian communities, can be found at the following website: www.statcan.ca:80/english/census96.
3. The project "Prise de Parole" was financed by the Conseil de recherche en sciences humaines du Canada (Principal investigators: Normand Labrie, Monica Heller, University of Toronto, and Jürgen Erfurt, Johann-Wolfgang-Goethe Universität, Frankfurt am Main; Collaborators: Annette Boudreau and Lise Dubois, University of Moncton). It is also financed by the program Transcoop from the German-American Academic Council Foundation (Principal investigators: Jürgen Erfurt, Monica Heller and Normand Labrie) and AUPELF-UREF (Principal investigator: Claudine Moïse, Université d'Avignon et des Pays de Vaucluse, France).

References

AbuKhalil, A. (1993) A note on the study of homosexuality in the Arab/Islamic civilization. *The Arab Studies Journal* 1, 32–34, 48.

AbuKhalil, A. (1997) Gender boundaries and sexual categories in the Arab world. *Feminist Issues* 15, 91–104.

Abu-Lughod, L. (2001) Is there a Muslim sexuality? Changing constructions of sexuality in Egyptian Bedouin weddings. In C.B. Brettell and C.F. Sargent (eds) *Gender in Cross-Cultural Perspective* (3rd edn) (pp. 198–207). Englewood Cliffs, NJ: Prentice Hall.

Agnihotri, R.L. and Khanna, A.L. (1995) Introduction. In R.L. Agnihotri and A.L. Khanna (eds) *English Language Teaching in India: Issues and Innovations* (pp. 12–28). New Delhi: Sage.

Ahmed, L. (1992) *Women and Gender in Islam: Historical Roots of a Modern Debate.* New Haven: Yale University Press.

Albó, X. (1995) *Bolivia plurilingüe: Guía para planificadores y educadores.* La Paz: UNICEF.

Al-Qardawi, Y. (1960) *The Lawful and the Prohibited in Islam* (trans. K. El Helbawy, M.M. Siddiqui, and S. Shukry). Indianapolis: American Trust Publications.

Alvermann, D.E. and Moore, D.W. (1996) Secondary school reading. In R. Barr, M.L. Kamil, P. Mosenthal and P.D. Pearson (eds) *Handbook of Reading Research* (Vol. 2, pp. 951–983). Mahwah, NJ: Lawrence Erlbaum.

Applebee, A.N. with Auten, A. (1981) *Writing in the Secondary School: English and the Content Areas.* Urbana, IL: National Council of Teachers of English.

Arnold, D.Y. and Yapita, J. de Dios (2000) *El rincón de las cabezas: Luchas textuales, educación y tierras en los Andes.* La Paz: UMSA/ILCA.

Arnopoulos, S.M. and Clift, D. (1984) *The English Fact in Quebec* (2nd edn). Kingston, ON: McGill-Queen's University Press.

Atkinson, D. (1997) A critical approach to critical thinking in TESOL. *TESOL Quarterly* 31, 71–94.

Atkinson, D. (1999a) TESOL and culture. *TESOL Quarterly* 33, 625–654.

Atkinson, D. (1999b) "I know I can never learn English": The learning of English by low-caste college students in Gujarat, India. Paper presented at the Annual Meeting of the National Academy of Education, Pittsburgh, PA, October.

Atkinson, J.M. and Heritage, J. (eds) (1984) *Structures of Social Action: Studies in Conversation Analysis.* Cambridge: Cambridge University Press.

Australian Bureau of Statistics. (1997) *Aspects of Literacy: Assessed Skill Levels (Australia 1996).* Canberra: Australian Government Publishing Service.

Bailey, T. (1997) Changes in the nature of work: Implications for skills and assessment. In H.F. O'Neill (ed.) *Workforce Readiness: Competencies and Assessment* (pp. 27–45). Mahwah, NJ: Lawrence Erlbaum.

Baker, C. (2001) *Foundations of Bilingual Education and Bilingualism* (3rd edn). Clevedon: Multilingual Matters.

Baker, C. and Prys Jones, S. (1998) Preface. *Encyclopedia of Bilingualism and Bilingual Education*. Clevedon: Multilingual Matters.

Bakhtin, M. (1984). *Problems of Dostoevsky's Poetics* (ed. and trans. C. Emerson). Minneapolis: University of Minnesota Press.

Ballinger, C. (1992) Because you like us: The language of control. *Harvard Educational Review* 62, 199–208.

Baquedano-Lopez, P. (1999) Narrating the collectivity: Language socialization of Mexican children in a Los Angeles parish. Paper presented at annual meeting of the American Association for Applied Linguistics, Stamford, CT, March.

Barth, F. (1969) *Ethnic Groups and Boundaries: The Social Organization of Cultural Difference*. Boston: Little, Brown.

Basu, A. (1989) Indian higher education: Colonialism and beyond. In P.G. Altbach and V. Sevaratham (eds) *From Dependence to Autonomy* (pp. 167–186). Dordrecht, Netherlands: Kluwer.

Bayley, R. (2002). The quantitative paradigm. In J.K. Chambers, P. Trudgill, and N. Schilling-Estes (eds) *The Handbook of Language Variation and Change* (pp. 117–141). Oxford: Blackwell.

Bayley, R., Schecter, S.R. and Torres-Ayala, B. (1996) Strategies for bilingual maintenance: Case studies of Mexican-origin families in Texas. *Linguistics and Education* 8, 389–408.

Baynham, M. (1993) Code switching and mode switching: Community interpreters and mediators of literacy. In B. Street (ed.) *Cross-cultural Approaches to Literacy* (pp. 294–314). New York: Cambridge University Press.

Béland, P. (1991) *L'Usage du français au travail, situation et tendances*. Québec, Conseil de la langue française.

Bell, J.S. (1997) *Literacy, Culture and Identity.* New York: Peter Lang.

Bell, J.S. (2000) Literacy challenges for language learners in job training programs. *Canadian Modern Language Review* 57, 173–200.

Berger, P. and Luckmann, T. (1966) *The Social Construction of Reality.* Harmondsworth: Penguin Books.

Berkey, J.P. (1996) Circumcision circumscribed: Female excision and cultural accommodation in the medieval Near East. *International Journal of Middle East Studies* 28, 19–38.

Bhabha, H.K. (1994) *The Location of Culture.* London: Routledge.

Bhatt, A., Barton, D., Martin-Jones, M. and Saxena, M. (1995) *Multilingual Literacy Practices: Home, Community, School* (Working paper # 80). Lancaster: Lancaster University, Centre for Language in Social Life.

Bloch, M. (1993) The uses of schooling and literacy in a Zafimaniry village. In B. Street (ed.) *Cross-cultural Approaches to Literacy* (pp. 294–314). New York: Cambridge University Press.

Blommaert, J. (ed.) (1999) *Language Ideological Debates*. Berlin: Mouton de Gruyter.

Borsuk, A. (1998) 75% in MPS poor enough for free lunch. *Milwaukee Journal Sentinel*, January 9, pp. 1, 14.

Bouhdiba, A. (1998) *Sexuality in Islam* (trans. A. Sheridan). London: Saqi Books.

Bourdieu, P. (1977) *Outline of a Theory of Practice*. Cambridge: Cambridge University Press.

Bourdieu, P. (1979) *La Distinction*. Paris: Les Editions de Minuit.

Bourdieu, P. (1982a) *Ce que Parler Veut Dire: L'Economie des Échanges linguistiques*. Paris: Fayard.

Bourdieu, P. (1982b) The school as a conservative force: Scholastic and cultural inequalities. In E. Bredo and W. Feinberg (eds) *Knowledge and Values in Social and Education Research* (pp. 391–407). Philadelphia: Temple University Press.

Bourdieu, P. (1984) *Distinction: A Social Critique of the Judgement of Taste*. Cambridge: Harvard University Press.

Bourdieu, P. (1985) The genesis of the concepts of habitus and field. *Sociocriticism* 2 (1), 1–24.

Bourdieu, P. (1986) The forms of capital. In J.G. Richardson (ed.) *Handbook of Theory and Research for the Sociology of Education* (pp. 241–258). New York: Greenwood Press.

Bourdieu, P. (1991) *Language and Symbolic Power.* Cambridge, MA: Harvard University Press.

Bradunas, E. and Topping, B. (eds) (1988) *Ethnic Heritage and Language Schools in America.* Washington, DC: Library of Congress.

Briggs, L.T. (1981) Politeness in Aymara language and culture. In M.J. Hardman (ed.) *The Aymara Language in its Social and Cultural Context.* Gainesville: University Presses of Florida.

Briggs, L.T. (1993) *El idioma aymara: Variantes regionales y sociales.* La Paz: ILCA.

Briggs, L.T. (1997) Vivir y hablar como un ser humano: Un relato de una mujer aymara. In D. Arnold (ed.) *Más allá del silencio: Las fronteras de género en los Andes.* La Paz: CIASE/ILCA.

Bucholtz, M. (1999a) Bad examples: Transgression and progress in language and gender studies. In M. Bucholtz, A.C. Liang and L. Sutton (eds) *Reinventing Identities: The Gendered Self in Discourse* (pp. 3–24). New York: Oxford University Press.

Bucholtz, M. (1999b) "Why be normal?": Language and identity practices in a community of nerd girls. *Language in Society* 28, 203–223.

Bustamante, M.M. (2001) La construcción de relaciones interculturales en un contexto socio-culturalmente heterogéneo: El caso de la comunidad de Montecillo (Tiquipaya). Master's thesis, Universidad Mayor de San Simón, Cochabamba, Bolivia.

Butler, R.O. (1992) Crickets. In *A Good Scent from a Strange Mountain.* New York: Henry Holt.

Calvet, L-J. (1998) *Language Wars and Linguistic Politics.* Oxford: Oxford University Press.

Cameron, D. (2000a) *Good to Talk? Living and Working in a Communication Culture.* London: Sage Publications.

Cameron, D. (2000b) Styling the worker: Gender and the commodification of language in the globalized service economy. *Journal of Sociolinguistics* 4, 323–347.

Camitta, M. (1993) Vernacular writing: Varieties of literacy among Philadelphia high school students. In B. Street (ed.) *Cross-cultural Approaches to Literacy* (pp. 294–314). New York: Cambridge University Press.

Canada (1969) *Royal Commission on Bilingualism and Biculturalism.* Ottawa: Queen's Printer.

Canagarajah, A.S. (1993) Critical ethnography of a Sri Lankan classroom: Ambiguities in student opposition to reproduction through ESOL. *TESOL Quarterly* 28, 601–626.

Canagarajah, A.S. (2001) The fortunate traveler: Shuttling between communities and literacies by economy class. In D. Belcher and U. Connor (eds) *Reflections on Multiliterate Lives.* Clevedon: Multilingual Matters.

Canessa, A. (1997) Género, lenguaje y variación en Pocobaya, Bolivia. In D. Arnold (ed.) *Más allá del silencio: Las fronteras de género en los Andes.* La Paz: CIASE/ILCA.

Castells, M. (1996) *L'ère de l'information: La société en réseau* (Vol. 1). Paris: Fayard.

Cazden, C. (1988) *Classroom Discourse: The Language of Teaching and Learning.* Portsmouth, NH: Heinemann.

Cazden, C., John, V. and Hymes, D. (eds) (1972) *Functions of Language in the Classroom.* New York: Teachers College Press.

Cerrón-Palomino, R. (2000) *Lingüística Aimara.* Lima: CBC/PROEIB Andes.

Chaiklin, S. and Lave, J. (eds) (1993) *Understanding Practice.* Cambridge: Cambridge University Press.

Chan, A. (1983) *Gold Mountain: The Chinese in the New World.* Vancouver: New Star Books.

Chen, Y. and He, A.W. (2001) *Dui bu dui* as a pragmatic marker: Evidence from Chinese classroom discourse. *Journal of Pragmatics* 33, 1441–1465.

Cheung, K. (1993) *Articulate Silences.* Ithaca, NY: Cornell University Press.

Chirinos, A. (1997) An experience of indigenous literacy in Perú. In N. Hornberger and J.A. Fishman (eds) *Indigenous Literacies in the Americas: Language Planning from the Bottom Up.* Berlin: Mouton de Gruyter.

Clyne, M. (1991) *Community Languages: The Australian Experience.* Cambridge: Cambridge University Press.

Clyne, M. (1997) Managing language diversity and second language programmes in Australia. *Current Issues in Language and Society* 4, 94–119.

Clyne, M. and Kipp, S. (1997) Linguistic diversity in Australia. *People and Place* 5 (3), 6–11.

Coates, J. (1986) *Women, Men and Language: A Sociolinguistic Account of Sex Differences in Language*. New York: Longman.

Cochran-Smith, M. (1984) *The Making of a Reader*. Norwood, NJ: Ablex.

Cole, P. (2000) *Philosophies of Exclusion: Liberal Political Theory and Immigration*. Edinburgh: Edinburgh University Press.

Comité interministeriel (1996) *La Français langue commune*. Rapport du Comité interministeriel sur la situation de la langue française. Gouvernement du Québec, Québec.

Connelly, F.M. and Clandinin, D.J. (1988) *Teachers as Curriculum Planners: Narratives of Experience*. New York: Teachers College Press.

Connelly, F.M. and Clandinin, D.J. (1990) Stories of experience and narrative inquiry. *Educational Researcher* 19 (5), 2–14.

Conseil des relations interculturelles. (1999) *L'Équité en emploi: de l'égalité de droit à l'égalité de fait*. Québec: Conseil des relations interculturelles.

Cook, H.M. (1999) Language socialization in Japanese elementary schools: Attentive listening and reaction turns. *Journal of Pragmatics* 31, 1443–1465.

Cook-Gumperz, J. (ed.) (1986) *The Social Construction of Literacy*. New York: Cambridge University Press.

Cope, B. and Kalantzis, M. (eds) (2000) *Multiliteracies: Literacy Learning and the Design of Social Futures*. New York: Routledge.

Coulmas, F. (1996) *The Blackwell Encyclopedia of Writing Systems*. Oxford: Blackwell Publishers.

Crago, M.B. (1992) Communicative interaction and second language acquisition: An Inuit example. *TESOL Quarterly* 26, 487–505.

Crago, M.B. and Allen, S.M. (1999) Acquiring Inuktitut. In O.L. Taylor and L. Laurence (eds) *Language Acquisition across North America: Cross-Cultural and Cross-linguistic Perspectives* (pp. 245–279). London: Singular Publishing.

Crago, M.B., Annahatak, B. and Ningiuruvik, L. (1993) Changing patterns of language socialization in Inuit homes. *Anthropology and Education Quarterly* 24, 205–223.

Crago, M. B., Eriks-Brophy, A., Pesco, D., and McAlpine, L. (1997) Culturally-based miscommunication in classroom interaction. *Language, Speech and Hearing Services in the School* 28, 245–254.

Cummins, J. (1992) Heritage language teaching in Canadian schools. *Journal of Curriculum Studies* 24, 281–286.

Cummins, L., Handscombe, J., Mckay, P. and Davidson, C. (1998) Do mainstream classrooms work for ESL learners? Paper presented at the annual meeting of TESOL. New York, March.

Dabène, L. (1994) *Repères sociolinguistiques pour l'enseignement des langues: Les situations plurilingues*. Paris: Hachette.

Daoust, D. (1987) Planned change and lexical variation. *Language Problems and Language Planning* 11, 148–165.

Davidson, A.L. (1996) *Making and Molding Identity in Schools: Student Narratives on Race, Gender, and Academic Engagement*. Albany, NY: State University of New York Press.

De Castell, S. and Walker, T. (1991) Identity, metamorphosis, and ethnographic research: What *kind* of story is *Ways with Words? Anthropology and Education Quarterly* 22, 3–20.

Delgado-Gaitan, C. (1990) *Literacy for Empowerment: The Role of Parents in Children's Education*. New York: The Falmer Press.

Department of Education (1997) *Languages Other than English in Government Schools, 1996*. Melbourne: State of Victoria.

Devine, J.F. (1996) *Maximum Security: The Culture of Violence in Inner-City*. Chicago: University of Chicago Press.

Dorais, L.J. (1997) *Quaqtaq: Modernity and Identity in an Inuit Community*. Toronto: University of Toronto Press.

Driessen, B. (1999) The Slovak state language law as a trade law problem. In M. Kontra, R. Phillipson, T. Skutnabb-Kangas and T. Várady (eds) *Language: A Right and a Resource; Approaching Linguistic Human Rights* (pp. 147–168). Budapest: Central European Press.

Duff, P. (1996) Different languages, different practices: Socialization of discourse competence in dual-language school classrooms in Hungary. In K. Bailey and D. Nunan (eds) *Voices from the Language Classroom: Qualitative Research in Second Language Education* (pp. 407–433). New York: Cambridge University Press.

Duff, P. (2000) Language socialization in high school social studies: The construction of knowledge in multicultural discourse communities. Paper presented at the annual meeting of the National Academy of Education, New York, October.

Duff, P. and Early, M. (1999) Language socialization in perspective: Classroom discourse in high school humanities courses. Paper presented at the annual meeting of the American Association for Applied Linguistics, Stamford, CT, March.

Duff, P. and Labrie, N. (eds) (2000) *Languages and Work:* Special Issue of the *Canadian Modern Language Review* 51(1).

Dunn, B.W. (1990) Homosexuality in the Middle East: An agenda for historical research. *Arab Studies Quarterly* 12, 55–82.

Early, E.A. (1993) *Baladi Women of Cairo: Playing with an Egg and a Stone.* Cairo: American University in Cairo Press.

Eckert, P. (1996) Age as a sociolinguistic variable. In F. Coulmas (ed.) *Handbook of Sociolinguistics* (pp. 151–167). Oxford: Blackwell.

Eckert, P. (2000) *Linguistic Variation as Social Practice: The Linguistic Construction of Identity in Belten High.* Oxford: Blackwell.

Eckert, P. and McConnell-Ginet, S. (1992) Think practically and look locally: Language and gender as community-based practices. *Annual Review of Anthropology* 21, 461–90.

Eckert, P. and McConnell-Ginet, S. (1999) New generalizations and explanations in language and gender research. *Language in Society* 28, 185–201.

Eisenberg, A. (1986) Teasing: Verbal play in two Mexicano homes. In B.B. Schieffelin and E. Ochs (eds) *Language Socialization across Cultures* (pp. 182–208). Cambridge: Cambridge University Press

Erikson, E. (1963) *Childhood and Society* (2nd edn) New York: W.W. Norton.

Erikson, E. (1968) *Identity: Youth and Crisis.* New York: W.W. Norton..

Erickson, F. and Schultz, J. (1982) *The Counselor as a Gatekeeper.* New York: Academic Press.

Erickson, F. and Schultz, J. (1997) When is a context? Some issues and methods in the analysis of social competence. In M. Cole, Y. Engestrom and O. Vasquez (eds) *Mind, Culture, and Activity: Seminal Papers from the Laboratory of Comparative Human Cognition.* New York: Cambridge University Press.

Fairclough, N. (1989) *Language and Power.* London: Longman.

Faltis, C.J. (1993) Editor's introduction: Trends in bilingual education at the secondary school level. *Peabody Journal of Education* 69 (1), 1–5.

Fanon, F. (1967) *Black Skin, White Masks.* New York: Grove Press.

Farah, M. (1984) *Marriage and Sexuality in Islam: A Translation of al-Ghazi's Book on the Etiquette of Marriage from the Ihyi'.* Salt Lake City: University of Utah Press.

Farr, M. (1994) Biliteracy in the home: Practices among Mexicano families in Chicago. In D. Spener (ed.) *Adult Biliteracy in the United States* (pp. 89–110). McHenry, IL: Delta Systems and Center for Applied Linguistics.

Farr, M. and Guerra, J. (1995) Literacy in the community: A study of Mexicano families in Chicago. *Discourse Processes* 19, 7–19.

Fernandez, S., Kipp, S. and Lotherington, H. (1997) Language maintenance: What is maintained and how? Paper presented at the Language Australia Annual Research, Review and Planning Forum, Victoria University of Technology, Melbourne, April.

Fernandez Kelly, P. (1995) Social and cultural capital in the urban ghetto: Implications for the economic sociology of immigration. In A. Portes (ed.) *The Economic Sociology of Immigration: Essays on Networks, Ethnicity, and Entrepreneurship* (pp. 213–247). New York: Russell Sage Foundation.

Fishman, J.A. (1966) *Language Loyalty in the United States: The Maintenance and Perpetuation of Non-English Mother Tongues by American Ethnic and Religious Groups.* The Hague: Mouton.

Fishman, J.A. (1972) *The Sociology of Language: An Interdisciplinary Approach to Language in Society.* Rowley, MA: Newbury House.

Fishman, J.A. (1991) *Reversing Language Shift: Theoretical and Empirical Foundations of Assistance to Threatened Languages.* Clevedon: Multilingual Matters.

Ford, C. and Thompson, S. (1996) Interactional units in conversation: Syntactic, intonational, and pragmatic resources for the management of turns. In E. Ochs, E. Schegloff and S. Thompson (eds) *Interaction and Grammar* (pp. 52–134). Cambridge: Cambridge University Press.

Foucault, M. (1995/1979) *Discipline and Punish: The Birth of the Prison* (2nd edn) (trans. A. Sheridan). New York: Vintage Books.

Franco, R. and Ochoa, S. (1995) *Wawas y wawitas: El desarrollo infantil en Cusco.* Lima: Asociación Pukllasunchis.

Gadrey, J. (2000) *Nouvelle économie, nouveau mythe?* Paris: Flammarion.

Gal, S. (1979) *Language Shift.* New York: Academic Press.

García, R.F. (2000) Yachay: Concepciones sobre enseñanza y aprendizaje en la comunidad campesina de Aucará, Departamento de Ayacucho, Perú. Master's thesis, Universidad Mayor de San Simón, Cochabamba, Bolivia.

Gee, J.P. (1990) *Social Linguistics and Literacies: Ideology in Discourses.* London: Falmer Press.

Gee, J.P. (1996) *Social Linguistics and Literacies: Ideology in Discourses* (2nd edn). London: Taylor and Francis.

Gee, J.P., Hull, G. and Lankshear, C. (1996) *The New Work Order.* London: Allen and Unwin.

Gendron, J.D. (1972) *The Position of the French Language in Quebec.* Québec: Éditeur officiel du Québec.

Gerrard, N. and Javed, N. (1994) A dialogue about racism and silence: Personal and political perspectives. *Canadian Woman Studies* 14 (2), 64–67.

Gilman, S.L. (1986) Black bodies, white bodies: Toward an iconography of female sexuality in late nineteenth-century art, medicine, and literature. In H.L. Gates, Jr (ed.) *Race, Writing and Difference* (pp. 223–261). Chicago: University of Chicago Press.

Gilroy, P. (1993) *The Black Atlantic: Modernity and Double Consciousness.* Cambridge, MA: Harvard University Press.

Godenzzi, J.C. (1997) Literacy and modernization among the Quechua speaking population of Perú. In N. Hornberger and J. Fishman (eds) *Indigenous Literacies in the Americas: Language Planning from the Bottom Up.* Berlin: Mouton de Gruyter.

Goffman, E. (1981) Footing. In E. Goffman, *Forms of Talk* (pp. 124–159). Oxford: Blackwell.

Goldberg, D.T. (1993) *Racist Culture.* Oxford: Blackwell.

Goldenberg, C. and Patthey-Chavez, G. (1995) Discourse processes in instructional conversations: Interactions between teachers and transition readers. *Discourse Processes* 19, 57–73.

Goldman, S.R. (1997) Learning from text: Reflections on the past and suggestions for the future. *Discourse Processes* 23, 357–398.

Goldstein, T. (1997a) Bilingual life in a multilingual high school classroom: Teaching and learning in Cantonese and English. *Canadian Modern Language Review* 53 (2), 356–372.

Goldstein, T. (1997b) *Two Languages at Work: Bilingual Life on the Production Floor.* Berlin: Mouton de Gruyter.

Gonzales, N., Moll, L.C., Tenery, M., Rivera, A., Rendon, P., Gonzales, R. and Amanti, C. (1995) Funds of knowledge for teaching in Latino households. *Urban Education,* 29 (4), 443–470.

Goodwin, M.H. (1990) *He-Said-She-Said.* Bloomington: Indiana University Press.

Green, J. and Bloome, D. (1997) Ethnography and ethnographers of and in education: A situated perspective. In J. Flood, S.B. Heath and D. Lapp (eds), *Handbook of Research on Teaching Literacy through the Communicative and Visual Arts* (pp. 181–202). New York: Simon & Schuster Macmillan.

Green, J.L. and Wallat, C.E. (eds) (1981) *Ethnography and Language in Educational Settings.* Norwood, NJ: Ablex.

Griffith, A.I. and Schecter, S.R. (1998) Mothering, education, and schooling (Introduction to Special Issue). *Journal for a Just and Caring Education* 4, 5–10.

Grin, F. (1996) The economics of language: Survey, assessment, and prospects. *International Journal of the Sociology of Language* 121, 17–44.

Guenena, N. and Wassef, N. (1999) *Unfulfilled Promises: Women's Rights in Egypt.* Cairo: Population Council, West Asia and North Africa Regional Office.

Guindon, H. (1978) The modernization of Quebec and the legitimacy of the Canadian state. In H. Guindon, *Quebec Society* (pp. 60–93). Toronto: University of Toronto Press.

Gumperz, J.J. (1982) *Discourse Strategies.* Cambridge: Cambridge University Press.

Gumperz, J.J. (1996a) The linguistic and cultural relativity of inferences. In J. J. Gumperz and S. Levinson (eds) *Rethinking Linguistic Relativity* (pp. 374–406). New York: Cambridge University Press.

Gumperz, J.J. (1996b) Introduction to part IV. In J.J. Gumperz and S. Levinson (eds) *Rethinking Linguistic Relativity* (pp. 359–373). New York: Cambridge University Press.

Gumperz, J.J. (1997) On the interactional bases of speech community membership. In G. Guy, C. Feagin, D. Schiffrin and J. Baugh (eds) *Toward a Social Science of Language: Papers in Honor of William Labov* (Vol. 2), *Social Interaction and Discourse Structures* (pp. 183–203). Philadelphia: John Benjamins.

Gumperz, J.J. and Levinson, S. (eds) (1996) *Rethinking Linguistic Relativity.* New York: Cambridge University Press.

Guskin, J. (1992) The context of bilingual education in Milwaukee: Complex ethnic relationships in an urban setting. In M. Saravai-Shore and S.F. Arvizo (eds) *Cross Cultural Literacy: Ethnographies of Communication in Multi-Ethnic Classrooms.* New York: Garland Press.

Gutierrez, K. D. (1995) Unpackaging academic discourse. *Discourse Processes* 19, 21–37.

Gyurcsik, I. and Satterwhite, J. (1996) The Hungarians in Slovakia. *Nationality Papers* 24 (3), 509–524.

Hall, S. (1997) The work of representation. In S. Hall (ed.) *Representation: Cultural Representation and Signifying Practices* (pp. 13–64). Thousand Oaks, CA: Sage.

Hardman, M.J. (1983) Andean ethnography: The role of language structure in observer bias. Unpublished manuscript.

Hardman, M.J., Vásquez, J. and Yapita, M.J. de Dios (1988) *Aymara: Compendio de estructura fonológica y gramatical.* La Paz: ILCA.

Harklau, L.A. (1994) Tracking and linguistic minority students: Consequences of ability grouping for second language learners. *Linguistics and Education* 6, 221–248.

Harklau, L.A. (2001) From high school to college: Student perspectives on literacy practices. *Journal of Literacy Research*, 33 (1), 33–70.

Hatem, M. (1986) The politics of sexuality and gender in segregated patriarchal systems: The case of eighteenth- and nineteenth-century Egypt. *Feminist Studies* 12 (2), 250–274.

He, A.W. (1998) *Reconstructing Institutions: Language Use in Academic Counseling Encounters.* Greenwich, CT: Ablex.

He, AW. (2000) Sequential and grammatical organization of teacher's directives. *Linguistics and Education* 11 (2), 119–140.

He, A.W. (2001) The language of ambiguity: Practices in Chinese heritage language classes. *Discourse Studies* 3, 75–96.

He, A.W. (in press) Discipline, directives, and deletions: Grammar and interaction in Chinese heritage language classes. In C. Holten and J. Frodosen (eds) *Discourse Studies and Language Teaching: A Festschrift for Marianne Celce-Murcia*. Boston: Heinle and Heinle.

He, A.W. and Keating, E. (1991) Counselor and student at talk: A case study. *Issues in Applied Linguistics* 2, 183–210.

Heath, S.B. (1980) The functions and uses of literacy. *Journal of Communication* 30, 123–133.

Heath, S.B. (1982a) Protean shapes in literacy events: Ever-shifting oral and literate traditions. In D. Tannen (ed.), *Spoken and Written Language: Exploring Orality and Literacy*. Norwood, NJ: Ablex.

Heath, S.B. (1982b) Questioning at home and at school: A comparative study. In G. Spindler (ed.) *Doing the Ethnography of Schooling* (pp. 103–131). New York: Holt, Rinehart and Winston.

Heath, S.B. (1983) *Ways with Words: Language, Life, and Work in Communities and Classrooms* Cambridge: Cambridge University Press.

Heath, S.B. (1986) The functions and uses of literacy. In S. de Castell, A. Luke and K. Egan (eds) *Literacy, Society and Schooling: A Reader* (pp. 15–26). Cambridge: Cambridge University Press.

Heath, S.B. (1989) Learner as cultural member. In M.L. Rice and R.L. Schiefelbusch (eds) *The Teachability of Language* (pp. 335–350). Baltimore, MD: Paul H. Brookes.

Heinlein, R.A. (1961) *Stranger in a Strange Land*. New York: Putnam.

Heller, M. (1994) *Crosswords: Language, Education and Ethnicity in French Ontario*. Berlin: Mouton de Gruyter.

Heller, M. (1999) Heated language in a cold climate. In J. Blommaert (ed.) *Language Ideological Debates* (pp. 143–170). Berlin: Mouton de Gruyter.

Heller, M., Bartholomot, J.P., Levy, L. and Ostiguy, L. (1982) *Le processus de francisation dans une entreprise montréalaise: Une analyse sociolinguistique*. Québec: Gouvernement du Québec, Office de la langue française.

Henderson, W., Dudley-Evans, T. and Backhouse, R. (eds) (1993) *Economics and Language*. London and New York: Routledge.

Herdt, G.H. (1997) *Same Sex, Different Cultures: Exploring Gay and Lesbian Lives*. Boulder, CO: Westview Press.

Hoffman, D.M. (1996) Culture and self in multicultural education: Reflections on discourse, text, and practice. *American Educational Research Journal* 33 (3), 545–569.

Hogue, W.L. (1996) *Race, Modernity, Postmodernity: A Look at the History of the Literatures of People of Color since the 1960s*. Albany, NY: State University of New York Press.

Holmes, J. and Meyerhoff, M. (1999) The community of practice: Theories and methodologies in language and gender research. *Language in Society* 28 (2), 173–183.

hooks, b. (1992) *Black Looks: Race and Representation*. Boston, MA: South End Press.

Hornberger, N. (1988) Iman Chay?: Quechua children in Peru's Schools. In H. Trueba and C. Delgado-Gaitan (eds) *School and Society: Learning Content Through Culture*. New York: Praeger.

Hornberger, N. (1996) Mother-tongue literacy in the Cambodian community of Philadelphia. *International Journal of the Sociology of Language* 119, 69–86.

Hornberger, N. (1997) Quechua literacy and empowerment. In N. Hornberger and J.A. Fishman (eds) *Indigenous Literacies in the Americas: Language Planning from the Bottom Up*. Berlin: Mouton de Gruyter.

Hornberger, N. (1998) Language policy, language education, language rights: Indigenous, immigrant, and international perspectives. *Language in Society* 27, 439–458.

Hornberger, N. and Hardman, J. (1994) Literacy as cultural practice and cognitive skill: Biliteracy in an ESL Class and a GED Program. In D. Spener (ed.) *Adult Biliteracy in the United States* (pp. 147–169). McHenry, IL: Delta Systems Co. and Center for Applied Linguistics.

Horsman, J. (1994) The problem of illiteracy and the promise of literacy. In M. Hamilton, D. Barton and R. Ivanic (eds) *Worlds of Literacy* (pp. 169–181). Clevedon: Multilingual Matters.

Howes, C. (2000) Shy need not apply: No longer able to hide in the corner office, today's CEO must feed keen investor and public interest in his company. *National Post,* National Edition, October 14, p. D1.

Hoyle, S.M. and Adger, C.T. (eds) (1998) *Kids Talk: Strategic Language Use in Later Childhood.* Oxford: Oxford University Press.

Hughes, E. C. (1943) *French Canada in Transition.* Chicago: University of Chicago Press.

Hwang, D.H. (1990) *FOB and Other Plays.* New York: Plume.

Hymes, D. (1972) On communicative competence. In J.B. Pride and J. Holmes (eds) *Sociolinguistics: Selected Readings* (pp. 269–293). Harmondsworth: Penguin Books.

Hymes, D. (1974a) *Foundations in Sociolinguistics.* Philadelphia: University of Pennsylvania Press.

Hymes, D. (1974b) Ways of speaking. In R. Bauman and J. Sherzer (eds) *Explorations in the Ethnography of Speaking.* Cambridge: Cambridge University Press.

India Today (1997) August 18, 24–31.

Irvine, J. (1987) Domains of description in the ethnography of speaking: A retrospective on the "Speech community." In R. Bauman, J. Irvine and S. Philips (eds) *Performance, Speech Community, and Genre* (pp. 13–24). Chicago: Working Papers and Proceedings of the Center for Psychosocial Studies.

Jacoby, S. and Gonzales, P. (1991) The constitution of expert-novice in scientific discourse. *Issues in Applied Linguistics* 2 (2),149–182.

Jacoby, S. and Ochs, E. (1995) Co-construction: An introduction. *Research on Language and Social Interaction* 28, 171–183.

Jakobson, R. (1959). Boas' view of grammatical meaning. *American Anthropologist* 61, 139–145.

Jayaram, N. (1993) The education–employment mismatch: A sociological appraisal of the Indian experience. *International Perspectives in Education and Society* 2, 123–143.

Jayaram, N. (1997) India. In G.A. Postiglione and G.C.L. Mak (eds) *Asian Higher Education: An International Handbook and Reference Guide* (pp. 77–91). Westport, CT: Greenwood Press.

Jones, R.P. and Williams, J. (1998, May 22) Thompson tells MPS he wants results now. *Milwaukee Journal-Sentinel* 1, 7.

Joseph, J.E. and Taylor T.J. (eds) (1990) *Ideologies of Language.* London, Routledge.

Kachru, B.B. (1994) English in South Asia. In R. Burchfield (ed.) *Cambridge History of the English Language* (Vol. 5, pp. 497–553). Cambridge: Cambridge University Press.

Kanagy, R. (1999) Interactional routines as a mechanism for L2 acquisition and socialization in an immersion context. *Journal of Pragmatics* 31, 1467–1492.

Keefe, S.E. and Padilla, A.M. (1987) *Chicano Ethnicity.* Albuquerque: University of New Mexico Press.

Kennedy, J.G. (1970) Circumcision and excision in Egyptian Nubia. *Man* 5, 175–191.

Kerswill, P. and Wright, S. (1990) The validity of phonetic transcription: Limitations of a sociolinguistic research tool. *Language Variation and Change* 2, 255–277.

Khayatt, D. (1992) *Lesbian Teachers: An Invisible Presence.* Albany: State University of New York Press.

Kim, E.H. (1982) *Asian American Literature: An Introduction to the Writings and Their Social Context.* Philadelphia: Temple University.

Kingston, M.H. (1978) *The Woman Warrior: Memoirs of a Girlhood among Ghosts.* New York: Random House.

Kipp, S., Clyne, M. and Pauwels, A. (1995) *Immigration and Australia's Language Resources.* Canberra: Australian Government Publishing Service.

Kogawa, J. (1981) *Obasan.* Markham: Penguin Books Canada.

Kondo, D. (1997) *About Face: Performing Race in Fashion and Theater.* New York: Routledge.

Kontra, M. (1995/1996) English only's cousin: Slovak only. *Acta Linguistica Hungarica* 43 (3–4), 345–72.

Kontra, M. (1998) Language rights arguments in Central Europe and the USA: How similar are they? In D. Kibbee (ed.) *Language Legislation and Linguistic Rights* (pp. 142–178). Philadelphia: John Benjamins.

Kontra, M. (1999) Some reflections on the nature of language and its regulation. *International Journal on Minority and Group Rights* 6, 281–288.

Kramarae, C. (1981) *Women and Men Speaking: Frameworks for Analysis.* Rowley, MA: Newbury House.

Kramsch, C. (1998) *Language and Culture.* Oxford: Oxford University Press.

Krashen, S. (1999) Bilingual education: Arguments for and (bogus) arguments against. Georgetown University Roundtable on Language and Linguistics, May (on the Web at: http://ourworld.compuserve.com/homepages.JWCRAWFORD/Krashen3.htm).

Kreckel, M. (1981) *Communicative Acts and Shared Knowledge in Natural Discourse.* New York: Academic Press.

Kroskrity, P., Schieffelin, B. and Woolard, K. (eds) (1992) Language Ideologies (Special issue), *Pragmatics* 2, 235–453.

Kulick, D. (1992) *Language Shift and Cultural Reproduction: Socialization, Self, and Syncretism in a Papua New Guinean Village.* Cambridge: Cambridge University Press.

Kulick, D. and Stroud, C. (1993) Conceptions and uses of literacy in a Papua New Guinean village. In B. Street, *Cross-cultural Approaches to Literacy* (pp. 294–314). New York: Cambridge University Press.

Labov, W. (1972) *Sociolinguistic Patterns.* Philadelphia: University of Pennsylvania Press.

Lakoff, G. and Johnson, M. (1980) *Metaphors We Live By.* Chicago: University of Chicago Press.

Lamarre, P. (2000) Le multilinguisme des jeunes allophones québécois: Ressource sociétale et défi éducatif. *Correspondance* 6 (3), 6–9.

Lambert, W.E. and Taylor, D.M. (1987) Language minorities in the United States: Conflicts around assimilation and proposed modes of accommodation. In W.A. Van Horne and T.V. Tonnesen (eds) *Ethnicity and Language* (pp. 58–89). Milwaukee: University of Wisconsin System Institute on Race and Ethnicity.

Langman, J. (1997a) Identitás és nyelv: Fiatal magyarok a Felvidéken [Identity and language: Hungarian youth in the Highlands]. In I. Lanstyák and G. Szabómihály (eds) *Nyelvi Érintkezések a Kárpátmedencében, különös tekintettel a 'magyarpárú' kétnyelvűségre [Language Contacts in the Carpathian Basin, with Particular Attention to 'Hungarian-paired' Bilingualism]* (pp. 102–112). Bratislava: Magyar Köztársaság Kulturális Intézete and Kalligram.

Langman, J. (1997b) Expressing identity in a changing society: Hungarian youth in Slovakia. In L. Kürti and J. Langman (eds) *Beyond Borders: Remaking Cultural Identities in the New East and Central Europe* (pp. 111–131). Boulder: Westview Press.

Langman, J. (2002) Mother tongue education versus bilingual education: Shifting ideologies and policies in the Republic of Slovakia. *International Journal of the Sociology of Language* 154, 47–64.

Langman, J. and Lanstyák, I. (2000) Language negotiations in Slovakia: Views from the Hungarian minority. *Multilingua* 19 (1–2), 55–72.

Lankshear, C. and Gee, J.P. (1997) Language, literacy and the new work order. In C. Lankshear (ed.) *Changing Literacies.* Buckingham: Open University Press.

László, B. (1998) A (cseh)szlovákiai oktatásügy szerkezete, valamint közigazgatási és jogi keretei 1945 után [The (Czecho)slovak educational system, including the administrative and legal setting since 1945]. In L. Tóth (ed.) *A (cseh)szlovákiai magyar művelődés története 1918–1998. Vol II. Oktatásgy – közművelődés – sajtó, rádió, televízió [The history of Hungarian (Czecho)slovak development – public education – newspaper, radio, television]* (pp. 94–178). Budapest: Ister.

Latour, B. (1987) *Science in Action.* Cambridge, MA: Harvard University Press.

Lave, J. (1991) Situating learning in communities of practice. In L. Resnick, J. Levine and S. Teasley (eds) *Perspectives on Socially Shared Cognition* (pp. 63–82). Washington, DC: American Psychological Association.

Lave, J. and Wenger, E. (1991) *Situated Learning: Legitimate Peripheral Participation.* Cambridge: Cambridge University Press.

Lea, M.R. and Street, B.V. (1998) Student writing in higher education: An academic literacies approach. *Studies in Higher Education* 23 (2), 157–172.

Lee, B. (2001) Mutual knowledge, background knowledge and shared beliefs: Their roles in establishing common ground. *Journal of Pragmatics* 33, 21–44.

Lee, S.J. (1996) *Unraveling the "Model Minority" Stereotype: Listening to Asian American Youth.* New York: Teachers College Press.

Leki, I. (1995) Coping strategies of ESL students in writing tasks across the curriculum. *TESOL Quarterly* 29, 235–260.

Leki, I. (1999) "Pretty much I screwed up": Ill-served needs of a permanent resident. In L. Harklau, K. Losey and M. Siegal (eds) *Generation 1.5 Meets College Composition: Issues in the Teaching of Writing to US-educated Learners of English as a Second Language* (pp. 17–43). Mahwah, NJ: Lawrence Erlbaum.

Leki, I. and Carson, J.G. (1994) Students' perceptions of EAP writing instruction and writing needs across the disciplines. *TESOL Quarterly* 28, 81–101.

Lerner, G.H. (1995) Turn design and the organization of participation in instructional activities. *Discourse Processes* 19, 111–131.

Leung, C., Harris, R. and Rampton, B. (1997) The idealised native speaker, reified ethnicities, and classroom realities. *TESOL Quarterly* 31, 543–560.

Levine J. and Moreland, R. (1991) Culture and socialization in work groups. In L. Resnick, J. Levine and S. Teasley (eds) *Perspectives on Socially Shared Cognition* (pp.257–279). Washington, DC: American Psychological Association.

Levine, M. (1989) *The Reconquest of Montreal: Language Policy and Social Change in a Bilingual City.* Philadelphia: Temple University Press.

Li, D. (2000) The pragmatics of making requests in the L2 workplace: A case study of language socialisation. *Canadian Modern Language Review* 57, 58–87.

Libermann, K., Godínez, A. and Albó, X. (1989) Mundo Rural Andino. In X. Albó, K. Libermann, A. Godínez and F. Pifarre (eds) *Para Comprender las Culturas Rurales en Bolivia.* La Paz: MEC/CIPCA/UNICEF.

Lippi-Green, R. (1997) *English with an Accent. Language, Ideology and Discrimination in the United States.* London: Routledge.

Livia, A. and Hall, K. (1997) "It's a girl!" Bringing performativity back to linguistics. In A. Livia and K. Hall (eds) *Queerly Phrased: Language, Gender, and Sexuality* (pp. 3–18). Oxford: Oxford University Press.

Lo Bianco, J. (2000) Multiliteracies and multilingualism. In B. Cope and M. Kalantzis (eds) *Multiliteracies: Literacy Learning and the Design of Social Futures* (pp. 92–105). London: Routledge.

Lo Bianco, J. and Freebody, P. (1997) *Australian Literacies: Informing National Policy on Literacy Education.* Belconnen, ACT: Language Australia.

Lotherington, H. (2000) What's bilingual education all about? A guide to language learning in today's schools. Language Australia.

Lotherington, H. (2001a) ESL literacy and new media: Reshaping literacies in the age of information. *Contact* 27 (2), 4–11.

Lotherington, H. (2001b) A tale of four teachers: A study of an Australian late-entry content-based program in two Asian languages. *International Journal of Bilingual Education and Bilingualism* 4 (2), 97–106.

Lotherington, H. and Ebert, S. (1997) Plugged in: Using electronic media to maintain the mother tongue. *Australian Language Matters* 5 (4), 9–10.

Lotherington, H., Ebert, S., Watanabe, T., Norng, S. and Tuc, H.D. (1998) Biliteracy practices in suburban Melbourne. *Australian Language Matters* 6 (3), 3–4.

Lotherington, H. and Norng, S. (1999) Literacy and language expectations of migrant factory workers in suburban Melbourne. *Australian Language Matters* 7 (5), 11.

Lowe, L. (1996) *Immigrant Acts: On Asian American Cultural Politics.* Durham: Duke University Press.

Lucas, C., Bayley, R. and Valli, C. (2001) *Sociolinguistic Variation in American Sign Language.* Washington, DC: Gallaudet University Press.

Lucy, J. (1992) *Language Diversity and Thought: A Reformulation of the Linguistic Relativity Hypothesis.* Cambridge: Cambridge University Press.

Luke, A. (1995) Text and discourse in education: An introduction to critical discourse analysis. *Review of Research in Education* 21, 3–48.

Luykx, A. (1989) Language, gender and education in a Bolivian Aymara community. MA thesis, University of Florida at Gainesville.

Lukyx, A. (1998). La diferencia functional de códigos y el futuro de las lenguas minoritarias. In L. E. López and I. Jung (eds) *Sobre las huellas de la voz: Sociolingüística de la oralidad y la escritura en su relación con la educación* (pp. 192–212). Madrid: Ediciones Morata.

Luykx, A. (1999a) *The Citizen Factory: Schooling and Cultural Production in Bolivia.* Albany: State University of New York Press.

Luykx, A. (1999b) The historical contradictions of language maintenance: Bilingual education and the decline of indigenous languages. Paper presented at the Annual Meeting of the American Anthropological Association, Chicago, Nov.

Ma, S. (1998) *Immigrant Subjectivities in Asian American and Asian Diaspora Literatures.* Albany, NY: State University of New York Press.

Maclear, K. (1994) The myth of the "model minority": Rethinking the education of Asian Canadians. *Our Schools/Our Selves* 5, 54–76.

Marmen, L. and Corbeil, J-P. (1999) *Les langues au Canada: Recensement de 1996.* Canada: Ministère des Travaux Publics.

Markus, A. (1993) Identity in an ethnically diverse community. *People and Place* 1, 43–50.

Markus, A. and Sims, E. (1993) *Fourteen Lives: Paths to a Multicultural Community.* Clayton, Victoria, Australia: Monash Publications in History.

Matusov, E., Pease-Alvarez, L., Angelillo, C. and Chavajay, P. (forthcoming) Critical dialoguing: Emerging teaching/learning opportunities in a BU/UCSC-Links after-school project.

McAll, C. (1992) Langues et silence: les travailleurs immigrés au Québec et la sociologie du langage. *Sociologie et Sociétés*, 24 (2), 117–130.

McAll, C. (ed.) (1993a) *L'utilisation du langage et des langues dans quatre milieux de travail à Montréal.* Research report submitted to the Office de la langue française, Gouvernement du Québec.

McAll, C. (1993b) L'utilisation du langage et des langues dans quatre milieux de travail à Montréal. In C. McAll (ed.) *L'utilisation du langage et des langues dans quatre milieux de travail Montréal* (pp. 1–23). Montréal: Research report submitted to the Office de la langue française, Gouvernement du Québec.

McAll, C. (1996) *Les requérants du statut de réfugié au Québec: Un nouvel espace de marginalite?* Collection Études et recherches, no.16. Québec: MRCI.

McAll, C. (1997) The breaking point: Language in Quebec society. In M. Fournier, M. Rosenberg and D. White (eds) *Quebec Society: Critical Issues* (pp. 61–80). Scarborough, New York: Prentice Hall.

McAll, C., Fortier, J., Ulysse, P-J. and Bourque, R. (2001) *Se libérer du regard.* Montreal: Editions Saint-Martin.

McAll, C., Montgomery, C. and Tremblay, L. (1994) Utilisation du langage et des langues au travail: La reconstruction de la journée du travail et la cartographie sociolinguistique d'entreprise. *Terminogramme* 74, 1–7.

McAll, C., Montgomery, C., Tremblay, L. and Teixeira, C. (1998) *La conquête de l'espace : Langues et territoires dans l'industrie aérospatiale montréalaise*. Research report submitted to the Social Sciences and Humanities Research Council of Canada.

McAll, C., Teixeira, C., Montgomery, C. and Tremblay, L. (2001), "Plurilinguisme et nouvelles technologies dans l'industrie aérospatiale à Montréal," in S. Pène, A. Borzeix, and B. Fraenkel (eds) *Le langage dans les organisations*. Paris: L'Harmattan, Collection Langage et travail.

McAll, C., Tremblay, L. and Le Goff, F. (1997) *Proximité et distance: les défis de communication entre intervenants et clientèle multiethnique en CLSC*. Montréal: Éditions Saint-Martin.

McCarthy, C. (1993) Beyond the poverty of theory in race relations: Nonsynchrony and social difference in education. In L. Weis and M. Fine (eds) *Beyond Silenced Voices: Class, Race, and Gender in United States Schools* (pp. 325–346). Albany, NY: State University of New York Press.

McKay, S.L. and Wong, S-I.C. (1996) Multiple discourses, multiple identities: Investment and agency in second-language learning among Chinese adolescent immigrant students. *Harvard Educational Review* 66, 577–608.

Mead, G.H. (1934) *Mind, Self and Society from the Standpoint of a Social Behaviorist*. Chicago: Univeristy of Chicago Press.

Medina, M. (1988) Hispanic apartheid in American public education. *Educational Administration Quarterly* 24, 336–349.

Mehan, H. (1979) *Learning Lessons*. Cambridge, MA: Harvard University Press.

Mehan, H., Hubbard, L. and Villanueva, I. (1994) Forming academic identities: Accommodation without assimilation among involuntary minorities. *Anthropology and Education Quarterly* 25, 91–117.

Merriam, S.B. (1998) *Qualitative Research and Case Study Applications in Education* (2nd edn). San Francisco: Jossey-Bass.

Meyerhoff, M. (2002) Communities of practice. In J.K. Chambers, P. Trudgill and N. Schilling-Estes (eds) *Handbook of Language Variation and Change* (pp. 526–548). Oxford: Blackwell.

Michaels, S. (1981) "Sharing time": Children's narrative styles and differential access to literacy. *Language in Society* 10, 423–442.

Michaels, S. (1986) Narrative presentations: An oral preparation for literacy with first graders. In J. Cook-Gumperz (ed.) *The Social Construction of Literacy* (pp. 94–116). Cambridge: Cambridge University Press.

Milroy, L. (1987) *Language and Social Networks* (2nd edn). Oxford: Blackwell.

Milroy, J. and Milroy, L. (1985/1999) *Authority in Language: Investigating Standard English*. London: Routledge.

Milroy, J. and Wei, L. (1995) A social network approach to code-switching: The example of a bilingual community in Britain. In J. Milroy and P. Muysken (eds) *One Speaker, Two Languages: Cross-disciplinary Approaches to Codeswitching* (pp. 136–157). Cambridge: Cambridge University Press.

Miracle, A. (1976) The effects of cultural perception on Aymara schooling. PhD thesis, University of Florida, Gainesville.

Moll, L.C. (ed.) (1990) *Vygotsky and Education: Instructional Implications and Applications of Sociohistorical Psychology*. Cambridge: Cambridge University Press.

Moll, L.C., Tapia, J. and Whitmore, K.F. (1993) Living knowledge: The social distribution of cultural resources for thinking. In G. Salomon (ed.) *Distributed Cognition: Psychological and Educational Considerations* (pp. 139–163). Cambridge: Cambridge University Press.

Montgomery, C. (1993) Une journée typique dans la 'cité de la mode': L'utilisation des langues et du langage au travail. In C. McAll (ed.) *L'utilisation du langage et des langues dans quatre milieux de travail à Montréal* (pp. 24–53). Montréal: Research report submitted to the Office de la langue française, Gouvernement du Québec.

Murray, S.O. (1997). Woman–woman love in Islamic societies. In S.O. Murray and W. Roscoe (eds) *Islamic Homosexualities: Culture, History, and Literature* (pp. 97–114). New York: New York University Press.

Musallam, B.F. (1983) *Sex and Society in Islam: Birth Control before the Nineteenth Century.* Cambridge: Cambridge University Press.

Naik, J.P. (1982) *The Education Commission and After.* New Delhi: Allied.

New Indian Express-Chennai (2000a) TNLA: A story rejuvenated after Veerappan's twist. August 8, 3.

New Indian Express-Chennai (2000b) I've never had any links with Veerappan, I have urged him to release Rajkumar. August 13, 8.

Nolan, F.J. and Kerswill, P. (1990) The description of connected speech processes. In S. Ramsaran (ed.) *Essays in Honour of A.C. Grimson* (pp. 295–316). London: Routledge.

Norton, B. (1997) Language, identity and the ownership of English. *TESOL Quarterly* 31, 409–429.

Norton, B. (2000) *Identity and Language Learning: Gender, Ethnicity, and Educational Change.* London: Longman.

Norton, B. and Toohey, K. (2002) Identity and language learning. In R.B. Kaplan (ed.) *Oxford University Handbook of Applied Linguistics* (pp. 115–123). Oxford: Oxford University Press.

Nystrand, M., with Gamoran, A., Kachur, R. and Prendergast, C. (1997) *Opening Dialogue: Understanding the Dynamics of Language and Learning in the English Classroom.* New York and London: Teachers College Press.

Oakes, J. (1985) *Keeping Track: How Schools Structure Inequality.* New Haven: Yale University Press.

Oakes, J., Gamoran, A. and Page, R.N. (1992) Curriculum differentiation: Opportunities, outcomes, and meanings. In P.W. Jackson (ed.) *Handbook of Research on Curriculum* (pp. 571–608). New York: Macmillan.

Ochs, E. (1986) Introduction. In B. Schieffelin and E. Ochs (eds) *Language Socialization Across Cultures* (pp. 1–13). Cambridge: Cambridge University Press.

Ochs, E. (1988) *Culture and Language Development: Language Acquisition and Socialization in a Samoan Village.* Cambidge: Cambridge University Press.

Ochs, E. (1990) Indexicality and socialization. In J.W. Stigler, R. Shweder and G. Herdt (eds) *Cultural Psychology: Essays on Comparative Human Development* (pp. 287–308). Cambridge: Cambridge University Press.

Ochs, E. (1991) Socialization through language and interaction: A theoretical introduction. *Issues in Applied Linguistics* 2 (2), 143–147.

Ochs, E. (1993) Constructing social identity: A language socialization perspective. *Research on Language and Social Interaction* 26, 287–306.

Ochs, E. (1996) Linguistic resources for socializing humanity. In J.J. Gumperz and S.L. Levinson (eds) *Rethinking Linguistic Relativity* (pp. 407–437). Cambridge: Cambridge University Press.

Ochs, E. and Schieffelin, B.B. (1984) Language acquisition and socialization: Three developmental stories. In R. Schweder and R. LeVine (eds) *Culture Theory: Essays on Mind, Self and Emotion* (pp. 276–320). Cambridge: Cambridge University Press.

Ochs, E. and Schieffelin, B.B. (1995) The impact of language socialization on grammatical development. In P. Fletcher and B. MacWhinney (eds) *The Handbook of Child Language* (pp. 73–94). Oxford: Blackwell.

O'Conner, M.C. and Michaels, S. (1993) Aligning academic task and participation status through revoicing: Analysis of a classroom discourse strategy. *Anthropology and Education Quarterly* 24 (4), 318–335.

Ohta, A.S. (1999) Interactional routines and the socialization of interactional style in adult learners of Japanese. *Journal of Pragmatics* 31, 1493–1512.

Olivas, M.A. (1986) Introduction: Research on Latino students: A theoretical framework and inquiry. In M.A. Olivas (ed.) *Latino College Students* (pp. 1–25). New York: Teachers College Press.

Olneck, M.R. (1995) Immigrants and education. In J.A. Banks and C.A.M. Banks (eds) *Handbook of Research on Multicultural Education* (pp. 310–327). New York: Macmillan.

Omi, M. and Takagi, D.Y. (1996) Situating Asian Americans in the political discourse on affirmative action. *Representations* (Summer), 155–162.

Ong, A. (1999) *Flexible Citizenship: The Cultural Logics of Transnationality*. Durham, NC: Duke University Press.

Patrick, D. (1994) Minority language education and social context. *Etudes/Inuit/Studies* 18 (1–2), 183–199.

Patrick, D. (1998) Language, power and ethnicity in an Arctic Quebec community. PhD thesis, University of Toronto.

Patrick, D. and Shearwood, P. (1999) The roots of Inuktitut bilingual language education. *The Canadian Journal of Native Studies* 19 (2), 249–262.

Patrick, P.L. (2002) The speech community. In J.K. Chambers, P. Trudgill and N. Schilling-Estes (eds) *The Handbook of Language Variation and Change* (pp. 573–597). Oxford: Blackwell.

Pease-Alvarez, L. and Vasquez, O. (1994) Language socialization in ethnic minority communities. In F. Genesee (ed.) *Educating Second Language Children: The Whole Child, the Whole Curriculum, the Whole Community* (pp. 82–102). New York: Cambridge University Press.

Peirce, B.N. (1995) Social identity, investment and language learning. *TESOL Quarterly* 29, 9–31.

Penelope, J. and Valentine, S. (eds) (1990) *Finding the Lesbians: Personal Accounts from Around the World*. Freedom, CA: The Crossing Press.

Pennycook, A. (1994) *The Cultural Politics of English as an International Language*. New York: Longman.

Philips, S. (1972) Participant structures and communicative competence: Warm Springs children in community and classroom. In C. Cazden, V. John and D. Hymes (eds) *Functions of Language in the Classroom* (pp. 370–394). New York: Teachers College Press.

Philips, S. (1983) *The Invisible Culture: Communication in Classrooms and Community on the Warm Springs Indian Reservation*. New York: Longman.

Pichler, T. (1994) The idea of Slovak language-based nationalism. In T. Pichler and J. Gasparíková (eds) *Language, Values, and the Slovak Nation* (pp. 35–46). Slovak Philosophical Studies I. Washington, DC: Paideia Publishers and The Council for Research in Values and Philosophy.

Polanyi, M. (1962) *Personal Knowledge: Towards a Post-Critical Philosophy* (2nd edn). Chicago: University of Chicago Press.

Pon, G. (2000). Importing the Asian model minority discourse into Canada: Implications for social work and education. *Canadian Social Work Review* 17 (2), 277–291.

Pon, M. (1996). The social construction of Chinese masculinity in *Jack Canuck*. In J. Parr (ed.) *Gender and History in Canada* (pp. 68–88). Toronto: Copp Clark Ltd.

Poole, D. (1992) Language socialization in the second language classroom. *Language Learning* 42, 593–616.

Prior, P. (1995) Redefining the task: An ethnographic examination of writing and response in graduate seminars. In D. Belcher and G. Braine (eds) *Academic Writing in a Second Language: Essays on Research and Pedagogy* (pp. 47–82). Norwood, NJ: Ablex.

Probst, P. (1993) The letter and the spirit: Literacy and religious authority in the history of the Aladura movement in Western Nigeria. In B. Street, *Cross-cultural Approaches to Literacy* (pp. 294–314). New York: Cambridge University Press.

Quebec, Government of (1977) *Charte de la langue française*. Québec: Éditeur officiel.

Rampton, B. (1995) *Crossing: Language and Ethnicity among Adolescents*. London: Longman.

Renaud, J. (1992) Un an au Québec. La compétence linguistique et l'accès au premier emploi. *Sociologie et Sociétés* 24, 131–42.

Reynolds, L.G. (1935) *The British Immigrant: His Social and Economic Adjustment in Canada.* Toronto: Oxford University Press.

Rindstet, C. (2000) *Growing Up in a Bilingual Quechua Community: Play, Language and Socializing Practices.* Working Papers on Childhood and the Study of Children, Nr. 2000: 2. Linköping Universitet.

Rockhill, K. (1993) Gender, language and the politics of literacy. In B. Street (ed.) *Cross-Cultural Approaches to Literacy* (pp. 156–175). Cambridge: Cambridge University Press.

Rogoff, B. (1990) *Apprenticeship in Thinking: Cognitive Development in Social Context.* New York: Oxford University Press.

Romero, R. (1994) *Ch'iki: Concepción y Desarrollo de la Inteligencia en Niños Quechuas Pre-escolares de la Comunidad de Titikachi.* Cochabamba: Instituto de Investigaciones de la Facultad de Humanidades y Ciencias de la Educación, Universidad Mayor de San Simon.

Roy, S. (2000) La normalisation linguistique dans une entreprise: Le mot d'ordre mondial. *The Canadian Modern Language Review* 57 (1), 118–143.

Rummler, G. (1997) School racial disparities grow. *Milwaukee Journal Sentinel*, August 25, 4B.

Ryan, J. (1991) Observing and normalizing: Foucault, discipline, and inequality in schooling. *Journal of Educational Thought* 25, 104–119.

Said, E.W. (1979) *Orientalism.* London: Penguin.

Sapir, E. (1949). *Selected Writings of Edward Sapir in Language, Culture, and Personality* (ed. D.G. Mandelbaum). Berkeley: University of California Press.

Sarangi, S. and Roberts, C. (eds) (1999) *Talk, Work and Institutional Order. Discourse in Medical, Mediation and Management Settings.* Berlin, New York: Mouton de Gruyter.

Saville-Troike, M. (1982) *The Ethnography of Communication: An Introduction.* Baltimore: University Park Press.

Schecter, S.R. and Bayley, R. (1997) Language socialization practices and cultural identity: Case studies of Mexican-descent families in California and Texas. *TESOL Quarterly* 31, 513–541.

Schecter, S.R. and Bayley, R. (2002) *Language as Cultural Practice: Mexicanos en el Norte.* Mahwah, NJ: Lawrence Erlbaum.

Schecter, S.R. and Bayley, R. (in press). Language socialization in theory and practice. *International Journal of Qualitative Studies in Education.*

Schecter, S.R. and Cummins, J. (eds) (in press) *Imagination in Practice: Implementing Strategies for Teaching and Learning in Multilingual Classrooms.* Portsmouth, NH: Heinemann.

Schieffelin, B.B. (1990) *The Give and Take of Everyday Life.* Cambridge: Cambridge University Press.

Schieffelin, B.B. (1994) Code-switching and language socialization: Some probable relationships. In J.F. Duchan, L.E. Hewitt and R.M. Sonnenmeier (eds) *Pragmatics: From Theory to Practice* (pp. 20–42). New York: Prentice Hall.

Schieffelin, B.B. and Ochs, E. (1986a) Language socialization. *Annual Review of Anthropology* 15: 163–191.

Schieffelin, B.B. and Ochs E. (eds) (1986b) *Language Socialization across Cultures.* Cambridge: Cambridge University Press.

Schieffelin, B.B. and Ochs, E. (1996) The microgenesis of competence. In D. Slobin, J. Gerhardt, A. Kyratzis and J. Guo (eds) *Social Interaction, Social Context, and Language* (pp. 251–264). Mahwah, NJ: Lawrence Erlbaum.

Schiffman, H.F. (1996) *Linguistic Culture and Language Policy.* London: Routledge.

Schiffrin, D. (1997) The transformation of experience, identity and context. In G. Guy, C. Feagin, D. Schiffrin and J. Baugh (eds) *Towards a Social Science of Language: Papers in honor of William Labov* (Vol. 2), *Social Interaction and Discourse Structures* (pp. 41–55). Philadelphia: John Benjamins.

Schmitt, A. and Sofer, J. (1992) *Sexuality and Eroticism among Males in Moslem Societies.* New York: Harrington Park Press.

Schofield, J.W. (1986) Causes and consequences of the colorblind perspective. In J.F. Dovidio and S.L. Gaertner (eds) *Prejudice, Discrimination, and Racism* (pp. 231–253). New York: Academic Press.

Schultz, E. (1990) *Dialogue at the Margins: Whorf, Bakhtin, and Linguistic Relativity*. Madison: University of Wisconsin Press.

Schutz, A. (1967) *The Phenomenology of the Social World* (trans. G. Walsh and F. Lehnert). Evanston, IL: Northwestern University Press.

Scollon R. and Scollon, S. (1981) *Narrative, Literacy, and Face in Interethnic Communication*. Norwood, NJ: Ablex.

Scrase, T.J. (1993) *Image, Ideology and Inequality: Cultural Domination, Hegemony and Schooling in India*. New Delhi: Sage.

Shamim, F. (1996) In or out of the action zone: Location as a feature of interaction in large ESL classes in Pakistan. In K.M. Bailey and D. Nunan (eds) *Voices from the Language Classroom: Qualitative Research in Second Language Education* (pp. 123–144). Cambridge: Cambridge University Press.

Siguán, M. and Mackey, W.F. (1986) *Educación y Bilingüismo*. Madrid: Santillana.

Sinclair, J. and Coulthard, M.R. (1975) *Towards an Analysis of Discourse: The English Teachers and Pupils*. London: Longman.

Sleeter, C.E. (1993) How white teachers construct race. In C. McCarthy and W. Crichlow (eds) *Race, Identity, and Representation in Education* (pp. 157–171). New York: Routledge.

Sood, S.C. (1995) Needs of the Indian undergraduate learners. In R.L. Agnihotri and A.L. Khanna (eds) *English Language Teaching in India: Issues and Innovations* (pp. 167–178). New Delhi: Sage.

Spack, R. (1997a) The acquisition of academic literacy in a second language: A longitudinal case study. *Written Communication* 14 (1), 3–62.

Spack, R. (1997b) The rhetorical construction of multilingual students. *TESOL Quarterly* 31, 765–774.

Spedding, A. (1994) Open Castilian, closed Aymara? Bilingual women in the Yungas of La Paz (Bolivia). In P. Burton, K.K. Dyson and S. Ardener (eds) *Bilingual Women: Anthropological Approaches to Second Language Use*. Oxford: Berg.

Spolsky, B. and Cooper, R.L. (1991) *The Languages of Jerusalem*. Oxford: Clarendon Press.

Sticht, T.G. (1997) Assessing foundation skills for work. In H.F. O'Neill (ed.) *Workforce Readiness: Competencies and Assessment* (pp. 255–291). Mahwah, NJ: Lawrence Erlbaum.

Stratford, B.D. (1989) Structure and use of Altiplano Spanish. PhD thesis, University of Florida, Gainesville.

Street, B. (1984) *Literacy in Theory and Practice*. Cambridge: Cambridge University Press.

Street, B. (1993) *Cross-cultural Approaches to Literacy*. Cambridge: Cambridge University Press.

Street, B. (1994a) Cross-cultural perspectives on literacy. In L. Verhoeven (ed.) *Functional Literacy: Theoretical Issues and Educational Implications* (pp. 95–111). Amsterdam: John Benjamins.

Street, B. (1994b) Struggles over the meaning(s) of literacy. In M. Hamilton, D. Barton and R. Ivanic (eds) *Worlds of Literacy* (pp. 15–20). Clevedon: Multilingual Matters.

Street, B. (1995) *Social Literacies: Critical Approaches to Literacy in Development, Ethnography and Education*. London: Longman.

Street, B. and Street, J. (1995) The schooling of literacy. In B. Street, *Social Literacies Critical Approaches to Literacy in Development, Ethnography, and Education* (pp. 106–131) London: Longman.

Szigeti, L. (1995a) Oktatásügyünk helyzete [Our educational situation) *MKDM-Füzetek* 3.

Szigeti, L. (1995b) Danaoszi ajándék – avagy trójai faló? [Danaus' gift – or Trojan horse?] *Identitásunk Alapja az Anyanyelvű Oktatás [Mother Tongue Education is the Base of our Identity]* (pp. 1–6). Conference proceedings, May 20, 1995, Érséküjvár. A Mécs László Alapítvány Kiskönyvtára: Bratislava-Pozsony.

Tannen, D. (1984) *Conversational Style: Analyzing Talk among Friends*. Norwood, NJ: Ablex.

Tannen, D. (1986) Introducing constructed dialogue in Greek and American conversational and literary narrative. In F. Coulmas (ed.) *Direct and Indirect Speech* (pp. 311–332). New York: Mouton.

Tannen, D. and Saville-Troike, M. (eds) (1985) *Perspectives on Silence*. Norwood, NJ: Ablex.

Taylor, D.M., Wright S.C., Ruggiero, K.M. and Aitchison, M.C. (1993) Language perceptions among the Inuit of Arctic Quebec: The future role of the heritage language. *Journal of Language and Social Psychology* 12 (3), 195–206.

Teal, G. (1985) The organization of production and the heterogeneity of the working class: Occupation, gender and ethnicity among clothing workers in Quebec. Unpublished doctoral dissertation, McGill University, Montreal.

Tharp, R.G. (1989) Culturally compatible education: A formula for designing effective classrooms. In H.T. Trueba, G. Spindler and L. Spindler (eds) *What Do Anthropologists Have to Say About Dropouts? The First Centennial Conference on Children at Risk* (pp. 51–66). New York: Falmer Press.

Tharp, R. and Gallimore, R. (1988) *Rousing Minds to Life: Teaching, Learning, and Schooling in Social Context*. New York: Cambridge University Press.

The New London Group (1996) A pedagogy of multiliteracies: Designing social factors. *Harvard Educational Review* 66, 60–92.

To thi Dien (1998) Language and literacy in Vietnamese American communities. In B. Pérez (ed.) *Sociocultural Contexts of Language and Literacy* (pp. 123–161). Mahwah, NJ: Lawrence Erlbaum.

Tollefson, J.W. (1989) *Alien Winds: The Reeducation of America's Indochinese Refugees*. New York: Praeger.

Toohey, K. (2000) *Learning English at School: Identity, Social Relations and Classroom Practice*. Clevedon: Multilingual Matters.

Tremblay, L. (1993) L'utilisation du langage et des langues dans une entreprise du secteur biomédical. In C. McAll (ed.) *L'utilisation du langage et des langues dans quatre milieux de travail à Montréal* (pp. 1–23). Montréal: Research report submitted to the Office de la langue française, Gouvernement du Québec.

Tripathi, P.D. (1992) English: The chosen tongue. *English Today* 32, 3–11.

Tuc Ho-Dac (1997) Tonal facilitation of code-switching. *Australian Review of Applied Linguistics* 20 (2), 129–151.

Tudge, J. (1990) Vygotsky, the zone of proximal development, and peer collaboration: Implications for classroom practice. In L.C. Moll (ed.) *Vygotsky and Education* (pp. 155–172) Cambridge: Cambridge University Press.

Turnbull, M., Bell, J.S. and Lapkin, S. (2002) *From the Classroom: Grounded Activities for Language Learning*. Toronto, ON: University of Toronto Press.

United Nations (1983) *Five Studies on the Situation of Women in Latin America*. Santiago: United Nations.

Urban, G. (1991) The semiotics of state–Indian linguistic relationships: Peru, Paraguay, and Brazil. In G. Urban and J. Sherzer (eds) *Nation-States and Indians in Latin America*. Austin: University of Texas Press.

Vaillancourt, F. (1991) *Langue et statut économique au Québec, 1980–1985*. Québec: Conseil de la langue française.

van Langevelde, Ab. (1999) *Bilingualism and Regional Economic Development*. Utrecht/Gronigen: Koninllijk Nederlands Aardrijkskundig Genootschap/Faculteit der

Vasquez, O.A, Pease-Alvarez, L. and Shannon, S.M. (1994) *Pushing Boundaries: Language and Culture in a Mexicano Community*. New York: Cambridge University Press.Ruimtellijke Wetenschappen, Rijksuniversiteit Gronigen.

Vavrus, F. and Cole, K. (2002) "I Didn't Do Nothin": The discursive construction of school suspension. *Urban Review* 34, 87–111.

Velez-Ibañez, C. and Greenberg, J. (1992) Formation and transformation of funds of knowledge among US-Mexican households. *Anthropology and Education Quarterly* 23 (4), 313–335.

Vishwanathan, G. (1989) *Masks of Conquest: Literary Study and British Rule in India.* New Delhi: Oxford University Press.

Vygotsky, L.S. (1978) *Mind in Society.* Cambridge, MA: Harvard University Press.

Vygotsky. L.S. (1986) *Thought and Language* (ed. and trans. A. Kozulin). Cambridge, MA: MIT Press.

Wang, X. (ed.) (1996) *A View from Within: A Case Study of Chinese Heritage Community Language Schools in the US.* Washington, DC: National Foreign Language Center.

Wassef, N. (n.d.) *Da min zaman: Past and Present Discourses on Female Genital Mutilation in Egypt.* Cairo: FGM Taskforce.

Wassef, N. and Mansour, A. (1999) *Investigating Masculinities and Female Genital Mutilation in Egypt.* Cairo: The NGO Center for Population and Development.

Weedon, C. (1987) *Feminist Practice and Poststructuralist Theory.* Oxford: Blackwell.

Weedon, C. (1997) *Feminist Practice and Poststructuralist Theory* (2nd edn). Oxford: Blackwell.

Weigert, A., Smith Teitge, J. and Teitge, D. (1986) *Society and Identity: Toward a Sociological Psychology.* Cambridge: Cambridge University Press.

Weinreich, U. (1953) *Languages in Contact.* New York: The Linguistic Circle of New York.

Weinstein-Shr, G. (1993) Literacy and social process: A community in transition. In B. Street, *Cross-cultural Approaches to Literacy* (pp. 272–293). New York: Cambridge University Press.

Weinstein-Shr, G. (1994) Literacy and second language learners: A family agenda. In *Adult Biliteracy in the United States* (pp. 111–122). McHenry, IL: Delta Systems and the Center for Applied Linguistics.

Welsh, D. (1988) The social construction of Franco-Ontarian interests towards French language schooling: 19th century to 1980s. PhD thesis, University of Toronto.

Wenger, E. (1998) *Communities of Practice: Learning, Meaning and Identity.* Cambridge: Cambridge University Press.

Wertsch, J. (1991) A sociocultural approach to socially shared cognition. In L.B. Resnick, J.M. Levine and S.D. Teasley (eds) *Perspectives on Socially Shared Cognition* (pp. 85–100). Washington, DC: American Psychological Association.

Wertsch, J. (1998) *Mind as Action.* New York: Oxford University Press.

Whorf, B.L. (1941) The relations of habitual thought and behaviour to language. In L. Spier, A.I. Hallowell and S.S. Newmand (eds) *Language, Culture and Personality: Essays in Honor of Edward Sapir.* Menasha, WI: Banta.

Whorf, B.L. (1956). *Language, Thought, and Reality: Selected Writings of Benjamin Lee Whorf* (ed. J.B. Carroll). Cambridge: MIT Press.

Willett, J. (1995) Becoming first graders in an L2: An ethnographic study of language socialization. *TESOL Quarterly* 29, 473–504.

Willis, P. (1977) *Learning to Labor: How Working Class Kids get Working Class Jobs.* New York: Columbia University Press.

Willis, P. (1981) *Learning to Labour.* London: Sexton House.

Wolf, E.R. (1982) *Europe and the People without History.* Berkeley: University of California Press.

Wong, S-L.C. (1992) Centers: A meditation on Asian American identity and aesthetics. In L.C. Lee (ed.) *Asian Americans: Collages of Identities* (pp. 87–100). Ithaca, NY: Asian American Studies Program, Cornell University.

Wong, S-L.C. (1993) *Reading Asian American Literature: From Necessity to Extravagance.* Princeton, NJ: Princeton University Press.

Wortham, S. (1994) *Acting Out Participant Examples in the Classroom.* Philadelphia: John Benjamins.

Yee, M. (1993) Finding the way home through issues of gender, race, and class. In H. Bannerji (ed.) *Returning the Gaze: Essays on Racism, Feminism, and Politics* (pp. 3–37). Toronto: Sister Vision Press.

Young, R. and He, A.W. (eds) (1998) *Talking and Testing*. Amsterdam: John Benjamins.
Zénié-Ziegler, W. (1988) *In Search of Shadows: Conversations with Egyptian Women*. London: Zed Books.
Zentella, A.C. (1997) *Growing Up Bilingual: Puerto Rican Children in New York*. Oxford: Blackwell.
Zuengler, J., Ford, C. and Fassnacht, C. (1998) *Analyst Eyes and Camera Eyes: Theoretical and Technological Considerations in "Seeing" the Details of Classroom Interaction* (Series 2.40). Albany, NY: National Research Center on English Learning and Achievement.
Zuengler, J. and Mori, J. (2002) Microanalyses of classroom discourse: A critical consideration of method. *Applied Linguistics* 23, 283–288.

Index

n indicates a note.